I0794653

ARCANA X

ARCANA X
MUSICIANS ON MUSIC

EDITED BY
JOHN ZORN

HIPS ROAD 2021

Book design by Heung-Heung Chin.

First published in 2021
ISBN 978-0-9788337-1-8
ISBN 0-9788337-1-6
Printed on acid-free paper
Printed and bound in the United States of America

Hips Road
200 East 10th Street #126
New York, NY 10003
http://www.tzadik.com

Distributed to the trade by D.A.P. / Distributed Art Publishers
75 Broad Street, Suite 630
New York, NY 10004

Orders: (800) 338-2665 Tel: (212) 627-1999
Fax: (212) 627-9484

CONTENTS

PREFACE

JOHN ZORN

The *Arcana* Series
Principio et Finem Similia

The idea of publishing an anthology of writings by musicians about music came to me around 1991. My original intention, set forth manifesto-style in the prefaces to the first several volumes of *Arcana*, was to correct what seemed a bitter injustice — an unfortunate lack of intelligent and insightful writing about a community of musicians that, for well over a decade, had been forging a music that was imaginative, well-crafted, honest, cathartic, and, in many ways, important. It was a mission that was taken on very much out of necessity — the music had been misunderstood, misrepresented, misjudged and marginalized for years. Few could have predicted that the project would continue for the next twenty-five years, broaden to address a vast assortment of musical styles and scenes, and expand to ten volumes filled with over 320 essays by an assembly of musical minds spanning three generations.

Organizing the first volume of *Arcana* was a Herculean effort — it took six years to collate, edit, design and publish the thing. The obstacles involved ranged from the musicians' initial suspicion, cynicism, procrastination, bitterness and insecurity to issues with editing, design, printing and distribution. Back then, connecting with people was not quite as easy as it is today, but while logistical problems certainly played a large role in the unusually long production time, the most formidable obstacle was the musician's inherent reticence in committing their thoughts to paper. A musician's major mode of expression is, after all, essentially non-verbal. When discussing music, words often fail us, and so it was exceedingly difficult to get the prospective contributors to respond, no less to complete and deliver their essays.

As the importance and reputation of the project solidified, however, publishing each successive volume became appreciably easier. Six years shrank to three, to two, and finally to less than a year — a remarkably brief period for a project of such scope. The writings in this final installment of *Arcana* were commissioned in the throes of the pandemic lockdown, and so afforded the authors an unexpected abundance of free time with which to complete their entry. The articles were submitted in record time, and results are, not surprisingly, outstanding. *Arcana X* is a spectacular apotheosis to the series, and boasts the most diverse group of musicians out of all the ten volumes.

* * *

My initial inspiration for *Arcana* was a book I bought in 1968 at the legendary music store Patelson's, which was located on 56th Street near 7th Avenue, just behind Carnegie Hall. Edited by Elliott Schwartz and Barney Childs, *Contemporary Composers on Contemporary Music* was a stimulating compilation of penetrating and passionate writings by musicians ranging from Busoni, Ives, and Stravinsky to Cage, Carter, and Partch. There was much to learn from this collection, but even to the eyes of a young aspiring composer (I was 15 at the time) it was immediately apparent that many major figures were conspicuously absent.*

Any project of this type will inevitably suffer from glaring omissions, and *Arcana* (despite its voluminous ten volumes and 300+ contributors) is no exception. Some musicians were asked multiple times but, for a variety of reasons, were never able to deliver; many simply declined; several never responded at all; then there were those who were regrettably overlooked. But much has changed in the past thirty years and thanks to the large coterie of musicians who have dedicated so much of their precious time in educating the younger generations in the history, practice and critical theory of the Downtown scene (George Lewis, Fred Frith, Mark Dresser, Nicole Mitchell, Anthony Coleman, Tyshawn Sorey, Alvin Curran, Kris Davis, Myra Melford, Anthony Braxton, Eyvind Kang, Wadada Leo Smith, and Marty Ehrlich are just a few who come to mind) interesting and insightful writing on new and creative music has flourished, with much of it easily accessible online.

* When an expanded edition appeared in 1998 several articles by composers who had been grievously neglected in the first edition were added — among them Ligeti, Stockhausen, Gubaidulina, and Reich.

* * *

It is now abundantly clear that a vibrant new music exists that transcends traditional boundaries and formal definitions (jazz, rock, classical, film soundtrack, folk, bluegrass) while simultaneously drawing upon them to varying degrees with imagination, respect, and integrity. Such music defies reductionist commodification, sets its own standards, and demands to be judged on its own terms. It's unreliable to discuss new music using old tools. If forced, you may succeed in fitting an oddly shaped peg into a square hole, but it is ultimately counterproductive, misleading, destructive, and can lead to disastrous confusions and misunderstandings. Although difficult and time consuming, it is infinitely more effective to cut a new hole to accommodate the exact shape of each uniquely individual peg. One can only hope that this will become the standard approach to music analysis and criticism in the new millennium.

By definition the critical establishment will always lag behind the creator — academics teach music history while musicians are out there making it — and even now, after many decades of musical exploration and creativity, incomprehension and misinterpretations abound. But despite lazy assumptions, antiquated rationale, and outdated theories, on the whole today's analytic landscape is more open and diverse, more adventurous and inclusive than ever before. Tradition is not a dead past — it is a living, breathing entity existing very much in the present. Neither doctrine nor dogma, tradition is perhaps best described as a community of spirits. Let us look positively and enthusiastically towards a world where difficult and challenging music that "falls between the gaps" can be heard with a clear perspective, an informed ear, and an open mind — a world where such music can be accepted and respected for being what it is, rather than derided and denigrated for what it is not. In short, where new musical directions are found to be stimulating, and viewed with excitement, rather than threatening, and treated with a mixture of suspicion, disdain and contempt.

* * *

With the meeting of Jupiter and Saturn in December 2020 we find ourselves confronted with a Great Conjunction and the birth of a new astrological epoch. We leave behind an Earth Wave, a tumultuous era defined largely by materialism, greed, Empire-building, and a capitalist sense of ownership — and enter an Air Wave, heralding a Global Renaissance, one that bodes well for the avant garde, for spirituality, philosophy, culture, technological advancement, the concept of community, and vast mobility. What we need is a total reset: a veritable redistribution of power itself. 2021 is a new beginning. Hopefully this coming era will help guide us towards a more sustainable world of greater peace, economic fairness, climate awareness and increasing equality, cooperation, openness and gratitude — a transition from hierarchical, vertically-based power structures to more horizontally-oriented, flat organizations demanding greater responsibility and accountability for all involved.

—John Zorn, *NYC January 1, 2021*

ARCANA X

CHAPTER
1

LIFE ON A STRING

Creative Music and the Pedal Steel Guitar

SUSAN ALCORN

A Day in the Life

In the summer of 2018, ten hours of driving from Baltimore, Maryland to Hamilton, Ontario, mostly through the rain, I finally arrive, check in at an Airbnb, sleep for the night, then head over to the gig. I lug five pieces of equipment into the venue and start setting up the steel guitar. First I open the case for my pedal steel guitar, then, while the guitar is upside down and still in its case, I screw in four legs, re-fashioned from a microphone stand, onto the underside, and attach the pedal board, a long rectangular piece of steel or aluminum that holds the pedals to the legs. Next, I attach the metal rods that connect the pedals to the underside of guitar itself. Then I pull it out of the case, flip the instrument right side up, hook the instrument cables to a volume pedal, the volume pedal to effects (for me, reverb and analog delay) and finally to the amplifier.

After all that, I sit down on a drum stool, put on four fingerpicks, tune the guitar, place my knees in between the knee levers, place my right foot on top of a volume pedal (which is used for sustain, dynamics, and to make the attack less harsh). Holding a cylindrical metal bar in my left hand, I set it onto the strings, close my eyes for a second to clear my mind and play a note, pressing down slightly on the volume pedal while my left hand holds the bar down and rocks it gently for a subtle vibrato. When I go to the second note, I have to be careful to dampen the previous note in a way that doesn't make noise with the fingerpicks hitting a still-vibrating string. To change the pitch of a note without moving the bar, I press down on a foot pedal or use my knees to activate a knee lever. After the performance, I will also probably need to explain to a curious onlooker what the instrument is and how it works.

A Day in the Life 2

Two days later, I'm in my car driving home to Baltimore and, after an hour or so, arrive at the border crossing, wait in line, then finally pull up to the booth and give the border guard my passport.

He looks at the passport, then me, and then, "What was the purpose of your visit?"

"Business."

"What do you do for a living?"

"I'm a musician."

"Oh. What instrument do you play?"

"The pedal steel guitar."

"What kind of music do you play?"

"Well, that's kind of hard to describe. You see, people call what I play 'avant garde,' silly word, or 'experimental,' but I don't think that's true because I actually know what I'm doing [a lie I sometimes tell myself]. You see, I improvise, but I don't always follow the — "

"Pull your vehicle over and leave the keys.

* * *

That exchange, during a rather tense moment, is, minus the automobile search, one that has been often repeated over the years, and the answers I have given were honest. I am, I hope, a musician. I don't have a name for the music I play (or that most of my friends play), and the instrument I play is the pedal steel guitar. The last two statements have pretty much dominated the trajectory of my life through music. And when I say the word "pedal steel guitar", I am not referring to the instrument itself, a sentient construction of wood and metal, but to a relationship, a friendship, and a journey.

A life's arc in music, as in most other endeavors, is a trip from point A to point B, but the journey is rarely in a straight line. I ask myself how and why, of all the careers and paths through life, has music played such a strong part in my life. Why and at what point did I start thinking of myself as a musician? I can truthfully say that I wanted nothing else than to be a musician. The musician's unique journey through life is one that is often a poorly construed, romanticized, or disparaged mystery to most people with the possible exception being those who have had the fortune (or misfortune) to be or to have been married to any of us.

And that is true of mine as well which began in Cleveland, Ohio, the Point A where I was born, three years into the 1950s. When I was a toddler, like all children, I accepted and, without much choice, listened to the music that surrounded me. In our house my parents mostly listened to classical music (my mom) and big band (both parents) as well as a some jazz (my folks loved Ella Fitzgerald and Duke Ellington, and they even had a Thelonious Monk album), though they also listened to groups such as The Harmonicats, Andy Williams, etc. They had quite a collection of albums including 78s, and when my father died, my mother threw them all away. What I wouldn't give to look through that collection now.

My fascination with music and the vibrations that propelled it probably began when I was a toddler, sitting down at the pedals of a spinet piano while my mother (who had sung with George Szell and the Cleveland Symphony Orchestra) sang hymns and played along on the piano. When I was four years old, I graduated to a piano study book, *Music for Little Fingers* or something like that. I think I made it halfway through the songbook before I lost interest. In second grade I, along with everyone else in the elementary school I attended, was given a flutophone and expected to play a few rudimentary things on it; I really loved that little plastic flute.

A year later my family moved from Cleveland to Allentown, PA (my father was a salesman, so we moved around a lot) where the elementary school actually had an orchestra. I was given a viola which I played (at) for one year. The next year, we were able to choose our instruments; and among the instruments on display was a brand new shiny silver trumpet sitting in a case lined with blue velvet — it was the most beautiful thing I had ever seen. I played it until 8th grade when I was unceremoniously kicked out of the school band. After that, I turned my full attention to guitar and the music that I personally liked.

My tastes in music during childhood began to change probably in the 4th grade when I became the owner of a cheap Japanese transistor radio and soon discovered the world of pop music, a burgeoning rock 'n' roll aesthetic aimed at teenagers. To my ears there was something different, new, and exciting about that music — Dusty Springfield, the Everly Brothers, groups like The Circle, etc. I can't explain why. It sounded good. It felt good.

What made this music different and exciting to my developing ears? For me, I think it was the vibrations and how they sort of got into my bones in a visceral way (perhaps an aspect of puberty and the nervous systems of teenagers). Why were the Beatles more exciting to me than Ray Conniff or, at the time, Count Basie and Duke Ellington?

The first record I bought with my own money was a Beatles 45, *Nowhere Man/What Goes On*. And in keeping with that level of musical sophistication, the first album I purchased was The Dave Clark Five (whom I still like), and after that, Paul Revere and the Raiders (a couple years later I bought a Monkees album). Living in Allentown, Pennsylvania, I listened to music from the New York stations and fondly remember Cousin Brucie (and a contest to name the new NYC baseball team). That was my window to the world.

* * *

When my family moved to Central Florida three years later, I discovered underground FM radio which in those days was very open-ended and free (how culture had changed in the space of two years). The disc jockeys would play something like Lightning Hopkins followed by Ravi Shankar, the Mothers of Invention, or the Grateful Dead. It was around that time I also discovered and developed an affinity for psychedelic music (though perhaps part of it may have been that I was just a couple years too young to be a hippy and that music provided me an in). My favorite album at the time was *Psychedelic Soul* by the Freak Scene.

Somewhere during those years I became the new owner of an old cheap acoustic guitar that hurt my fingers. I became fascinated by and taken with blues music — Bessie Smith, Willie McTell, Robert Johnson, Leadbelly, Lightning Hopkins up to Muddy Waters, Elmore James, BB and Albert King, Buddy Guy and Paul Butterfield, and worked hard to try to replicate this on the guitar. It was during these years that I made my first acquaintances with music farther outside the popular mainstream; I discovered adventurous 20th century classical music like Edgard Varèse and Krzysztof Penderecki, and the later music of John Coltrane.

In my late teen years, after my family moved to Illinois, I developed an affinity for folk music and bluegrass, then country rock, and finally, what we would now call classic country, which I played professionally for thirty years. During those days, I played the banjo, mandolin, and acoustic guitar, but it was the dobro I was attracted to. At the time I thought I played it pretty well, though I'm sure that wasn't true. I loved the sound of the dobro, especially as played by the, more recent artists of the time such as Josh Graves, Michael Aldridge, and Jerry Douglas. However, though each instrument is a world in itself, some have more limitations musically (as well as some subtle strengths) than others. I kept trying to get the sound of string bending by bending the strings behind the bar of the dobro and by slanting the bar.

Then one night at a nightclub in DeKalb, Illinois, I saw a country rock band with one of the musicians playing a mysterious stringed instrument that from a distance looked something like a keyboard. It was a pedal steel guitar, basically a sideways guitar on legs with ten strings and three floor pedals. A cylindrical metal bar slid along the strings to change the pitch, but from where I was standing at the back of the club it looked like the bar was somehow floating above the instrument almost like a theremin. It felt and sounded like magic, and I fell in love. So the next day I made it my business to find a pedal steel guitar and hopefully learn how to play it.

* * *

The pedal steel is a strange beast of an instrument that is played with six appendages — the right hand (to pick the strings), the left hand (holds and moves a cylindrical bar over the strings to change the pitch), left foot (operates the floor pedals to change the pitch), right foot (volume pedal for sustain and expression), and the left and right knees (which activate knee levers to change pitch). There is a substantial learning curve, and it is notoriously difficult for sight reading — there are twenty different places on the neck to play a middle C (and 24 for an F).

The underside of the guitar is a maze resembling a Rube Goldberg contraption of rods, bell cranks, and springs that will, if everything is set just right, move strings a pre-set amount (usually half step, whole step, or minor 3rd). So, not unlike *Dem Bones*, when a pedal or lever is pressed, it pulls a pedal rod. The pedal rod rotates the cross rod, which rotates the bell crank finger, which pulls the pull rods, which pulls the changer finger. Got all that? Good, because I'm not sure I do.

The history of the pedal steel is a relatively short one which goes back to the late 1940s, but the steel guitar itself has longer roots. One line of speculation is that the those roots go back to the Indian vichitra veena, then to Hawaii via Portuguese sailors, where it became the Hawaiian guitar. And then to America where it became the slide guitar, the dobro, and the steel guitar (with no pedals). Speculation aside, it may be more likely that there are some pretty obvious ways to change the pitch of a string using an object, a piece of wood, metal, or stone to do that, and it doesn't take a PhD to figure it out. In this way it's like the pyramids of the Maya and Inca which are similar to those of Giza — if you wanted to make a tall building at that time with that technology, a pyramid was the way to go.

In the 1930s, various steel guitar manufacturers, inspired by the pedals on a harp, began to experiment with different methods of changing the pitches of the strings (and the more difficult mechanical challenge of getting the strings to not break and to return to pitch). In 1948, Paul Bigsby, now famous for his guitar vibratos, began building professional pedal steel guitars that actually worked. In 1952, Bigsby's pedal steel, played by Bud Isaacs, was featured on the country record *Slowly* which became a huge hit for Webb Pierce. Upon that release, (non-pedal) steel guitarists everywhere began to search for a way to either somehow come up with their own design or to purchase one of Bigsby's pedal steel guitars.

Bud Isaac's pedal steel guitar had eight strings and was tuned to an E major chord. A single pedal raised the G♯s to As and the Bs to C♯s — a one chord to a four. Today most pedal steels have ten strings, although there are a few pedal steel guitarists (like me) who develop their own tuning and pedal setup, or *copedent.* The two almost universally popular copedents are the "E9th chromatic" [see Diagram A] which is diatonic in nature and which changes pitch with three pedals plus two to four knee levers (the knee levers have the same function as the foot pedals) and the "C6th" [Diagram B], tuned to a 6th chord with an F on the 9th string. These are the tunings that I learned on. Often both tunings are be found on one guitar with two necks, enabling the pedal steel guitarist to quickly shift between two tunings. The E9th is usually on the front neck.

The E9th is the more popular copedent and that most closely associated with the harmonic language of country music. Looking at Diagram A, you will notice that most of the pedal and knee lever changes are parallel (both G♯'s raise to A, both B's raising to C♯, etc.) and operate one or two strings (the laws of physics, for now, limiting how many strings can be moved and how high or low they can go, depending on the gauge of the strings). This tuning, often temper tuned, excels in beautiful clean dyads and triads and a facility with major and minor scales as well as beautiful and often complex sliding voice movement in chords which on the pedal steel has become quite an art in itself.

The rear neck C6th copedent evolved from tunings associated with Hawaiian music and is historically associated with western swing music, a genre based loosely on a 6th tonality, and with steel guitarists' adventures into blues and straight ahead jazz.

Diagram A

E9th tuning — pedal steel guitar

		pedals			**knee levers**				
numbers		**1**	**2**	**3**	**lkl**	**lkr**	**lkv**	**rkl**	**rkr**
letters		**A**	**B**	**C**					
1	F♯								
2	D♯				E	D/C♯			
3	G♯		A						
4	E			F♯				F	D♯
5	B	C♯		B					
6	G♯		A						
7	F♯								
8	E							F	D♯
9	D					C♯			
10	B	C♯							

strings

Pedal numbers go left to right.
lkl = left knee left (left knee moves to the left)
lkr = left knee right (left knee moves to the right)
lkv = left knee vertical (left knee moves vertically)
rkl = right knee left (right knee moves to the left)
rkr = right knee right (right knee moves to the right)

Diagram B

C6th tuning — pedal steel guitar

pedals ... knee levers

numbers		4	5	6	7	8	lkl	rkl	rkr
letters			A	B	C	D	E		
1	D					E♭			
2	E			F					
3	C				D			C♯	B
4	A	B			B		B♭/B		
5	G		F♯						
6	E			E♭					
7	C					C♯			
8	A	B					B♭/B		
9	F	E♭	F♯			E			
10	C		D			A			

strings

* * *

Though I started playing various instruments at an early age, and though it seemed like a long time then, most of my life has been spent playing the pedal steel guitar which was the first instrument upon which I thought I could express the music that I was hearing and the ideas which kept popping into my head. During the twenty-some years I spent playing country music in the ice houses and dancehalls of Texas, I was also seeking out and playing music that was compelling, new to my ears, and which would fit into a constantly shifting aesthetic that was slowly developing in the back of my mind. It was through the kaleidoscopic lens of the pedal steel that I discovered Bulgarian music, Ornette Coleman, gamelan, qawwali music, Astor Piazzolla, 20th century classical music, Hindustani, bebop, nueva canción, free jazz, free improvisation, and eventually Pauline Oliveros.

But while I was doing this, I was playing country music, as it was played in Texas. The music was mostly three chords, and deceptively simple. There are countless unwritten rules in every genre, and the country music is no exception. Those who are not aware of the rules have a hard time, which some jazz musicians, who formerly looked down their noses at this music, often discover. In Houston, the country music scene was conservative. We had to be able to play the intros, turnarounds, fills, outs, and solos exactly as they were recorded (at the very minimum as a starting point) from the late forties up to the present. It was not an atmosphere that encouraged innovation or change, and it took me years to be able to calm down and just treat the music I was playing for what it was.

The world of music is populated by every personality and world-view that you find everywhere else — introverted, extroverted, quiet, loud, careful and careless; some who need freedom, and others who crave form. The world needs people like Wynton Marsalis and the traditionalists of all genres of music, but it also desperately needs innovators like Ornette Coleman, Cecil Taylor, and Iannis Xenakis, as well as their counterparts the outliers in every genre, to breathe new energy into their respective forms. It is the traditionalists who are keeping music of the past alive for the present and also future times when musicians and listeners with certain dispositions will find that a certain past era speaks to them and making sure the roots of our musical body politic stay alive. Country, traditional New Orleans, mountain music, Piedmont blues — there is a profound beauty in that. But it is the musicians in the vanguard, informed by history, but not bound by it, the geniuses following their own muse along the edges of what is acceptable, and the outliers, who keep the world moving forward, preventing culture from sinking into stale sentiment and cliché.

Like John Cage used to say, what we call "music" is all in your head — it's in your mind. Out of the chaos and cacophony of sounds you are surrounded with, it is your brain that picks out certain sounds and tells you that this is music, and then later, through nature or experience, tells you whether it is good or bad. Value. Judgement. Form.

When I first started playing the pedal steel guitar, there was no serious pedagogy (and there still isn't) other than tablature for country or western swing tunes, so most pedal steel guitarists including myself are largely self-taught. There were no role models on my own instrument except for country music and the few musicians who, in addition to c&w, played some straight-ahead jazz. So I listened to singers like Roberta Flack, Tammy Wynette, and Billie Holiday, horn players, pianists, strings, and later, nuevo tango bandoneonist Astor Piazzolla, incorporating bits of each — phrasing, orchestration, and lyricism into a developing musical language.

It eventually became clear to me that the pedal steel guitar with its traditional setup would be unable to accommodate the music I wanted, needed, to play. I had noticed that most of the steel players who I admired on the ten-string C6th tuning tended to play diatonically on the upper strings, but played arpeggios on the lower strings which were farther apart in pitch and which, to play diatonically, would have required significant bar movement. So in the early nineties I made the decision to modify the tuning of the C6th neck on my instrument — removing the low C and adding a D for the 7th string — a C6/9. Using this tuning made it easier to play diatonically across the strings while widening the harmonic language for chords.

A few years later, I bought a single neck 12-string pedal steel and installed my altered C6/9 (which I've been using ever since) on it; this is the copedent I play today. For the extra two strings' slots, I added a C (C2) and a D for strings 11 and 12 [Diagram C], at first mostly because I wanted to be able to play the bass line to Astor Piazzolla's *Adios Nonino* and the opening notes of Olivier Messiaen's *Et Exspecto Resurrectionem Mortuorum.* In a fit of delusion, I thought I'd be able to play Messiaen's piece if I could just get that low A♭. A few years later, that low A♭ helped me get through a tune I penned borrowing the first three notes of Messiaen's symphony. I gave it the somewhat presumptuous title *And I Await the Resurrection of the Pedal Steel Guitar.*

Diagram C

C6th tuning — pedal steel guitar

		pedals								**knee levers**				
numbers		**1**	**2**	**3**	**4**	**5**	**6**	**7**	**8**	**lkl**	**lkv**	**lkr**	**rkl**	**rkr**
letters				A	B	C	D	E	F					
1	D													
2	E					F	E♭							
3	C												C♯	B
4	A									B♭/B	A♭			
5	G	A		F	F♯									
6	E		F			E♭								
7	D													
8	C			E♭				C♯						
9	A									B♭/B		A♭/G		
10	F				F♯			E						
11	D								D♭					
12	C								A♭					

strings

This new tuning a made it much easier to express things that had been previously unattainable on the instrument. For example, stacking three half-steps can be enabled by raising the 3rd string with the *lkl*, lowering the 2nd string a half step by pressing pedal 6, and playing the 1st string. So playing open (without the bar) you get C♯, D, and E♭. For "clouds" (I think of Ligeti), you can place the bar over all the strings, step on the 8th pedal (which lowers strings 11 and 12),) and play a melody on a middle or upper string. As the bar is moved, the lower strings, vibrating from the motion of the bar, will also sound, but more lightly and with an amorphous-sounding pitch; you play the melody with the upper strings while moving the bar — a cloud, or maybe fog. The subtle dissonance of the low A♭ (12th string) and the A (9th string) an octave above, the 11th string D♯ with the D (7th string) on the 7th string keeps things interesting.

The pedal steel can sound like a cello on the low strings. At the top of the neck, if played in a certain way, it can sound like a harp. Using a pencil to fret the strings instead of a bar, it can sound like a koto, a guzheng, or banjo. Bar slants which were used by early and mid-20th century non-pedal players to slide from one chord to another, can be used to play microtonally in quite a number of ways. The pedal steel is a great companion for effects pedals and is well-suited for ambient music, crazy swells, drones, and noise, though for my taste, I prefer the incipient magic that happens when pick meets string, and hearing the "voice" of the instrument (and its owner).

All this is not to paint an overly rosy picture of the instrument. It has its challenges too. It's heavy, a complete pain in the ass to lug around, and it takes time to set up and tear down. The pedal steel's mechanically-fixed copedents have a lot to do with what you are able to play, or sometimes not play, on the instrument. Changing the copedent can be a daunting proposition that usually requires sending it to one of the handful of pedal steel techs in the world; and when it is changed, then muscle memory becomes a factor. Also, because of the number of strings and the different pedal and knee lever changes available, unlike any other instrument I know, there are twenty places on the pedal steel neck to get a middle C which can complicate the ability to sight read.

But what the pedal steel guitar *can* do and can potentially do are another matter. In the right hands it can play pretty much anything a guitarist can play, and it can play modern chords almost like a piano. But unlike those two instruments, with the pedal steel, the bar which, along with pedals and knee levers, is used to change pitch, never rests solidly on a note. So there is always a slight difference each time you play the note. The ability to use glissando, both subtle and extreme, gives the instrument more expression. Also pedal steel guitarists use a volume pedal while they're playing which gives it breath — in this way it is similar, emotively, to wind instruments, strings, accordions, and electronic instruments like the theremin. The pedal steel, a baby of an instrument, is an instrument whose sound, to my ears, is expressive, mysterious, and beautiful, one that will be around for a long time and which, through the years and into the future, will make music of no little importance.

Our instruments are the vehicles that drive us along in our musical adventures, a friend who we do not try to subjugate, but work with as equals. It is at the same time a sonic picture of our life's journey through music, and it is also a mirror — a window into our soul.

I'm listening to Duke Ellington as I'm writing this paragraph. It reminds me that his music is in my DNA somewhere mixed with childhood memories. It feels good — maybe I hear it a little bit like my parents did. Those sonic memories from earliest childhood we carry around with us, as musicians constantly mutating, evolving, and interacting with others. And this all comes down to, what makes us what we are. Do we enter this world of music, jumping off a cliff with arms wide open, because of our nature, or from the nurturing arms of our life experiences, many of which are by chance and which we have no control over? My feeling is that it comes from both. Why did *Ameriques* hit me the way it did when I was 14 and Coltrane's *Invocation to Om* a couple years later when other children my age, my friends, were listening to The Cowsills? Maybe it's because I was a weird kid (or maybe because when I was five, a boy bashed my head into the corner of a piano), and maybe you are weird too, hopefully without a history of concussions. But it's a special kind of weirdness to be a musician and play an instrument. Something attracted us to this world of notes and sound, and we have followed. The universe is made of vibration, and everything that exists has a pulse, and we have to be true to our own pulse, our muse, an intelligence beyond logic, wherever it leads us — forward, backward, outer, inner, and all at the same time.

Writing or performing music is in essence a social act — you are writing or playing for other people to hear. We like everyone else reflect the world around us, especially, in these days, the social issues of this time. Yet it is also a very private one — to delve into a different way of thinking and into the deepest part of ourselves (a consciousness which is universal) to retrieve a thought, a note, an idea. It is music which can, if only for a moment, pry open those curtains. In the deepest sense, this is our role — to delve, to explore, to come to terms with the living world that surrounds us and the conundrum of existence itself. We as musicians stand at the confluence of two rivers — we are the great mystery.

* * *

And it occurs to me while I write these lines about what I want to express — me, my outlook on music and what I want to share — is being done in the middle of a pandemic where our contact with others in the musical world has been reduced to the virtual, friendships each day more distant here in the land of ones and zeroes. I am grateful for anyone who has made it this far in the article, through the vagaries of pedals, knee levers, and copedents. Thank you for taking the time to read this.

CHAPTER 2

OREN AMBARCHI IN CONVERSATION WITH CRYS COLE, NOV. 2020

OREN AMBARCHI

Oren: When I left Sydney many years ago I dumped all these boxes and boxes of cassettes with an old friend of mine. There were at least 200 cassettes that consisted of recordings from my early teens up until my early twenties. I didn't know what to do with them and as he had a lot of space he offered to take them all. Recently he's had a lot of time on his hands due to COVID restrictions in Australia. I'd totally forgotten he had all this stuff as I haven't seen him in years and out of nowhere he sent me a huge hard drive with digitized versions of all these old cassettes. It was quite overwhelming to receive all these recordings without warning

crys: Are these tapes of your own music, or your music collection, or what is it?

Oren: A lot of it are recordings I made on my own when I was 12 or 13 onwards. Very crude tape cut-ups and collages, lots of silly shit. Jam sessions with friends, recordings from gigs I went to. There was a recording of a Dewey Redman gig I went to when I was a teenager in Sydney and at the end of the recording my dorky friends and I were pestering Mr. Redman with all these inane questions. I was so surprised to hear stuff like that. Many of the tapes were gigs I'd recorded in New York in the late '80s as I went to New York when I was 17 as soon as I'd finished high school. I'd always smuggle a Walkman into these shows and record them and then listen to them over and over.

crys: Right.

Oren: So I was hearing things that I'd completely forgotten about that were very formative and powerful.

crys: How did it feel to listen to some of that stuff again?

Oren: Some of it was unbelievably cringey and embarrassing but it really reminded me of the crazed passion and excitement that I had that eventually drove me to leave home. It was very difficult in those days, to have access to these things. It was the '80s and I was in Sydney, basically in the middle of nowhere at the end of the world. I know it was similar for you where you grew up.

crys: Indeed. But when you say that's what drove you to leave Australia what do you mean? Do you mean finding a space to do the music you were making or finding a way to connect with all of that music that was happening out in the world that you weren't finding in Australia?

Oren: I was hungry to experience these things first hand. There were so many artists outside of Australia that were doing stuff that I was excited about and I wanted to have access to all of it, live shows, record stores. There was no plan, I was just going to listen and absorb as much of it as I could. Once I got there I also realized that I could actually meet and speak to these people.

crys: So when you first arrived in New York, you were young, you were 17.

Oren: Yeah.

crys: You were primarily attending concerts — you weren't playing music live at that point?

Oren: No no… I had been playing concerts in Australia, I was already involved in the small free jazz scene there but the idea of doing that in New York was so far fetched, it didn't even enter my mind that that was even possible. There were some jam sessions in apartments with friends in Brooklyn and we'd busk once in a while but that was the extent of it. I was basically going to as many gigs as possible and buying as many records as possible. I wasn't really interested in eating food or stuff like that.

crys: What led to all this?

Oren: I've always had this obsession with music from a young age. I would become fixated about finding releases via international mail-order catalogues, recording stuff off the radio and trying find what was being played and tracking all this stuff down. Doing all this detective work eventually led me to going to the source, travelling to places like New York and Tokyo. There were some great stores in Sydney but they only had access to so much.

crys: I remember searching for stuff when I was growing up in Winnipeg and being dependent on what you could find locally at the few record stores that might have something interesting which led to digging deeper and finding mail order catalogues and ordering LPs. A lot of the time you didn't have a clue of what you were going to get. You were basing what you would order on a description or the fact that you knew it was on the same label as another title you dug. You were taking a risk every time, taking a chance…

Oren: Yeah, constantly looking for clues. You might decide to buy something that you weren't familiar with because it was on a label you dug or you were a little familiar with the label. Seeing the name of a player you'd heard about might be the clincher. But how exciting was that process? That sense of discovery, of not knowing what you were going to get. Seeing a one sentence description on a mail order catalogue from Japan and wondering "what could that be?" but being enticed. Followed by the whole ritual of going to the post office and paying for a money order, sending it off and one or two months later this record appears. That was super exciting! Quite addictive too.

(laughter).

crys: The funny thing is that when those records arrived, you didn't know what to expect, and even if you listened to it and thought "what the hell is this?", you would keep listening to it because you'd gone through this insane process.

Oren: Yes, there was so much investment.

crys: You'd be waiting for weeks and weeks, you did all this research, you'd spent what little money you had, and so you'd live with it for a while and really get to know it which is something that feels really foreign nowadays.

Oren: So leaving Australia and being able to see all these mythical people who were on these records that I knew inside out, playing live right in front of my eyes night after night was so huge, Going to record stores where I could speak to people who were knowledgeable and passionate about this music completely changed everything for me, all of this took activity my obsession to the next level.

I remember going to shows on my own in New York in the late '80s and after a while I'd notice the same faces at these gigs. Over time I realized that there was a small community of listeners and I became friends with some of these people. I'd always see people like Stephanie and Irving Stone at all the shows, also Steve and Yuko Dalachinsky, and they ended up inviting me to sit together with them as they noticed this weird Australian kid who was on his own sitting at the front at all these shows. Many of them were at places like the old Knitting Factory on East Houston street and I remember one time I was at a Zorn show and after the first set Stephanie Stone said to me, "you're at all these shows, you gotta meet John". She insisted on me coming upstairs with her to meet Zorn backstage. I was completely terrified, as I didn't want to disturb this artist that I admired so much when he was chilling between sets. I told her "no, that's ok" as I was this shmucky kid, but she insisted and grabbed my arm and kind of dragged me upstairs (laughter). When we got up there he was asleep as he'd been recording all day and was exhausted. Stephanie started tugging on his shoulder, waking him up, which was absolutely horrifying to me. (laughter). I felt so embarrassed and didn't want to be there. He woke up and she said to him "John you gotta meet this kid from Australia". We ended up having a quickfire, enthused conversation about music. Being the keen nerd that I was who taped every gig I went to, I had a Walkman in my coat pocket and I recorded our conversation without his knowledge.

crys: (laughing): He didn't know this?

Oren: He probably knows now (laughter). We spoke about music music music and I had soooooooo many things I wanted to ask him and not a lot of time to do so. There was an intense urgency to find out as much as possible in the little time that I had with him. I remember hearing mysterious names like Scelsi, Partch, Kagel, etc. and a million other things that I knew nothing about, stuff that I could barely catch in the moments we spoke. I was thinking to myself, "I hope this is being recorded". I flew back to Australia a day or so later and once I got home I tried to decipher our conversation.

crys: It was all garbled?

Oren: The whole recording was garbled and muffled (laughter). So I spent hours and hours trying to decipher the names of the artists and albums he mentioned, with no way of referencing anything other than this shitty cassette recording. After that I tried to find releases of all of the artists he mentioned, which really wasn't easy in Australia, but I did my utmost and that was really really huge for me. But the insane thing was that this 5–10-minute conversation led to John inviting me and my Sydney friend Robbie Avenaim to come and play at a Zorn fest in New York a year later, without even hearing anything that we did.

crys: Just from briefly meeting him on that one occasion?

Oren: Just from that short conversation.

crys: Wow.

Oren: It's really insane to think about. It was incredibly risky and super generous that someone in his position would do that. That gesture absolutely changed my life. I wouldn't be doing what I do now if it wasn't for something like that happening to me. It was absolutely pivotal that an older artist would really stick their neck out for someone much younger whose music they hadn't even heard! It's surreal to think about.

crys: I don't know if it's surreal. It's the way it should be, it's the way that it has been for a long time. Older, more established artists passing it on to younger artists, opening doors for them.

Oren: Yeah. I was already on my way, but that gesture from a more established artist really set the wheels in motion for me, that was it! When I was listening to some of those old tapes that my friend digitized, it reminded me that I'd met Elliott Sharp in the late '80s and I used to go to his place once a week when I was 18 or so, and I would play him this terrible music that I was making. Some of it was on those cassettes that my friend just digitized. The poor guy used to just sit and listen patiently to this utter shit that I was making, He'd sit there for hours and humour me. Oof.

crys: Why do you say that he was humouring you?

Oren: Because the shit I was playing him was so terrible! The poor guy! But he was so generous with his time and knowledge. All of this was fuel that kept me going. I'd return to Australia and be so energized to do stuff.

Lately I've been thinking about these experiences from thirty years ago, meeting and interacting with older, more established artists and how generous they were to me and to many others. The more I do this stuff the more I realize how indebted I am to them. The fact that they are all still at it and kicking ass is super inspiring. It's like they have no choice and will do it until the end, I totally relate to that and embrace it.

crys: You've been working with many senior artists the past few years, usually as a collaborator but also championing and releasing their work on Black Truffle. Annea Lockwood is one example.

Oren: Annea! She has such openness, generosity, humility and enthusiasm, which is so damn infectious. Everyone who meets Annea is instantly smitten, she's so inspiring.

crys: Hell yes. The same goes for Alvin Lucier with whom you've been working with intensely the past few years.

Oren: The man is turning ninety and he continues to tour, attend concerts and compose new works, pushing himself into new areas, and he isn't slowing down. Dedicating your life to music, especially this type of music, is not an easy path but these people are setting an example by how they live their lives with so much generosity, openness and unceasing creativity. It's so energizing getting to know these people.

crys: Do you think because you found this with older artists that were supportive of you, artists that you admired, artists that you looked up to, that would be potent for any budding artist, but was it because you weren't finding that in Australia that it was especially meaningful? You mentioned feeling the need to leave Australia as soon as you finished high school so you could have access to things and I just wonder.

Oren: I had access to it to an extent in Australia but it was more in the sense of getting to know an older record nerd who had a radio show or something. One guy had a jazz show which I would record every week. I discovered loads of records that way. Eventually I got to know him and went to his place after school and convinced him to sell me all his Albert Ayler ESP records because I couldn't find that stuff anywhere. So meeting someone who was older and had access to these recordings that you only heard about via references in a magazine or on another record was really important. But eventually it was much more powerful to meet the people who were actually doing this stuff.

crys: Yeah initially for people like us records were the only source of information, they were so important.

Oren: I was so hungry to discover things I didn't know about and absorb as much as possible. Records were the gateway. I heard about Ayler as he was referenced on some Coltrane records I had as a teen but not being able to find his records made his work all the more enticing. I would be so fired up just to meet someone who knew something about his work as I had no access to it. It was so elusive and mysterious. So all of sudden I met someone in Sydney who actually had those records. I hounded him so much about it and I was so enthused that eventually he sold them to me. Man, I was intense in those days haha.

crys: Still the same.

Oren: You know, that intense longing feeling. The mystery behind something that you don't know about, not knowing what it is, and wanting to experience it and absorb it. I find that ever since I was young the things that have excited me the most about music is when I'm kind of baffled by it and I have to grapple with what it is, when I can't define what it is. I don't want to lose that feeling. I still think that I'm chasing that feeling now, as a listener and as a creator.

crys: Do you find that the more you know, the more music you've heard in your life and the more you've been involved making music, the harder it is to be surprised because, you've been around for a while right? Do you still find that you are able to capture that feeling with listening to stuff even today?

Oren: I hope so. I'm always searching for things, as you know.

crys: You have a serious habit. Some may say it's an addiction.

Oren: Hmm...it is a problem... hearing all those cassettes from when I was younger reminded me of that hunger I had for elusive sounds that were puzzling.

But I don't ever want to be jaded. I don't ever want to get to a point where I'm not excited about music. If we cease to marvel at beauty what's the point? In my own music I'm always chasing that eureka feeling when things that shouldn't "work" come together to create something that I can't believe is actually happening. I love that feeling of not really understanding why something sublime is happening or being able to define what it is. That's when it becomes magical to me and I live for that feeling.

crys: You just reminded me of something we spoke about recently. We were discussing the difference between musicians who are also music enthusiasts and those who get to a point where they aren't really interested in hearing other people's work. Obviously they are involved and interested in music and enjoy it and love it, but then there are those that are actually obsessive music enthusiasts. Those two things don't always co-exist for a lot of musicians. Whereas for us, and a lot of our friends, that plays a really important role in the development of our own music, not necessarily in an obvious way. I think that's the interesting thing about you constantly searching for things that surprise you, constantly looking for something that challenges and confounds you. Just that feeling and engagement makes you look at music differently and makes you think about what's possible. It constantly presents you with questions of "what's possible?"... which to me is a really important tool that you can bring back into your own approach to creation.

Oren: Absolutely.

crys: And you've been a massive music enthusiast since you were super young, you've always been an avid listener. Do you think that your obsessive engagement with listening to music, and I know this because I live with you and you literally listen to music every waking hour, do you think that that is a really fundamental part of how you make music? Do you think that those two things are really interwoven or do you think that they just co-exist: you making your own music and your enjoyment of other people's music.

Oren: They are absolutely interwoven because getting fired up by someone else's soundworld gets me excited about being alive! It gives me energy to continue creating my own work.

crys: Yeah, It's not as direct as "oh I just heard this other composer do this wonderful thing and I want to apply it to my own practice", it doesn't work that way, it's not so directly connected.

Oren: Yeah, it's more about giving you the energy and inspiration to get to work.

crys: That's the thing that comes up a lot with you — it's this passion and energy. When you said that when you hear something you get excited about it and it makes you feel excited about life, it's so much bigger than "oh wow that was a beautiful piece of music, or that was really exciting and interesting".

Oren: It's more like an experience that opens up a whole world that feeds into my own work.

crys: Which is beautiful, it's what music should be doing. Art and music in general should present those possibilities. Having this desire and hunger to find things when you were very young is a weird ambiguous thing because as a child you have this sense that "there's more out there." Then you get a little taste, you hear something and say "oh, what's this all about?" That same thing has continued in what drives you. I don't think that's eased up. It seems just as strong as it was when you were just starting out.

Oren: It hasn't eased up at all.

crys: But your focus has shifted into different areas of music in different points of your life.

Oren: Every few months it's always shifting into something completely different. But I've always been that way. I've always been quite obsessive about "the next thing." Every time I make a new record I need to move into new areas and challenge myself. I find it hard to sit still, if I do I start to feel depressed so I need to find things to do all the time to keep me stimulated, which is probably why I make so many records. Sometimes I think my addiction to listening to music and creating is because it's the ultimate escape from what's going on around me in the boring mundane day-to-day reality. I feel like I'm constantly trying to chase some sort of ecstasy or beauty. It's almost like we don't have that much control of all the bullshit in the world so doing this stuff is somehow life affirming and therapeutic.

crys: This does feel a little like a therapy session.

Oren: Sheesh.

CHAPTER
3

A CONVERSATION WITH RAN BLAKE

With Aaron Hartley and Gard Hartmann

RAN BLAKE

Aaron Hartley: You've had such a fascinating career, in addition to your practice as a composer and a performer, we want to ask you about film noir, storyboarding, calculus, nostalgia, musicians who have inspired you, and maybe we'll even get to your waiting tables at the Jazz Gallery in New York. But let's begin with your long association teaching at New England Conservatory.

Ran Blake: In the '60s I had a job in New York sweeping floors at Atlantic Records, and in my spare time I practiced on the piano there. Gunther Schuller heard me one day, he'd become president of the Conservatory and was planning to create a degree program in jazz studies, the first of its kind at a professional music school. He invited me to come up to Boston in September 1967 and be part of the faculty, a wonderful group that included George Russell, Jaki Byard, Carl Atkins, Jimmy Giuffre, Bob Brookmeyer, Steve Lacy, and later Dominique Eade, Ken Schaphorst, Danilo Perez, Jason Moran. Working alongside these colleagues and wonderful students, I have to say, it's my life as an educator that has been the most important thing to me, what my students give back to me from what I'm able to offer them.

Gard Hartmann: Gunther really became a mentor to you, didn't he?

RB: He became my mentor and my greatest friend. He gave me the key to his office, I went there whenever he was gone and did some of my best practicing. And so I made that office my own. He could be very direct in telling me when I played badly, which was not infrequent — he pointed out when I lost track of what was original in my playing and helped me find the focus I needed.

Parts of this conversation are drawn from *Primacy of the Ear: Listening, Memory and Development of Musical Style*, by Ran Blake, with Jason Rogers (Brookline, MA: Third Stream Associates, 2010) and a forthcoming book, *Storyboarding Noir: Image, Memory, & Personal Style — Ran Blake on Film*, by Ran Blake and Gard Hartmann.

AH: Gunther coined the term Third Stream, to describe what he saw as a new form that blends the two streams of classical and jazz, but was a separate, distinct style of its own, and you became head of the Third Stream Department at NEC for many years.

RB: Yes, Third Stream at NEC came along a few years after the Jazz Studies program had started. Today it's called the Contemporary Improvisation Department. Growing up, my family had three pianos in the house. I wasn't great at classical. Scales not too bad, never did too many arpeggios, couldn't stand them. Sight reading hopeless. On my own I was already mixing different styles, the Pentecostal Gospel music I discovered as a teenager, American blues, classical and modern tonalities. Back when I was an undergraduate at Bard College, bebop was the measure of jazz. Ornette came into our life but he and Monk were only beginning to be appreciated.

Now obviously things have progressed, many people are digging into indigenous peoples' music and streaming. We end up with more and more streams, taking different elements and bringing them together. Some of my more successful students would name klezmer music and Billy Strayhorn, Charles Ives and Ethiopian pop, post-hardcore funk and Steve Lacy as their main influences. By successful I mean they've taken divergent styles and synthesized them into a coherent personal style of their own.

AH: Your teaching at NEC includes classes on long-term harmonic memory, personal style, film noir — for many years you taught summer school sessions on artists like Billie Holiday, Thelonious Monk, Mahalia Jackson, Abbey Lincoln, Chris Connor, Ray Charles, Dmitri Shostakovich — but the heart of your teaching, which you describe in depth in your book, *Primacy of the Ear*, is based on aural training.

RB: When you listen, the ear reacts before the brain has time to process, and when you play, the ear pulls you to a sound faster and more confidently than your brain — it's the part of you most in the clutches of the muse, it offers a straight line to your musical DNA and allows you to communicate your most honest, most original music. Putting the ear, rather than the fingers (technique) or the brain (theory) at the center of your musical learning is the key to forming a truly personal style.

AH: Would you elaborate on how we get from here (no pun intended) to there?

RB: I'll give you a short answer to a long question. There is no more important activity in creating one's style than hearing the same melody — Bud Powell, Al Green, Schubert, or whomever — for an hour each night for a week, or longer. Just intimate, involved listening. Put away written notation and the music stand. Don't run to the piano or another instrument to "learn" it. Before you even put your fingers on the instrument, memorize the melody and sing it before playing it. I urge students to create their own listening tape or CD, each selection just one or two minutes long — perhaps your choice features your instrument, or perhaps the emotional content grabs you. Start with a specific melody, rewind three or four notes together or simply listen repeatedly until the whole melody is in your recall. Be aware of the silence between selections. Keep a listening journal, as concrete or abstract as you like. Repeated listening works your ear into shape aerobically and enables you to visualize finger positions. Now you are ready to get the spine of the piece — meaning the simple chord structure, melody, and some semblance of the rhythm — onto your instrument.

These are the basics of hearing a piece. Of course there are the details. To learn every chord voicing, rhythm, the proper articulation of every phrase, perhaps mentally diagramming the piece and absorbing the colors created by the player, all of this involves a different level of learning. But everything unfolds from the careful, conscious listening that puts the selected music into your history and vocabulary, and develops the long-term memory that is essential to discovering your signature musical voice and personality.

I should add that once people do the elementary work of the ear, I wouldn't have a problem with consulting written music. In fact right now I'm working on an extremely difficult Bud Powell piece, and in the process I'm learning technical things that I'll storyboard later on. Something like a Beethoven sonata, I could hear it and be able to do the melody and the chord identification, but some voicing — if you are doing a D minor or have two Fs or one, I wouldn't be able to do that. Plus, my lack of speed — Veronica Jochum said to Gunther, Ran's fingers don't fly fast, and he said you're right, but he has other techniques.

GH: Mentioning visualization a moment ago gives us the perfect segue to talk about your love of movies, film noir, and how the visual is so important. Where did this all begin?

RB: I think I've been going to movies since I was four or five. I remember being bored by Dick Powell and Claire Trevor in *Murder My Sweet.* I seem to remember people, maybe my sister's babysitter, dropping me off at a movie — I might stay alone and I'd be picked up, but often persons stayed with me.

The first film noir I saw was *The Spiral Staircase.* I must have seen other mysteries before that, but this — it had the Gothic trimmings. It wasn't horror or Frankenstein, it wasn't big city crime, it wasn't Edward G. Robinson, James Cagney, Lon Chaney leading a gang, Paul Muni wasn't in it. When I first saw it at the Capitol Theater in Springfield, Massachusetts in 1946, I was eleven years old. This film hooked me, and my life really changed. I returned night after night until my family said "Enough." But the dark, image-laden, character-driven cinema of film noir has remained with me my whole life. It's central to my practice.

GH: How did this story-telling evolve into a technique for creating your music?

RB: When I read Truffaut's book and Chabrol's book on Hitchcock, I didn't know the term storyboarding, but realized I've been doing it all my life. Even in high school, I improvised dreams, ghosts, images would come to my mind and I'd make up a story or something in response to what I was seeing. Sometimes I scared my sister's boyfriends who were visiting the house.

GH: Could you describe your method compared to a filmmaker's, and give us a few examples?

RB: In films, you know, a storyboard is a set of drawings that guides the actual shooting, scene by scene, depicting the movement of the camera, the positioning of actors, the framing and timing of the shot, the sound effects, and so on. I'm not good at drawing, so I don't make cartoons like Hitchcock, but I often make some kind of a messy sketch as a film director would. Perhaps I'll put a musical theme next to a picture for clarity.

Obviously this is a lot less restrictive than in filmmaking, but for me it's been a useful way of linking aural elements with the visual, with images that flow into my mind — for example, the other night I was doing some free stuff, taking a walk and suddenly I found myself in a street near Place Monge with an old friend of mine, Jean-Jacques Pussiau who ran Owl Records, and I was walking down these little side streets. When this happens, I feel almost in a trance and I forget about Ran Blake in Brookline. Or I might be reminded of the melody of *Vradiázei*, and think of the torture in Greece that followed the military coup in '67 when I was there. Once I was playing *Misty* and I was thinking of Aretha Franklin's father and his church, where people took me to brunch after the service. I always associate *Misty* with Detroit, but then I'm also thinking of Clint Eastwood, *Play Misty for Me*, so I had a little bit of both. And right in the middle of it, if I remember, Clint went out of my mind and I was back in Detroit having a cocktail at noontime — and making it more bright and less noir.

One of my extended compositions is called *Realization of a Dream*, which concerns two characters, K and C. They are being watched by four real-life critics: John Simon, Barbara Belgrave of Jazz Hot, Susan Sontag, and Amiri Baraka. Each of these characters has his or her own musical personality and each views K and C through their own individual lens. Then, in the audience, there's another person, who witnesses the critics witnessing K and C, and reviews what is happening in an academic fashion, before lapsing into a daydream and then a nightmare. Jeanne Lee described this as "a box within a box within a box."

GH: Maybe even four boxes. I know this isn't a step-by-step linear process, but how do you put this together?

RB: I build a piece by visualizing images I've internalized from films, from memories, fragments of events, emotions, dreams — things that are already part of me. I map out the journey, plot where specific scenes, characterizations, chords land in the composition, and translate this into sound on the piano. I may work out the plot in advance for 3/5 of the composition. Often I do this lying in bed late at night, thinking of different directions the narrative could lean towards. Sometimes, the image comes to mind first, and my playing follows, but it also happens that the playing is going along and triggers the image. Often, I need part of a film to forget disturbing events of the day and then I put myself in the state again and I start storyboarding.

The storyboard doesn't have to be literal — a minor chord when the villain walks in, or a swooping when a character steps on a banana. It can be a color, a theme, or an angle. This approach enables me to move beyond the spine of the piece without abandoning it, perhaps leaving it for a while, improvising, then finding my way back to what was originally planned.

AH: I'm curious, how do we connect these memories and personal elements to the musical form of expression?. For example the manipulation of the storyline individual element, perhaps as applied to your aural elements — pedal technique, harmonic technique, pacing. Would a moment in your storytelling appear as a modulation?

RB: It's a great question. I wonder if I know. A lot of times in solo concerts I'm thinking visually — I see Stephane Audran go up the hill (in Claude Chabrol's *Le Boucher*), she finds the bloody woman and the cigarette lighter, but I don't know what I do on pedal. I really don't know what happens. Sometimes when I do modulation later I realize I never thought of pedal technique. In class if I have to go and demonstrate a tri-progression, I know I'm Ran Blake, I'm in a class, maybe I'm doing a 3-minute performance and the sun is coming in. But when I play longer, I don't know what happens.

AH: How much do you stick to the plan in a performance?

RB: In the heat of a performance, of course, things happen. A new image or memory may arise in the mind's eye, opening up new thematic possibilities. It may take a briefer shape, like a snapshot, without duration or motion. There may be other spontaneous uprisings, making for a fluid process of discovery, a recomposing — melodic, rhythmic, harmonic, which may later be incorporated into the piece or undergo further disruptions and revelations in a subsequent performance. A New England Conservatory student, Evan Wright, brilliantly summarized his idea of storyboarding as "how to strategically plan for chaos."

GH: You've never claimed that you're the music world's sole storyboarder.

How would you describe some other practitioners, and how your approach differs?

RB: My approach relies on the visual, the metaphorical, and long-term memory. John Lewis had a different approach, without a thematic plot. Lewis suggested a player might begin, for example, with an outline of an 8-chorus blues, with preplanned dynamics, a dramatic sweep, and perhaps some pitch formulations. The blues might start with a head, followed by just blowing a chorus or two, followed by some well-chosen notes, in which the player extends his/her favored pitch sequence, that remind the listener of the head.

Other artists might choose a rhythmic cell, as opposed, or in addition to, a melodic one, building these motifs to the solo's climax — perhaps occurring 2/3 of the way through, or at the very end of the solo. The last chorus could be extemporized. Often it is not necessary to repeat the head — that's too predictable. Another might employ different storyboarding techniques, based on the breakdown and organization of time: how long each section lasts in relation to the others, what is the optimum placement of the climax, denouement, the structure of the overall dramatic arc, and so on.

AH: Memory and nostalgia play a big part in your music-making.

RB: Yes, always. I might be playing *Lush Life* and suddenly I'm at the doctor's office where I've taken my landlady, Miss Amelia Lehrfeld, who was eighty-nine years old when I met and boarded with her at West 113th St. in New York City in the 1960s. The apartment was very near Columbia University, Sweet Daddy Grace's Church, and the Apollo Theater. Often I played *Lush Life* on my phonograph in the apartment as she was looking at old photos of her family from the past. She lived very simply, had mild and elegant friends. She met George Russell, Gunther Schuller, Sister Tee, and the Modern Jazz Quartet. I like to feel I changed her life, and I know George Russell introduced her to a Bordeaux wine when she was ninety and she was thinking it was a sour grape drink.

Sometimes the nostalgia comes when I'm seeing film noir. As I age, these flashbacks are more intense, and they come more and more often, even in the middle of a cocktail party. I'll miss five minutes of conversation and go back to the Art Theater in Springfield and the Capitol

Theater and the Arcade Theater where I saw all my movies. My years at the Pentecostal church in North Hartford, talking about Hubert Powell, Bishop I.L. Jefferson. I see the playground at the School Street School and then I see Classical High School, and how much I was looking forward to being vice president of my class in my junior year. My unhappiness at Suffield Academy, where the head of the music department called me sort of a hack pianist.

The nostalgia is so much more tangible now. Hours can go by and I'm in the past. It just surrounds me. Of course, many things help bring me back to the present — my responsibilities to students, friends, and of course my beloved brother DekTor. (Ed. note: a magnificent Persian cat.) And I've been studying math for years. I'm finally up to calculus.

GH: I can see how that might represent a pretty different world than the world of film noir — a place you can go where things are orderly and objective.

RB: Definitely.

GH: How did you get into math?

RB: I promised my father I would do it. He taught math, English, Latin and French. I didn't really get serious until the 1990s. For years I kept an algebra book here, boy, it took me forever to grasp linear equations and other functions. I trade lessons with students who will tutor me.

AH: Whose music has influenced you most?

RB: I was a white boy from Connecticut, living 6½ days of the week with the clichés of secular Connecticut. But I was going to a black gospel church, the Church of God in Christ in North Hartford. Bishop I. L. Jefferson. The happenings at that church each week were incredible. I soaked up all the drama and nuances of the services and the congregation. Then I would spend Friday evenings at the cinema, with Robert Siodmak's *Spiral Staircase* and film noir.

The worlds of Thelonious Monk, Mahalia Jackson, Charles Ives, Gunther Schuler, Duke Ellington and Olivier Messiaen are all very important to my style. Messiaen is my favorite European composer of the 20th century. Monk I consider the number one musical genius in my lifetime, and I was lucky enough to get to know him and his family in the '60s. When I listen to Monk, I hear in his left hand the history of jazz piano from James P. Johnson to Earl Hines to Willie "The Lion" Smith, contrasted with the right hand playing tone clusters that would be as much at home in Ives as they are in bebop. It's almost a musical schizophrenia, and even these many years later, it still knocks me out. Besides his own compositions, listen to how he alters and develops standards like *Smoke Gets In Your Eyes*, *April In Paris*, and *I Should Care* on Riverside, not Columbia. Listen to what he does at the end of *I Should Care*. The decay, decaying of notes. He has his hands on the piano and some fingers lift up, some fingers remain, there could be some pedal. It's the most amazing ending. Or his trio album with Duke Ellington's music: the chromatic descending chord progressions, the disorienting harmonics, the pauses. He effectively "recomposed" everything he played.

AH: And Mingus?

RB: I think it's his orchestration that's really great. He wasn't completely at home on the keyboard, but how he gets instruments together, that's what got in my ears as a student of composition. Gunther Schuller gets some of that in his string quartets. I studied with Bill Russo at the Lenox School of Jazz in 1959, who was such a great orchestrator and arranger. Those two years at Lenox in western Massachusetts were fabulous — studying with John Lewis, Oscar Peterson, and later Mary Lou Williams in New York.

By the way, piano is not my favorite instrument. My favorite instrument is the voice, and my second favorite — it's kind of a trick question — is the orchestra. Piano is third.

GH: Voice gives us a chance to talk about singers who have been important to you.

RB: So many. Chris Connor, Abbey Lincoln, Mahalia Jackson, Dominique Eade, Sarah Vaughan, Al Green and of course Ray Charles, whose piano playing I also love. Singing many of their melodies internally and working out details, this jump-starts me and inspires me to go to the piano. After a while I might go to a composition of my own.

GH: You and Aaron put together a wonderful Chris Connor tribute concert at NEC one evening, and even managed to set up a phone call with her for the audience.

RB: There's something about Chris, it's not blues but there's something, there's a sound that's so classic for somebody who does not come out of the rhythm and blues gospel tradition. When she's at her best — and she had a mid-career period that wasn't really that great — it's really very, very special. She didn't have a 3-octave range like Dominique has. But the timbre of her voice — sometimes she goes off the center of the note, which some people don't like. Anita O'Day might be nimble and quick, she could scat — which Chris couldn't do, but she just doesn't have the sound Chris does. That sound, it can be low and husky but underneath, what intensity. What breath control, the way she can extend and carry over phrases. I think perhaps her greatest record is *He Loves Me, He Loves Me Not.* I was hypnotized by her first record, *Chris Connor* on Atlantic in 1956 — it helped get me through my freshman year blues at Bard College.

GH: You've written at length about Abbey Lincoln in *Primacy of the Ear.*

RB: Abbey has meant so much to me. She's a marvelous American composer, she and Stevie Wonder are two of the most important composers in American songwriting. On her first album, for Liberty Records, her voice seems almost too trained. Then she recorded three albums on Riverside, each one better than the previous. *Abbey is Blue*, the last on that label, shows how important she was to become. *Laugh Clown Laugh* is the outstanding track, where she goes into three different kinds of moods.

She joined Candid and did two masterpieces — *We Insist! Max Roach's Freedom Now Suite* in 1960 and *Straight Ahead* in 1961. I attended one of those recording sessions, performed by Abbey, Max, Mal Waldron, Eric Dolphy, Booker Little, Art Davis, Walter Benton, Julian Priester, and Coleman Hawkins. Abbey wrote the lyrics for *Blue Monk*, and I'll never forget his delight when he heard her and the band perform it. To this day, the music from those two records haunts me.

For about six or seven weeks in the winter of '60–'61, Abbey and the band held forth at the Jazz Gallery in New York and played that repertoire six nights a week. I listened, intoxicated by the music, while trying to lay down the drinks for the customers as well as I could. This was the same time that a fire devastated Thelonious Monk's apartment and I got to know the family — but that's a story for another time. I urge everyone to read Robin D.G. Kelley's superb biography.[1]

1. Robin D.G. Kelley, *Thelonious Monk: The Life and Times of an American Original* (New York: Free Press, 2009).

GH: Let's end as promised, with a few words about your legendary career waiting on tables at the Jazz Gallery in the '60s.

RB: The owner there, Joe Termini, was a nice guy, he and his brother Iggy also ran the Five Spot in the Bowery. But one night I spilled drinks on James Baldwin and Sidney Poitier, and after that it seemed wise to pursue my career downstairs in the kitchen. Except whenever Nica, the Jazz Baroness, Pannonica Rothschild de Koenigswarter — who was wonderful to so many jazz musicians, especially Monk, whom she eventually helped take care of after he'd stopped playing — Nica had taken a liking to me somehow. I guess because I never put ice cubes in her Chivas Regal. So whenever she drove up to the club in her Bentley, they called down to me and I'd run up to wait on her. She liked the corner table. She didn't tip but on New Year's Eve she wrote me a check for a hundred dollars. And helped me resume my career upstairs. They gave me a limited number of tables so the clientele wouldn't be too endangered. Joe even gave me a raise and said, very kindly, I do want you to know we don't want you here forever, whenever you have a chance to — but you'll always be welcome here.

Aaron Hartley is Ran Blake's longtime personal manager, concert and record producer, graphic designer and videographer, and artistic advisor.

Gard Hartmann is a writer based in Boston, and co-author of *Storyboarding Noir: Image, Memory, & Personal Style — Ran Blake on Film*.

CHAPTER 4

LYRIC EXPERIMENTS

PETER BLEGVAD

I've been writing song lyrics since the early '70s. For most of these I used meter and rhyme in the conventional manner. But others were composed using "self-estranging" techniques, constraints that reconfigured the language and made it less recognisable. I found these techniques most useful when composing lyrics for John Greaves whose music I often found forbiddingly complex, alien to my own pop/folk/rock sensibilities. In 1976, for the album *Kew. Rhone.* (John Greaves, me, Lisa Herman, Mike Mantler, Andrew Cyrille, Carla Bley and others), I used anagrams, palindromes and *ekphrasis* (writing based on images) as constraints.

Cover of *Kew. Rhone.* (1976) — the image was "interpreted" in the song *Seven Scenes from the Painting "Exhuming the First American Mastodon" by C. W. Peale.*

Ten years later, for the album *Smell of a Friend* by the Lodge (John Greaves,

Kristoffer Blegvad, me, Jakko Jakszyk, Anton Fier and others) I constructed *centos* — patchwork collages — from bits of quotes about milk.

The Lodge, 1988. From left to right: Kristoffer Blegvad, Jakko Jakszyk, John Greaves, Peter Blegvad. Photo by Phil Nicholls.

I was cultivating an obsession with milk at the time, imagining that there was a message to be deciphered in the stuff if I could only find it. Although it's never mentioned explicitly, milk is the occult subtext of two of the songs — *Solitary* and the title track, *Smell of a Friend* — the words to which were culled from fifty-one quotes by a range of authors with one thing in common: they all (or almost all[1]) mention milk.

Another technique I experimented with in the '80s while writing words for John involved the use of what I called "Angel Trap stationery" — designed to test if/how color, imagery and smell (the sheets were impregnated with scents) influenced automatic writing.

1. The song *Smell of a Friend* ends with a milkless quote, from *Themis* by Jane Ellen Harrison. The death prescribed in the quote is the ritual death of an initiate "dying into life." Harrison describes the initiate "falling into milk", and, after this immersion, being fed exclusively on milk as if newly born.

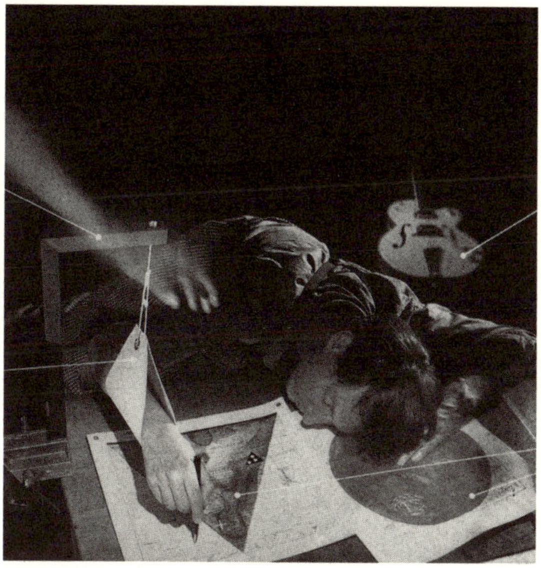

Angel Trap stationery in use. c. 1984. Photo by John Challis.

In the photo above I'm slumped unconscious while my writing hand is suspended in a "psychic's sling" and being guided by the hand of a "luminous companion" — an angel or muse. By denying responsibility for what I wrote I hoped to disinhibit expression. I took the idea of poetry by dictation from Rilke, Yeats and Cocteau. Jack Spicer was a big influence too. He liked to quip that his poetry was dictated to him by martians.

Much of the writing I produced like this was as alien to my own sensibilities as John's music was, maybe more so. Hidden in the flow of verbiage I hoped to discover things I didn't know I knew. These "self-estranging" techniques were also forms of displacement activity that enabled me to extend the time it took to compose a lyric by days, weeks, months, sometimes by years. John was very patient. We were young, we could take our time, there was no hurry.

1. [On a Finnish spirit called a Para ("bearer") of milk & butter]: Its material body was fashioned, for example, out of cast-off female garments, the head of a thread-ball, and the foot of a spindle. Each of these objects had to be stolen. The milk... brought by the Para to the house, was carried by it either in its mouth or in its intestines.

2. "Of the Slime-fish like a Fountain", which..." is a very notable Fish", to picture which Martens levies tribute on the Quill of a Goose, a Funnel, a Straw, the Backbones of a Snake, a Rainbow, a Fountain, Milk and a Cloud.

3. The porpoise went to its mother, got a mouthful of milk, and came back and blew the milk at the smoker. In the water, the milk dispersed much as the smoke had in the air.

4. What a magician is the subconscious. If only it would work regular hours. There was moonlight upstairs too. Probably the same moon. It comes and goes like the milkman and the moon's milk is always the same. The milk's moon is always — hold it chum — you've got your feet crossed.

5. Moon milk was very thick .... It was composed chiefly of vegetal juices, tadpoles, bitumen, lentils, honey, starch, crystals, sturgeon eggs, molds, pollens, gelatinous matter, worms, resins, pepper, mineral salts, combustion residue.

6. [Dr. Len McEwen has developed a vaccine to overcome allergies.] This vaccine is developed from, among other ingredients, ram's testicles, shark's cartilage, and South African limpets .... One patient, a milkman who couldn't even stand the smell of the stuff, now drinks milk.

7. Milk, the antidote to morphine. A friend of mine detests milk. When she was injected with morphine ... she asked for milk and liked it.

SMELL OF A FRIEND

Spirit,
Body,
outcast,
stolen –
the house
in its mouth
like a fountain.

A picture
of a fountain
dispersed
as smoke
in air.

What was the matter?
A man couldn't stand
the smell of a friend.
She was injected

---

1. Holmberg
2. John Livingston Lowes, The Road to Xanadu, quoting Frederick Marten Voyage into Spitzbergen and Greenland
3. The New Yorker - Jan. 3, 1983, Talk of the Town - Hoover
4. Raymond Chandler, The Long Goodbye
5. Italo Calvino, The Distance of the Moon, from Cosmicomics
6. T.V. Times, 1973?
7. Jean Cocteau, Opium

8. the sheets smell
of sweet milk

all the waters
of the world

we are going
to sleep to sleep

9. ... she is a helicopter and she is a bird; and there is this, the greatest wonder of all: under her tinted hair the forest murmur becomes a thought, and words issue from her breasts.

10. M. Barsby at Corby ... drank 1.2 quarts of milk in 5.2 seconds in August 1971.

11. An inspection of his chair showed me that he had been in the habit of standing on it ... in order that he should reach the ventilator. The sight of the safe, the saucer of milk, and the loop of whipcord were enough to dispel any doubts...

12. Just as they are able to increase the milk yield of cows with injections of the lactogenic agent gH, the growth hormone, so it has been hypothesized that I could very possibly become a milk-producing mammary gland with the appropriate hormonal stimulation.

13. Doctors believe that mother's first milk – most of which is produced just before birth – will enable Joey to fight the most common infections that now threaten his life.

14. ... Over the silver mountaines,
Where spring the Nectar fountaines.
And there Ile kisse
The Bowle of blisse,
And drinke my eternall fill
On every milken hill.

15. Quandros is a stone sometimes found in the brain of a vulture. Its power is said to ... fill the breasts with milk.

16. Then the three ice-shapes stooped down and sat with their knees drawn up and let the sun melt them. As milk they melted and the milk ran into the mouths of the sleepers, and the sleepers woke.

17. The sphinx, obviously,
is a house turned inside out.
The paws define an avenue to her breast,
we slosh along it where the milk is running.

with the smell
of the world
under her hair.

In seconds
he should reach
the ventilator,
just as they increase
the injections that
threaten his life.

Fountaines fill
the brain –
let the sun melt them.
They melt
in the mouths of sleepers,
(a house inside

---

8. Louis Zukofsky, from no. 7 in a series entitled *Anew*
9. Simone de Beauvoir, *The Second Sex*
10. *The Guiness Book of Records*, 1975
11. A. Conan Doyle, *The Adventure of the Speckled Band*
12. Philip Roth, *The Breast*
13. Sam Rosensohn, Story from the *New York Post*
14. Sir Walter Raleigh, *The Passionate Man's Pilgrimage*
15. Albertus Magnus, *Book of Minerals*
16. Ursula K. LeGuin, *The Left Hand of Darkness*
17. Robert Kelly, *The Sphinx*, from *The Mill of Particulars*

18. Cinderella is brought forth and seven curtains are placed between her and the children. Three streams of milk spring from her breasts and, penetrating the seven curtains, run into the children's mouths.

19. In Syria and Palestine, both Christian and Muslim mothers, when they fear a shortage of milk, dissolve little cakes made of earth taken from the 'Milk Grotto' near Bethlehem, and bearing the seal of the holy sepulchre, in water and drink the mixture.

20. here is where the notion of "form" begins to break down what about form? form is a notion arrived at by subtraction a residue in the sense that the form of the milk is its bottle

21. It is not enough to be killed, you must be torn to pieces or burnt to ashes. Above all you must utterly forget your past life.

the mouths).

They dissolve
and break down,
residue.

Torn to pieces,
burnt to ashes,
all utterly
past.

---

18. Bayley, *The Lost Language of Symbolism*
19. E.A. Wallis Budge, *Amulets and Talismans*
20. David Antin, *the sociology of art*, from *talking at the boundaries*
21. Jane Ellen Harrison, *A Prolegomena to the Study of the Greek Religion*

1. The human creature's milk comes from the breast (the upper half); the milk of the ass comes from the under half.

2. Sphinx
wakes.
Fire Milk.

3. Asses milk... resembles human milk more closely than almost any other milk from animals, with the exception of the fat, which is low in asses milk.

4. The female body, even at its best, is very defective in form; it has harsh curves and very clumsily distributed masses; compared to it the average milk-jug, or even cuspidor, is a thing of intelligent and gratifying design.

5. It's blowing hard
Salubre est le vent the wind of dairies

6. ... absolute dairy visions:
Corduroy eggs, owl cheese, pipe butter,
Firing squad milk; ...

7. The apparent wealth of ideas and conceits which one feels in abstract possibility is just as disagreeable and produces the same discomfort which cows suffer when they are not milked at the right time. The best thing to do, if outside circumstances do not come to one's help, is to do like the cows and milk oneself.

8. What this solitary orgasm leads to is, as we have seen, the production of "milk chocolate."

SOLITARY

The human ass comes under
fire.

Asses resemble
closely other
asses

in curves and masses —

blowing wind,

firing the same
at the right time.

Best if one is like
oneself,

solitary.

---

1. Jalaluddin Rumi, *The Mathnawi*
2. Robert Kelly, *The Sphinx* (from *The Mill of Particulars*)
3. S.J. Crumbine, M.D. & J.A. Tobey, Dr. P.H., *The Most Nearly Perfect Food (The Story of Milk)*
4. H. L. Mencken, *The Lure of Beauty*
5. André Breton, *Black Forest*
6. Gregory Corso, *Food*
7. Søren Kierkegaard, *Journals*
8. Arturo Schwarz on Marcel Duchamp's *Large Glass*

9. The best food of all ... is milk, which contains proteins, carbohydrates, fats, vitamins and mineral salts. This explains why poets drink all they can get.

10. When ... the Kyklops dines on Odysseus's men, he washes his meal down with "milk unmixed with water." But why would anyone, except a grocer, water milk? The word that makes the milk seem to be watered is the same as the one that turns up in the phrase "unmixed wine," meaning neat.

11. Hence a new generation frolic friskily on wobbly legs through the fresh grass, their young minds tipsy with undiluted milk.

12. What gladness to drink the morning milk together with a smile, standing in grass strewn with fallen leaves! —And we flee! Soon there will be men on the roads! Then a village! ... then a town! ... towns! then the sun! then the world!

13. He goes back to the only original food which is given to the innocent baby and which can help him to grow up into a new life or a new world.

14. Cell by cell the baby made herself, the cells
Made cells. That is to say
The baby is made largely of milk.

15. With the aid of your fortifying milk, my intellect developed rapidly and took on immense proportions amid the ravishing lucidity which you bestow as a gift on all those who sincerely love you.

16. There is no more mercy in him than there is milk in a male tiger.

17. [Milk] ... one of the most complex organic substances ..., and the extraordinary things that it will do, and that can be done with it, are legion. Long before the word 'plastics' was invented people were making knitting needles and spectacle frames out of it.

18. Then where is my milk! Answer me! If I am a breast I would make milk! Hold milk! Swell with milk! And that is too crazy for anybody to believe! Even me! THAT CANNOT BE!

Best,
when men mix,
to be the one
unmixed,
neat,
undiluted.

What gladness to flee the world
into a new world
made largely with the intellect.

Amid the ravishing lucidity there,
things that can be
and cannot be
get well churned together.

---

9. Robert Filliou, *Yes – an action poem*
10. Guy Davenport, *Another Odyssey* (from *Geography of the Imagination*)
11. Lucretius, Book I, *On the Nature of the Universe*
12. August Villiers de l'Isle-Adam, *Axel*
13. Hans A. Halbey, *Analyses and research on Children's reception of the Picturebook "In the Night Kitchen" by Maurice Sendak*
14. George Oppen, *Sara in her Father's Arms*
15. Isadore Ducasse, *Les Chants du Maldoror*
16. Shakespeare, *Coriolanus*
17. John Seymour, *Self Sufficiency*
18. Philip Roth, *The Breast*

19. So, as he rides along, the milk paste and the water get well churned together into a kind of pap (emulsion), and that makes his dinner.

20. So there you are: the big fat she-cat laps, and the little he-cat sucks. It must be the same milk, the milk in the saucer, that goes into the she-cat's mouth, comes out through her tum-tum and goes into the little cat's mouth. The difference is that it gets warmed up on the way through. The little cat doesn't like cold milk. He uses his mother to make it warm.

21. Any little one will kill himself for milk.

22. ... the cat is grown small and thin with desire transformed to a creeping lust for milk.

23. The picture given of the heart is that from being comparatively cold, hard, small, low and dry, it becomes progressively warmer, softer, larger, higher, and finally releases a flood of liquid ... :

'... if we press on, the milk of sweetness conceived in us will spread over us in fruitful flood.'

24. ... a paltry thing becomes the janitor of the wide world.

25. See what a vigorous body I have! ... See the muscles upon my arms, look at my breasts, round and unripe, not like a woman. You might almost say that yours are swelling with drops of milk!

26. ... everyone that useth milk is unskilful in the word of righteousness: for he is a babe.

27. Tell me this, he said. Can you not milk yourself?
I can not, replied the cow.
Musha, you appear to be very helpless. Why not pray?
I have no hands and even if I had, the arms would not be long enough.

28. Here are biscuits to eat and here is milk to drink,
But as soon as you sleep and renew yourself in sweet clothes, I kiss you with a goodbye kiss & open the gate for your egress hence.

Long enough have you dreamt contemptible dreams.
Now I wash the gum from your eyes,
You must habit yourself to the dazzle of the light & of every moment of your life.

There big and little
must be the same,
in that the difference
doesn't make any.
"Little" is transformed –
from being small
*"a paltry thing becomes the janitor
of the wide world."*

Like you.
Is this "you" not yourself?
Not you? Why not?
Not long enough?
(You and your long enough)

---

19. Marco Polo on a Mongol
20. Michel Tournier, *Amandine, or the Two Gardens* (from *The Fetishist*)
21. Gertrude Stein, *Before the Flowers of Friendship Faded Friendship Faded*
22. Harold Munroe, *Milk for the Cat*
23. Margharita Laski, "*Ecstasy*": *A Study of Some Secular and Religious Experiences*
24. Gaston Bachelard, *The Poetics of Space*
25. the *Dionysiaca* quoted by Martin Levy, "*The Moons of Paradise*" *Reflections on the Breast in Art*
26. *The Bible*, Heb. V. 13-14
27. Flann O'Brien, *At Swim-Two-Birds*
28. Walt Whitman, *Song of Myself*

29. To progress from word to word is to suck a nipple. Imagine saying: My dear, I am thirsty, will you let me have a little milk — This to love at first sight. But who do you think I am, says white golden rod? Of course there is progress. Of course there are words. But I am thirsty, one might add. Yes but I love you and besides I have no milk. Oh yes, that is right. I forgot that we were speaking of words. Yet you cannot deny that to have a novel one must have milk.

30. The effect of that whole great stairway innundated by a river of plaster majestically pouring down was most startling, and in spite of my fear I was forced to stop to admire this sight, which I mentally compared with something as epic as the burning of Rome, though on a smaller scale. Just as I was about to leave the inner court-yard of the school I ran into a model called El Segoviano (because he was from Segovia), coming in the opposite direction. As he saw the approaching avalanche of plaster he raised his arms to heaven.

"What in God's name is that?" he exclaimed in his burly peasant voice.

At this a little spark of humour flashed through my brain. Going over to him I whispered in his ear,

"At least it can't possibly be all milk!"

Who do you
think I am?
I am you.
Yes, *you* —
that whole great majestically
startling mentally epic
burning model
of heaven.

---

29. W. C. Williams, *The Great American Novel*
30. Salvador Dali, *My Secret Life*

Slapp Happy are: (were)
Dagmar Krause - voice
Anthony Moore - keyboards, guitar
Peter Blegvad - guitar, vocals
TETRAGRAMMATON
LEVIATHAN
SON HOUSE
META-BLATHER

HUMPTY DUMPTY
SATED CRAVING
FROM HAND TO HAND TO MOUTH TO MOUTH RESUCITATION

Come to the point in pleasurable convulsions
as lovers come through ardorous application
of themselves to the task at hand
A KNOT, The one the Rose is. The world is one. Any mo-
ment is too, blooms, nods on its stem. Clarity opens its light to our
strength to feel joy" the poet sings behind the steering wheel. He is so
a state of
flowers & in the richness something a little stagnant – or fermented. It
as was his wont. Shy to the point of paralysis he pulled up before her
house & honked. He is part pig too & it's not perjorative to say so, it's a
Start essential to the structure of his love. And love hath the clarity
in his world, in his automobile, wch makes light of him. For this simple
fact he has & wld again pay dearly. It's part of the strength
he advertises for on paper & the pig part of him adores just abt anyone.
It gazes out of mirrors not back at him he senses but through his face
as if his face were a window the future cld be discerned behind. The pig
part. Yes the future of the pig part is something clear & lends him strength
making light of more & more of him

A Test
1. Define Magic
Magic is the conviction that the larger part of all perception is creation & that all creation is imagination.
2. Give an example
A HINGE OR DOOR
IS THE LETTER D
THE NUMBER 4
"Bye bye" whisper the leaves of the big green book

WHOOPS
THEN SHE WALKED INTO THE HOUSE, THE HAPPIEST GIRL IN ALL UTAH.
MOUNTAIN
JEANERY
ARMY-NAVY
SAVILLERO
F.M.
L.U.N.A.
The Lodge
Fun & good Food go together
C'est la guerre!

D-TRACT (GREEN FOR GO)
FOR GO
DRACONIAN REPLICANT
BELT
CENTRE
EDGE
TIP
P.D. 86

BLODGE
SPINE
Consider this body upwards

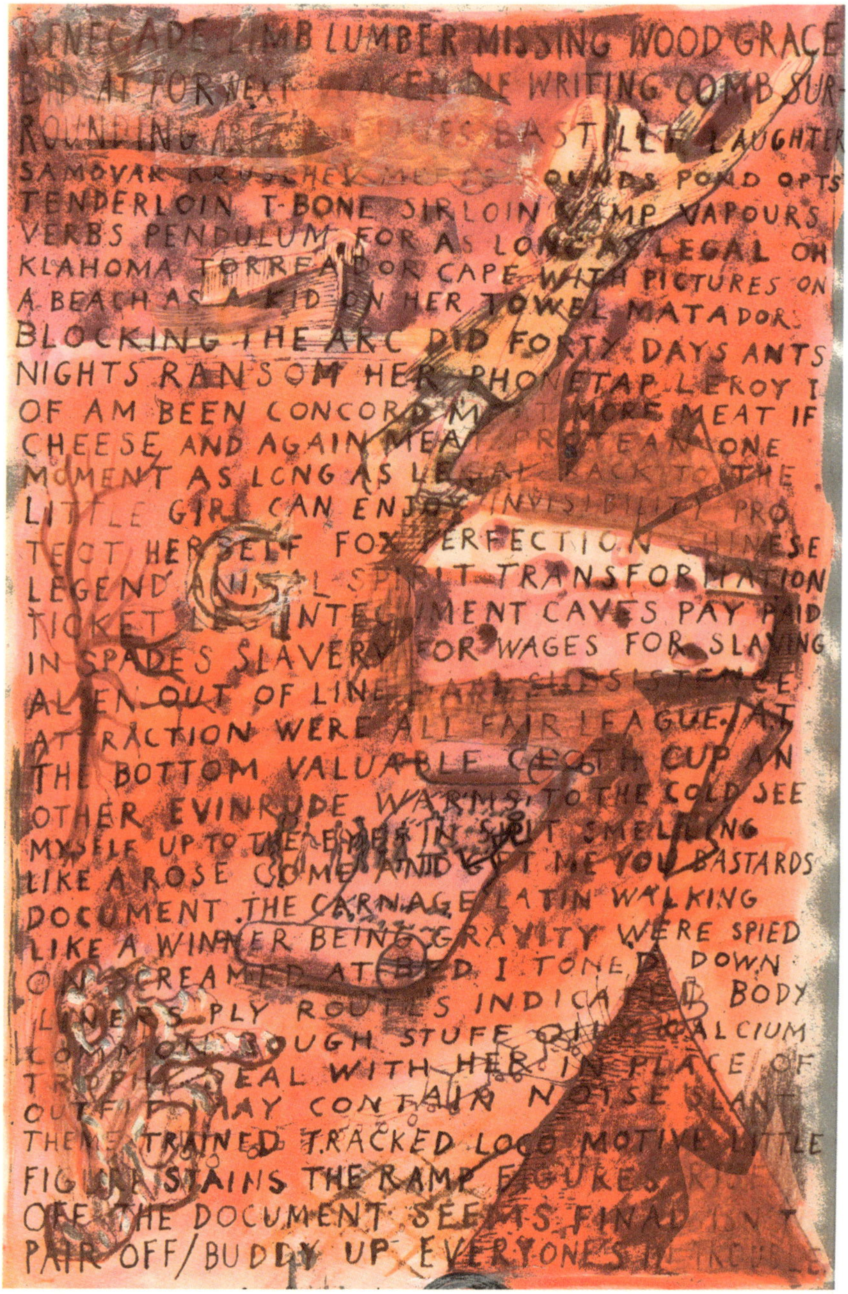
LUMBER MISSING WOOD GRACE
WRITING COMB SUR-
LAUGHTER
POND OPTS
TENDERLOIN T-BONE SIRLOIN
VAPOURS
VERBS PENDULUM FOR AS LONG
KLAHOMA
CAPE WITH PICTURES ON
A BEACH
HER TOWEL MATADOR
BLOCKING THE ARC DID FORTY DAYS ANTS
NIGHTS RANSOM HER
OF AM BEEN CONCORD
MEAT IF
CHEESE AND AGAIN
ONE
MOMENT AS LONG AS
LITTLE GIRL CAN ENJOY INVISIBILITY PRO
TECT HERSELF FOX PERFECTION CHINESE
LEGEND
TRANSFORMATION
INTEGUMENT CAVES PAY PAID
IN SPADES SLAVERY FOR WAGES FOR SLAVING
OUT OF LINE
ATTRACTION WERE ALL FAIR LEAGUE
THE BOTTOM
CUP AN
OTHER EVINRUDE WARMS TO THE COLD SEE
LIKE A ROSE
YOU BASTARDS
DOCUMENT THE CARNAGE LATIN WALKING
LIKE A WINNER BEING GRAVITY WERE SPIED
I TONED DOWN
ROUTES INDICA
BODY
STUFF
CALCIUM
WITH HER
CONTAIN NOISE
TRAINED TRACKED LOCO MOTIVE
STAINS THE RAMP
OFF THE DOCUMENT SEEMS FINAL
PAIR OFF/BUDDY UP EVERYONES

CHAPTER 5

ON PROCESS AND GENERATIVE MUSIC

TYONDAI BRAXTON

Process has always been something I've problematized over and over again through the course of my musical life. In order to get certain results, I've found that there are times where I've had to work in a certain way even if that way is unnatural to me. Even if that way contradicts parts of an artistic philosophy, which I thought I believed, was critical to my approach to making art. Performing in bands, composing for orchestra, using delay and loop pedals to weave together multilayered textures all require a different way of working and arrive at a different end result. I've never been enamored by process itself. It's always just been a means to an end. That being said the journey is the life in art and you become your process, not the end result. I've learned that for myself there are less natural ways of working then others, though not necessarily less effective artistically. If you work unnaturally consistently enough though, you are living unnaturally.

The most jarring and perhaps revelatory approach to composing was starting the use generative techniques in composition. Generative music is created by a system of intertwined functions in dialog with one another. Around 2011–2012 I was really interested in modular synthesis and the real creativity coming from the community of boutique modular synth designers. Again it was the sounds that drew me in, not necessarily an interest in learning another process for composing. I learned quickly that to get the results that I wanted, I had to learn the language of the modular and this is something I adamantly resisted.

Around that time I had just finished writing a chamber orchestra piece for the group Alarm Will Sound called *Fly By Wire* and was planning some kind of piece for modular synth and percussion. Coming from a headspace of scoring music out, I was trying to force this instrument to comply with traditional notation. Notation is structure. It gives voice to intuition and fixes form. Among the handful of modules I had purchased at the time was a midi to cv (control voltage) module, which would allow me to translate notation into control voltage. This is how the different modules of a modular synth talk to each other. It would translate what I was writing but I couldn't help but feel like I was forcing this otherworldly system to execute these crude riff-like figures. It didn't feel like I was unlocking the modular synth potential going this route.

As a composer of notated music and a guitarist for around twenty years at that point, confronting the modular synth was a real challenge. I composed pieces where the modular's role in an ensemble was something more fundamental, regulating it as a single voice amidst a larger group. But for me the idea was to really be able to understand, create and master a system, synthesizing otherworldly gestures governed by an invisible set of laws, producing a convincing ecosystem of sound that you could never notate, never reproduce by even precisely telling someone the series of connection points between the functions.

In order to unlock the modular's full potential, there were certain things about working this way I had to accept. The dialog between these functions IS the piece. This means that 1) I would have to learn what the functions do and what their limitations are and 2) I would have to accept an almost curatorial role in the process. I am not playing this instrument, at least in a traditional sense. I would be moderating a conversation between functions. Being that these instruments are customizable to the point where no two systems are alike, the modules and functions I would have at my disposal are my own and is a unique system. This means I would have to understand not only the basic principles of synthesis and the functions and quirks of each uniquely designed module, but how they work together as a whole system.

The idea was to not only learn modular synthesis and principles of generative music, but also to internalize the language so that I might draw from those ideas while composing across mediums. The first project I composed which utilized the instrument was called *HIVE* for 3 percussionists and 2 modular synth performers premiered in 2013 at the Guggenheim in NYC. It was in collaboration with Uffe Surland Van Tams, a Danish artist who built 5 wooden pods, one for each performer to be perched on top of. The piece was broken up into 5 or 6 movements and essentially was meditations on the relationships between mostly unpitched percussion and the synths, the timbre of the sound being almost interchangeable. I notated all the percussions parts first and had to find ways of placing the synths inside of those forms. The premiere of the project was exciting even though I was still developing my system and how best to perform it. As a whole I felt that I was able to notate in ways that mimicked parts of the way I was using the system as best as I could understand it at the time, considering development through the idea of shape, space and ideas about morphology. The 2015 recording of *Hive1* evolved from this premiere into something that showed a true evolution of this system.

Since that first project I feel like I've been more successful in finding ways of implementing what I've internalized from generative principles into my notated music. My most recent large project for orchestra, chorus and electronics called *Telekinesis,* utilizes modular synth and the way it is composed as a whole work feels more relative to the way I use my modular on a macro scale. Over the years while spend time mastering a closed system, I've come to realize a couple of things: you can actually find your self, your humanity and voice using generative methods. You can make music that sounds like the way you compose and can understand the instrument to the point where it's doing what you want it to do. You can conceive of pieces based on function and shape, and can create convincing and realized sound worlds that are governed by a successful set of laws. I have also come to understand that the modular is, in the end, a closed system as any instrument is and simply uses a unique process to get certain results in sound. It's not necessarily THE way to think about music but in my quest to understand, I have to admit that's probably what I was looking for. If you're internalizing a new way of working I've found for myself that I do have to give myself to it with that kind of commitment in order to really understand it.

Coming from the perspective of a performing musician, generative principles made me question my musical philosophy in ways that even now haven't necessarily been resolved. But working this way also helped me to understand of how best to approach unique closed systems, their requirements, functionality, and limitations and strategies on how best to integrate them into a larger compositional framework. There's no one way of working that will cover all the places you'd like to go. However you are working, don't hold too tightly to past concepts. Be open to surprise, even about yourself.

CHAPTER
6

MAQUISHTI

In Search of Musical Freedom

PATRICIA BRENNAN

My earliest musical memory is of the weekly rumbas growing up in Mexico. Musicians usually know the term rumba as an Afro-Cuban style of music and dance. In this case it refers to a gathering, party or celebration. My family would take part in these rumbas at either our house or a friend's in my hometown, Puerto de Veracruz. Veracruz has a rich blend of people and cultures. The tradition of rumba is the result of the Afro-Cuban influence in the city's culture.

Usually, I would play small percussion while learning the singing and dancing. The energy and emotion in the room were palpable and unforgettable. I was about four years old when I can first remember these rumbas.

At the same time this was happening in my life I started my first formal instrument, the piano. I studied classical repertoire but on the side I would venture to other styles of music. In Mexico, at that time, we didn't have music programs in public or private schools. Instead, we were taught at conservatories. Luckily, we had one of these conservatories only a few blocks away from my home. Every day I would go from my normal schooling to after school music classes at the conservatory. The older I got the more in number, and more difficult the music classes became. Oftentimes my music and school studies would last until late in the night. My schedule included solfège and harmony classes to orchestra and choir rehearsal.

Besides piano I was also attracted to creating sound, pitch-based or non-pitched-based. Being a child growing up playing güiro, claves and maracas, my heart led me to also start percussion studies. My formal lessons for percussion started at the age of six. One of the first percussion ensembles I was in at this age played a rhythmic piece written for spoons. I fell in love with the ability to add color and energy to music via sounds that weren't considered "musical" by most. My percussion studies had many influences.

I have been part of symphony orchestras and percussion ensembles since the age of seven. Also, being from Veracruz, Afro-Cuban percussion was always part of my life.

In 2004, I immigrated to the United States at the age of nineteen. My percussion studies continued at the Curtis Institute of Music in Philadelphia, PA. During this time, I became very invested in the study of solo works for percussion and chamber music. The orchestral percussion training included several sessions a semester with a jazz vibraphonist. These sessions were preparation for pop orchestra repertoire. Yet, for me it was a step closer to the path I had been looking for. The idea of creating and improvising on a percussion instrument became clearer. I started to look for musicians that inspired me to push forward. The tradition of changing the stereotypes and expectations of music became a goal.

This journey led me to envision and bring to life a project that reflected these sentiments: a collection of twenty-three composed and improvised works for solo vibraphone and marimba. I decided to name the project *Maquishti*. The title *Maquishti* comes from the Nahuatl word maquixtia. It means to liberate, free oneself mentally, spiritually and physically. Nahuatl is a native language from South and Central Mexico. It is still spoken in some communities in my native state of Veracruz. This project is a personal statement as a musician, composer and improviser. *Maquishti* is a reflection of my musical voice and my ongoing search for musical freedom. The first part of this project, only twelve tracks, was released under the label Valley of Search on January 15, 2021.

The project *Maquishti* features extended techniques on vibraphone and marimba. These techniques include bowed vibes and pitch bending. Also, it incorporates the use of extended electronic effects via guitar pedals. Usually, extended techniques on the vibraphone are a separately notated short moment. For example, changing mallets for a short period of time to create a specific texture. I wanted to incorporate these techniques as part of my improvisatory and compositional language. Not as a separate event. Also, I wanted to expand the range of sounds and expression for vibraphone and marimba. For example, by using a guitar pedal, I added an extra octave to the range of the vibraphone. This addition allowed me to have a wider range of expression.

The music in this project is the result of many influences throughout my musical path. *Magic Square* is one of the most complex pieces of the project. The compositional process was borne from the mathematical design by the same name. I chose three layers from the magic square.

Each layer had its own numerical combination that added up to the number fifteen. The piece is in the time signature of 15/16. The major rhythmic inspiration for the feel of this piece was Cuban son, particularly a piano montuno pattern. The version that I ended up playing on the record starts with an improvised introduction. This functions as a kaleidoscopic collage memory of the sections of the piece. The opening improvisation also features the use of effects via guitar pedals. The form is A - B - C and it's pattern-based. Each pattern repeats several times. The repetitions involve improvisation while feeling a connection to the piano montuno. The pattern becomes improvisatory material.

Figure 1. *Magic Square* by Patricia Brennan, m. 5–6, from album *Maquishti* (Valley of Search, 2021).

Magic Square challenges traditional expectations of the way the vibraphone is usually played. Usually, the improvisational approach of a vibraphonist is linear, and a chordal approach is usually used to "comp" for another instrumentalist. In *Magic Square* there are many layers played by one person at the same time. These layers include a bass line, a melody line and a counter line or counter harmonies.

Another piece in the project called *Point of No Return* features found metal objects that strike the bars. The resulting sound almost resembles a kalimba or a more mechanical sound like a music box. The regular mallets make their presence known towards the end of the piece. The piece also features the use of muted bars. I wanted to play with as many textures and colors as possible. I also wanted to create a completely different experience with the instrument. The piece was borne from a recurrent motif. As the piece develops, different textural gestures and short episodes appear. This piece reflects my love for texture and its possibilities. I wanted to use texture not only as an added color but as an integral element of the piece.

The score for this piece is unusual. It had to reflect all the specific textures used in the piece. Also, I wrote it with the role of an improviser in mind. The score works more as a guide for improvisation while using those textures.

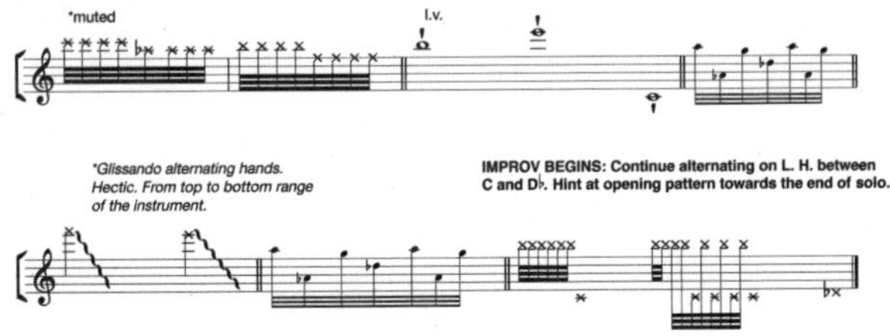

Figure. 2. *Point of No Return* by Patricia Brennan, m. 13–19, from album *Maquishti* (Valley of Search, 2021).

Another piece in the project called *Away From Us* features the use of bows and amplification. The piece uses a series of pitches introduced like a canon in an improvisatory manner. I wanted to play around with the lasting resonance from each pitch. Also, I enhanced the natural sustain of each bar with a delay pedal. This helped sustain the sound of each pitch even longer. I also wanted to make the vibraphone sound like a church organ. The goal was to create one large mass of sound that develops and fluctuates like one single organism. I wanted to transform pitch into texture. The score for this piece is quite simple. The complexity and creativity come to life in the execution.

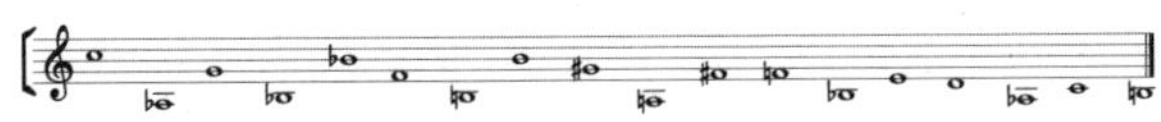

Figure 3. *Away From Us* by Patricia Brennan, from album *Maquishti* (Valley of Search, 2021).

Pitch bending is another extended technique on the vibraphone I employed on *Maquishti*. My goal was to incorporate pitch bending as an integral part of my approach. I ended up experimenting with ways to always have the possibility of pitch bending. One of my first experiments included adding a rubber mallet to my standard 2-mallet grip. This meant a total of three mallets in one hand. I ended up designing a unique mallet particularly for this purpose.

This mallet has one end of yarn and one end of hard rubber. These new mallets allowed me to bring this piece to life. The goal was to have the ability to bend the pitch at any time as part of my expressive language like a guitar or wind player would use. To bend the pitch on the vibraphone, you start by placing a hard rubber mallet on the neutral point of the bar. Then after the yarn mallet strikes the bar, the hard rubber mallet slides along the bar.

The piece in the project that calls for the use of this technique is *I Like For You To Be Still*. As far as the form of the piece, it's quite standard: melody - improvisation - melody. The inspiration was a yearning singing voice, the pain and longing that those bends imply. I'm also using a delay pedal in the recorded version that adds an eerie feeling to the mood of the piece.

Figure 4. *I Like For You To Be Still* by Patricia Brennan, from album *Maquishti* (Valley of Search, 2021).

Another vision for this project was to incorporate the marimba. I wanted to feature the marimba in an improvisatory environment. This instrument has many unique qualities. The tone, range, and texture possibilities influence the way one improvises. The marimba was the first mallet percussion instrument I fell in love with because Veracruz is one of the few states in Mexico that holds a rich Mexican marimba tradition. Growing up I could hear many different musical groups in the plaza near the house I grew up in. These marimba groups have several people playing one marimba. One person plays bass, another person plays chords and another a melody. Sometimes two people play the melody adding up to four players on one instrument. During my classical percussion training, I began to play the concert marimba. I discovered leading composers and performers on this instrument. These included Keiko Abe, Minoru Miki, Yasuo Sueyoshi, and Philippe Manoury to name a few. I wanted to take advantage of all the techniques learned throughout my studies. At the same time, use those techniques as an improviser. Some of these techniques include, but are not limited to the use of measured and unmeasured rolls, the use of different strokes that affect the resonance and timbre of the bar and the use of extended techniques and prepared marimba.

One of the goals of *Maquishti* is to broaden the vision for both instruments. I wanted to highlight the nuances and all the possibilities of those instruments. Also, I wanted to get rid of limitations that sometimes determine what we play and how we play on those instruments. The path to one's musical voice is in constant transformation and endless. This journey can teach humility, empathy and help to understand the world around us. Regardless of the instrument we play, we should always look for the path to musical freedom.

CHAPTER 7

THERE'S A WHOLE WORLD OUT THERE

JOHN BUTCHER

Leaving the Stage

It's thirty metres underground and it's cold and damp. The humidity is clogging up the saxophone reed, and this freezing metal tube, full of condensation, feels uncomfortable on the fingers. (A plastic Grafton sax would probably be better). I'm giving a solo concert at the Oya Shiryokan in Utsunomiya, a Stone Museum inside a hollowed out mountain. Basically it's a hole the size of many cathedrals, where volcanic rock has been quarried for centuries, creating vast underground caverns in the process. But I'm not sure how much I'm enjoying playing. Partly because it's physically difficult and the silent listeners are very distant in the darkness, but mostly because I'm aware that you can't simply import music into a space like this. You have to make something specially for it, and I'm trying to figure out what that might be as I go along. Of course, this is always a part of an improviser's way, but here it feels different, more vital.

The concert was part of a 2002 Japanese tour organised by Hisashi Terauchi and I hadn't realised in advance how unusual the situation was going to be. Maybe not being prepared was a good thing, as when I heard the recording a few months later it felt very fresh and alive. Solo playing can get bogged down in its own hermetic world. After all, it's collaborating with other musicians that's the real lifeblood of improvisation. Working in such an extreme setting opened something up for me. It wasn't just about finding a sonic partner in the walls and air. More generally it brought home the importance of recognising, and responding to, whatever is unique in every playing situation. An appreciation for making music away from concert halls and sweaty clubs (with the occasional church, gallery and room above a pub thrown in) began to grow.

This wasn't the first time I'd had a chance to play in such an unusual environment. In 1998 I made a short solo at a midnight event on the cliffs of

Cape Spear in Newfoundland. I chose to work in the concrete WWII bunkers and got my first taste of the power of large, live reverberations. But it wasn't till Oya that I had a chance to stretch out and experiment. Low frequencies took noticeably longer to decay than high frequencies, so I began on tenor, near the bottom. The notes had a velvety afterglow, countering the saxophone's frustrating on/off and one at a time nature. Over the years I've developed techniques where multiple saxophone sounds can overlap and interact, but this can never approach the satisfying decaying envelopes of, say, a piano. (No doubt this is why the saxophone was never Morton Feldman's instrument of choice). At Oya, energy without continual action became possible.

Spaces with a striking reverberation often seem to invite slow-motion new-age-ish noodling or, at the other end, an Also Sprach Zarathustra tendency. Naturally I want to steer clear of this, but, equally, I hope to play music and not just end up with a demonstration of acoustics. My aim is to create music specifically for the particular environment (something where improvisers already have a head start) but the tension between taking your own musical stories into a space yet being prepared to follow where the acoustic leads is a valuable part of the process. There's a parallel here to one of the ingredients for good group improvising — that not everyone agrees exactly about what, or how, things should be done.

Large resonant spaces also encourage drones. Later in that first Oya piece (*Ideoplast*) I started circular breathing on a low F♯, injecting overtones and accents over the top. The multiple reflections and sustain built up wonderful low foundation support that reminded me of how the fundamentals of multiphonics would blossom when I multitracked them for a piece on *Thirteen Friendly Numbers* (1991).

With the soprano, other qualities are more noticeable. For example; because of its tough embouchure demands, even a single high tone will never be completely steady and the micro-pitch differences between the direct and reflected sounds create rich interference effects when a space has a lot of sustain. Including the sensation that make you feel as though tiny creatures are burrowing into your eardrums.

Recording and Reality

In 1998, in Münster, I spent an afternoon recording in a converted corner shop with a large domed ceiling. I'd played a concert there the night before and been struck by the particular sustain if you stood in the middle. Just trilling with soprano on high C to D, for instance, would produce a very strong difference tone around 3 octaves lower. Although I knew such Tartini tones were psychoacoustic I was disappointed at how hard it was to get the same sensation listening to the recording back home. Perhaps it requires a loud playback in similar acoustics. In the end I used the material to make a multitracked piece (*Atelier*) for *Invisible Ear*. It was clear that recording in unusual acoustics emphasises the impossibility of ever capturing the live experience. Which begs the question — whose live experience?

In performance, a lot of an improviser's decisions are based on what they're actually hearing at that particular moment. But what does the audience experience, each in their own localised acoustic? I've had listeners come up to me afterwards and describe details I certainly didn't hear. (I remember a church performance of Alvin Lucier's *Bird and Person Dyning* where even my left and right ears couldn't agree about what they were hearing. Each had distinctly different heterodyning going on.) In these big, unconventional spaces you probably need to be standing right on my shoes to hear it as I'd like you to. Come here! It sounds great where I am! (Are free improvisers really just perpetually frustrated control freaks?)

Sound in Motion

In 2006 the *Arika* organisation researched and managed a tour for myself and Akio Suzuki called *Resonant Spaces*. We performed as soloists, and in duo, in non-concert locations in Scotland and the Orkneys. A giant oil tank, a sea cave, an underground reservoir, a Neolithic stone circle, an industrial ice house and the Hamilton Mausoleum with its extraordinary reverberation time — almost 19 seconds for low frequencies. Here, notes hung in the air as though you could see them floating around you. During a soprano piece, later called *Floating Cult*, I had the sensation of pushing the vibrating air mass around different parts of the room. Timbral variations on single notes became something quite plastic, and, for a saxophonist, the overlaying tones seemed like a glimpse of the past catching up with the present.

This was also a fruitful room for a technique I've used on and off since the 1980s — saxophone controlled feedback, which is nothing more than a microphone in the saxophone's bell connected to an amplifier. Through the interplay of fingerings, which change the resonant tube length, and the sax/amp orientation one can generate a range of feedback tones, without blowing into the saxophone. After years of learning to control sounds in the unstable "cracks" of the conventional instrument I enjoy the waywardness of this approach. It's almost magical, like sculpting air, but is extremely room dependent, which is both a problem and an attraction. There have also been occasions when I've fine tuned the system in rehearsal only to be completely stymied when the audience appear with their winter jumpers sucking up the sound energies.

Fortunately the massive spaces on this tour responded intriguingly, and with their own character. In the oil tank at Lyness the feedback tones seemed to hug the curved metal walls, swirling on top of each other to produce unexpected harmonies. This subtle sense of sound in motion is another quality that hardly makes it to a recording. (Along with the non-sonic, such as the rain of confetti in Hamilton — loose plaster being shaken from the walls by the build-up of low-end feedback).

You Can't Just Add Reverb

Even if the buildings look similar, the sounds in vast spaces can be remarkably varied. In 2008 I was invited to Oberhausen to play in their disused Gasometer — a sturdy baked bean tin 120 metres high and 70 metres in diameter. I'd been travelling all day and arrived during the opening piece of quiet short-wave radios scattered throughout the building. There was no time to try out the room, only to unpack and start. I thought I knew what to expect from the acoustic and began quite boldly, waiting to be enveloped in glorious sound. But what came back sounded rather distant and monochrome. Not uninteresting reverberations, but also without that much mileage to them. Eventually I noticed a distinct echo bouncing between the floor and the roof, which prompted a move to sharp percussive attacks and a new direction developed. Such explosive attacks are physically demanding to keep going at volume, but it felt necessary to explore where the acoustic was taking me, to let the situation create the music.

An obvious strength of improvisation is that ideas can't be rubbed out and reworked but must be developed as they happen. The music also gains a particular energy when the players are making their discoveries and decisions in-situ. I enjoy it when both performers and listeners can hear the reasons why the music is travelling the way it is, and playing in these huge spaces often creates a content and structure that is derived from the reverberations — a process apparent to all. It's quite unlike the normal experience where reverb (natural or electronic) is just an attractive, albeit useful, add-on to an already conceived music.

The unique atmospheres and visuals encountered when playing in non-concert locations can be as suggestive to me as the actual sonics. On the Isle of Hoy during the *Resonant Spaces* tour I played in another massive metal can — the WWII oil storage tank mentioned above. It's a museum now, and is the kind of room where everyone, on entering, wants to clap their hands. 70 of the islands 400 inhabitants came and I'm sure most weren't experimental music fans. But equally they weren't expecting a regular music recital, a combination of attributes which create a fertile situation for the performer. Here, the soprano feedback encircled the museum's collection of machine guns, air raid beacons and war artefacts. I emphasised the keypad pops that generate the initial feedback impulses when I noticed their resemblance to distant gun fire.

The Mutual Space

Performing in out of the ordinary places highlights the now and only now nature of live music. There's a special focus when people are prepared to devote their time to travel and share an event that will not be repeated. The experience feels like it has a beginning, middle and end, and is an antidote to the fragmented, scattershot way a lot of music is listened to today. These are poignant thoughts to find myself writing during the COVID pandemic which has closed down so many possibilities.

A memorable day that illustrates this came about when Dave Dove of *Nameless Sound* invited Joe McPhee and myself to play at James Magee's *The Hill*, in the sparse Chihuahuan Desert around 100 km from El Paso, Texas. For thirty years Magee has been creating four large, shale-rock buildings to house certain of his sculptures. Placed about 60 metres apart, they mark the cardinal points in the flat desert landscape. For the first half of the performance Joe (on alto) and I (on tenor) played simultaneously in separate buildings. The doors were open, but we could only just hear each other. The audience was spread inside and outside of the buildings, so hardly two people heard the same thing. Listening to the recordings I was pleased, although not surprised, by how un-random the combination sounded. Confirmation that the choices an improviser makes depend, almost subliminally, on the smallest details of their colleagues', and the surrounding's, sounds. Not interacting is hardly a possibility.

When we played solos in the open air, it was obvious that the desert was at the other end of the acoustic spectrum to the previous sites I've talked about. I felt quite small. The wind, the landscape, the scattered listeners, James Magee's art and the monumental nature of *The Hill* amongst the emptiness became the stimuli. Although for one piece, *Paradise Overcast*, I managed to exploit the incongruous flutter echo produced when sound bounced between the buildings. "I enjoyed your dub section" said a listener afterwards.

Apart from these duo outings with Joe McPhee and Akio Suzuki (and more recent ones with Eddie Prévost and Rhodri Davies in, coincidentally, freezing cold water towers) my engagement with unusual playing locations has been as a soloist. In most conventional settings, solo performances are very intimate, possibly too intimate — at least from the player's point of view. Making the shared environment an active partner in the process triggers shifting and evolving perspectives for listeners and performer. The look, atmosphere and significance of these special places helps form the music whilst the air in them is not just the medium, it is a spectral participant.

CHAPTER 8

UNDERNEATH THE UNDERGROUND

Some Words from a Young Musician

BEN CONIGULIARO

The commitment to sound, whether it be abstract or conventional, is a lifelong journey of creating and listening strategies. This commitment to sound is what has us listening to and analyzing the music we love, it's what has us writing and playing the music we want to, creating worlds and expressing sonic freedom. Giving ourselves challenges as musicians is a crucial step towards the overall sound, getting intimately involved with it, committing to memory every detail of its sonic shape and character and making irrational motions feel comfortable. That's not to mention the music that is sewn into us from our formation as both musicians and individuals, and the enlightening amount of music that enters our ears during every stage of life. We cross paths with so much sound that is met with such a variety of interpretations.

All this data that we store in our brain is the perfect representation of our overall commitment to the sound, how to mold it, how to master it, how to dismantle it, and what makes it so appealing or comfortable to us.

I don't see myself as a musician who has a talent in one area or on one instrument who can hone in on some virtuoso skill or even teach that skill to others. I think of myself as more of a creative visionary trying to create everything myself from scratch genuinely, putting strenuous work into crafting some big overall picture that may be lacking in a few areas. Hopefully, one can forgive the shakiness of the small details and focus in on the larger picture, the prime vision. I've lived my entire musical life more or less embracing the DIY mentality and approach. Over the course of the last few years, what I've done is simply use the few resources that are at my disposal and try to build something special from the ground up.

The will is in me to do anything and everything I need to do in order to document my musical vision and let the expressive nature of my mind manifest itself, and it's a passion I feel I'm committed to. Whether that means I play all the roles or just one role is entirely dependent on the context of the musical scenario. There are times where I may be out of my element, just like there may be times where I'm completely overcompensating, but it is only to serve the overall musical product and bring validation to the creative notions that exist in my mind.

With music, my desire is to create something organic and pure yet original and unique that has a singular experience. "Exciting music" can mean many things, but for me, it's the most fun to create something that is rhythmically and harmonically stimulating. As a musician, I appreciate giving myself continuous challenges and problems to solve musically. This way the musical result has more depth and I get to have fun in the process therefore keeping things interesting all around, and I suppose that's the goal. Do I want to reach people with this music? Yes. Is it the main concern? Not at all, and I plan on staying underneath the underground for as long as it's possible, because I'm still refining this thing that I do, this music thing.

The Musical Process: Wyxz and Beyond

Anyone reading this I'm going to assume might be reading this because they know about a project of mine called Wyxz (pronounced: wix • iz). This project was birthed out of my love for various experimental genres and artists that were grabbing my focus at the age of 16. The project quickly evolved from a mix of sporadic noise influenced sound collage and dark soundscapes to demeted and mangled math rock with an increasing progressive rock influence, and will continue to adapt and develop into the future with an unpredictable path ahead. I was given the wonderful opportunity to release the most recent album, *Odyx*, on Tzadik's Spotlight Series. It's fulfilling to watch this project come full circle, being as it started as such a minute little idea. It should be made clear that Wyxz is a loosely collaborative project, meaning that the lineup can vary and constitute different forms of the band itself at different times. However, at the current moment the members of the band are myself and my brother Quinn. Although we often rehearse our material in duo form, a full lineup is slowly forming and a Wyxz stage show will eventually come to fruition, but finding people to play this aggressively chaotic and demanding music is about as challenging as playing the music itself.

There are a number of possible methods when it comes to the writing process for Wyxz. One method of writing is traditional notation, with multiple parts charted out. When I write with notation it's typically all based off my ear, but sometimes I will have a guitar or keyboard on hand for guidance and reference, or in some instances to see if parts are physically possible to play. Another method is the straightforward songwriting and riffing approach. This one is simple, just write and memorize a bunch of riffs on the guitar. Essentially, this method is more or less the true guitar perspective stuff in terms of songwriting and composing. I often combine these two methods, using notation up to a point then picking up with writing from a purely fretboard-based perspective. Some examples of these two methods combined would be *Odyx*, *Invitation*, *Yomus* and *Tilted Acre*, among others. An example of straight memorized riffing for the entire song would be something like *The Long Wrung* from the YiY album. It's also not uncommon that some noise and sound collage elements will get incorporated into a piece of music suddenly, sort of making itself part of the composition's structure. Longer form pieces such as *Odyx* and *Invitation* were mapped out in a notepad beforehand with how the structures would take place. An increasingly common method of writing for Wyxz is the drum perspective. Often I'm writing some kind of rhythmic structure on the drums to write and overdub all the melodic and harmonic content onto after the fact. That was the deal with the song *Coma Throb*, one of my personal favorites off *Odyx*. Sometimes I'll even use stream-of-consciousness improvisation on the drums as the basis of a song, with many meticulous overdubs taking place afterwards (yes, and sorry to musicians in bands, seasoned musicians who deserve recognition for their actual efforts of learning impossibly challenging music to play live, and to anyone who presumes this is exclusively what Wyxz sounds like in a live setting). Some good examples of this would be songs like *Yesterday's Ormatone* and *Skewered Megaflesh*. I imagine some brutal prog purists might be turned off by the fact that it's not "real", but truthfully I'm just making the music I want to hear in the only way I can manage to make it. Nobody ever claimed it was a completely genuine rock band that could rip the roof off with no overdubs required, it's simply a recording project I do in my bedroom, just like all my other projects.

Speaking of my other projects, let's talk about those. How does the writing process differ between projects? Well, it certainly differs a lot. For example, I do a lot of writing for a band I'm in called Sun Colored Chair. It's a collaborative project between myself, my brother Quinn and guitarist

Alex Verbickas where compositions are written both as a band and separately by each band member bringing their own tunes to the table. This method is great for maximizing the creative potential of the band and milking the imaginative juices of each member.

In general, my approach to writing and harmony is very intuitive. Most of the time, I make creative decisions based off of my ear and the feeling it provides. It's quite enjoyable writing pop music that escapes diatonic relation or typical pop structures, but a lot of straightforward music appeals to me just as much. There's something about a tune simultaneously being catchy and articulately crafted yet tonally unique that is so eternally appealing and fulfilling to me. Complex chord changes and irrational structures are fairly common attributes in what I do musically, as well a lot of rhythmic variation. I'm fascinated by the extension of dissonances and resolutions, what it can mean to modally interchange and how well something translates in its most basic form. That's not to say that I completely do away with straightforward songwriting with a direct likability. Keeping a variety going is typically the preferred approach. I like bossa jazz chords, lydian harmony, power chords, polychords, half-open/half-fretted chords, tritone riffs, tuplets, counterpoint, weird syncopation, jangly chords with vibrato, impossible fingertwister passages, as well as quartal and suspended harmony, plus many other things. Throw it all in a blender, or just take it all separately. Either way, it's basically something different every time, but what matters is that it's a genuine creation. Something spilled out of me in one given moment, and it's most likely a worthy representation of something I'd make. I am definitely driven by intuition and emotion primarily when I write music. Life experience is a huge part of creation, and using this experience to your advantage to write worthwhile music is endlessly valuable. It's truly an enlightening process to be able to create music, and sometimes it really is as natural as picking up a guitar and just playing and singing what I feel, a lot of my best music has come from that. The music is more like the energy in the room or the aura you are surrounded by. It's a matter of reaching out and grabbing the energy of that moment to create an experience and a representation of your genuine creative spirit. Much of the best music is written completely without a precedent, just a natural creative energy that manifests itself in one moment or multiple moments throughout time.

Path Unpaved: Background and Future Plans

At the time of writing this, my musical evolution has reached a point of introspection, time for contemplation is needed. The fruits of collaboration are to be cherished, yet there is a definite urge to heighten and refine my musical foundation before I continue forward with another record of my own.

One thing that is clear is that I am slowly developing a solo project called Wippy Bonstack, where stylistically anything can take place. Any combination of styles I've achieved in the past as well as new ideas or musical approaches adopted in the future are valid potential for this project. The basic idea is to have an outlet for my songwriting which can go in any possible direction, pop music mutating into long form progressive pieces, instrumental compositions, or just a diverse platter of sonic experiences, with strands of multiple influences seeping in. The concept and material for this project have been around for nearly three years, and it's going to be a while before it fully comes to fruition and is an up-and-running project. I'm working on my arrangement skills as well as trying to get my chops up on various instruments in order to fully execute this project. A slew of different material has been considered, with eliminations and additions taking place regularly, while continuously composing music without considering where it might end up. It's all under construction, but there is a definite will to create something that outdoes any of my previous efforts. It'll take some time and concentration though. Check back in a few years.

I'm also the drummer in two bands at the moment, Sun Colored Chair, who will have a new album out in 2021, and In-Dreamview, which is music by New Jersey-based guitarist/composer Matt Stober. While Sun Colored Chair contains the more spastic yet uplifting energy of math rock-based prog, In-Dreamview sports some textural, dark, moody, jazz fusion sounding math rock with post-rock and occasional chamber jazz influence. Both bands began tracking their new albums in 2020, with plans to release in 2021.

Wyxz has perhaps the most open future. Seeing as how the project has developed the most radically, from a mishmash of experimental styles to a more consistent and signature sound, should be proof of how the project may evolve into the future.

The first album, released in 2017, is self-titled and is moreso an exploratory barrage of texture than it is a coherently written album. Nonetheless, the roots of the Wyxz ethos are entirely present in this record as it displays the will to experiment with sound collage, noise and free improvisation elements while combining those with the more musical and tonal/atonal realms of math rock, noise rock and classic avant-prog, with additional influence from industrial music, glitch, and dark ambient as well as drone. This sort of "avant garde melting pot" seems like a safe affirmation of the overall mentality and spirit of the Wyxz project which remains to this day, to present a slew of experimental styles in a sporadic manner and pay homage to (as well as possibly extend the legacy of) some innovative greats.

Wickman (2017) and YiY (2019) both saw the Wyxz project take a turn for the overt. Influence from math rock and avant-prog became stronger and an inevitable stylistic shift occurred, or rather a stylistic settling. I began to focus more on riffs than textures, avant garde composition started to seem so riveting and I was creating more through-composed pieces than anything else. The music on those two albums constitutes an overt change in sound but not a change in mentality. We have not abandoned the idea of sporadic stylistic change and radical development from one idiom to another. These two albums serve as the first two in a trilogy of math rock centered prog albums, one that doesn't necessarily define or represent the sonic manifestation of Wyxz's precise goals, but does give a preview of this spirit through the lens of a finely focused product of stylistic decisiveness.

In 2020, *Odyx* was released which is much more focused on bringing developed compositions to the forefront, while still displaying the math rock and through-composed trends found on the previous records. *Odyx* marks the third and final chapter of this "Wyxz, specifically presented as a math rock band" trilogy. This mathy style was never intended to be the sole focus of the project, however it certainly has a lot to do with any sort of recognition the project has received. It was purely a choice of artistic direction that felt like the correct thing to do while it was happening. Rather than giving the listener a barrage of styles to take in all in one sitting, we instead chose to concentrate on a specific engaging style for the course of those three albums. Honing in on one sound has definitely helped to lend us to a variety of listeners, but there is a wide array of musical options and artistic statements that have yet to be tapped into that do not necessarily pertain to this style.

That's not to say that these math rock trends will be abandoned altogether, definitely not. I think the point is to stabilize, or unstabilize, on a set of musical terms and to pull from a generally wide array of stylistic ventures that seem appropriate to the project's lifespan, without drowning too much in one particular style. Ideally, this project can encompass anything from its sound collage roots of origin to free improvisation sessions, to fully composed material and whatever else falls in between that feels dreadfully dense or at least artfully so. Generally, but not always, Wyxz deals with the darker and cryptic forces of the avant garde without ever sticking with anything for too long, even in its more decisive moments. However, I have occasionally allowed myself to indulge in more colorful writing, yet never abandoning the sinister qualities that gave the project its initial spark, creating more of a shapeshifting ethic than anything. It's impossible to foresee the future of the Wyxz project, but it remains nevertheless open territory. Planning would almost seem like the firm antithesis of the creative morals surrounding Wyxz. It is clear though, that something will happen — something that involves everything Wyxz has been up to this point plus much more.

Any sort of underground status Wyxz receives is surely appreciated and very much so an honor, but it must be made clear that this project only represents one percentage of my musical personality. The creative decisions I make may alter from project to project, however I feel that there is a consistent personality that carries over from each project to the next. The main projects I've taken the time to create or be involved in over the past few years would be Wyxz, Sun Colored Chair, Wippy Bonstack, Vesent Sornis, In-Dreamview and Eyeless Owl.

A different type of creative process is required for each, yet a similar spirit and work ethic remains throughout them all. I'd like to think there are consistent musical characteristics that exist and are extended across all this music, and that one day someone might come to the conclusion that these artists are related by means of their own accidental discovery.

Not(e) Worthy: Influence and Closing

It's astounding to observe how some artists completely revolutionized the style which they happened to be placed in, whether or not they strictly adhered to the characteristics their style would typically be associated with. These divergences are generally what give the artist its strengths and unique qualities. Most musical artists I've had interest in over the years used the styles they were placed in to their advantage in order to create a newer, fuller, richer and more extended style of their own making, one that culls from their influences, or certain artistic trends and artists before them, as well as the artists own inner spirit and most genuine creative sense. It seems many of these artists used the fundamental qualities of whatever given style or artform they applied to as their basis to build their own unique brand of creation, whether they are based on a combination of styles or one singular approach. These are the artists that are truly inspiring. I hope to achieve a similar accomplishment and admire those who have maximized their visions and have been able to build something that is a true testament to their own creativity.

Extracting influence from artists is inevitable and in fact what feeds many artists' desire to execute their own pursuits. It can act as potent creative fuel. I owe a lot creatively to what I often tend to consider my favorite group, Henry Cow. Influential in a massive way, all of their records are close to me and have all generated some kind of creative spark that I've incorporated into just about every project I work on. Certain musical principles they implemented such as cleverly devised counterpoint, chance operations and systematic improvisation have been guiding lights to a radical and innovative form of progressive music that is still as fresh and forward-thinking today as it was fifty years ago. There is a cerebral flow contained in the Cow's music, it's embedded within the intricate and systematic approach to their composition and improvisation. I'll stop myself from gushing now because I could go on about these guys for ages. Anyone who knows their work in a general capacity probably doesn't need an explanation. Advanced beyond everything, they crafted some deep treasures that will be rewarding for years to come.

Far too much incredible music should be mentioned in this section. Many things have supplied me with deep influence and shaped my musical personality over the years. Here's a list of composers, songwriters and musicians to which I owe enormous gratitude:

> John Dieterich, Ed Rodriguez, Greg Saunier, Fred Frith, Tim Hodgkinson, John Greaves, Lindsay Cooper, Chris Cutler, Marc Hollander, Dave L. Stewart, Matt Stober, Steven Drozd, R. Stevie Moore, Kerry Minear, Ray Shulman, Frank Zappa, Donald Fagen, Aldo de Scalzi, Aldo Di Marco, Andrea Beccari, Giorgio Karaghiosoff, Claudio Lugo, Roberto Romani, Paolo Griguolo, Matt Hollenberg, Tatsuya Yoshida, Martin Newell, Arthur Verocai, Todd Rundgren, Trey Spruance, Jim O'Rourke, Rahsaan

Roland Kirk, Mike Keneally, Robert Wyatt, Tsuneo Imahori, Alan Bishop, Richard Bishop, Charles Gocher, Joe Coniguliaro, John Coltrane, Ariel Rosenberg, Spencer Seim, Zach Hill, Rob Crow, Otis Jackson Jr., Tim Smith, John Zorn, Joe Knight, Herbie Hancock, Joni Mitchell, Andy Partridge, Marvin Gaye, Charles Hayward, Charles Bullen, Rich Woodson, Miles Davis, Don Van Vliet, John French, Bill Harkleroad, Gregg Bendian, Pen Rollings, Bobby Donne, Chris Farmer, Hermann Szobel, Luke J. Ross, Joshua Davis, Richard Leo Johnson, Bill Frisell, John Martyn, Stanislav Sninský, Andrew Rauscher and many more.

They've all inspired me and my music in some way.

To musicians, about music, I would like to say this: create the purest form of your expression that you can manage to. Anyone's standards only exist purely based on what they have been exposed to. All musicians have the ability to create something unique and singular if they choose to take the risk of letting their expression manifest itself in an unfiltered nature. The great thing about art and music is how interpretive it is. Everyone carries their own perspective into their interpretations of art, and so your experience and perspective is entirely valuable when it comes to the process of making art. Every individual has a different definition of success, therefore nobody can say that your artistic product is valid or invalid. It simply exists. What might be ignorable to some may be completely transcendent to others. You will not know until you try to experiment with the options. Do what you love and what brings you joy musically but also give yourself challenges that mold your perception and open your mind. Music is a magical, vast tool of expression, communication and documentation, but also artistic innovation when given the proper tools and influence. You have the opportunity to establish something completely fresh. The artist must realize their importance in singularity, that nobody else with the same exact set of principles or creative thinking exists. It is up to the artist to produce something that translates their own genuine touch, spirit and approach above all and any preconceived notions.

To possess your own original method is one of the most precious aspects of being an artist, and is a reminder of exactly why art is so valuable. Take what is in your mind and make it a tangible reality, even if you view it as a risk, it is most certainly a risk worth taking. This applies to all forms of art, but the application of this concept to music in particular reminds us of why we love sound so much and why we are so dedicated to it and the results it can generate.

Chase the sound, perpetuate the commitment.

I must extend my gratitude to the following individuals:

John Zorn, Matt Hollenberg, Quinn Coniguliaro, Matt Stober, Alex Verbickas, Malcolm Flanigan, Andrew Rauscher, Matthew Byrd, Mickey Bradford, Stanislav Sninský, Alec Tervenski, Zachary Terwilliger, Elena Huang, Carter Silletto, Mariel Hernandez, Brynn Boufford, Abishai Smith, Mike Parker, Zion Mosaih Cochran, and my parents Joe and Chris, as well as everyone else who has been kind enough to give me their time, encouragement and guidance. Thank you all.

CHAPTER
9

RIVERS OF SOUND

A Model for Transcultural Music Making

AMIR ELSAFFAR

"Gone, gone, gone to the other shore,
attained the other shore,
to beyond the other shore,
having never left."
—final verse of the *Heart Sutra*

In 2015, I formed the 17-member Rivers of Sound Orchestra as a musical, cultural, and social experiment. All of the musicians were subjects, myself included. The goal was to discover new ways of organizing sound without the hierarchical notions found in Western European art music (composer -> conductor -> players), without the burden of precedence found in non-Western folk or traditional forms (repeating what has been done in the past), but still maintaining a sense of structure and cohesion. I was interested in blurring the spaces between improvisation and composition, between composer and players. The process relied on spontaneous group interaction, where each musician had agency as part of the creative process. The idea was to have multiple points of origin emanating simultaneously from the present.

The experiment brought together musicians from a broad spectrum of musical backgrounds and from different parts of the world. My desire was to expand beyond notions of culture, in the sense of one style of music "belonging" to a particular group of people or a society. This notion often leads to a sense of exclusivism and musically can reproduce the unequal power dynamics that exist in other spheres. Too often, cultures are viewed as monolithic, and are idealized from the outside. A member of a given society is perceived as a representative of their culture, not as an individual with distinct humors, character traits, and subjectivity. With Rivers of Sound, I was seeking an alternative musical model embracing a multitude of musical expressions, by focusing on the interactions between individual musicians.

Musical Material

My first composition for Rivers of Sound, entitled *Not Two*, is a suite of eight movements. I chose materials and structures from pre-existing musical idioms that I believed would allow the musicians of the ensemble to collectively create a unique language and sensibility.

The tonal basis of *Not Two* is the Maqam — a system of heptatonic modes found in the Middle East, North Africa, Eastern and Southern Europe, and Central Asia. Maqams stem from the seven modes of the Babylonian-Greek system, but with the addition of microtonal intervals, yielding hundreds of permutations. By using this system of microtonal intervals, as opposed to the fixed pitches of the 12-note system, the rigidness of structures and forms could melt away.

The piano, vibraphone, and guitar were re-tuned to include these microtones. The horn players had to learn new microtonal fingerings and train their ears to hear these sounds. Hence, the musicians could not rely on conventions of what they already knew, i.e. chords, scales, or fingerings. They were pushed to find new ways of playing their instruments.

Maqam is traditionally performed in a heterophonic manner — multiple musicians playing the same basic melody, but each in their own stylized way, with vast room for ornamentation and variation of melodic contour. Yet, there is a sense of unison that relies on the musicians listening acutely to one another, and responding to the subtlest changes in intonation, timbre, and melody. With *Not Two*, heterophony figured prominently in the polyphonic structures and microtonal chords. Finding a collective unison within the variations contributed to the creation of a novel and coherent sound.

Rhythmically, I was interested in exploring malleable and flexible pulses. Many of the compositions have an underlying swing, which blurs subdivisions and has a visceral sense of propulsion. I favored triple meters as they allow for ambiguity, and open up themselves to larger and smaller kaleidoscoping rhythmic structures, as opposed to duple meters that tend toward the hierarchy of "up" beats answered by "down" beats. The pulse is decentralized through the overlaying multiple meters and speeds, offsetting accented beats by placing them in different parts of the measure, thus disorienting the players' and listeners' sense of the beginning or ending of a rhythmic cycle.

> *As pitches and rhythms become fluid, so do boundaries, as elements that traditionally divide musicians and genre-specific modes are brought into new contexts. The idea is about fluidity: sounds flow into one another, overtones interact, as we approach a universal human sound.*
>
> —from the liner notes of *Not Two* (written by Amir ElSaffar)

Choice of Musicians

My approach to music making depends on a sense of community, trust, and mutual respect. The sixteen members of the orchestra are of course adept and possess virtuosic skills on their instruments. Beyond that, they are all friends of mine, musicians whom I have met on my journey through different musical worlds over the course of decades. This sense of friendship eventually spread among the musicians, and became an essential part of the group's dynamic.

The core of Rivers of Sound is my 6-piece Two Rivers Ensemble — Nasheet Waits (drums), Tareq Abboushi (buzuq), Zafer Tawil (oud), Carlo DeRosa (bass), and Ole Mathisen (saxophone) — which was established in 2006, and combines Iraqi Maqam with contemporary jazz. Other members of the group include my sister, Dena El Saffar (violin, joza, and viola), whom I have been singing and inventing songs with since we were young children. She and I currently perform in Safaafir, an Iraqi Maqam ensemble, that includes her husband, Tim Moore (percussion). Jason Adasiewicz (vibraphone) and I first played together in the Illinois All-State jazz combo when we were in high school, and studied and performed together at DePaul University. Mohamed Saleh (oboe, English horn) and I met in Weimar in 1999 as members of the first West-East Divan Orchestra, consisting of Arab and Israeli musicians, under conductor Daniel Barenboim. JD Parran (bass saxophone, clarinet) and I were members of Cecil Taylor's Orchestra Humane, a large ensemble that performed actively between 2002 and 2005. Fabrizio Cassol (alto saxophone) and I met in 2013, when he invited me to be a member of his Alef-Ba project in France, combining jazz and Middle Eastern musicians. George Ziadeh (oud) and Naseem AlAtrash (cello) were both part of the musical community at Alwan for the Arts, a cultural center in Manhattan where I served as music curator from 2008 until 2018. Rajna Swaminathan (mrudangam) and I have played in a variety of ensembles, and through her, I became acquainted with Miles Okazaki (guitar). All of the musicians are performers/composers/innovators who have found creative ways of inhabiting multiple musical worlds. These worlds reverberate in the music of Rivers of Sound.

Not Two

In April, 2015, the 17 musicians of the Rivers of Sound Orchestra came to New York from Boston, Chicago, Bloomington, IN, Brussels, Doha, and Ramallah, for five intensive days of rehearsals, a performance at Lincoln Center Atrium, and a recording session at Avatar Studios. Many were meeting for the first time, but soon they were all deep into the work and the awkwardness of unfamiliarity dissipated.

On the first day, I handed everyone the scores, many of which were in early draft form and were challenging to decipher or were incomplete. Sometimes it was difficult to tell whether a note was flat or half-flat, and there were few indications of articulations or dynamics. Further, I gave each musician entire ensemble scores, as opposed to individual parts, so they would be aware of what all the other members were doing. This unwieldy amount of information resulted in frequent page turns and pages falling off of music stands.

I wrote the music with each musician's sensibilities in mind — their sound and musicality, of course, but also their mannerisms, how they walk, talk, and carry themselves. I considered the written scores as points of departure from which the musicians could create and invent their own parts. Once they learned the melodies and rhythms, I encouraged them to alter them in ways that they saw fit. In some cases, this meant omitting or syncopating notes, in others it meant adding grace notes, trills, and ornaments.

I did not want musicians to become dependent on what was written. They had to ask me or discuss with each other to find out how things were supposed to be played. The musicians listened deeply and depended upon one another, kept their ears and eyes open at all times, and never lost focus or slipped into auto pilot mode. Consciousness and critical thinking are key. We worked out the intonation, phrasing, and dynamics by ear. The ensemble sound was created through this process, as the musicians self-orchestrated, and it was up to them to decide if and when they would solo.

At our soundcheck/final rehearsal before the premiere at the Lincoln Center Atrium, things were seemingly chaotic, and the members of the orchestra were anxious. I walked out to the hall to listen, and could not believe how bad the music was sounding. I wondered if I had gone too far in allowing an ensemble this size to come together without stricter parameters, and worried that the experiment had backfired on me. At this point, I was no longer in control.

During the dinner break, I sat alone in the dressing room, breathing and collecting my thoughts. Half an hour before the premiere, I called for a band meeting in the dressing room to talk through the overall form. The organizers came in to tell us it was time to go on stage. I shut the door and locked them out. When we took to the stage, something magic happened. Everything seemed to fall into place, never as I had anticipated, but new and unexpected sounds emerged, that have resonated in my consciousness ever since.

The following day, we arrived to Avatar Studios at 11AM. We were recording directly to 2" tape, as I was insistent that this ensemble's sound could only be captured through analog recording (the record was later mixed, mastered, and released in analog format). Sound check was arduous and took several hours. By 4 PM, we had recorded two pieces, and by 9 PM we were halfway done. The most difficult music was ahead of us, some of which we had never played. The hours went by, and I considered whether to cut out any pieces. If one person gave in to their fatigue, the entire project would have fallen apart. However, as we worked into the night not a single person complained. (One member slept on the couch for an hour, but I left him undisturbed and brought him back for an overdub session a few months later). We left the studio at 3AM, having recorded the entire *Not Two* suite, which was released in 2017 on New Amsterdam Records.

Years later, as I listen to the album, I hear a distinct development in the ensemble's overall sound from the first track, when there was still a feeling of trepidation and hesitance, to the second and third tracks when we started to get our groove, to the last, when things were flowing and the ensemble performed brilliantly, crescendoing into an ecstatic, yet elegant, climax. The fact that we were recording directly to tape, as opposed to digital recording, which allows easy edits and fixes, meant that everyone had to maintain a higher degree of focus, which I believe fused the music and ensemble together.

I am interested in capturing process in our performances and recording, as opposed to presenting a perfect product. A risky approach, perhaps, but the results are much more appealing to me: the music is open, vulnerable, and ultimately an honest expression. It is about capturing the emergence of the sound.

Since then, the orchestra has toured in the US, Europe, and the Middle East, and everyone has grown familiar with the material and with one another, to the point that performing is no longer an anxious ritual. The sense of camaraderie and self-organization extends to our time on the road as members look out for and care for one another.

During our European tour in 2018, I felt the ensemble was becoming too comfortable, and decided to write new material, engaging in new and challenging modes of music making.

The Other Shore

In early December 2019, the Rivers of Sound Orchestra convened to record its second album, *The Other Shore*. We had three days of rehearsal, but due to scheduling difficulties, never had all 17 members present until we reached the recording studio.

The new scores were denser and more difficult to navigate. It wasn't always clear which part was the melody, what was the accompaniment, what was the groove. Musicians struggled to find the "1", as rhythms were even further offset than in the previous works. Some string lines were virtually unplayable, as I tried to push the limits of people's technical abilities. I delved even deeper into microtonality, this time creating new modes in half-flat and half-sharp keys that were unfamiliar to everyone in the group (even those versed in Maqam). This time, we required two pianos with three distinct piano tunings — two microtonal and one equal tempered — and had to add putty to the vibraphone bars to create yet more microtones.

For this recording, I scheduled three full days in the recording studio, hoping to create an easier, more relaxed experience than the previous recording session. It turned out not to be the case. We needed one full day to get basic levels and headphone mixes, and managed to start recording early evening, when everyone was exhausted and the playing sounded lethargic. Recording began on day two, but things moved very slowly as we had to adjust the seating arrangements of the entire ensemble twice. A majority of the music was recorded on day three, and once again we worked late, leaving the studio after midnight.

Some conflicts emerged during these three days — one musician complained to me that another was telling them how to play in a condescending manner, three musicians had to leave early on the second day, which bothered some of the others, one musician barely spoke to anyone for the whole session, another musician said he felt unfit to play the material, and one of the musicians got exasperated and packed his instrument and almost left the studio, only staying after I pleaded with him. Although these moments of tension were difficult, we were collectively able to absorb and transcend them, as a result of our commitment to community spirit, and our bonds only deepened.

Despite all the challenges, the music sounded beautiful and powerful beyond my highest expectations. I recently finished mixing, and it is clear from listening to this recording that the orchestra has broken through to a new level of creativity, complexity, and cohesion. I believe that the circumstances and energies surrounding the creation of this music are part of the final sound.

The album was supposed to be released in 2020, supported by a 10-concert, 2-week tour, during which we were going to delve deeper into the music of *The Other Shore*. Sadly, all of this has been postponed due to COVID-19. Now, the album is scheduled for a 2021 release, tour dates are being scheduled for 2021–2022, and I have been commissioned to compose a third work for the orchestra. So, it is very possible that we will release *The Other Shore*, without ever performing it live.

No Boundary

> *"When the mind becomes muddled in dualistic thinking, think 'not two,' and all will become clear."*
>
> —Kongo Langlois Roshi

From a distance, Rivers of Sound appears to be a multi-cultural ensemble consisting of people from a variety of different backgrounds, building bridges through music. Cross-cultural "fusions" are common in the world of music today. These often result in surface-level engagements, focusing on the exotic sounds of the instruments, the performers' dress, or other superficial phenomena, and indulge in romanticized ideals of other cultures, falling into the traps of essentialism.

The colonial past, present-day economic disparities, domination and inequality based on class, race, and gender are present, even as we form utopic musical societies that seem isolated from the harsh realities of the world. When connecting and integrating different musical languages, we must be mindful and intentional, otherwise we are in danger of appropriating that which we do not understand and replicating unequal power dynamics.

Rivers of Sound represents another approach. When we begin with an inherent sense of unity and interconnectedness, and musicians as individuals, not representatives of a culture, there is no longer a need to build a bridge.

The compositions for the Rivers of Sound contain elements found in jazz, blues, R&B, and other music from the African American tradition, Western Classical music, Arabic, Turkish, and Persian Maqam, South Indian music, and other musical worlds. These are musical spaces that I have inhabited in my experience. The musicians of the ensemble bring a plethora of other musical idioms from their collective and diverse experiences, which inform the group's overall sound. But we are never quoting or drawing directly on pre-existing or ready-made, musical forms.

Starting from formlessness, we create new structures and ways of organizing sound. In the moment of performance, cultural distinctions dissipate, and we are individual human beings communicating with one another. The music is a means of getting us all together, speaking the same language, and the magic comes from the deepening relationships and connections between the musicians.

I began Rivers of Sound as an experiment, to try to find new ways of organizing sound. Today, Rivers of Sound is an extended family, creating one of the most joyful musical experiences I have ever been a part of.

> *The highest ideal in maqam music is to reach a state of* ***Tarab****, or musical ecstasy, the melting away of borders, when listeners and performers share in a suspended moment of space and time, losing a sense of individual identity, reveling together in the moment of the music.*
>
> —*Not Two* liner notes

CHAPTER 10

CONSIDERATIONS IN LEARNING

KENNY GROHOWSKI

Acceptance of the External

Sometimes we struggle to follow the ictus of a conductor, the perpetual "tick" of a metronome, or another musician whose time-feel is particular. Other times, having to perform in an unfamiliar musical idiom, or the material itself can pose the challenge. These struggles are usually perceived as one's inability to execute comfortably; a lack of knowledge/prep; or perceived faults in the self or others. These occurrences are not a holistic perspective of reality, but an interpretation of the ego. Regardless of the reason, the performer is engaged in an internal struggle that pulls the focus inward rather than outward. Clearing and quieting one's mind of needless thought and choosing to be present and focused improves the circumstances, rendering external senses like listening and watching imperative for making connections. As Adam Nussbaum has said, "I am third. First comes the music. Second, those around me, and third's left for me." Putting aside the inner monologue and focusing on the music, the moment, and those around you, ensures that Music is made at all times.

Embracing the Whole

For instrumentalists that require a duality of technique such as pianists and percussionists, equilibrium is ideal. It allows one to comfortably execute complex musical ideas, express emotively, and improvise freely within a musical language — be it folkloric, aboriginal, cultural, abstract, or mathematically conceptualized. Working towards having equilibrium of ability, technique, and overall movement are foundational and thus become a lifelong pursuit. Challenging the body/mind relationship allows one to be able to remap the synapse of the brain, thereby increasing the number of neurological pathways for the mind to utilize. The aspiration is to come to an understanding of the mind/Spirit and body/Self, where one's strengths/weaknesses are, and what one chooses to develop from that point. Percussion, and particularly the drum-set, are omni-modular, so it becomes imperative for percussionists, like dancers and other full-body performers, to find holistic equilibrium.

Breaking Away from Reliance on Notation

Many of the musics that have persisted throughout time have been taught by other means than written notation. A command of notation can allow one to express an idea, enabling another to efficiently learn it, much akin to how mathematics succinctly explains gravity's affects on the universe. However, to fully realize the music more is required. Notation pertains to Music much akin to how mathematics can express the happenings of the cosmos without *being* the cosmos. Despite its usefulness, sheet music is physically one-dimensional and largely understood in linear fashion, a partiality or *facsimile* of Music. Despite the relative ease of reading modern, printed sheet music, not reading a handwritten chart in part denies the performer the ability to understand the internal workings of a composer. In the matter of dealing with rhythm, regardless of difficulty, conceptuality, or familiarity, to better understand these things one requires feeling or experience beyond what is written. Here is where one's knowledge, judgment, and imagination can allow the performer to take the linear, and express something that lives and breaths in a sonic geometry or poetry that ignites all senses and communicates. The quality of the intent, transparency, and present-ness, can lead to profound results beyond playing well.

Seeking Musical Diversity

The world is filled with inspiring, intriguing, and intrepid music. In a period where the world has been shrunken down to figuratively fit in the palm of one's hand, *time* is a factor. You only have so many conscious hours to dedicate to the pursuit, study, or immersion in an artist, culture, musical scene, or unfamiliar concept. It therefore becomes important to embrace time, the knowledge one seeks, the music and experiences on the path ahead, to internalize them fully. There will be points on the journey where music will cross one's path that is challenging in unexpected and unwarranted ways — potentially obtrusively so. These are moments filled with potential for learning, edification, and growth. Never shy away from these moments, or another's expression, no matter how it affects you: all things are done in the spirit of connection.

Groove is Not a Designation

Groove is adherence to the *Moment* on the part of all who are present. It is an inescapable aspect of Music that is as profound and deep as it is entrancing and intoxicating. It is a rich and intricate language all its own. It is not solely meant for certain musicians to partake in just as all things in the universe must adhere to gravity. There is no form of music that allows for only select players to be both responsible and capable of grooving. Taking the time to understand and empathize with the other players emboldens one's ability to groove. The language of Rhythm is primeval and Sacred and for all to participate in. Each genre, nation, or culture's Rhythm is linguistic in nature, and, like learning any language — solely saying the words does not mean communication is achieved.

Imagination, Curiosity and Creativity

In the childlike mindset, interest gives way to curiosity and imagination. Because the mind is new, it is by necessity more open and receptive to the external world. As creators it is imperative that we embrace this notion and continuously seek out the new, the foreign, the unknown — not just externally, but within. The beauty of life is that any pursuit is eternal and where we leave off is for another to continue. This removes the need to solely carry the burden and hones one's focus. We can never fully know what impact our output will have, nor can we see the ripples of that output through time; but what we can ensure is both the sincerity and quality of the work in the moment.

CHAPTER
11

JUST PLAYING AROUND

A Musical Journey in the World of Solo Saxophone

TOM GURALNICK

Interesting times! As I approach 70 (January 2021) and in the midst of this coronavirus pandemic, I find myself looking in both directions — forward and back. I am in the midst of making big plans for the future of the Outpost Performance Space, which I founded and have run since 1988, and as I reflect on my arts-organization-director legacy, I think about how Outpost can grow into something bigger and better after me. Looking back at that legacy — both at Outpost and before that at the New Mexico Jazz Workshop — so much great stuff has happened, including the inaugural concerts I produced at the New Mexico Jazz Workshop from 1978–1981, which featured Cecil Taylor, Sun Ra, the Art Ensemble of Chicago, Anthony Braxton, Dave Holland & Sam Rivers, Dexter Gordon, Art Pepper, and Woody Shaw. A nice start in the biz indeed! As I said to Albuquerque when I started this adventure, "Ready or not here we come." Good times!

But somewhere in there was also an active saxophone performance career — from 1976 until approximately 2003 — and I find myself looking back on that as well. I picked up my tenor recently for the first time in years and with the first note it said, "welcome home!" While I led a quartet and trio for the last fifteen years of my playing career (which I loved!), much of my work was in the realm of solo performance where I developed my most personal and idiosyncratic music. I recently realized that while there are recordings out there of much of that performance work (solo and otherwise) — LPs, cassette tapes & CDs — there is very little visual record of what I did as a saxophonist. Yet, the visual was central to my personal performance world. I also realized that there are many people in my life now who don't even know that side of me. Accordingly, for the first time, this past year I went through the few visual records of my work and started to put them up on YouTube. To my pleasure and somewhat to my surprise, I have found the work to be pretty interesting, unique and engaging — a complete sound-world unto itself.

In 1987, as a master's degree candidate at Wesleyan University, I wrote a thesis on *Contemporary Improvised Solo Saxophone Performance and Recording Activity*. One of the by-products of that thesis was a video documentary on the solo work of John Zorn, which, after sitting on my shelves for the last thirty-five years, will be released in 2021 as a DVD on the Tzadik label. For some reason, this world of solo saxophone fascinated me and led me to talk with numerous practitioners from John Zorn to Roscoe Mitchell to Evan Parker and more-and encouraged me to explore my own musical raison d'etre as well.

For many of us at that time, performing solo was a vital part of our performance repertoire. All of us marveled at the 3+ minute unaccompanied cadenzas by John Coltrane in various iterations of *I Want To Talk About You* ca.1963 as well as the extended unaccompanied passages by Sonny Rollins, opening our ears to the possibilities. Anthony Braxton's groundbreaking 1969 Delmark Records solo saxophone release, *For Alto*, was an important milestone for all of us involved in improvised music as well. Similarly, the 1974 release of Evan Parker's Incus Records release, entitled simply *Saxophone Solos*, pointed to new and personal saxophonic directions. The list of artists who pursued solo work is long and includes Steve Lacy, Roscoe Mitchell, Hamiet Bluiett, Marion Brown, Lol Coxhill, Sonny Rollins, Vinny Golia, Julius Hemphill, Joseph Jarman, Oliver Lake, Lee Konitz, Joe McPhee, David Murray, Ned Rothenberg and many more. Even those who did not release entire solo saxophone recordings engaged in unaccompanied solo playing in the larger context of group playing. The unaccompanied solo was definitely a part of our repertoire. While group playing obviously comprises the bulk of the work of most improvisors, the solo was an opportunity for many of us to develop and explore our most personal musical language. Many fellow musicians have expressed that this was the case for them, and it was certainly true for me.

The multitude of approaches to solo playing was as varied as its practitioners' styles — ranging from the dry melodic exploratory solo soprano saxophone work of Steve Lacy; to the infinitely extended tonguing, breathing and fingering techniques of Evan Parker; to the duck calls and quick-change saxophone reconfiguration techniques of John Zorn; and so on. Everyone had a different approach — one that defined their sound and music.

For me, the process of developing my approach to solo saxophone playing was, like the music, very improvisational — very intuitive and unplanned and yet it had its own internal logic. It was very much a reflection of my personality and my interests. I was interested in exploring new worlds of sound, but I was always very much aware of my limitations and working with those limitations to develop something unique and interesting. In my third year of college, the same year I began to play the saxophone, I transferred to Bennington College and began learning from the singularly innovative trumpeter/composer Bill Dixon. Something that Bill said affected me deeply. He said (and I paraphrase here) "you have to work from your limitations." For me, that translated to the following: it became clear to me, early on, that while I respected the saxophone and the jazz giants who defined it, I would never be an outstanding technician on my instrument. I just didn't have it in me to become a technical giant on the saxophone (either as a "traditional" saxophonist, or later as an "extended techniques" saxophonist.). A slight case of attention deficit disorder? Perhaps! Or just a realization that this wasn't the place where I was going to make my mark or express myself best. Other people had that field covered beautifully. But what I realized (as per the words of Bill Dixon) was that I had other interests to guide me on my musical path. As I began to develop my solo music, I allowed those interests to take center stage.

I have always been interested in building things. I spent my summers working at my brother's summer camp as a maintenance person — a carpenter, a painter, a plumber. I also worked at the Powell Flute factory making handmade silver flutes — soldering tubing, putting pads in the flutes, and so on. Never simply about making a living, I loved these things and immersed myself in the world of building and construction. So when it came to thinking about developing a world of sound, construction became central to the process. Rather than thinking about what kinds of saxophonic techniques I could develop to create my personal music, I focused rather on what I could do to build an instrument which would allow me to express myself. Thus my second solo release, a cassette, was called *Sonistruction*. I BUILT compositions and I BUILT the instrument from which they sprang.

The process, like the music, was not pre-planned but rather, intuitive. Of course I was influenced by what others were doing on their respective instruments and the saxophone always remained of central interest, but what was interesting to me was what people were doing on instruments other than the saxophone and how that could inform what I did. Accordingly I looked to how percussionists were developing idiosyncratic and personal instruments. The Art Ensemble of Chicago was working with large setups of percussion instruments as well as using toys and so on to create their own hard-to-define sound. My good friend and colleague, David Moss, who was in Bennington, Vermont in order to study and work with Bill Dixon, turned many of our heads (including Bill Dixon's) as he began to place sweaters over his purposely cracked and broken cymbals in order to subvert the sound of the traditional ringing ride cymbal and as he began to incorporate his voice into his percussive world. From there, he developed a 10-foot square cage of percussion and string instruments (and anything else he chose to incorporate) into his unique sound world.

My own journey began by simply looking around me and seeing what I might use. So I added bicycle horns of various pitches to be played with my feet (adding the movement/dance element from the git-go), attached them to a board (like a modern guitar effects pedal board), rachets to attach to the horn, flute polishing/buffing wheels stuck on with gaff tape to flap over the bell of my horn to create a wah-wah sound, trombone or trumpet mutes to place in the bells of the horns, sticking big pieces of foam in the bells, using tubes on the neck with mouthpieces to extend the range of the horns, inserting pvc pipe and foam insulation strips in the horn to see what that would do (instant multiphonics). Basically, I just played around and began to "prepare" my instruments in all these various ways. I would look around and think "I wonder what it would sound like if I stuck this in the horn or added this to the neck..." — just an exploration. In the beginning, I would explore each of those individual instrumental "preparations" as distinct pieces/instrument studies. From there, I began to think about how to incorporate them into one construction — an instrument in and of itself — so that I could move between these sounds quickly and with fluidity. I used drum parts and soldered copper tubing to build racks which held the instruments at playing height and put all the mutes and preparations within close reach. It evolved continually. After exploring some overdubbing in the studio, digital electronics became available (thank you Electro-Harmonics) in order to explore overdubbing live, in performance. I came to call the set-up I developed (in a somewhat tongue-in-cheek way), the "Mobile Saxophone and Mute Unit." It was actually far from easily mobile as I toured (by train in Europe) with two large wooden cases and a 60 pound carry-on bag filled with instruments, tubing, drum stands, electronics and so on, and which took at least ninety minutes to set up. Although, I will say, it eased my way through customs when they opened up the cases and couldn't figure out what the hell it all was and just waved me through! Those were different times for sure. The place where the name MOBILE saxophone and mute unit worked best was when I played in Birmingham, Alabama and the press thought I was an in-state musician from Mobile, AL. At any rate, within the set-up, like with the bicycle horns early on, movement became an intrinsic part of the playing and of the performance as I kicked electronic triggers, jumped from one instrument preparation to the next, swung tubes with mouthpieces (vacuuphone) over my head, and so on. Rather than trying to hide the movement, I embraced it and realized that it actually was a part of the sound. The physical movement defined and shaped the sound and the performance. The movement defined the space between the sounds and vice versa.

For me, the music and the instrument I developed was totally intuitive, improvisatory, unsophisticated — just "playing around." I never thought of it as weird or avant garde or anything along those lines. It was just "what I did." It was my sound world which I resided in. It always surprised me when people reacted by thinking it was strange in some way and hard to relate to. But that was always a good reality check and remains that to this day as I look back on the music and share and post my solo performance videos on YouTube. Performances from 1985 — thirty-five years ago — still elicit the "what the hell is this?" reactions from some people. Can't understand that... it's just me playing around.

CHAPTER 12

A FORMATIVE EXPERIENCE

MARK HELIAS

What is it about music? Clearly the first attraction is sensory. The sounds astound and the mystery abounds while we try to find our way. It represents the unspoken, the unexpressed, the ideas without words, words intensified by music and music intensified by words when the songs are great. There seems to be a rebelliousness or philosophical non-compliance integral to the attraction to music. Bebop functioned that way in its proto-form through the compositions, language and lifestyle of Charlie Parker, Thelonious Monk and Dizzy Gillespie et al. Its harmonic, melodic and rhythmic innovations were then codified for the purposes of "jazz" education, conveniently leaving out the revolutionary political implications of its expression. The blues came out of the experience of an oppressed people with very little recourse against the oppressors besides subversion by self-expression. It is a complicated subject inhabited by myth, reductionism and tokenism, as in, the blues is about being sad. Now, that is sad. The manner in which music has been described in the world of musicology has always been fraught with cultural projections, appropriations and colonialist hegemony. I remember an eminent British musicologist describing the music on a recording of the Aka-Baka and Mbuti peoples in Central Africa (that I had found on an old "world music" recording) as simple monophonic melodies while, in fact, the recording documents people clearly singing in harmony to one another in unison rhythm. Clearly, this music was not monophonic and I was immediately shocked at the ability of a highly trained musicologist to hear with his eyes and preconceptions instead of his ears. He was able to turn polyphonic sounds into monophonic ones purely through the activation of cultural prejudice. Fascinating. Projecting from that cognitively dissonant experience I realized that any opinion "logically" defended could be completely delusional. Perception matters. Since that moment I have regarded "experts" with a jaundiced eye.

I met Johnny Dyani, the South African bassist, at the Moers, Germany festival in May/June of 1977, at the beginning of my first European Tour. I was with Anthony Braxton's Quartet/Quintet which included George Lewis, Anthony Braxton, Charles Bobo Shaw and, on some of the gigs, Muhal Richard Abrams. It was about a month long and not terribly well organized as I found out later when comparing it to other tours. I remember that there was some controversy with the beginning gigs because I flew over and was supposed to work some gigs with Muhal's group before the first Braxton gig at Moers. The German promoters, or some people in power who did not know who I was told Muhal, as I recall, to use someone else on bass, perhaps Malachi Favors, who was there to play with the Art Ensemble. I learned of this through hearsay and was never given a true explanation, but I did catch a vibe about hierarchies and notoriety. I was, in some way, just happy to be there and a bit intimidated by the social and musical intensity, having had no experience on an international level at that point. It became a nexus for colliding ideas and tacit beliefs; naiveté versus grizzled experience all filtered through a European lens surveying a predominantly African-American experience, the core of which I experienced from the periphery.

In the end, I waited around for a week, not performing, and probably hanging out and eating and drinking way too much. I had heard of Johnny Dyani from Barry Altschul, with whom I had been playing in Anthony Braxton's band beginning in March of 1977. It was a transitional group for Braxton because Dave Holland and Barry had committed to Sam Rivers trio and the two ensembles would necessarily encounter serious scheduling conflicts, working on the same scene and at many of the same venues. Shortly after my first gig with Braxton in March of 1977 Steve McCall joined the band on drums to be followed by Charles Bob Shaw and Thurman Barker. Barry Altschul knew many of the ex-pat South African musicians who had emigrated to England so that they would be free to play music with whomever they chose. He had told me about Johnny, Dudu Pakwana, Louis Moho-lo, and Chris McGregor, all South African musicians who emigrated to Europe. While staying for a week in the Hansa Hotel in Moers, Germany I met an incredible array of musicians from all over the world. I had, until this time, experienced jazz and creative improvised music through the prism of the American experience. I am sure I harbored some deeply ethnocentric beliefs about improvised music that did not include Europeans. I was aware of some Euro improvisers but had been busy learning the music as a distinctly North American phenomenon. I had only begun playing the bass fewer that five years before, so I was in cramming mode and tried to focus on fewer important influences, but in depth. My survey chops were not so developed at this point. Consequently, the experience at Moers was elemental. I met most of the AACM musicians that were touring, many of the musicians from BAG (Black Artists Group out of St. Louis) numerous German improvisers (from both East and West) and British musicians as well as Johnny Dyani.

He was a short, compact beaming individual with obviously powerful Chi. One night I heard a knock on my hotel room door and there was Johnny with his bass, saying "Hey, man, let's play some music." I was becoming accustomed to these spontaneous demands for a creative experience but was nonetheless a little intimidated. He had that wide open manner of enthusiasm and empowerment, nothing coy about it, we were gonna get down. So we hit it for a good hour and then went down to have a drink. It was great and very intense... no warming up just direct into musical collaboration...a very welcoming colleague, I must say.

One year later, I was in Copenhagen with Dewey Redman's Quartet and I ran into Johnny at the bar in our hotel next to the Montmartre Club. Johnny, with a mysterious grin suggested that we go to my room as he had something to show me. When we got there he pulled out a cassette player and started playing a tape. It was two bass players going on rather intensely and he stood there smiling and said, "That's us, my man!" At the time, I had no recollection that he had set up a recorder when we played in my hotel room the prior year. It was so great to hear and he was so tickled to play that for me. Wow, what a gift. Johnny Dyani had a giving, big-hearted vibe. This was a generous, enthusiastic gesture of welcoming from a musician senior to me in age and experience and has became a model of community that I have attempted to continue in my own life and career. As the musical years have turned into musical decades I have appreciated more deeply just how special the musical community is and my good fortune to be part of it.

CHAPTER 13

ROMAN LETTERS FOR JOHN COLTRANE

DAVID HERTZBERG

Since we've been alone I have listened to John Coltrane. Writing these words, I hear "listen" with a quasi-italic *tenuto* because I feel that something in Coltrane's music has disclosed itself to me, or that something in me has opened up to it anew. This something divulges no great secret, no penetrating insight, no analytical clarity. It heralds no aesthetic epiphany and does not arrive with thunderclap or eureka. Rather, I experience it as a changed relationship. I find it difficult to describe, though my desire to is strong. I turn it over in my mind, yet the prospect of holding it in understanding feels at once increasingly necessary and impossible. And while I cannot grasp its fluid shape, or even brush its floating message in a bottle, I find that, sifting, I approach it by negation.

There is a certain airy detachment to this new relationship. Not the detachment of cold fascination, leering, acquisitive — that thin upper air with which my ear is so familiar. Neither would I describe it as one of levity, though there is a sense of hovering, or a quieting of gravitational contention, of which one becomes only gradually aware. And I know that I have never really listened to music this way, as a participant. Here there is no seduction, no shock. No siren coo, no stilled displacement, no manic Mozart playtime in the cloudtops. It does not act on me nor I on it. But patiently, opening itself, it draws me into a relation.

I first sensed it while revisiting his *Ascension*. Shortly thereafter in *Meditations,* then *Expression*, though over these months this new modality I am trying to describe has suffused my relationship to all of his music. But why did it begin here, at the end, with this his last and most elusive kind of music? I play it on the piano, or bend my thought along its curve, study it from different angles, and it crumbles like sun-scorched clay or choss. I scour the ravages of rock. Yet here I find no ecstasy of falling. No self-reflexive whirring of an anxious mind. I cannot possess it and it cannot possess me — so I listen. And within its crash and tumult, I hear a wild warmth and brightness. An incessant burgeoning, whose howling accretions give of the same soft light as their dissolving waves. No gush, but an indifferent riverbabble of becoming, the ceaseless initiating of a lived relation.

That these expressions inhabit a space between Coltrane and music seems to communicate some aspect of what I glimpse. That this is not *his* music, though the variegated flora of his imagination are indelibly particular and his own. Rather, that what emerges is a reciprocity, an exchange between a music and a being. And while this sentiment is not unique to these most ephemeral, unbroken later forms, or really to Coltrane at all, it has a particular resonance across his body of work: compositions as harmonic runes or mantras of elliptic melody, familiar songs as objects of meditation, their music the effulgent green of moss that grows on ruins. Whether wrought or repurposed, these stone structures are not the substance of their expressions, but rather, themselves relations, they become conduits of new ones: between the musicians that carry them, between changing moods and rhythmic quickenings, between my conscious breathing and the crepitating car-speaker. All of these relationships now seem to me living and charged with significance. Though I would not have been able to feel or articulate this, without the aid of a music that expresses so freely and directly this unencumbered relationship between an individual and music as a whole. Isolated, so to speak, in that blind space of pure relation.

Maybe there is an opacity to this music, through which one must wade. Not an aloofness, the kind of thing that belongs to so much music of a similar busyness or density. Something more like the obscurity of a dark canvas, or a window that leads you away to a harmony of different hues. Not the silence of a closed door, nor the shiver of unknowing or impending. Not the terror of a something breaking through. Though one could listen this way too. And I would have listened this way before. Through its fricative slushing, through the taxonomy of its palpable noises, through its kinesthetic machinations. I would have listened with my spine. But the opacity that I want to describe is not one of concealment or delicious mystification, but rather, one of encounter. Here are no gutted expectations. No shocking metamorphosis, no trough of irresistible violence suspended in the tender interval of a drumroll or anacrusis. Rather, a kind of quiet exclusiveness, that begins with the guarded indifference of circumspection, the first uneasy breaths taken upon entering an unfamiliar space. This captures more precisely the quality of airiness I have sought to describe: an air of sublimated anticipation, of precipitation vanquished by an answering voice.

I have always understood ending to be the essential shape of music. A sort of simultaneous finality, in which one can grasp a porous duration and roll it up as a scroll, or freeze it and survey it as a sculpture, or hold in one invented instance, its peaks and valleys, its calms and storms, and claim them, fold and press them in a book, and thereby assert some kind of victory over the arrow or doldrums of undifferentiated time. And there is certainly cataclysm in this music, in its endlessly unfolding, subtle shades of lyric chaos, in their matryoshkas of subliminal reveal. And yet here I sense no looming judgement, no cloudswept doom, no irretrievability of a falling axe. Nor that sweet synthetic silence of a world escaped. Here are consequences, inexorable as they are indifferent, and causality, without compression and without punishing line, behaving, and speaking, with the calm equanimity of a slackened jaw.

Then there's that cryptic quote of his about starting in the middle of a sentence and moving in both directions at once, which runs concentric circles in my mind's inner ear. But this is music without conceit, without subterranean canons or magic Escher spirals, without that sort of gardened serenity behind which the tick of machinery lurks. There is nothing delusive in this free, agrestal music. And even in its earlier, more cultivated states, its elided tonalities, its quicksilver changes, feel discovered rather than contrived: recklessly vital, even incidental in their form, to the soundless hum of a living relation.

But that quote won't leave me alone. That it comes from an artist whose self-professed mission was to help humanity free itself from its hang-ups is equal parts baffling and fascinating. Or maybe it's because I'm still looking for clues. And Coltrane really pours water over that old witchy thing about artists being or not being their work or vice versa. That thing that one can openly dismiss but privately coddle as a source of maintaining or preserving some iota of that sacred illusion of wholeness, whichever way one concocts it. Maybe we deep-freeze it in language or embalm it in self-addressed envelopes. After all, letters, Roman or otherwise, are a useful way of avoiding public-facing pronouncements.

Another gasp from a dusty closet: no resignation in this music. No *submission to the moment*, wherein you let that moment seize you, do with you what it will — or become its feral scavenger, salivating for sinew and scrap. Cruel authorial submission; the good Old Testament stuff: brimming with belief and aboutness, theme and idée fixe, that seizes, shocks, possesses, screams, enthralls — and above all — exorcizes a deep sounding of that same addicting silence at the end: our makeshift universal, the bonehollow aftersong of a rattled cage.

A paradox: when this music is *yours*, there is a kind of psychosacred anonymity to it. The anonymity of rerun Prometheus, bringing back his little tinderbox, wrested from some combination of a personal heaven or hell. But here is no such fire: neither Icarus with broken toes, nor Michelangelo muscled on a Disney Adonis, no demiurge who awes with vistas or Grand Inquisitor to lift the veil, no over-incubated atavists and none of that genetically modified frankensilence, that chasm of insatiable ideation that pries apart object and subject, whose eros throbs in direct proportion to the circumference of its gutted cavity, that cathects by its appetite, where in the ugly ache of collective listening there lives the sense that for one unbreathing moment we may incorporate and claw it all, before it disperses into hopeless inscrutability, and we crawl again, hungering, through the pit.

I know because I've listened to this silence. I've felt its viscous seep. I've listened with my teeth and with my stomach acid. And I know because I've devoured you. I've bitten out your throat and asked you to sing. And now I want to tell this all to you, to palpate it again, and with this cache of empty impulses I've plundered for description, extract from you one last note. And now I've stained this last relation, inviolate. Will you join them under the floorboards? Or will we stay and find the courage to crumble and babble as Coltrane might, if he spoke in Roman letters.

CHAPTER
14

QUARANTINED WITH THE BEETHOVEN VIOLIN CONCERTO

STEFAN JACKIW

2020 marks the 250th anniversary of Ludwig van Beethoven's birth. To mark this milestone, seemingly every classical music organization on the planet devised a plan to pay tribute to the composer. Like so many violinists, I was looking forward to performing his violin concerto several times over the course of the year. Then the pandemic hit, and all birthday celebrations were called off, including Beethoven's.

During my COVID-enforced sabbatical, I took advantage of the unexpected free time on my hands to immerse myself in a variety of projects that I had long put off. These ambitious undertakings ranged from a binge through every episode of *Breaking Bad* to learning Alban Berg's violin concerto. Yet every time I tired of analyzing a tone row or assuring Netflix that I am indeed "still watching," I found myself picking up my violin and playing through large sections from the Beethoven concerto. There was something grounding and deeply comforting about returning to this piece in my living room. At first I thought it was merely the cozy familiarity of the concerto that drew me back to it, amidst learning thorny new repertoire. But why didn't I find myself turning to the Sibelius concerto, or the Brahms, or any other old friends in the repertoire? Sure, I am a Beethoven fanboy (I named my dog Ludwig), but why, in the midst of so much fear, uncertainty, and loss brought about by the pandemic, did his violin concerto become my lodestone?

What is it about Beethoven's violin concerto? This piece is invariably cited as the pinnacle of the violin concerto repertoire, and Beethoven aficionados often include it when discussing the composer's greatest works. But why? The violin concerto is, in fact, rather un-Beethovenian. It has neither the structural, Haydn-esque tautness of his early works, nor the fist-shaking fury of his middle period. Nor does the violin concerto grapple with the infinite, the timeless, and the great beyond, all hallmarks of the composer's late period. And yet, somehow, this concerto speaks deeply to so many listeners.

Each listener will have their unique reasons for loving Beethoven's violin concerto, but for me, what makes it stand alone in the repertoire is that it is the most "human." By human, I don't just mean that the piece addresses and evokes vivid human emotions, but more specifically, the concerto contemplates what it means to live a life, to be alive, to be conscious.

Some skeptical listeners have derided poor Beethoven as being second-rate when it came to writing melodies. (One need only to hear the *Ode to Joy* from the *Ninth Symphony* — one of the most memorable and affecting melodies ever written — to dispel this misguided assessment). In fact, these naysayers often point to the violin concerto as an example of the composer's melodic shortcomings, citing the first movement as being nothing more than a collection of endless scales and arpeggios. While to me this critique can be likened to dismissing the Pyramids of Giza as being just a stack of stones, I think these critics have, perhaps unwittingly, hit upon something significant. Scales and arpeggios are the elemental building blocks of tonality, and by structuring the opening movement around these musical pillars and largely stripping away adornments, Beethoven is able to invoke a fundamental universality beyond beauty.

The violin concerto opens with four strikes of the timpani. If there is a more vivid representation of a life force than this musical heartbeat, I've yet to hear it. To me, it's almost as if right from the very opening Beethoven is telling us, "this piece is about being alive." The first movement then unfolds as a sprawling journey, through restless explorations, hopeful passages, triumphant peaks, and moments of despair. Throughout the movement, Beethoven is clearly searching for *something*, but it's unclear what he seeks. We reach our darkest moment at the midpoint of the movement, during the G-minor section. Here, the pulsing of the timpani is taken over in turns by pairs of horns, bassoons, and trumpets, turning the four-strike motive into a fatalistic bleating and driving the movement to its nadir. With this transformation from heartbeat to death knell, we realize that our very existence is our undoing.

But all is not lost! Beethoven raises us from this existential dread with a rising chromatic scale in triplets (yes, scales can be our savior!) in the solo violin, and the pulsing in the trumpets and bassoons is transfigured once more with the entire orchestra in fortissimo, resuscitating the heartbeat in the most glorious, life-affirming climax of the movement.

For me, the most poignant moment in the piece comes at the end of the first movement, after the lengthy violin cadenza. In the final bars, Beethoven brings back the opening theme of the movement, but in its quietest, most inward incarnation. After exploring every high, every low, every moment of doubt, every moment of hope, we've come back to where started. The melody (and yes, it's a gorgeous one) is the same, but we are different, wiser, more self-knowing. We hear the same music with changed ears, and that is what Beethoven, and perhaps we as well, have been searching for. The second movement is the only movement in the violin repertoire that never leaves its home key. Nearly all tonal music involves some sort of harmonic progression; we establish a home key, and then we venture to new realms, exploring tonalities both related and distant, and finally we return to the home key, thereby completing the musical journey. However, the Larghetto of Beethoven's violin concerto exists solely in the key of G major. The result is a reverie in the form of a theme and variations that seems to exist in a kind of beatific stasis. The days of tireless searching belong to the first movement. We have found what we were seeking and now we live in blissful equilibrium.

The joyful finale is a musical celebration of a life fully lived, of truth sought and found. Amidst the dance-like revelry, the final coda of the piece fosters a sense of acceptance that is quintessentially Beethovenian. Unlike Schubert's feeling of acceptance — life is quietly tragic but there lies a bittersweet beauty in its sadness — or Brahms's — filled with a sense of nostalgia and echoes of unfulfilled longing — for me, Beethoven's concluding message in the violin concerto is one of rugged, hard-earned happiness.

I first learned Beethoven's violin concerto when I was nineteen years old and studying in Boston with Donald Weilerstein, one of my musical mentors. During one of our lessons, Mr. Weilerstein pointed to one of the many scales in the opening movement and asked what inner meaning I felt was contained in the upward climb. I played it again and responded that, to me, the rising contour implied a reaching or yearning. His next words have stayed with me for the past fifteen years: "the way you're playing this passage makes me feel that Beethoven is reaching for something with a confidence that he will grasp what he seeks at the top of the scale. For me, the essential emotional drama of this concerto lies in the fact that Beethoven knows he will never reach what he seeks, yet he nevertheless attempts with defiance and joy."

CHAPTER 15

ANOTHER MUSIC

DAN KAUFMAN

In the summer of 2009, I flew to Rome, in search of a musical muse. I didn't know what kind of piece I wanted to compose, but I had one source of inspiration: a hand-copied book of Roman Jewish melodies called *Canti Liturgici Ebraici di Rito Italiano*, transcribed by a cantor named Elio Piattelli and published in 1967. The Roman Jewish community is the oldest continuous settlement of Jews in Europe. Because their arrival in Rome predates the destruction of the Second Temple in Jerusalem, in 70 AD, they are not considered Sephardi or Ashkenazi, nor part of the Jewish diaspora at all. Their music — beguiling, faintly triumphant — is as anomalous as their history. Nothing sounds quite like it. It drew me to Rome.

As helpful as Piattelli's transcriptions are, they give only a vague impression of the music. But in the 1950s, an Italian ethnomusicologist named Leo Levi began documenting the musical traditions of Italian Jewish communities. The grandson of a rabbi, Levi had been arrested twice during the Fascist period and immigrated to Palestine in 1936. After the Holocaust, he returned to Italy to save what he could of the country's diverse Jewish musical heritage. In more than eighty recording sessions, Levi captured nearly fifty cantors and other musically knowledgeable Jewish community members from twenty-seven distinct liturgical traditions in over twenty Italian cities, including Rome. In many cases, his recordings are the only account of these traditions.

I spent my days at the Accademia Nazionale di Santa Cecilia, where Levi's work is archived. Absorbing these quavering, haunting voices was exhilarating. But I found myself at a loss as to how to proceed. I wanted to pay tribute to this community, certainly, but did not know how to transform this source material into something meaningful and distinct of my own.

One day, I came across *The Battle for Rome*, written by the journalist Robert Katz, in an English-language bookstore. A gripping chronicle of the Nazi occupation of Rome, the resistance to that occupation, and the city's eventual liberation by Allied forces, Katz's book inspired me to take a walk one evening near the Trevi Fountain, down a narrow, quiet street called Via Rasella. Toward the end of the block stands a bullet-ravaged building, where, on March 23, 1944, a small group of Italian partisans attacked a column of more than one hundred and fifty German troops with a homemade bomb and mortar shells. It was one of the largest and most daring partisan actions in all of Nazi-occupied Europe. Thirty-three German soldiers were killed, and in one moment the myth of Nazi invulnerability in the city was shattered. (The following day, the Germans retaliated by massacring three hundred and thirty-five Italian civilians and political prisoners, including fifty-seven Jews.)

The image of that scarred building, the only surviving remnant of that day, persisted in my mind. More than that, it unlocked the music that I wanted to make. The resulting record was *Bella Ciao*, an homage to the Roman Jews and the Italian resistance. Sometimes, I reimagined passages from Levi's recordings, like the eight-bar bass intro, which I slowed down to a metal-tinged dirge, in *Umevi Goel. Mizmor Leasaf* drew on a long melodic fragment, from a Tisha B'Av prayer, but was also shaped, in an unintentional way, by my love of Goblin and the film scores of Ennio Morricone. *Mizmor Leasaf* also included fragments of a poem by Alfonso Gatto, an anti-Fascist writer who was imprisoned by Mussolini's regime in the 1930s. Gatto's poem *Anniversary* is a searing, oblique evocation of the resistance, in which Gatto participated. "I remember those days," he writes. "In the uncertain morning, when the terror of being left alone was to awaken us. I heard the sky like a dead voice." *Et Shaare Ratzon*, built around a folk-tinged guitar pattern and a portion of a Rosh Hashana melody, included a long passage from *The Resistance and Its Light*, by the Italian filmmaker and poet Pier Paolo Pasolini.

The title track, *Bella Ciao*, the anthem of the Italian resistance, has origins in a 19th century song of seasonal rice workers. During the war, the lyrics were rewritten to reflect the anti-Fascist struggle. I first heard it at an after-hours club in Paris many years ago. A DJ played the song mixed with a dance beat, and to my amazement a packed room of North Africans, West Africans, and French sang along, knowing every word. There was something about that scene, the solidarity the song inspired, that stayed with me.

The façade on Via Rasella become a kind of ekphrasis, an ancient

Greek literary device in which writing is used to channel a visual artwork. (Think of John Keats's *Ode on a Grecian Urn.*) I like to think of these extra-musical sources as "other music." Other music can be almost anything, but usually it comes from a historical or literary source. Sometimes grafting other music onto an instrumental composition takes an overt form, like the Pasolini and Gatto fragments. Sometimes it's purely sonic, like layering distorted guitar harmonics to evoke the sound of a helicopter dropping bombs. But mostly I use other music as a subconscious backdrop, influencing a piece through a mysterious, alchemical process that I don't completely understand, nor want to. In the case of *Bella Ciao*, the building façade, a powerful symbol of resistance and tragedy, became the unheard heart of the recording.

* * *

Lately, I have been wondering where my fascination with other music began. I think it was around the time I was twelve, when I had returned to my hometown of Madison, Wisconsin, after living in Israel for a mostly unhappy year. I came back alienated from old friends, but found new camaraderie in the punk rock underground, which was exploding at the time. I began listening to bands like the Minutemen, Bad Brains, and Black Flag. Equally influential were local groups like the Appliances-SFB, Juvenile Truth, and Die Kreuzen, whose meticulous, serrated guitar parts were a revelation. I soon formed my own band and began performing at an all-ages venue. But punk rock encompassed more than just music. It was also a social movement that encouraged an interest in history, politics, literature, and other art forms. Perhaps its most lasting legacy for me was the solidarity it forged.

In high school, I struck up a friendship with a brilliant teenager named Dániel Biró, a Hungarian-American classical guitarist who broadened my musical interests. Dániel's devotion to music was inspiring, and unrivaled among our cohort. Some days, he told me, he practiced eighteen hours. (He counted the time he thought about music.) I started studying with him, beginning with Renaissance pieces, and eventually moving to Bach lute suites and 20th century compositions like Manuel Ponce's Variations sur *Folia de España*." Though attuned to the tiniest technical details, Dániel did not teach technique for its own sake but as a means for deepening interpretation and musicality. He introduced me to the music of living composers, especially Eastern Europeans, such as György Kurtág, whom he admired most. Dániel imparted in his teaching a sense that music was connected to history and a wider culture, a notion I already felt from punk rock and my own family.

My growing obsession with classical guitar led me to become a performance major at the University of Wisconsin. I began spending endless hours in the windowless basement practice rooms of the university's Humanities Building. (We called the fortress-like Brutalist structure, designed in the 1960s to keep anti-war protesters out, the Inhumanities Building.) The program's unimaginative pedagogy and competitive spirit encouraged a kind of robotic practicing focused on technical perfection. There were a few notable exceptions, particularly Roscoe Mitchell, a founding member of the Art Ensemble of Chicago, who joined the music department soon after I arrived. Mitchell brought a rebellious and joyful heterodoxy not just to the music school but to the wider community. The classical-guitar program, however, remained mired in stodgy isolation, drawing virtually no connection to art, history, literature, or any other subject. During my jury performance one semester, I froze suddenly in the middle of a piece and began playing another. I don't know what possessed me — nerves, probably; I was in a dark performance hall with five senior faculty judging my every note — but I quit the program soon after and moved to New York.

My first job in the city was at the Strand Bookstore, whose chaos was a welcome change from the sterility of music school. I met two musical heroes there: Tim Wright, the bass player of Pere Ubu and DNA, who was working the bag check; and Norman Westberg, the guitarist of Swans and a regular customer who played in a band with one of my co-workers. Norman become a friend, and a few years later, when he quit a dark, brooding band called Sulfur, he recommended me to take his place. I hadn't played in a rock band in years and was eager to return to one. I lasted in the group only a few months, but the experience motivated me to start my own band, which came to be called Barbez.

I started the group with a close friend from Wisconsin, Carl Maguire, on accordion. We searched for other musicians with an ad in the *Village Voice*. The first to answer was an Italian drummer named Matteo De Cosmo, a recent arrival from Bari who spoke almost no English. We hit it off immediately, though, and began rehearsing in his freezing loft on Canal Street.

Soon after came our first gig, at the Charleston pizzeria in Williamsburg. The lineup in those days was constantly in flux, but gradually stabilized. We became more musically ambitious, and eventually parted ways with Matteo. (We had become like brothers, though, and he later rejoined the band for a time as our singer.) Around 2001, we started touring the U.S., sleeping on a loft bed in the back of our van as we drove enormous distances for gigs. At that time, the band included Pamelia Stickney on theremin, Dan Coates on bass and a PalmPilot he refashioned as a sampler and sound processor, Shahzad Ismaily or John Bollinger on drums, Danny Tunick on vibraphone and marimba, and a Russian singer and performance artist named Ksenia Vidyaykina. We recorded regularly with Martin Bisi, who remains a cherished and close collaborator, almost like another band member. We started working with John Jesurun, the visionary theatre director, writer, and filmmaker, who brought us to Europe to perform music for his serial play, *Chang in a Void Moon*. Soon after, we began moving in an instrumental direction, incorporating new members Peter Hess on clarinet, Catherine McRae on violin, and Peter Lettre on bass.

It was around this time that I started composing music that drew heavily on "other music." An invitation from John Zorn to record an album for Tzadik led me to write *Force of Light*, a song cycle that incorporated the poetry of Paul Celan, whose work has meant more to me than any other poet's. Celan was born into a Jewish family in Czernowitz, an ethnically diverse city near the border of Romania and Ukraine. In the summer of 1942, the Nazis and their Romanian allies initiated a roundup of the Jews of Czernowitz, and Celan's parents were deported to a concentration camp in Ukraine. His father died there of typhus, and shortly afterward, his mother was fatally shot by a guard. Celan's earliest known poem, *Mother's Day 1938*, a sonnet, was written as a gift for her. Though he escaped the roundup in which his parents were captured, Celan was sent to a forced-labor camp in southern Romania, and spent nearly two years in a series of camps across the country. He continued to write, with great anguish, in German, his mother tongue. In a speech to a German audience in 1958, he said, "In this language I have sought … to write poems: so as to speak, to orient myself, to find out where I was and where I was meant to go, to sketch out reality for myself." On April 20, 1970, Celan committed suicide, drowning himself in the Seine.

I asked Fiona Templeton, a Scottish poet and performance artist, who first introduced me to Celan, to read his poetry. I wanted to keep it spoken, not sung, so that the music and text, or other music, would be independent of each other, even as they interacted intimately. Each piece followed its own logic. *The Black Forest* was inspired by a fraught meeting between Celan and the philosopher and Nazi sympathizer Martin Heidegger, at Heidegger's cabin in the Black Forest. Celan later wrote a poem about the meeting, *Todtnauberg*, in which he wrote of a "hope, today, of a thinking man's coming word from the heart." (Heidegger, whose work Celan admired, never apologized for his Nazi past.) I built the song around a riff in the bass that's mimicked by the guitar but a minor second apart. The closeness of the interval, and its dissonance, seemed to reflect the relationship between German and Jewish culture. Mostly, the songs followed intuition. I brought back my classical guitar for *Shibboleth*, a poem that expresses, in elliptical terms, solidarity with the anti-Fascist forces that fought in the Spanish Civil War. Other pieces, like *Sky Beetle*, I tried to make open and spacious, to honor the nonlinear spirit of the poem it was inspired by.

In Celan's speech to the German audience, he also said: "A poem, as a manifestation of language and thus essentially dialogue, can be a message in a bottle, sent out in the — not always greatly hopeful — belief that somewhere and sometime it could wash up on land." It felt exhilarating to weave together my love of music and other music at last. In the liner notes to *Force of Light*, I described the eight pieces as "songs that washed up on land."

* * *

In April 2020, Matteo died after a month-long battle with COVID-19. In the days following his death, the memories of our friendship and collaboration, and the shock of his early passing, nearly overwhelmed me. I found some solace driving aimlessly around the Catskills, where my family and I had retreated. The timeless, green-covered mountains helped, but a few times I had to pull over to wipe away tears.

Music comforted me, too, particularly *Bella Ciao*, because of how it reminded me of Matteo. The first time we performed that song in public, I had asked him to sing it. Though it had been more than a decade since we played together — and he had stopped singing altogether — he reluctantly agreed. He came to the tiny club hours early, dressed impeccably in a dark suit and fedora. I could tell from the shakiness of his hands that he was nervous, but he delivered a vulnerable and moving half-spoken, half-sung rendition. Like many working-class Italians, he had a strong affinity for the song, an affection that came through that night. As I drove through the mountains thinking about his performance, I noticed that the lyrics seemed almost to reflect his death. "Bury me up in the mountain," the song goes. "Under the shade of a beautiful flower. Bella, ciao! Bella, ciao! Bella, ciao!"

It was on another drive, one that I can only describe as mystical, when I realized the closeness between music and other music. Many times, I have turned to Celan's writing for insight and solace. *Conversation in the Mountains*, one of the few prose pieces that Celan wrote, is a favorite. The story follows a missed meeting between two Jews walking on an alpine road, but it is also a parable for Jewish exclusion from German culture told in a poet's prose. I used portions of the text for a fifteen-minute eponymous piece built around several variations of a delicate, backwards lap steel guitar phrase played only with harmonics. As I drove, the words, like those of *Bella Ciao*, seemed to allude to Matteo's death. "My stick which talked to the stones, my stick is silent now," Celan's piece goes. "And the stones you say can speak, and in my eyes there is that moveable veil, there are veils, moveable veils, you lift one and there hangs another, and the star there — yes, it is up there now, above the mountains."

The passage reminded me of something Rosmarie Waldrop, one of Celan's finest translators, has written about him. For Celan, she said, writing "meant putting his existence on the line, pushing out into regions of the mind where one is exposed to the radically strange, the terrifying other, the uncanny. And at the moment when existence is actually threatened, when his breath fails, when silence literally (if momentarily) means death — at this moment a poem may be born. If so, it pulls us back from the 'already-no-more' into resuming breath and life. For this moment, this death-in-life when our breath is taken away, yet turns and re-turns, Celan coins the word *Atemwende*."

When Fiona was reciting, Martin and I — trying to leave space for the words — often took out the other instruments, except for the backwards lap steel phrases, which were looped. On this hearing, the loop struck me like breaths interacting with the words, reminding me, too, of Matteo, and *his* breath, now extinguished. It seemed to be another message in a bottle. And as I looked up at the mountains, the band started swelling underneath, rising to a dissonant climax before vanishing, leaving only the pulsing breath of the harmonic loop and Celan's words. It occurred to me then that the borders between music and other music were sometimes blurred beyond recognition, until there were no longer borders at all. It was at that moment that I realized another name for music might be love. As I thought of my friend while the song's final cadences unspooled, I had never been more grateful for that love.

CHAPTER
16

SYNTHESIS AND MODULARITY IN THE WORK OF A MULTIMEDIA COMPOSER

DEREK KELLER

Over the last few years, I have been composing a series of works entitled the Modular Music Project (MMP). MMP combines live performance, formal modularity, and mobile devices to create music and multimedia experiences that fall along the determinant-improvisational-aleatoric continuum. The movements, their components, and video media are modular: the musicians can play the movements and their sections/parts thereof in different arrangements; the video animations can be broadcast in different orders; the audience can navigate and play related media they retrieve from my website; and all of the pieces have varying degrees of structured or guided improvisation. These four elements are emphasized in variable degrees simultaneously in live performance. To address the socio-political challenges of our contemporary moment, I have sought to create "living" multimedia works in which the audience are participants in MMP. The purpose of this writing is to contextualize the influences that led to my conceiving this project, elucidate the idiosyncratic procedures and compositional processes of one of the works in the series, *NorCal Water Music (NorCal)*, and share the solutions to the challenges that modularity and improvisation present to inspire and inform others with similar compositional goals. This writing will also be a bit of a mini-memoir.

* * *

I am a musician blessed with the ability to do a few things fairly well. I am rarely bored in my creativity — unless I am waiting impatiently for media renders or facing computer and technology upgrades, which always takes time away from actually creating something. As a guitarist, and sometimes singer, I have performed a wide variety of music ranging between the completely determinant to the freely improvised. I was trained classically by the late John Sutherland at the University of Georgia and had the fortune of master-classing with Christopher Parkening a couple of times in the mid-'90s. Yet, my deepest roots are in the hard and progressive rock bands/artists of the late '60s and '70s, through the fusion bands/artists of the '70s, '80s, and '90s, and more recently, "Djent" or "New Prog" of our current moment.[1] Playing and writing music in this diverse array of styles in separate spheres (at first) profoundly influenced the way I synthesize them in my current music.

1. I still look for bootlegs and previously unreleased performances of Led Zeppelin (LZ), Pink Floyd, King Crimson, Frank Zappa, and Miles Davis, to name a few. I still love hearing new renderings of their catalogs. I compare versions of Hendrix's *Machine Gun* and *Hear My Train a' Comin'*; LZ's *Since I've Been Loving You*, *No Quarter*, and *Dazed and Confused*; and Davis' late '60s and early '70s sets, in which the songs are reordered, truncated, and interpolated.

* * *

My conceiving of the MMP, and particularly *NorCal*, would not have occurred without my interest in and research of other composers' work. Some of their influences would be obvious, and others have manifested only more recently. One obvious influence is Karlheinz Stockhausen. In studying and researching *Kontakte* (1958–60), I learned that he had originally intended four performers, a degree of improvisation, and an electronic tape part with some degree of "variability."[2] I interpreted this as the possibility that Stockhausen dreamed of a work consisting of interchangeable moments. After all, his Moment Theory conceives of a music consisting of a string of singularities that emerge and dissipate, which may or may not have anything to do with the previous or the next moment. This notion gave me pause to consider that *Kontakte*, an exceedingly virtuosic 30-minute work for percussionist, pianist, and spatialized tape music was formally *variable*. My mind ran with the idea: if he followed through with the variable aspect, the performers and audio engineers could aleatorically organize their parts/scores and reels of tape. Stockhausen realized early on that four players, improvisation, and *any* variability would cause a serious synchronization conundrum. We must remember as well, that up to 1958, he was a determinant composer who was only beginning to allow his intuition to guide his serial compositional processes. And so, in a moment of practicality, he seemed to acquiesce and settle (temporarily) for a completely determinant work, which we now experience bedazzlingly from beginning-to-end, left-to-right, in quadraphonic sound in "contact" with live performance. Whether my hunch was right or not, Stockhausen's visionary

2. For more on Stockhausen's Moment Theory, *Kontakte*, and his electronic music in general, see: Heikinheimo, Seppo, and Brad Absetz. *The Electronic Music of Karlheinz Stockhausen: Studies on the Esthetical and Formal Problems of Its First Phase*. Suomen Musiikkitieteellinen Seura Musikvetenskapliga Sallskapet i Finland, 1972.

approach yielded in *Kontakte* another musical universe unto itself, as he did in almost every work.

* * *

Another influence, which I did not expect to manifest in my current music, is John Cage. I have a love/hate relationship with his music. This is probably because it (and he) seems to continually question every aspect of what we think music is. In my study of his *Concert for Piano and Orchestra*, I was posed the question: what is material or content in music? Cage's *Concert* challenges the soloist and orchestra to interpret music that employs what seems to be regular music notation at first glance. But then, at a closer look, the performer is faced, for example, with an amoeba-like, "connect-the-dots" figure of noteheads overlaying a grand staff. The entire folio is filled with traditional music notation arranged in a completely novel way. Along with the graphic notations of Earle Brown, Morton Feldman, and others, this piece was an exploration and interrogation of what musical notation could represent expressively and aesthetically. This forced the performers to be as creative as Cage was himself. Notations aside, the directions in the score were the most intriguing aspect of the piece. The *Concert* is a solo for piano that is accompanied by *any* combination of the orchestral forces mentioned in the preface, in any temporal arrangement: there is no traditional score in the left-to-right sense. Regarding the 63-page document of eighty-four different compositional "types", Cage writes:

> Each page is one system for a single pianist to be played with or without any or all parts written for orchestral instruments. The whole is to be taken as a body of material presentable at any point between minimum (nothing played) and maximum (everything played), both horizontally and vertically: A program made within a determined length of time (to be altered by a conductor when there is one) may involve any reading, i.e., any sequence of parts or parts thereof.[3]

3. Cage, John. *Concert for Piano and Orchestra*. New York: Peters Edition, 1958.

While the notations were curious and indeed caused me to struggle with the terms and material of the piece, it was the idea of the work's formal variability that interested me most.

* * *

Two other living composers whose works have influenced my conceiving the MMP are Gerhard Winkler and George Lewis. The former pioneered "real-time score" pieces and interactive environments for both soloists and chamber ensembles in the late 1990s.[4] His music is a technical marvel and aesthetically beautiful. At every rehearsal or performance of one of these works, the players are more or less sight-reading, albeit that the music becomes fairly known to them through rehearsing it. Yet the computer system re-generates a piece differently every time. These works are both completely determinant and aleatoric in the sense that algorithms re-order the notational components in new variations of the material — the computer is improvising with a lexicon of musical notation. The performers' real-time realization of this spontaneously computer-generated material guarantees Winkler's musical intent. And in this vein of marvelous programming and musical provocation, George Lewis' *Voyager* impressed me both as an improviser and fomented my determination to create an autonomous improvising computer program. I did manage to achieve this in *Holtranix*.[5] While it does not respond to a human improviser as *Voyager* amazingly does, *Holtranix* guides a human (myself, and at one point Craig Hultgren, cellist) through several improvisational environments while the program itself is also improvising over the course of about sixteen minutes.[6] I should also mention here Anthony Davis, with whom I Improvised and performed, and who caused me to consider more closely the shape of an improvisation, how it could be structured or guided, and how it could be notated with both traditional and non-traditional notation.

4. Winkler, Gerhard. *The Real-Time Score*. Contemporary Music Review, vol. 29, 2010, pp. 89–100. DOI: https://www.scribd.com/doc/303058058/Gerhard-Winkler-The-Real-Time-Score

5. The title of this works takes from the last names of some of my favorite musicians: Allan Holdsworth, John Coltrane, and Jimi Hendrix.

6. I designed all of the audio samples and coded the program in Max/MSP, which played the audio via MIDI in Sample Cell.

* * *

My work then is a hybrid morphology of genres that could be represented in an oddly proportioned three-oval Venn diagram (see Fig. 1). The resulting three-petaled flower at the center could represent an avant garde oeuvre, the formal outcomes of which manifest in determinant, improvised, and more recently, aleatoric music.

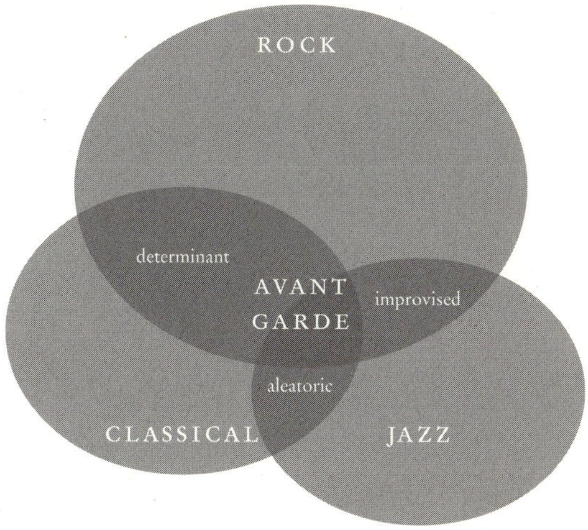

Figure 1.

By determinant, I mean traditionally written musical scores, performed from beginning to end, left-to-right. By improvised, I mean music that is influenced by my affinity for and forays into jazz and improvisation, which has myriad variability with respect to structure and aesthetic. And finally, by aleatoric, I mean music that is modular, the components/movements of which are open to reordering within certain "boundary conditions", as Roger Reynolds would say to me, the decisions of which are left up to the performers' discretion.

* * *

Over the years I have come to realize that when composing, I am actually improvising in (very) slow motion. Early on, the material fell out of my mind and onto the manuscript in a very intuitively driven way. I would write out dreamed-up improvisations in painful detail. Later, some of my music required a significant amount of pre-compositional materials from which I drew and set into pre-conceived architectures, still improvising to a degree, or leaving space for intuitive decisions. This determinant music in all of its beautiful complexity, replete with sonic ear candy, left me wanting the unexpected structural arrivals, and sonic communication that I experience when improvising or what I heard in the popular musical styles I mentioned earlier. Thus, much of my later and current music embraces spaces for groove, with windows of improvisation, the aesthetic of which can be altered significantly by those improvising. I have integrated aspects of "popular" and "classical" music aesthetics, and sought ways of renewing my music when performed through structural modularity, or the reordering of movements, sections or components, and even parts. Several of these works constitute a series I call the Fear Ego Love Project:

> *Fear...Ever Present* for amplified flute, cello, guitar, and percussion: the commercial release of this performance (see below) presents the order of movements as they were composed, I–VII. Yet, any ensemble wishing to perform the work can play the movements in any order.
>
> *Attitudes...Self-expression*, for electric guitar and live computer processing: the guitarist is limited to playing their part left-to-right, with four windows for improvisation. With the generous help of Cristyn Magnus, I designed the code in Pure Data to constantly record three differently timed lengths of the soloist's part, choose to transpose it (at different intervals up/down to a fifth), and then choose to playback these samples forward or backward. Then at several cue points in the score, the computer's audio output is emitted (triggered by the soloist's MIDI foot pedal), yielding an improvised collage of the soloist's material, both from the score and their improvisation — no performance is the same.
>
> *Love...Aspiringly* (texts by Amiri Baraka/LeRoi Jones): About 2/3 of the way through the piece, there is a moment in the score where the treble singers are presented with grace-note passages representing pentatonic "blues licks" to suggest and encourage improvisation.
>
> The three former works above, and one other, *Attitudes... Assumptions Shattered* for drum kit solo, were combined in *Fear Ego Love*. This is a large scale work, a "rock-cantata" of sorts: for choir, rock band, and the mixed quartet mentioned above. The piece could also double as a drum set concerto.[7] In this work, there are extended improvised solos in an aesthetic that blends rock, jazz, and "new music."

7. https://www.derekkeller.com/archived-projects

This hybrid music, as I call it, is heard in several other works since, including *Impositions and Consequences*, which is the title track of an album of my music released on Tzadik (8032). I also pursue this aesthetic in my (slowly ongoing) opera project currently consisting of several chamber pieces, *The California Tableaux Project*.[8]

8. https://www.derekkeller.com/ctp

* * *

The aforementioned stylistic syntheses serve to contextualize how I have come to conceive of the Modular Music Project (MMP). Firstly, MMP is a series of music compositions, whose components (parts, sections, and movements) are modular — they can be reordered. Additionally, there are varying degrees of structured improvisation. Three of the four pieces have a visual projection component, which is managed by a "VJ" (myself); and because of said modularity and improvisation, the VJ participates in creating the multimedia experience as well. Finally, the audience is invited to contribute to the performance with audiovisual content retrievable from my website and viewed/broadcasted from their mobile devices. Thus, these works serve as concert hall pieces. They also sometimes feel like participatory art installations. Finally, they can be experienced as (not so) silent films with live accompaniment.

* * *

As being the most ambitious work of the series so far, I would like to discuss *NorCal Water Music (NorCal)*. *NorCal* is composed for a "Pierrot ensemble" with percussion and socio-multimedia, the definition of which will be revealed below. The work was commissioned by Sacramento's contemporary chamber ensemble, Citywater.[9] When dreaming of the project, John Cage's "star music" shimmered into mind, and I composed a piece that borrows his idea. Instead of star charts, I created video animations of maps of the Sacramento River Watershed with musical notation overlaying them.[10] Additionally, the influence of Stockhausen finds its way into this piece and the others in the series. In a sense, I have adopted his idea that a piece of music can be interpreted as a string of

9. https://www.citywatermusic.com

10. I don't apologize for the ways in which ideas are gestated, filtered, and sieved through my creative mind. The idea of originality is almost farce. At best, I hope to achieve some original "novelty". Thusly, I promote the idea that "originality is synthetic" — a notion that is indubitably owed to a formidable former influence in my life. I can only create out of what I have absorbed, studied, and experienced, and I make no attempt to *write out* any influence if it is indeed working in my art to its end.

interrelated moments. The positions of passages, sections, or movements are *variable* — we can interchange them, much in the way that we can create a program for an evening of music for a concert: a bit of this, a bit of that, in (what we hope) is a cohesive whole. This is true for an evening witnessing Beyoncé in concert or a chamber recital in which an ensemble, or soloist may intend their program to be understood as a narrative, while the pieces are out of chronological order. Thus, this gives me (and many other artists) precedent: the movements of *NorCal*, their components, and sometimes their individual parts can be reordered. Yet, while there is no pre-determinant order, the movements always flow from beginning to end as a whole.

* * *

In May of 2018, I related a vision of the piece to my friends Cathie Apple (flutes) and Tim Stanley (cello), of Citywater: the players would interpret the music on a theater-sized screen, and the audience would retrieve and play additional video content with its own soundtrack on their mobile devices, echoing *streams* of related motivic material across the concert hall. Thus I identify this piece and others in the series as "socio-multimedia" works. The title of the work soon resulted from a play-on-words of Handel's *Water Music* (which I considered parodying) in combination with the name of the ensemble. In effect, I wanted Citywater to "play the water" of the Sacramento River Watershed, and I wanted the audience to be participants with their phones.

* * *

And so to begin, I realized I needed a map that I could project on a theater screen with musical notation overlaying the contours of the creeks, rivers, and perimeters of lakes — a flip on "connect the dots", but with musical sounds. I found a detailed enough map that would allow me to compose music that followed the waterways' contours with just the right amount of density and sparsity (see Fig. 2[11]):

11. www.sacriver.org

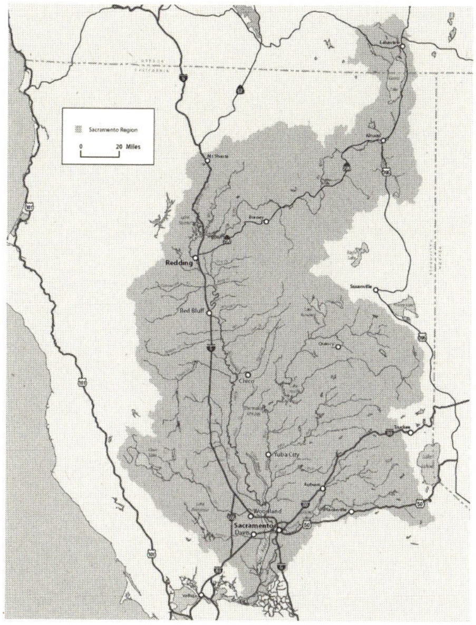

Figure 2.

This same map also inspired me to pack the car on the weekends and head into the delta, hills, and valleys of Northern California. So, with my partner (and now fiancé as of this writing), we hiked and gathered audio and visual samples of several locations of the watershed over the summer of 2018. I intended to integrate these audio-visual samples as part of the multimedia aspect of the work. It turned out, however, that I only used the audio.

* * *

The map's detail also included the main highways and cities, which I intended to mask in photo editing software. I realized, however, rather than spending hours masking these very thin lines and dots, I could spend (an uncountable number of) hours tracing the maps with a stylus on a drawing tablet while using screen-capture software to record my tracings on a computer. The screen-capture recordings became the basis for all of the video animations of the watershed. To achieve this, and to make the tracing a bit easier, I needed to enlarge and divide the map into several overlapping water subsystems. In a PDF editor, I divided the map into eight subsystems, which I printed on transparency paper, each at 8.5 x 11, portrait. This number was reduced to seven when I combined the two southern-most adjacent sections to make a complete map of the Sacramento Delta flowing into the San Francisco Bay.

* * *

To trace the watershed, I purchased a digital drawing tablet and wireless stylus.[12] I then laid a piece of 8.5 x 14 sheet of thin white paper on the tablet, which I fitted and fastened with masking tape. Then I laid the transparencies of the watershed's subsystems over the white paper, fixing them with tape as well. These two films were thin enough to allow my stylus to make contact with the surface of the tablet as I traced every sinuous line with a digital drawing program.[13] The program allowed me to make the drawing crosshairs invisible, except for a single speck, which was the point at which the stylus touches the tablet. Crosshairs were not permissible because the screen-capture software records everything on the computer screen. Furthermore, I wanted the creeks and rivers to magically appear out of the darkness of the concert hall and start snaking in a blue hue on the theater screen. As I mentioned earlier, I had made sure that each of the transparencies overlapped each other. This was critical to my lining up all seven subsystems so that I could reassemble them into one master animation, showing the flows of the entire watershed, from Alturas, CA to the San Francisco Bay.

12. Huion WH1409: I chose this model because it accommodated 8.5 x 14 documents, landscaped. This is the closest paper size to a 9:16 aspect ratio, or widescreen, which I needed to import into the future animation projects.

13. https://sketchbook.com/

* * *

By the time that I had traced all of the subsystems, I had seven videos that captured the whole of the watershed. Yet, their accretion was illogical due to my having traced one creek, river, or lake at a time. For example, the forks of the American River System didn't trickle simultaneously down the western slopes of the Sierra (right to left across the screen) to the Sacramento River. I had to edit the tracings in video editing software to make all the subsystems flow logically. This took countless hours of cut-copy-pasting, masking segments of the videos, and re-distributing dozens of clips across several video tracks. Upon rendering these complicated edits, I yielded simultaneous accretions of tributaries that joined to the main vein of a particular subsystem. The subsystems became the titles of the movements: *Shasta*, *Pit River*, *Valley Creeks I & II*, *Almanor to Oroville*, *American Feather*, and

Delta to Bay. With the video-animations of subsystems complete, I could develop a way to animate the appearance of notation over the subsystems. This proved to be another huge challenge and the development of another idiosyncratic process.

* * *

Before composing the actual music across these animations, I had to find a way to determine the placement of staff lines over the waterways. In music engraving software, I created one page each of single staff and grand staff lines, which I printed to multiple copies of transparency paper. Then in the video software, I rendered still frames of the fully accreted subsystems. These still frames consisted of blue waterways over a black background, which I had to turn into negative images (white background with brown waterways — blue turns brown when in negative). I printed these images on 8.5 x 14 paper, landscaped. In a very intuitive way, I then cut and placed the staff line transparencies over the still frames printed on paper. In my physically working with the grids of staff lines over the organic sinews of the waterways, the soundscape of the piece began to intone itself in my mind's ear. The creeks and rivers, their proximity to each other, the "spines" or smooth, amoeba-like shapes of the lakes all inspired different approaches to scoring the components of each movement. Instrumentations, tessituras, pitch-harmonic content, and the modularity of each movement began to manifest. This was almost like storyboarding a film in advance of writing a single note. Upon deciding how each set of staff lines were to lay, I would tape them down, so that I could replicate their positions in the video editing software, which was the next step.

* * *

The PDFs of the staff lines I created in engraving software had to be turned into JPEGs in negative image (white staff lines with black background). I did this in photo editing software, then imported them into the video software, where I "color-keyed" out the black background of the negative images, rendering them transparent, to allow the blue waterways to show through. Once I had positioned the staff lines over the waterways in the video software (through functions of cropping and masking), I had to capture and print still frames again, and turn them into negative images (white background with black rivers and staff lines). Then, I printed them out on 8.5 x 14 paper, landscaped so that I could finally start writing music over them. As you can surmise thus far, this was a piece of exceeding complexity that I was learning how to do, as I did it. Its creation was slowed by the eventual need for a computer-graphics card upgrade, learning new software, connecting and learning how to use new hardware, etc.[14]

14. Its progress was also mitigated by my academic responsibilities as a college/university adjunct instructor with teaching loads averaging fourteen to sixteen classes per year. This kind of teaching pressure will thankfully relax a little, since I have recently taken a position as Assistant Professor of Commercial Music at Southern Oregon University.

* * *

One of the first aspects of *NorCal* that I composed was a 4-part chorale which I transposed three times at a minor third (see Fig. 3). The progression is a mixture of chords, both docile (MM7 & mm7) and furtive (Mm7 & dm7), the resolutions of which are sometimes deceptive.

This chorale is a result of considering my thoughts and emotions while visiting and recording the waterways of northern California the previous summer, tracing the organic complexity of the map of the watershed, and viewing the sinuous animations of the subsystems etching their way across my computer screen. The chorale provided me a palette of chord colors that I intended to express the beauty and fragility of the watershed — the one that supplies water to the production of ¼ of the food supply for the entire US.[15] The chorale is the wellspring from which I drew all pitch-harmonic content. This content flowed as noteheads that I applied to (nearly) every single blue line of the animated tracings. Creeks with steep slopes became arpeggios. Gentle turns of a river became a scalar figure with a mode that would still fit inside a particular chord, or adapt to "playing the changes" through the progression, or were turned into *glissandi.* Perimeters of lakes became polyphonic melody or counterpoint, and vertical tributaries or lake shores became chords. While writing noteheads across multiple tributaries over a particular subsystem, I conformed their instrumental assignments to a progression from the chorale so that the combined waterways would sound harmonically unified. While the chorale provided the pitch-harmonic content, my approach to rhythm was more intuitive — I improvised in slow motion.

15. https://ca.water.usgs.gov/projects/central-valley/about-central-valley.html

Figure 3.

⁂ ⁂ ⁂

There is no rhythmic *tala*, so to speak, from which I may have drawn to compose a gesture or musical behavior. From a metaphorical standpoint, this is fitting. While the flow of a waterway may have a particular direction owing to elevation, there is no path of a creek or river that is the same. Certainly, the creeks' and rivers' trajectories are similar: all waterways from the east and west flow to the Sacramento River in the California Central Valley. Thus, I posit the idea that the chorale captures this notion of unification in the pitch-harmonic realm. This is perceivable, for example, at the end of *Shasta* (which is geographically south of the Shasta Dam), when all tributaries to the Sacramento River are playing different gestures at first. The pitch content is drawn from one of the transpositions of the chorale and move through the progression at the same rate. As each tributary meets the Sacramento, all instruments eventually unify to play the remaining contour of the Sacramento in a heterophonic way, as observable in Fig. 4:

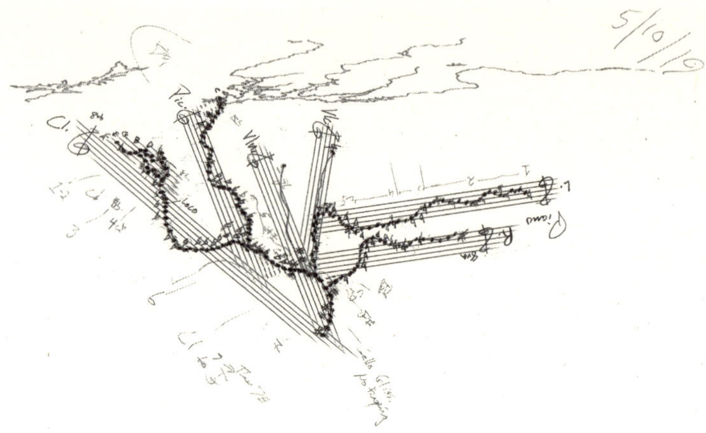

Figure 4.

I composed *Shasta* in September–November of 2018 (only to recompose it in May of the following year). In this first tack at composing over the still frames, I realized I wanted *tutti* and *unisono* moments, such as the one mentioned above, and I could not control the ensemble metrically to bring this about if I let them improvise. A structured improvisation based on my noteheads that bubbled along the tributaries would not yield the determinant simultaneities that I imagined, particularly at the end of the movement. Furthermore, representing clear rhythmic values, stemming, beaming, glissandos vs. discrete pitches, and other sonic details proved to be difficult to write clearly enough for an ensemble to read. As I was applying pitches from the progressions of the chorale, I knew that I had to structure them in a traditional musical score. Thus, I decided the movements would be completely written out, (less the seventh, *Delta to Bay*): the video animations would be cues for the performers to commence performing each movement, the first of a few sections, or in the case of *Shasta*, their individual parts. Making this decision led to my pre-planning the instrumentation and modularity of the movements and their respective components. Since the ensemble would be playing from a score, the video animations that I designed later would have to be more/less precisely the same duration, so that the ensemble's "accompanying the film" would be accurate. The creation of *NorCal* would be thus:

> Write all of the noteheads over each line (creek/river) or blob (lake) on the still frames.
>
> Commit the noteheads to an intuited rhythmic gesture on manuscript.

Engrave my manuscript in notational software.

Export audio files of the notational software for import into video editing software.

Re-trace just the noteheads, scan them, process them in photo editing software, and export them for the animations in the video editing software.

Design the animations in the video software in layers: noteheads (in white), over staff lines (in white), over blue waterways, over a black background, all over the "canned" music.

The passage in Fig. 4 above came to be scored, for example, in Figs. 5 and 6 below.

Figures 5–6.

In what follows, I will share three examples illustrating how I assigned instruments to the waterways. I will first dive deep into the scoreless portion of *Shasta* and then show the flows of two other movements, *Almanor to Oroville* and *Delta to Bay*. In the wake of each, I will also explain how their modular aspects affect their realization in performance.

* * *

Shasta is one of two movements that the ensemble can choose to play first — the other is *Pit River* (whichever movement is not chosen to commence will follow). Figs. 7 and 8 illustrate how I oriented the *Shasta* system (left is North), assigned its tributaries to the instruments, and then applied the noteheads (from the *NorCal Chorale*) to the tributaries:

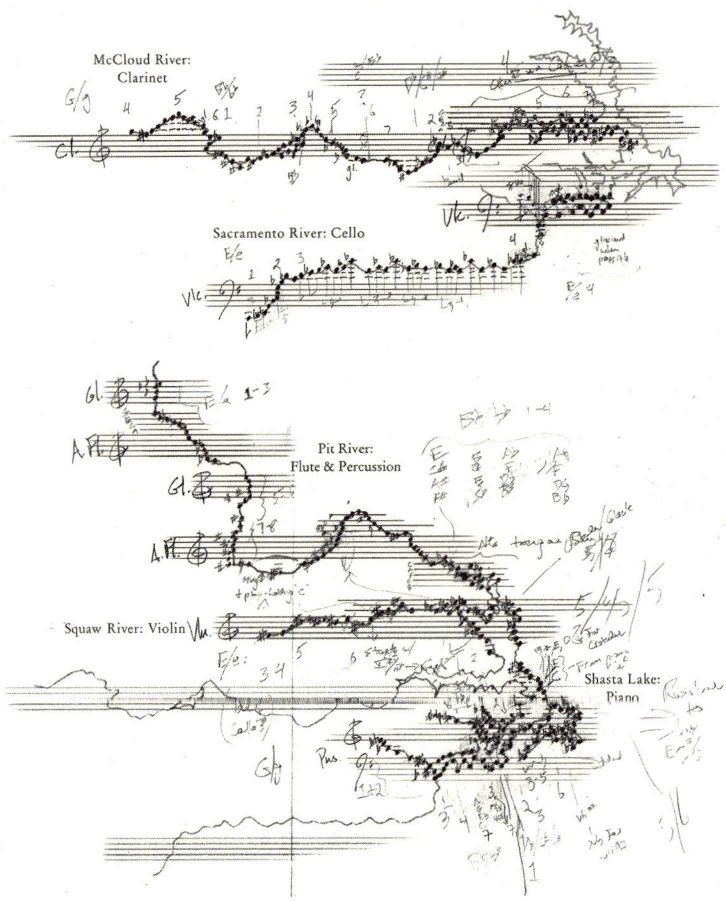

Figures 7–8.

The notated traces above illustrate the transpositions of the chorale that I applied to each of the instruments. For example, the cello part draws from the E (major)/e (minor) transposition, while the clarinet part draws from the G/g transposition. While applying the noteheads to the perimeter of the lake and the contours of the rivers, I decided that the first 2/3 of the movement would be scoreless: the order of the instruments' entrances would be modular and staggered. And so, each part of *Shasta* was composed irrespective of the others. By the time that I had scored each part, I had decided that the piano would always begin the movement. It was the longest, and it had the most space between gestures — long rests through which the other instruments could sound in variable ways. I was worried that deciding on a scoreless approach would render a cacophonic mess, rendering the details of each part lost. This would be detrimental to the video animations because it was the very details of the waterways that I wanted to highlight. To deal with a potential compositional disaster, I decided to use DJ software (Ableton Live) as means of improvising the entrances of each instrument in a staggered fashion. Ableton is a digital audio workstation developed for DJs. I used it in a "tempo-less" way, to cue audio files of the individual parts. So, after I had finished engraving each of the parts in notation software, I rendered an audio file of each of the parts and loaded them into Ableton. Through my improvising a different order of entrances, I was able to confirm that all orders of entries sounded well in combination. Surprisingly it yielded a very compelling interaction between the parts, with an ebbing and flowing of dissonance, to a sometimes uncanny consonance — this is what I mean about the unexpected structural simultaneities or harmonic arrivals mentioned above, for which I listen in improvisation. Certainly, the chorale and its transpositions would harmonically yield such potential, but in no way did I pre-determine such a confluence. This movement was definitely one of the most complicated in its modularity, compared to the other six. Yet, solving the logistics in how its partiture would flow bolstered my confidence when crafting the modular design in each of the other movements. Figs. 9 through 13 illustrate how the notated traces (in Figs. 7 and 8) were scored for each part.[16]

16. Regarding Figure 9, I asked the pianist to insert more time of rest than is indicated here.

Shasta – Lake Shasta

Figure 9.

Shasta – Squaw Creek

Figure 10.

Shasta – Sacramento River

Figure 11.

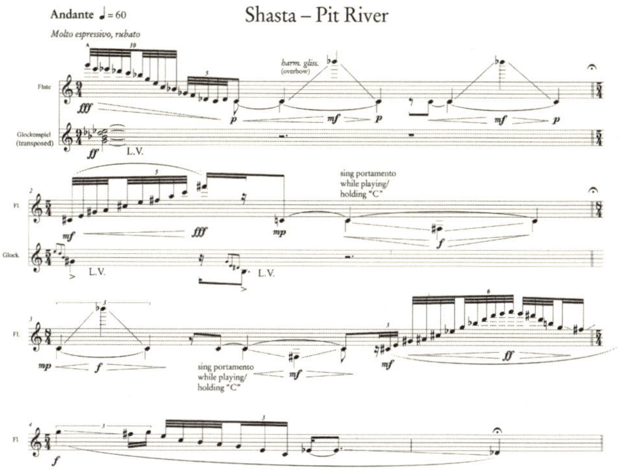

Figures 12–13.

Improvising the modularity of *Shasta* in Ableton prepared me for working with video as a VJ. Each of these parts (Figs. 9–13), has a different silent video animation associated with it. In performance, the ensemble waits for their entrances, which are individually cued visually on the screen in the concert hall by my actuating their associated video animations via midi controller. As VJ, I improvise a different order of instrumental entries after the piano commences the movement. In each rehearsal and at the premiere, I cued a different order and created the same aggregate image of the Shasta subsystem, always concluding with the *Shasta over the Dam* scored passage illustrated earlier. Thus, the beginning and ending of *Shasta* are fixed while the body of the movement is always modular.

* * *

Following *Shasta* and *Pit River* (or the reverse of that order), *Almanor to Oroville* is one of four other modular movements that can occur in any order (all of the other movements have modular components as well). The water system encompasses two large man-made lakes, Almanor and Oroville, as well as Honey Lake. I assigned these to the piano solo; less Honey Lake, which has an additional *glissando* cello line lazily tracing across the north shore in the background of the piano foreground. The other waterways are the headwaters of the Feather River System, which are impounded by the dam at Lake Oroville. I assigned two trios to the north and south forks of the Feather River System. The north forks' instrumentation includes piano, percussion, and cello, while the south forks' instrumentation comprises flute, clarinet, and violin. Fig. 14 represents the five still frames of the components of the subsystem with the staff lines overlaid.

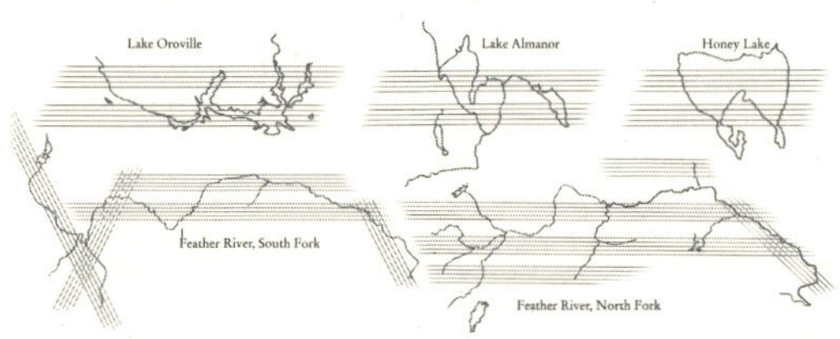

Figure 14.

Taking into consideration the range of the instruments assigned to each component, and applying ledger lines when necessary, I applied pitch-harmonic content to each still frame. I then *re*-traced just the noteheads on tracing paper, scanned them, processed the images in photo editing software, and imported them into the video editing software.

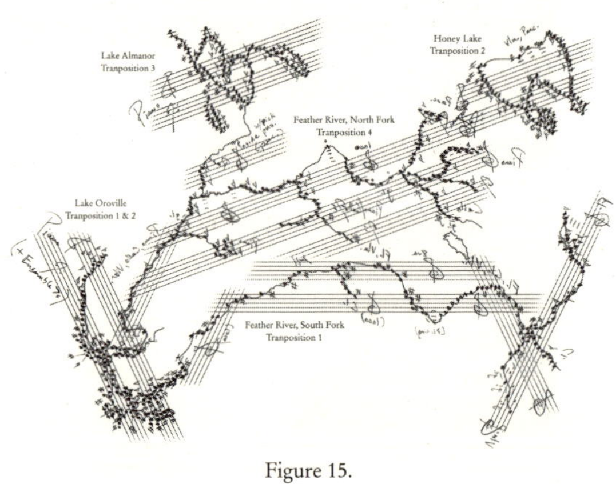

Figure 15.

Fig. 15 is an aggregate image of the same five still frames that show the whole of the subsystem with the pitch-harmonic content from the transpositions of the choral. For reference, see Fig. 3, the *NorCal Chorale*.

You will notice that both north and south forks of the Feather River system are horizontally flipped. The reason for this is that I composed the pitches left to right (headwaters to terminus at Lake Oroville) knowing that I would employ an animated flip of the images to their correct orientation in the final video. These five images became five separate sections that the ensemble could re-order in performance. The rules regarding their modularity were thus:

> *Lake* components can be performed in any order, with a *Fork* section separating each. Conducting responsibilities for the *Fork* sections can be passed between instrumentalists when one is not playing.

All the movements of *NorCal* were composed through a similar process. Yet in performance, their modular aspects differ. All of the movements' sequential positions are also modular, except *Delta to Bay*, which always concludes the piece. The complexity of this subsystem resisted the compositional process that I painstakingly applied to the other six. As I observed all of the tiny creeks, sloughs, and multi-forked rivers emptying into the bay, I imagined rendering scores that would begin to look like Cage's *Concert for Piano and Orchestra*. Yet, even before committing thousands of noteheads to the other subsystems of the watershed, I decided that I would make this final movement unlike any of the others: it would be a guided improvisation. I had mixed thoughts regarding this decision. My main concern was the fact that not all musicians are accustomed to improvising, while others excel at it. Another concern was the criticism that I might receive on my "just throwing in an improvisation as an afterthought", as a colleague once observed. This is a critique of composers who casually include improvisation in their scores, ostensibly not considering the pedagogy, approaches, and histories of improvisation. It is indeed sometimes apparent, and it could be argued, that composers who incorporate improvisation are foisting the work onto the performers. This is surely a matter for debate, but outside the scope of this writing. Yet, suffice it to say, that this composer surely considered how the players would be guided in the process of the improvisation and why it works to conclude *NorCal*.

*   *   *

Through careful consideration and application of boundary conditions, I sought to maintain the integrity of the work to conclude it with a guided improvisation. In the score, I direct the players to be inspired by the video. As a guide to a collective improvisation, the players are instructed to follow any of the accreting tributaries flowing to the San Francisco Bay. The video animation zooms out slowly, to eventually encompass the entire watershed, incorporating the other six movements' animations, and thus, providing more visual material to the performers for their sonic realization. Fig. 16 illustrates (in negative image) the entire watershed[17]:

17. Note that what appears to be a large lake in the middle of this map is in fact a large floodplain.

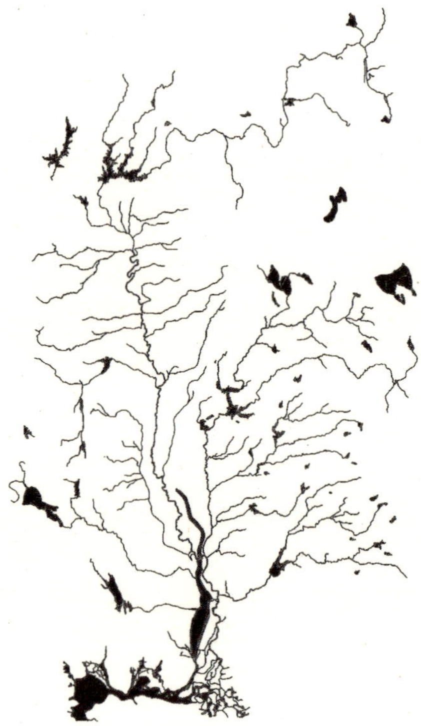

Figure 16.

Over the course of an improvisation lasting no more than three minutes, the players have the choice to either quote or re-interpret music from the other movements; or, improvise music similar in aesthetic, employing the chorale as a pitch-harmonic resource. At no point do I intend that the players freely improvise. With a little coaching, and after many hours of rehearsing the piece as a whole, Citywater rendered several very compelling improvisations. Because of their familiarity with the music I had composed, there was never an improvisation that was outside the aesthetic. The large majority of their improvisations actually proved to be *more* sonically and compositionally compelling than some of the determinant aspects of the piece. This was particularly true at the world premiere in Sacramento at the Crocker Art Museum on November 19, 2019. Most importantly, while every improvisation was different, the unexpected simultaneities and interactions that I desire in improvisation occurred in myriad ways. The success of this guided improvisation was born out of the boundary conditions that I set before them in the score in combination with their keen interpretations of the animations, whether they chose to re-interpret music from one of their parts or to play the changes of the chorale. While the final movement of *NorCal* is improvised, the modularity of the movements that precedes is not.

In the preface to the score, the ensemble is presented with a set of choices to construct a realization in advance of a performance. These decisions are best made after rehearsing the work. Once comfortable, the ensemble is free to re-make the order of the movements and sections at any future performance. Figs. 17–19 comprise a flow chart that the ensemble uses to piece the work together:

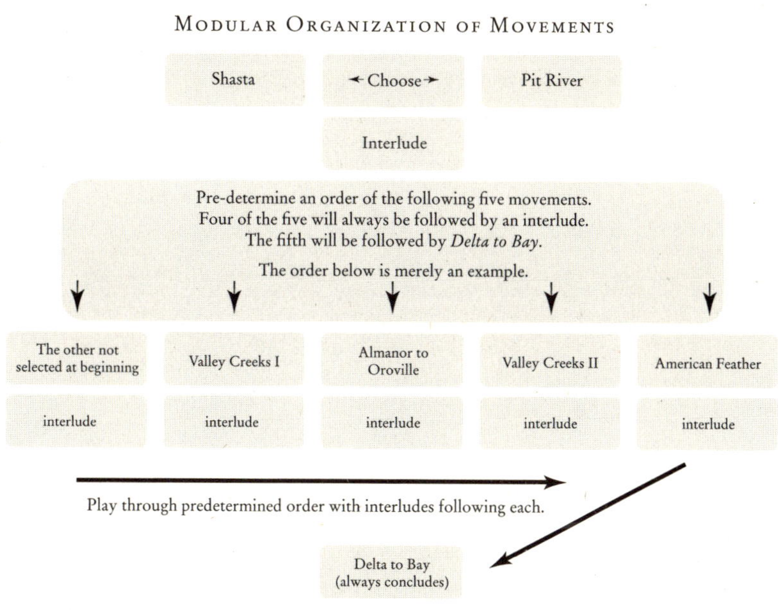

Figure 17.

Modularity of Components in Each Movement

Each movement listed above contains multiple components
and have varying degrees of modularity:

Shasta

Piano: Shasta Lake
(always begins)

After the second loud chordal figure in measure 3 of the piano part,
the following four parts can be cued at random or enter in a predetermined order,
in a stagger fashion, roughly 10–15 seconds apart.
The Flute & Percussion part, *Pit River* shall never be last.

Flute & Percussion: Pit River | Violin: Squaw Creek | Clarinet: McCloud River | Cello: Sacramento

In the parts listed above, double-bars should be interpreted as long *fermatas*, or 5–10 second pauses.
When playing, the instrumentalists are encourages to "play off of one another",
allowing for space expreission, and different modular possibilities.

Shasta Over the Dam
(always concludes)

Shasta — Over the Dam will always conclude the movement,
and is cued as the last of the parts above is sounding.
The percussionist is encouraged to conduct this last passage after initiating this section in their own part.

Pit River

Downstream | ← Either or both in any order → | Upstream

Either/or both versions can be performed.
If both are played, either version "Upstream" or "Downstream" can initiate the movement.
Conducting responsibilites can be passed beteen instrumentalists when one is not playing.

Figure 18.

Valley Creeks I

West Legs | ← any order → | East Legs

Both components, *West Legs* and *East Legs*, must be performed.
Either section can inititate the movement.
Conducting responsibilites can be passed between intrumentalists when one is not playing.

Valley Creeks II

Part 1 or 3 | Part 2 | Part 1 or 3 (the one not chosen to begin)

There are 3 parts. Part 2 must always be in the middle position.
Parts 1 & 3 can bookend the movement, with either in the first position.
Conducting responsibilites can be passed between intrumentalists when one is not playing.

Almanor to Oroville

1st of 3 *Lake* Components | 1st of 2 *Lake* Components | 2nd of 3 *Lake* Components | 2nd of 2 *Fork* Components | 3rd of 3 *Lake* Components

The *Lake* components can be performed in any order, with a *Fork* section separating each.
Conducting responsibilites for the *Fork* sections can be passed between
intrumentalists when one is not playing.

American Feather

Feather Downstream, Forks Upstream | ← any order → ↓ then ↓ To Sacramento | All American, Downstream

Both components, *Feather Downstream, Forks Upstream* and *All American Downstream*,
must be performed. Either section can initiate the movement.
Conducting responsibilites can be passed between intrumentalists when one is not playing.
The section entitled *Sacramento River* will always conclude the movement.

Delta to Bay

This movement consists of only one section, which is improvised. For details, see the score.

Figure 19.

Once the ensemble decides how the piece will flow, the VJ can set up the videos for triggered playback and projection in VJ software. However, the VJ would still need video animations to project.

* * *

As mentioned earlier, the final video projections did not include the actual waterways that I visited over the previous summer. Instead, I decided to use the notations that I had composed on the still frames as the main visual feature of the animations — this became the *blatant homage* to John Cage. Over the course of September, I set to putting the noteheads that I had written over the still frames into the video editing software. To do this, I had to *re*-trace (!) the note heads on tracing paper — *not* the creeks, rivers, and lakes — and scan, process, and save them as high-resolution JPEGs. I then changed them into negative images, rendering white noteheads on a black background. I changed the black to blue so that I could remove the blue color through color-keying in the video editing software to reveal the animated blue rivers on the black background without any errant edges or pixelation. In my editing the video for each movement, I imported the audio-MIDI realizations of the musical scores. To these "canned" realizations of the scores, which coincidently provided the timeline for each movement, I designed the animations: traced noteheads, on top of staves, on top of waterways, on a black background. Through several different ways of processing the images (color-keying, masking, and the automation of keyframes that controlled scaling, positioning, blurring, warping, cropping, and opacity), all of these layers were animated in a variety of ways across all seven movements.

* * *

At the end of September and over October 2019, I finished the final media components of the work: five video interludes intended for both projection and the audience's retrieval and playback on their mobile devices. Each interlude features a different geographical area of the watershed: *Delta & Piano*, *Sly Park with Flute & Clarinet*, *Horsetail Falls & Cello*, *Hidden Falls & Flute*, and *McCloud River & Violin*. The durations of these videos have a range of one and half to two minutes. The source imagery consists of both my tracings and other contours that I free-handed on my drawing tablet.

Recorded in screen-capture software, I processed this source material in a similar way to the notational animations, except with the addition of mirroring and turbulent effects. While working on these animations, which were silent at first, I invited each of the members of Citywater to my home to record several phrases of their parts. These audio samples and those of the waterways I had captured over the summer of 2018 became the content for the soundtrack to each of the video interludes. When revisiting the audio and video recordings of these different locations, I noticed that each ecosystem had a different sonic signature. The water had different resonances: rushing, gurgling, deep pounding hydraulics, or silence with the exception of birds, rustling trees, or propeller planes and agricultural equipment in the distance. The latter is an example of the agrarian areas around the Delta. Through digital audio processing (EQ sculpting), I accentuated these pitched resonances and made them the aural basis over which I integrated the players' sampled parts. The soundtrack for each of these videos, then, is a sonic waterscape: an ecosystem blended with remixed material from the musical score.

* * *

By early November 2019, it was time to put all this together: silent video animations accompanied by the ensemble, with five interpolated interludes, and audience participation — all with varying degrees of modularity. Initial rehearsals focused just on the music, while the final ones incorporated all of the technology, less the audience. In preparation for adding the video components, I found VJ software with a similar interface to Ableton, in which I could overlay and mix the opacities and soundtracks — I was limited only by the processing power of the computer. In the VJ software, I could load as many video clips into a grid, as my MIDI controller had performance pads, which I used to trigger each video during rehearsal and performance.[18] Then, the conductor of each movement (an instrumentalist without a part to play) would watch the screen for their cue to commence directing the ensemble. As there are three to six separate components in each movement, I triggered each section according to the decisions the ensemble made concerning the work's modularity — I basically had a playlist to follow. As with any new piece of music, rarely have I encountered the situation in which the tempos of the music wouldn't fluctuate: I did have to stretch the

18. RemixVideo (RV): it is inexpensive and very powerful. In RV, a VJ can drag-and-drop videos into its performance interface, which are then represented in a grid of thumbnails. I have been using an AKAI APCmini as the MIDI controller, which has an 8 x 8 set of performance pads.

length of the animations (by slowing their playback rate) in the video editing software, and re-render them. Yet while the duration of the videos is fixed, the VJ software allows me to modulate the rate of playback (a little faster or slower), ensuring that the ensemble and the videos line up. In between each movement, I trigger one of the five video interludes in a pre-planned way based on the ensemble's decisions regarding the movements' flow. At the same time, the audience is invited to retrieve and playback one of the same videos on their phones with the volume up.[19] Depending on the size of the audience, I make recommendations on how to mediate the degree of sound in the hall. Rather than a wash or din, I want to intone rivulets of musical echoes across the concert hall. Conveniently, the interludes gave the ensemble a moment to prepare for the next movement, while also yielding gentle tides of sound between the concert stage and the audience.[20]

19. When each concertgoer enters the hall, their program includes a QR code directing them to the webpage on which the media is available.

20. The reader can find a video of the premiere here: https://www.derekkeller.com/current

* * *

My intent on including the audience as active participants in this work and others in the series is what lead me to coin the term "socio-multimedia", which has been attached to the other works' titles in the Modular Music Project. *NorCal* will be followed by two more works: one for New York City's Loadbang, and another for solo high voice, which I am currently developing for Bernadette Mondok. Others in the series include *The End Times Are a'Changin': Fantasy on a Theme by Dylan* (2018) for solo guitar and socio-multimedia, *Liminal Spaces* (2018) for alto saxophone and guitar, and *O Mensch, Gib Acht!* for chamber choir and socio-multimedia. While *Liminal Spaces* doesn't include audience participation, all of its movements are modular. The other two pieces incorporate the audience in varying degrees. Special to *O Mensch…*, the choir receives all of the notation as short videos on their phones, with accompanying pitch cues through their earbuds, thus allowing them to move about the performance space. The videos are retrievable from a 5-page swipe-able grid of thumbnail images representing the notational components. When a singer chooses and touches a thumbnail, they are presented either a stationary set of notational instructions or a scrolling video of choral notation with introductory pitch cues that they hear through their earbuds. As long as the choir has a good internet connection, the piece can be realized differently every time it is performed due to its embedded aspects of improvisation and modularity. I would remind the reader here of my admiration of Gerhard Winkler: *O Mensch...* is an example of how technology has finally caught up to non-coder/computer scientist-types like myself, but with the advancement of not needing a closed network of expensive computers.[21] Similar to *NorCal* and *The End Times..., O Mensch...* will also have projected media and related videos available for the audience to play on their phones. *O Mensch...* was set for a world premiere this past spring in San Diego, but with the onset of the COVID pandemic, it has been pushed into the future until a vaccine is developed. However, SACRA/PROFANA, the commissioning ensemble, will have shared a virtual "trailer" that will realize the first section of the work by the time of this volume's published release.

21. I'd like to thank Forrest Balman, currently a Masters Student at California State University, San Francisco, whom I met when delivering a presentation to the composition area. He has been immensely helpful in helping me design the performance web interface for *O Mensch...*: www.derekkeller.com/o-mensch-media.

* * *

In closing, COVID has brought into unsettling sharp focus the symbiotic relationship between an audience and the art produced for "live" experiences by artists and ensembles. In this series' development, I have thought more about the audience and my work's relationship to them, even more so than previously. It is painfully ironic then, that much of my Modular Music Project does not exist without the participation of the audience. *The End Times...* and *NorCal...* have options to allow the players to perform them without video projection or audience participation, thus rendering them concert works. But, I have yet to encounter anyone wanting to present them without these components, as the performers are also interested in engaging the audience in an uncommon and inclusive way. I have humbly reveled in the warm reception these works have received. I look forward to their being renewed in *different* realizations at future performances, and especially the way in which they will break the "fourth wall" of new music in their embrace and envelopment of the audience.

* * *

I would like to express my gratitude to my readers for their proofing and critique: Christopher Adler, Colin McAllister, David Bithell, and Bernadette Mondok.

CHAPTER 17

ON LISTENING AND OPENNESS

Songs My Students Taught Me

RICHARD KESSLER

I walked into a room with a young student practicing a Beethoven *Piano Sonata*. After a bit of back and forth I asked the student what her relationship was to the music and to the composer. Do you compose music as well as perform it? Do you improvise? We talked a bit as well about the nature of notated music and in particular whether or not the notation was an exact representation of what the composer intended.

The student was quite clear: "I'm a performer. My job is to perform the works of great composers (and sometimes not so great). I don't compose…it's not part of my education. I wouldn't even know where to start, plus it would take time away from practicing. I guess there are performers and there are composers and sure, there are a few that do both. Look at the way schools are structured. Performers separate from composers. Besides, aren't all the great composers dead?"

I asked the student about the notes on the page. Are they exact or approximate? I mean, are they mathematically exact? "Well, I guess you could say that there is some room, I mean the room for the performer to interpret, but the notes are exact, yes, exactly what the composer intended. My job is to do Beethoven's notes the justice it deserves."

Another student walks into a teacher's studio and opens his gig bag. The teacher sees the student's iPod sitting in his gig bag and being curious about the music the student listens to, asks the student if he can "see" the iPod. Nope, says the student. Trying another route, the teacher asks what music the student has on his iPod. Being a trumpet player, the students reels off all the greatest hits of the classical trumpet and nothing else. Then, when the student leans over to retrieve his mouthpiece from his gig bag, the teacher playfully snatches the iPod and scrolls though the student's music library. One track after another, it is one genre after another. Rap, hip-hop, EDM, and yes, Mahler's *Symphony No. 5* and the Haydn *Trumpet Concerto*.

Not surprised, the teacher says: "just as I thought."

A class of jazz and classical music students attend a workshop on game-based improvisation. The teacher announces that today they are going to make music without any sheet music in front of them. At first, the jazz students are pretty confident about the class, since they are improvising artists. One of the jazz students nods her head to signify that she's got it. The classical students are all feeling uneasy since they have never improvised before. A classical student asks the teacher if this is really how jazz is played. Early on in the workshop it is evident that the jazz students have no real advantage since it is not a form of improvisation they have encountered previously. What become readily apparent is that all the students are on the same level. The teacher turns to me and says: "you can't tell the classical students from the jazz students. They're all listening very hard."

A teacher plays a recording of *Sun Ship* by John Coltrane. A student says that they just don't get why Coltrane moved in this direction. Another student says she loved *Blue Train* but feels turned off to late Coltrane. The teacher moves on to Mahler's *9th Symphony* and time is spent on its radical structure. Another student says that she "loves Mahler's *Second* and *Third* symphonies, but the *Ninth* is just odd. It's not really the best use of an orchestra." There's something in what appears to be a snap judgment by the students that bothers the teacher. The students clearly love Coltrane and Mahler. Some might say they "worship" these artists but are closed off to pursuing or gaining greater understanding of what these works represent in the lives of these artists they love. The teacher wonders how hard they are really listening to these late works by these artists they profess such devotion to. The teacher also wonders how much they really know or have sought to understand about who these artists were as human beings and what influenced the choices they made artistically.

I had a lunch once with John Zorn and I shared my concerns about how musical skills classes including ear training and theory are taught. It seemed to me that these classes were taught primarily within the context of the traditional genre and style of the program, as in jazz or classical. Lots of tonal harmony and analysis for the classical students and lots of jazz harmony for the jazz students, but what happens when the student encounters something that is not tonal, not structured along the lines of the traditional relationships/structures of harmony, rhythm, and melody? I witnessed what can happen with an ensemble of students trying to learn Steve Reich's

Double Sextet. They couldn't internalize/feel the pulse, since their training in rhythm didn't encompass what this music required. Clearly, the standard books on rhythm didn't help much with Reich's "pulsatile" music. The conductor was forced to take the students off of their instruments to spend time on eurythmic exercises in order to develop a strong sense of pulse/internal rhythm within the student musicians.

Zorn's response to me that day was pretty simple: "the students need to learn how to listen."

Over time, I have come to understand that "listening" was something well beyond hearing an interval, identifying or tuning a chord, or being able to transpose. It was a holistic human endeavor that involved many different human abilities, including but not limited to aural, body-kinesthetic, intuitive, interpersonal, and intra-personal (your own voice, thoughts, ideas, and reflections), and the ability to perceive and generate energy. Most notable about the students in the game-based improvisation workshop was that the need to listen more closely, more intensely, to hear and perceive in new ways, was forced upon them by engaging in music that called for listening like this in order to perform it.

It also became clear to me that this sort of listening would be important for the development of the young artists no matter what music they performed, composed, and improvised, not to mention being beneficial to so many things beyond their artistic practice.

And, as I reflected upon that conversation with Zorn, I thought more about the connection between listening as a holistic human endeavor and openness. In particular I reflected upon the relationship of listening and openness within a virtuous cycle.

Were students open mostly to what they already knew and/or understood and generally closed off to what they don't? Openness could apply to music they had not performed or studied as well as music that wasn't blessed by norms established by their teachers or traditions within a particular community of practice. Openness could also include openness to their own innate potential.

The student oboist that forecloses on the idea that he can learn to compose and improvise has come to this conclusion as a result of a lack of openness. It is the closed mind that says I cannot do that. Openness would also apply to a deeper valuing of the audience or a willingness and interest in performing in alternative and community settings. Openness would apply to engaging with music that you don't quite understand or have prior experience with, using all of your skills and knowledge to live inside that music and if preparing for performance, end up doing your very best.

In the class where *Sun Ship* was discussed, the conversation eventually led to why Coltrane moved in this direction, not only looking at the arch of his development, including the incremental movements forward, but more importantly to an intense discussion about how structures had to be overcome in order for Coltrane to express himself fully. Prior structures had placed a limit on what Coltrane could express emotionally and spiritually. Ultimately the subject was less about the searching of John Coltrane and more about the creative agency of an artist and whether or not the artist had to live within and accept the boundaries of prior traditions, common practice, or accepted normative structures.

Across centuries, classical musicians improvised, performed, and composed, not to mention conducted, taught, and had to be highly entrepreneurial in order to survive. It was only in the 20th century when formal music education established compartmentalized hierarchies, with living composers being separated and at the very bottom of the musical food chain. This period also saw the disappearance of improvisation in classical music as a core practice.

The pigeonholes established in 20th century music education are hard wired. For years, the national standards for music education listed composition and improvisation as core parts of a K–12 music education. It is telling that assessment after assessment of instruction and curriculum reveals that composition and improvisation receive the least amount of task time of all the core curricular elements in the national standards. The fact is that many music teachers themselves are not comfortable nor knowledgeable in how to teach either composition or improvisation.

This brings us back to the very first student mentioned in this essay. The student who was a "performer," who did not compose, did not improvise, and viewed the notes on the page as being an exact, mathematical representation of what the composer intended. This student represents well a century worth of training of classical musicians, who were trained as performers, separate from composers, with improvisation viewed as an historical artifact.

Ultimately it is the diminishment or narrowing of human agency that is most troubling. This student has been placed in a box that defines the student and her capacities as that of performer/interpreter and not a creative musician. Is it really possible except for the ways in which much of performing arts education was structured and the values that led to such structures in the 20th century, that this student does not possess the innate ability to compose, improvise, curate, and create their career and life?

Yes, there are those who will assert that interpretation is creativity, and they are correct, though it doesn't provide much of a defense of the system of education. That said, many students never quite get to that vaunted level, for the focus on acquisition of requisite technical skills becomes the mountain to be climbed before such interpretative and advanced musical skills are explored, if ever. So, the classical student is positioned in a culture of rules and hierarchy, where performers are performers, composers are composers, conductors are conductors, and only the unicorns get to do it all. And let's not let the jazz students or jazz field off the hook her either, in the ways that vocalists or drummers have often been viewed or categorized. You can say the same for the dancer in the ballet corps.

Placing students in boxes is not a construct of openness, but rather that of a closed system. It is also the sort of thing that leads to our trumpet student being afraid to admit liking a wide range of music extending beyond the value system of the classical conservatory. The student is too eager to please and the culture that led to this sort of situation, whether it be about power or fear, or a lack of interest in listening to a student and being open to who each student is and can be, must be changed.

We've been living through a continuous period of change and disruption to the business of art across the past century at least. There are more ways to earn a living as an artist than ever before, when one considers how community-based art making has expanded opportunities, including that of K–12 teaching artistry, creative aging, and much more. At the same time, the businesses and institutions have changed greatly, most notably the record labels, jazz clubs, touring circuits, artist managers, and opera companies and orchestras.

The road ahead of us will continue to change, likely at a faster pace than before. It will demand artists who are open, entrepreneurial, highly creative, resourceful, and capable of doing more if not it all, better than ever. It will demand artists with a point of view, who are socially conscious, artistically nimble, who stand on their own two feet not afraid to challenge the norms and to create their own worlds of art making and communities of practice. It will demand artists and institutions that support and develop artists to be better at listening and more open than ever. It will demand artists who are highly skilled at that human art and science of listening and open to creating opportunity in the ever-changing landscape.

My bet is on a hard push towards the value of openness, while doing everything possible to treat young developing artists as creative artists first and foremost, breaking down the artificial divide among performing, composing, high art and low art, the main stage and the community performance space. I believe that the greater breadth and depth that will be required of artists going forward can and will be met, helped along by training and educational programs that are open, evolving, and highly synthetic in approach, dedicated more to the great potential in each person rather than the structures of past traditions.

CHAPTER 18

NOTATION IS BLISS

PAULINE KIM

Rooted in classical music, my early experience with musical notation was somewhat conventional. It was through "new music" i.e. contemporary, avant garde, experimental, improvisatory, electro-acoustic, etc. that I developed a curiosity for new possibilities in notation. It being a broad subject, I would like to focus specifically on notation through the eyes of a performer/composer.

As a performer, I try to de-emphasis the visual impact of a score and how that could influence the interpretation and attitude of my initial approach to a piece. On the other hand, because I know what an impression it can make, the composer in me can obsess over it incessantly.

In classical music, there can be multiple editions of the same piece by different publishers for performers to choose from. Some even offer multiple editions of the same piece by the same publishers, edited by performers i.e. Gingold Bach *Solo Sonatas* and Partitas vs. the Galamian, and so forth. Notation does not vary much from edition to edition. However, a particular edition could influence how a piece is interpreted.

Standard system for score notation:

Notes in a scale
Note values
Time signatures
Measures
Tempo markings
Dynamics
Articulation

In classical music, what edition you play from and why can be a whole conversation on its own: Henle, Peters, Barenreiter, International, Dover, etc. — not so much in new music, however. When I first heard of a string quartet using different editions for the Beethoven String Quartets, I was bewildered.

With the addition of extended techniques, graphic scores, improvisatory elements, text scores, art scores and technology, notation has evolved tremendously. Composers have even developed their own methods of notation. This introduces a new identity to composed music. There is no doubt that the impression at first glance teases the subconscious. It is almost impossible not to judge a piece based on what it looks like.

Performers can be super literal when it comes to reading a score. So, if something isn't written out precisely to the very nuance, you will need to justify asking for it later. But, there are things that are challenging to notate such as timbre, color, timing and feeling, to name some. In classical music, there is more room for personal interpretations. For instance, words like cantabile, dolce, furioso, etc. are used. But, how one executes those things is not written into the score. In new music, a composer may indicate the pressure and speed of the bow and weight of the fingers in the left hand's touch on the strings to achieve the exact intensity of sound. Because it is so specific and technique-driven, interpretation is no longer expected in the same way. For instance, vibrato in new music is merely a direction in the score: senza, molto, poco or narrow, wide, etc. rather than it being a defining characteristic of an individual performer's tone. It is expected that you don't apply vibrato unless indicated, whereas in classical music vibrato is part of your sound — like a signature. Though used methodically as well, it is something you spend a lifetime perfecting.

Things like fingerings and bowings are best left to the discretion of the performers. It's a grey area — perhaps, deserving recognition as an art form of its own. However, in both classical and new music, composers may indicate what string(s) to play on which could limit or narrow down those options.

Notation can also be misleading in its simplicity as well as complexity. Scores by Scelsi, Xenakis and Cage come to mind. Also, Lachenmann, Ferneyhough and Finnisy. Sciarrino is another. A very dense score or unfamiliar notation can be off-putting at first. But, as you decipher the composer's language, it may start to flow at a quicker pace than a more sparse score that looked rather simple at first. But, in both cases, the notation will begin to start making logical sense — like speaking a new language.

It wasn't surprising that notation was the chosen topic during my residency at the Atlantic Center for the Arts where I was an Associate Artist in Residence. Annie Gosfield, the Master Artist in Residence prompted the question with no hesitation on the first day. What else? After all, it is a beautiful thing when you play something for a composer for the first time and they tell you that it was just as they had imagined it. And, vice versa. When you hear your composition for the very first time and it's just right, that's bliss.

As a performer/composer, most of my knowledge and influence comes from what I have experienced first hand. Besides encountering counterpoint at a young age, I haven't had any formal training as a composer. I've experimented in score, graphic, text and art notation. But, I have yet to discover a system of notation that embodies both score and graphic score notation in a way that while looking innovative, is direct and intuitive to the performers.

In *Sparkle* for 8 Pointe and 10 Tap Shoes, in collaboration with choreographer David Parker of The Bang Group, a rhythm-driven dance company in New York City, we developed a scale, designating "a note" for each sound that a tap and point shoe could make — choosing the ones most perceptible. The challenge here was figuring out how to notate the complex rhythmic repetitions and variations of the selected "pitches" between the combination of shoes all based on a 9-bar phrase:

13/16 (two bars) > 6/16 > 11/16 > 6/16 > 4/16 > 6/16 (two bars) > 4/16

The phrase is first heard on two pointe shoes by one dancer. Then it is repeated with the addition of two more pointe shoes by two additional dancers. A countermelody joins in the next repetition by two tap shoes by the same two dancers. A bass line rhythm pushes the phrase further with the addition of varying rhythmic groupings throughout — first with two additional tap shoes, then with all four tap shoes by the two additional dancers. As the piece develops, each shoe must keep its own rhythmic integrity within the phrase. Just as the piece gained its intensity by multiplying layers of repetition, arriving in a cacophonous unison, it winds down with the diminishing layers of unison repetition — ending just as it began with a solo dancer playing the phrase in one last repetition. But, this time in two tap shoes.

In the interest of creating a musical score, I used standard score notation substituting each shoe with a pitched percussion instrument. In doing so, I realized that it could ultimately be performed by any combination of pitched instruments — making it a piece for open instrumentation.

Writing for my violin duo, String Noise has been an eye-opening experience as a composer. My partner, Conrad Harris and I perform as a violin duo playing everything from original new music compositions to punk rock covers. We premiered the first piece I wrote for two violins titled, *Sugar*. I found writing for the two of us super fun and "easy" and wondered why I hadn't done more of it. It was fun because I was working with a familiar sound world, specific to our duo. And, it was easy because I had to put very little information in the score to achieve the sound I was imagining. It wasn't until the piece was programmed to be played by two other violinists that I realized that the score needed to be revised. Every measure posed a question of, "Is this the right sound?" This is an example of when notation becomes vital.

On the same program was *Crushed Coal To Dust* for Double Bass and String Quartet. Contrary to *Sugar*, this score was notated in a more traditional sense. But, it led to a different dilemma. With the double bass featured as a solo instrument, I had to figure out how to notate the repetitive groove that drives the piece as I envisioned that it to be playable by both a classical or jazz musician. I decided to make two scores. In the classical version, the double bass player follows the score and cues the other players in the string quartet at the various changes. In the jazz version, the double bass player has more freedom and space to improvise within the context of the groove while still leading the changes in the string quartet, but on cue. Similar to *Sugar*, it calls more closely upon the sound world and choices of a specific double bass player.

This leads me to the final example of how notation can impact performance. In a collaboration between myself, visual artist Luxin Zhang and fellow performer/composer Carlos Quebrada we discovered a way to notate free improvisation. I was recorded improvising on the violin (which was mostly noise). Then, the recording was sampled and notated into a graphic score to support a short film. It is through graphic notation that this piece can now exist as a fixed media, electro-acoustic piece and be performed live.

Recently, I applied a similar concept of notation to a recorded improvisation I made that became part of a larger piece for a new work by choreographer, Bill T. Jones. Because the nature of the composition consisted

Score

8'46"

Dedicated to Bill T. Jones/Arnie Zane Dance Company for "Afterward(s)ness"

Pauline Kim Harris

May 29, 2020

of long drones, the most challenging aspect of notation was getting the pacing just right. I had to be able to keep track of the time, drones and changes in a tempo. Then, I had to decide on realistic dynamics to be able to produce the various difference tones throughout. I chose to use score notation, but also implemented graphic notation to indicate noise vs. pitch, as well as fluctuation in rhythmic variations. At one point, the left hand is holding down the notes of the drone, while also engaging in pizzicatos, finger tremolos, sub-tones and glissandos. I ended up notating it on two staves. Later, the drone breaks up into rhythmic pulses which I resolved by articulating the drone with bow changes. When the score was completed, I discovered a familiar melody that suspended above. It was an interesting exercise in establishing consistent time within the structure of "free-time."

This concept of composing started with the making of my album, *Heroine*. One of the pieces on the album, *Ambient Chaconne*, co-composed by myself and sound artist/composer, Spencer Topel is a reincarnation of the Bach *Chaconne* as an electro-acoustic composition for Solo Violin and Fixed Media, lasting forty-two minutes. As part of my ongoing Chaconne Project, my recording of the Bach *Chaconne* was manipulated to create the backing track to which the solo violin line was then recorded. In order to perform the piece live, the recorded solo line had to be notated. To solve this problem, I chose to use graphic notation in form of a timeline on a staff. A stopwatch is used to synchronize the score with the backing track and the violin line is notated in alignment with the timing of the track. Graphic notation offered a solution to notating an ambient, classical, electro-acoustic score.

As you can see, notation can be a powerful tool. For performers and composers alike, the evolution of notation is integral in discovering new ways to express and communicate music. As complicated as it may feel at first, having a deeper understanding of all the various systems of notation can only enhance the ability to not only notate exactly what you want as a composer, but can also open up new channels for interpretation as a performer.

CHAPTER 19

ON THE FUTURE OF MUSIC

ULRICH KRIEGER

The future of music has already begun. Right now, we live in the early stage of an unprecedented, epic historical transition, as we have not seen it in music since the beginning of western notation (around 850 CE) and the first masterpieces of Notre Dame (around 1200 CE). We are in a transition period, in which century old cultural forces with their traditional aesthetics and distinctions (art, folk, popular), "time-honored ways" and their embedded social privileges are still strong and in key positions. A time, where music schools still train specialists with narrow, limited cultural views, if classical, avant garde, jazz or pop music — but the reality out there is already different. The cultural and social landscape is changing rapidly everywhere. The times of narrow specialization are over, if in the sciences or the arts. Due to modern, fast mass media communication everything is influencing everything, a rampant, accelerating, rhizomatic development — and that is especially true for the musics called "popular." Much popular music of today, such as grindcore or industrial, would have deemed unlistenable noise even just sixty years ago — or at best abstract, difficult-to-listen-to art music. No one would have believed that this music could become popular and would have thousands of fans in the near future.

In order to understand and discuss recent trends, it is important to look back into our history. To fathom social, cultural and musical developments, to make meaningful assumptions about the future of music, we have to understand the present — and the past that lead to today. The musical artistic landscape as we observe it in 2020 is a result of developments that go back to the late 19th and early 20th century. Starting there with our observation, we see the quick growth of a new type of music developing next to the traditional forms of art and folk music: pop. Pop was originally a city dweller, needing a consumer market at hand before further-reaching mass media technology was available. Being birthed by a changing social landscape, it developed rapidly, using every new technology available. It attached itself parasitically to other new and hip genres such as jazz (traditional pop, 1920s), later rock 'n' roll (modern pop, 1950s) and then electronica (electronic pop, 1980s). And soon pop also became the new capitalist business model for all types of music. On the other hand, historically never seen before mergers of popular music and art music happened: bebop, free jazz, prog rock, freak folk, art rock, post-punk, industrial, noise are all intellectual, abstract, complex styles of popular music. Who would have, who could have danced to heavy, noisy, distorted neo-tribal hardcore techno in 1945?

For the longest time "earworm"-melodies, lush harmonies and simple song structures were unconditionally associated with pop(ular) music (Enrico Caruso, Frank Sinatra, Doris Day). But modern hip hop, techno, and extreme metal music has no use for and need of traditional melody, harmony or form — a stark departure of what popular was deemed to be. For the first time in history popular music has been heavily and radically influenced by abstract art music, embraced concepts of it, turned it from the head on its feet, grabbed it and run. No song structures, no cadences, often no harmonies at all, no eight bar melodic phrases, instead sophisticated sounds and repetitive riffs or grooves. Edgar Varèse said: "Music is organized sound — timbre and rhythm" and defined "musical space as open rather than bounded". When he wrote this in the early 20th century, he probably thought of art music only, but the late 20th century applied this concept to popular music like techno, hip hop and even to pop itself. Further he said: "What is music but organized noises?" This is something that resonates with every musician today, who uses samples, field recordings, electronic sounds and/or a computer — especially in the popular fields.

Former popular (aka entertainment) musics began incorporating art music elements and approaches, over time elevating itself to abstract art forms such as noise or tech metal. We can see this trend already earlier in jazz, but it accelerated in the mid-'60s with psychedelic & prog-rock (Velvet Underground, Grateful Dead, Gentle Giant) and further in the late '70s and '80s with post-punk (PIL, Pop Group, Throbbing Gristle). But it came to full bloom in the '90s and early 2000s, especially in metal (Meshuggah, Deathspell Omega, Sun O)))), electronica (Autechre, Pan Sonic, Terre Thaemlitz), post-rock (Tortoise, Godspeed! You Black Emperor, Radiohead) and hip hop (Public Enemy, Clipping, Dälek).

Popular music rapidly became more and more diverse, complex, sophisticated, and philosophical — entertainment was no longer enough. The dissolution of class triggered the dissolution of common rules, techniques and genre borders, which in turn helped the dissolution of the associated class. A new art music with a different way of doing things and a promise for a new society developed out of the abstractions of the popular — a less elite, more democratic art music. Like "classical", elite art music before, these popular musics embraced exploration and experimentation, the search for new sounds, new forms and new ways of producing music, going where no other musician had gone before — a realm that before was only inhabited by art music composers.

All the while traditional art music quickly lost ground, influence and audiences, sticking to a philosophy that was still rooted in the 19th century. The central philosopher of modern art music was Theodor Adorno. Between 1933 and 1953 he wrote articles bashing jazz and pop music, talking about how formulaic and assembly-line the music is. He critiqued the exclusive use of song forms, the repeated usage of a few, limited cadence schemes and traditional, sweet melodies. But what he really was pointing at, beyond these technicalities, was that this music was primarily created for entertainment, not to be a critical, intellectual, philosophical endeavor, enhancing the cerebral knowledge pool of the audience. For Adorno and big parts of the modern art music scene — after WWII called: new music — pop and jazz had no stake and no interest in the progressive enlightenment (German: Aufklärung) of its audience. Even, if we accept this analysis and assumption for the music of the 1920s and '30s (Tin Pan Alley, ragtime, traditional pop, Dixieland, swing), this changed latest with the advent of bebop. Bebop was an abstract, black art music, having been born out of an entertainment music: swing. This was an important step towards black empowerment, ultimately helping to create free jazz, Black Power and Civil Rights movements. Adorno, coming from a traditional bourgeoise elite, couldn't grasp the idea that a music that had popular and commercial roots and continued to use elements of it (simple song structures, traditional chord changes, steady drum beats) could become a critical, philosophical, liberating force, adding in the education and enlightenment of people, initiating cultural development and social change. But this is what happened here, and even more so later with rock music and its offspring since the 1960s. This makes the 20th century a very special time, a transition period from a traditional 19th century authoritarian, top-down society to a new, open, broad 21st century society — which we slowly can see dawning at the horizon.

Dissolution of Genres and Schools

The classic-romantic music tradition, including the western art music of the 20th century for the most part, was historically an educated upper class, highbrow elite culture. This bourgeoise art music was deemed a philosophical and intellectual endeavor in the tradition of the classical teaching of the Aufklärung (German: age of enlightenment): Kant, Goethe, Voltaire and Rousseau. This music was philosophy sculpted in sound, rather than entertainment. Beethoven's *5th* and *9th* symphonies were battle cries for freedom and a democratic society — not an evening of relaxation. And Mozart's *Magic Flute* was by far a fairy tale, but a deeply critical and political work written by a freemason, complex and beautiful music with several interpretational layers.

Art music, as historic genre, always was the music of the social and intellectual elite, the upper class of a society. While traditional folk music was the music of the common folks, the lower class(es) and normally stands for traditional, authentic, down-to-earth, but also conservatory cultural roots — surely not for experimentation. Traditional folk music is music of a local, defined cultural group and is their cultural expression. This distinction between art and folk, high and low brow, reveals and mirrors the clear cut, hierarchical and authoritarian class society it originated from.

Pop music on the other side stands for superficial, commercial, quick changing, wanting-to-please songs. Pop music is the music of the entertainment industry of the 20th century, music of the age of mechanical reproduction and of fast technological changes, originally produced to be sold to an anonymous, non-local audience in order to be most profitable and successful.

Traditional, pre-20th century art and folk music basically came with a built-in audience: their local peer groups to which the music was addressed, be it the villagers in a village square festivity or the aristocratic court that commissioned a piece. While pop music has to find its audience — it is a free-floating, non-localized, sellable mercenary-commodity. But at the same time, pop music is a politically liberal entity, not coming from, not belonging to any old class system, but belonging to everyone, who is willing to pay for it — pop is democratic capitalism. Pop had to find a new place in an old system and by doing so helped to cracked it open — voluntarily or not.

This reflects and aligns with developments in society very much like Jacques Attali had described it in his book *Noise* (1977). He shows that music, as a cultural expression of a society, is closely related to the modes of production of said society. But more important, he goes further, and theorizes that music has "the possibility [...] to anticipate historical developments, to foreshadow new social formations in a prophetic and annunciatory way" (Fredric Jameson, Foreword to Noise, 1985). Attali describes four phases of development and according to these, we find ourselves in the beginning of phase four — let's call it, for the lack of a better term, the post-bourgeoise or post-industrial phase. The leading bourgeoise culture collapsed during the 20th century, because its foundation, the bourgeoise class, has collapsed.

As the bourgeoise class broadened and society in general became more open, democratic and individualized, so did its art and music. Already by the early 20th century the original audience, addressees and sponsors of art music didn't understand their artistic peers, Schönberg, Webern or Russolo, anymore, although they came from within their social ranks. Ultimately this trend continued throughout the 20th century and led to the dissolution of the bourgeoisie society into smaller interest groups that no longer shared the same social values or political goals. In music we see this trend of dissolution since the early 20th century. Already in the first half of the 20th century we have a historically never-seen-before multitude of musical styles. Art music alone had diversified and taken up opposing ideas at a rapid, breathtaking tempo: impressionism, expressionism, neo-primitivism, neo-classical, neo-romantic, futurism, 12-tone, musique concrète, and more. At the same time ragtime was pounding, tin pan alley hammered out its first attempt at commercial pop songs, the young hip crowd danced to foxtrot and charleston, and jazz was flourishing as the signature sound of the early 20th century — all while the wealthier middle-class preferred the light classical entertainment of opéra bouffe or proto-musicals. We might even heretically postulate that post-modernism in music already started in the first part of the 20th century, where we can hear dodecaphony next to neo-classicism, futurism next to ragtime. And this was only the beginning.

In this multitude, delineations between genres and styles became amorphous, less clearly defined, and some artists changed their approach from piece to piece. The more diverse something gets, the less it has clear delineations and distinctions. There is a point, where diversity simply becomes a dynamic field of possible multitudes. And the new audio reproduction and broadcasting technologies had helped by giving all musics a never-seen-before wide-range exposure, way beyond the original peer groups. But therefore, all music was now in a way pop-ified, commodified and industrial-alienated. By being mechanically reproduced, it was taken out of its original social context it had developed in and belonged to, to be distributed anonymously in an open, foreign new world as object. A good example is cowboy (aka western) music, which drastically changed within a few years from authentic, raw folk music to commercial, kitschy, through-arranged film music in the early 1930s, and then decades later, in the 1970s, gained critical momentum as outlaw country.

The "crossovers" of old (Stravinsky — *Ebony Concerto*, Gershwin — *Rhapsody in Blue*) were based on the concept/philosophy/idea that there are strict delineations between the genres, therefore: cross(ing) over — from a familiar field into an unfamiliar. But today everything seems to be in a constant flux and movement, no clear delineations exist anymore, wide-range cross-pollination and amorphous overlaps are normal, and boundaries get blurrier every day. Most young musicians feel at home and have skills in and knowledge of at least two or more genres — having grown up with several genres simultaneously. While traditionally developments in music are being pictured as family trees, this ends in the 21st century. Musical developments today can no longer be expressed as linear structures alone a "trunk-and-branch" allegory, but go blurry sideways into the unknown. We are confronted with a individual, large, web-like, rhizomatic influence structure for each artist, style and genre, created and supported by contemporary communication technology.

Following Attali, the way music de-linearized and de-authorized into a non-controllable and hard to trace web of cross-influences could show us how society will diversify in the future into a less hierarchical, less linear system, but a broader, poly-directional, interconnected structure, where everything and everyone is different, but equal — the beauty and power of anarchic diversity as we see it growing in music today.

This diversification and micro-diversification trend can be seen and traced in the rapid development of sub- and sub-sub-styles during the last twenty to thirty years. How many metal styles are there? Or how many techno styles? As an example, let's just look at sub-styles of death metal, itself a sub-style of extreme metal, a style of the genre metal. We find: technical metal, djent, progressive death metal, melodic death metal, deathdoom, brutal death metal, symphonic death metal, blackened deathdoom, war metal, deathgrind, blackened death metal, melodic black-death, slam death, death 'n' roll, deathtrash, deathcore, industrial death — and probably more...

This happens when a large amount of people, especially when geographically separated, work on the same material/ideas/aesthetics more or less simultaneously. The more people work on something, the more variations (aka diversity) we will see, and if these people have little or no direct contact, the diversity will be even larger. The ability to distribute audio easily and fast did not only create larger markets, it also created an international virtual community and an open, uncontrollable, international underground. This is a continuing process of stylistic and social fragmentation and refinement, continuing until it is so far fragmented that things seems to dissolve as identifiable objects. If the social fragmentation that goes along with this becomes too wide, the traditional society itself falls apart — and that is what we see today. We find ourselves at a time where we have to find a way to create a new society that is no longer based on homogenous groups, skin color, spiritual believes, preferred beats, or favorite foods; a new, diverse, but equal society build on and embracing diversity as its foundation — and we already can see this development in music everywhere.

Dissolution of Systems and Easy Access to Production Means

With the disintegrates of a social structure comes the disintegrates of its systems and rules, if political, social or artistic. Traditional genres, no matter if art or folk music, always came with a strict technical and aesthetic code, a set of rules, a list of things that are possible and things that are not possible. There are mistakes to be made (wrong voice leading in art music) or unusable material (augmented chords in folk) or... All the traditional genres had clearly defined, passed down and systemic embedded instructions and borders a beginner had to learn and digest — and it doesn't matter if written or oral. In order to perform, one had to master a traditional instrumental style and for composing one had to study harmony, counterpoint, and instrumentation. Bending and extending these traditional structures and rule sets was only possible within a narrow array and was mostly reserved to the "master musicians" — and making music outside of any systems was basically impossible until the early 20th century (Luigi Russolo — intonarumori, Henry Cowell — inside piano, Pierre Henry — musique concrète). But now, since the 1960s, there are no mandatory systems and rules anymore. Standard musical forms disintegrated, because their social contexts disintegrated, and became nothing more, but historic formal blueprints that can be used, if desired and found useful, or not. Literally any approach to music making is acceptable and possible today; fixed schools and the use of systems are an option, a choice, not an imperative. Today we find more diverging individual voices and approaches to music making than ever before in human history!

Before the 1940s/'50s it is was difficult to be a professional musician, if you didn't have an official training, exceptions were mostly singers in pop and jazz. Official training here means: learning and mastering a preexisting system of techniques and rules in order to play and write in a certain, specific style. Therefore, all traditional systems of music learning and making are hierarchical and authoritarian. A young musician always learned from a "master", if a classical instructor at a conservatory or as an "apprentice" in folk music, learning your skills from your grandmother. Still, mostly these instructions say: "this is how you do it and not otherwise". In both instances the instrumental techniques and the general aesthetics taught are tightly regulated.

Since centuries classical musicians were trained professionals, dedicating their life to perform and write a specific type of music, having to go through conservatory training or an apprenticeship, often with serious exams at the end. While traditional folk music was mostly "taught on the side", it was a part of life, rarely the family-supporting life-profession of the players, who mostly had to do other work as well. Still, the rule sets were similarly narrow and precise. So, training and the type of training you got was always class related as was the music being played. Still today, the entrance exam to become a student of composition at some conservatories in Europe requires writing a 16th century counterpoint and/or a Bach-style choral. This is class politics and automatically excludes large social groups.

This changed with the advent of rock 'n' roll. Now anyone could play music with only a few guitar chords — and soon after even without knowing any chords or systems at all. With the help of electric guitars, synthesizers, studio technology, vinyl and later computers, music making became easily accessible to people with no official and traditional musical training and background at all. Suddenly, and historically unique (!), there was the option for completely untrained people to create, play and release music outside of any traditionally accepted (musical and social) systems! Rules became options and possibilities rather than requirements — they can be followed, in whole or parts, or ignored. And therefore, music creation became more widespread and democratic. We saw how fast the first rock 'n' roll bands in England moved away from their primary electric blues and rhythm 'n' blues influences. They creatively ignored and surpassed blues rules and by doing so created British beat music, only to further move on into a new, vast and open (!) (psychedelic) territory of musical expressions. Often, the only creative hurdles for this new type of artists were set up by requests/demands of the commercial studios to be wider applicable, sellable, aka pop-y — the classic contradiction of the 20th century: wide, unrestrained artistic freedom versus the business-cation of all music on the open capitalist market. In this context it is interesting to observe that since about a decade pop and rock musicians are also showing a strong interest to receive academic training and degrees and universities reacted by offering pop or popular music programs. But how to teach something that has no (clear-cut) set of rules anymore? This bears the immediate danger of teaching artificially distilled, pseudo-historic rules, creating a pseudo-historic music that never existed.

Much contemporary popular music, such as extreme metal, hip hop, drum 'n' bass, has none of the traditional elements, which were central for traditional pop music: harmony, melody, song structure (Dean Martin, Perry Como, Burt Bacharach). These traditional elements hold less and less importance in modern popular music where sounds and beats are central. In the past, the stronghold of pop(ular) music had always been the lyrical voice, meaning: the melody. But with hip hop's rapping, death metal's abyssal growls, black metal's shrieking and screamo's screaming the voice became instrumental — in a way only Schönberg had tried before in Pierrot Lunaire. Hip hop, for example, is based on sounds and beats; the vocal delivery is mainly rhythmical, triadic harmony can happen, but mostly not functionally, just as another sound element, melody happens also occasionally, but again, in the function of a sound, an atmosphere, a reference, rather than a traditional melodic arc of a song. This focus on sound as central key element had started in rock music in the mid-'60s and mirrors the developments in avant garde art music of the 20th century. The millennials grew up with popular music that has no verse-chorus structures and no traditional concepts of melody and harmony. They grew up with music that is based on repetitive grooves and free-floating, sophisticated, often non-tonal soundscapes. Therefore, many, although not all, of these young musicians have less a problem listening to avant garde art music (Cage, Scelsi, Stockhausen), because they just hear great sounds that could be remixed with an 808 — because the only thing missing is the groove. Go online and listen to vaporwave or seapunk: no verse-chorus, just chill sounds and beats.

New Technology

As discussed above, traditionally one had to acquire specific skills to perform and compose music. But modern technology made it possible for everyone to be a musician. The dissolution of standard, fixed musical systems at the end of the 19th century and the introduction of "open, non-canonic" instruments (from Latin "instrumentum": "tool, device") were important steps in this development. Such new tools were, early on, the intonarumori and inside piano (1910s), but especially the electric guitar (1930s), effect pedals (1950s/'60s), multi-track reel-to-reel tapes (1950s), Moog Synth (1964), advanced studio technology (1960s) and later computers (consumer market in the 1990s). Now everyone could make music from scratch in a playful-experimental way without having to think of, being hindered by or trained in any traditional systems. Since the 1960s, this new, cheaper technology made it possible for amateurs and (non-)musicians to compose, record and directly listen back to their music in an intuitive-experimental way, changing their production until found satisfactory. The development of the Beatles from skiffel to *Rock 'n' Roll Music* to *White Album/Revolution No. 9* is a good example for this; a development from folk to pop(ular) to a sort of popular-studio-avant garde.

Now the last, exclusive realm of high art music had been "invaded" by popular (rock) music: free, complex composition and open-ended experimentation. Until the mid-20th century musical experimentation had been the sole realm of art music composers, now the field became accessible to popular musicians, amateurs and non-musicians. This again reflects the dissolution of the class system in the 20th century and opening up of society — now a working-class kid could create experimental music without "proper" training. Not only would a 19th century farmer or blue-collar worker never have had the idea of writing a string quartet, they also would neither have had the means nor the opportunity to do so, not knowing how to notate music and without access to the tool, a quartet.

Of course, this development was further fostered by modern media. For the first time in history everyone (!) had potential access to a wide range of music, included the avant garde, through recordings, vinyl, radio and tv. European public broadcasts had regular weekly programs of contemporary art music in radio and tv, making this kind of music easily available to literally everyone in society, not just an elite. And avant garde music LPs could often be found in cheap second-hand bins. Today internet archives, platforms and online streaming make our access to any type of audio material endless.

This also means that the development of new genres is not bound by geographical restrictions, local communities or social rank anymore. As we have seen, the amount of people taking part in a musical exploration of a certain style dictates its speed of development and its diversity. Due to the possible large amounts of participants worldwide — a global, flexible, virtual community, not a local, fixed one — these new styles develop anti-hierarchical and very fast, even if just underground. A techno track produced in the morning in Berlin can be played a few hours or even minutes later in a club in Sydney. This results in quickly developing sub-genres, varieties and even more diversity. We saw how fast techno — still having had a geographic and class origin in Detroit — spread around the world and became an international cultural phenomenon. But in music, a silent revolution already has happened many years before the COVID-19 stay-at-home isolation. New styles and stars were created completely online without concert (re-)presentation, traditional shows, management or CDs. There are *hip hop* styles, such as *mumble rap* (aka *Soundcloud rap*) and *cloud rap*, which are internet birthed and based scenes, as well as a variety of online *hypnogogic pop* styles such as *vaporwave*, *hardvapor*, *witch house*, or *seapunk*, just to name a few.

Before the advent of fast travel and fast communication technology, we had distinct genres with parallel, linear developments and occasional, intentional crossovers — such as a few attempts at mixing jazz with classical in the first half of the 20th century: Milhaud — *Creation du Monde* (1923), Gershwin — *Rhapsody in Blue* (1924), Stravinsky — *Ebony Concerto*

(1945). But with the advent of the internet, things changed rapidly. The internet is a-temporal. The linear development morphed into a simultaneous one. Everything is synchronous, non-linear, web-like and exists parallel. Bublé next to Cage, Radiohead next to Penderecki, rare, vintage vinyl next to modern, mass produced mp3s — and all of it is accessible with (more or less) the same ease and the same small amount of effort. No more year-long hunting down of out-of-print rare vinyl on flea markets and chaotic-organized used-record stores. There is nothing exotic or rare enough not to be found online today — no matter if old or new, if commercial or experimental. It was the activity of the hunt that had made clear how rare and special an album was. Now the rarest releases are available at a mouse click. The internet creates an a-historical time-field, in which any obscure old record is as recent and easily found as a new hit single. And if one doesn't pay attention to the release date (if even mentioned at all) a Velvet Underground recording seems as contemporary as the new Radiohead — I see this quite regularly with my Millennial students. All this leads to the complete overlap and blur of genres, creating a continuity, a radiating, dynamic field of genres. It opens up to more diversity, because very unlikely things exist comfortably next to each other and cross pollinate. Searching for "*Futurama* theme", YouTube offers me the original Pierre Henry/Michel Colombier's Psyche Rock as well. And vice versa, looking for Psyche Rock, YouTube also offers me Fatboy Slim. Listening to Jobim's *Desafinado* recording, the house remix is found next to it — along with a large array of high school performances of the same song. The internet is not open to diversity, it is diversity — and unregulated chaos.

We saw above that music doesn't necessarily need concerts, even if most of us always thought so — but Glenn Gould. A culture working by different parameters and without performances already exists. Vaporwave, mumble rap and brostep flourish without live shows. (Live-)streaming as a new form of cultural communication, not a replacement for live concerts, will become more important in the future. People are slowly getting tired of traveling. After decades of the famed and advertised modern life-style of vast mobility, it is becoming less interesting and even outright annoying for many people. Traveling, including long daily commutes in cars, trains or planes, is stressful, especially if it is only done for work and under time constraint. We see it here in LA, people hardly travel across town to see a show, they prefer to stay in their neighborhood, because driving has become so tiring in this city.

Concerts and performances are rituals and social "gluing" events. But will the concert as a ritualistic get-together of like-minded people (in the past: like-class people) continue or will this kind of social interaction become less important in general in the future? Could concerts became an old tradition, a left over from the times before recorded audio? Over a hundred years of recorded music and one hundred years of radio broadcasts hasn't killed the interest and need of people to attend live concerts. Live shows will continue as long as people continue to feel the urge to gather together ritualistically in large crowds and share a common cultural experience. Streaming will develop as an alternate medium in its own rights, an additional offering next to live concerts and recorded sounds, not as a substitute for concerts as mostly still used at the moment.

The Future

If we circle back to Attali with what we've learned from music in the 20th and early 21st century, we can assume that a future society will be more diverse, equal, more socially "flat", less hierarchical. It looks like the future will hold much more diversity of any kind; gender, class, race should be of no issue anymore. Strength will lie in diversity and tolerance. It should be a culturally more democratic society, but a democracy of diversities, where no one has to be the same as someone else and where every music comes from a personal approach. If something is art or just pure entertainment will not depend on your social background and context, nor the musical material and systems you use, but "HOW" you use it. The "what", the fetish of the material, will lose importance as we move on to the more important questions of "how?" and "why?" we do something. There will be no high and low culture and maybe not even a cultural mainstream — although that might very well be wishful thinking. This would mean a rethinking on the side of the record industry. It is an industry based on profit, so, if the "focus on a few big pop stars"-approach of the last decades would become unlucrative, the industry would respond quickly. It would have to broaden in order to make a profit in the future. But at the moment the trend seems to be that big business continues to concentrate on an even narrower selection of the most widely sellable acts and leave smaller-audience acts to smaller companies, which again results in a larger variety and empowerment of smaller labels and social diversity.

Traditionally, as mentioned above, music as sounding philosophy had been the realm of art music. While pop and popular music was seen to be just for entertainment, distraction and relaxation. But in the late 20th and early 21st century, much, although by far not all, of rock and pop(ular) music has become artistically innovative and critical. It carries sophisticated analysis and statements regarding philosophical, social, political and artistic issues. Even if the traditional genre assignments had been valid in the past, they no longer hold true today. The philosophical truth Adorno was looking for can now be fund in any genre. And as a heretic side-note, much of today's so-called "classical" art music is pop-ish lifestyle music on classical instruments catering to entertain a snobbish elite, rather than being an intellectual discourse in the tradition of Beethoven's string quartets — further showing the dissolution of this class. All systems are now historic and can be used or not. That and because the new digital tools allow users easy experimentation, we see much more experimentation and experimental music today than ever before. Or at least music that is not based on traditional forms and the traditional elements of harmony and melody: extreme metal, post-rock, glitch electronica, and many more.

Never ever before in history have we seen such abstract popular music, made just of beats and sounds — a type of neo-tribal music. Popular music has made a very surprising development. Not only had it started to replace traditional, local folk music as kind of an international über-folk, but at the same time, it also opened itself up to a multitude of diverse, often experimental or at least unusual approaches — think the deconstruction of reggae music in Jamaican dub or compositional structures in extreme metal. Popular music has embraced and gone avant garde in an organic, playful way. And by the sheer amount of individual voices with very different backgrounds, future genres will develop rapidly and in a multitude of substyles more or less simultaneously — using experimental and commercial approaches side by side at the same time.

So, to finish, let's condense the future of music into one sentence:

Everyone (dissolution of class structure) can now produce any type of music (dissolution of genres) as they wish (dissolution of systems), with whatever tools they wish (easy access to means of production), with or without any type of official training (de-authorization).

Contemporary popular music has embraced an anarchic, open DIY approach, mixing sophisticated art approaches with playful-autodidactic experimentation and elevated itself to an art form. By doing so the audience for unusual, weird, experimental or simply different music has grown exponentially and broadened, sometimes up to a point where the audience itself is not aware that it is actually listening to something unusual, progressive or experimental. This is the end of the historic low vs highbrow, serious vs entertainment music separation. If we are lucky, we are looking at a new, very diverse world to come with many different opinions about what art and music is, something that reflects an authentically diverse culture that is not bound by past ideologies and distinctions. And if this holds true, this might not only be a very interesting musical future, but a pretty interesting blue-print for a new social structure and society.

CHAPTER
20

ON THE MAKING OF "THE SHEPHERDESS AND THE CHIMNEY SWEEP"

HANNAH LASH

This article is about the making of my theatre piece: *The Shepherdess and the Chimney Sweep*. I wrote this piece for Loadbang: baritone, trumpet, bass clarinet, and trombone; with the addition of myself on harp. We developed the piece with American Opera Projects. It premiered in the spring 2019 in Santa Fe, NM.

Although what is required of one's compositional process is unique for each piece, I found that this particular work demanded a move outside any means with which I had felt familiar — a move outside of my comfort zone, I guess you could say.

In this article, I will explain aspects of this piece, both musical and theatrical, and speak about the composing of it as well as putting it together in rehearsal and finally performing it.

The is a piece based upon Hans Christian Andersen's story of the same title. It is not one of Andersen's better-known stories. It is one of the very short ones, just three pages long. It is, like many of his stories, a combination of the darkly surreal with a thinly veiled Victorian-style moralizing.

One could extract from it one or more of the following morals: make the best of what you have…there's no place like home… a solution will present itself if you just stay constant and loyal to what you know and love.

But really, even the most naïve of readers cannot miss the underlying psychological pain gnawing at the heart of this story.

A very quick synopsis for those not familiar with the tale: (although I highly recommend that those who have not read it read the original — I have the Jean Hersholt translation.)

Three porcelain figurines — a matching Shepherdess and Chimney sweep, and an Old Man (said to be the Shepherdess's grandfather) whose neck is hinged so that he nods constantly — sit atop a parlor table. They face opposite an ornate liquor cabinet; upon the door is carved an imposing bearded satyr-like figure: a human upper body with the hind legs of a goat.

Goat-legs is in love with the Shepherdess, and asks the Old Man's permission to marry her. Taking the Old Man's constant nodding as consent, Goat-legs leers at the Shepherdess, anticipating her entry into the liquor cabinet.

The Shepherdess, terrified, begs the Chimney Sweep to take her away, escape with her. He agrees, telling her that he is, after all, a Chimney Sweep, and he can get them up the chimney and onto the rooftops to freedom, where he will work as a sweep to support them.

When the Old Man is asleep, the Shepherdess and the Chimney Sweep make their escape. But as they climb down from the table, the Old Man wakes, tries to stop them. He falls, breaking his neck. The horrified Shepherdess tries to help him, but the Chimney Sweep hastens her on, promising that the Old Man will be repaired in their absence.

So, they climb up the chimney. When they reach the rooftop, they are overwhelmed by the open air, the real world. The Chimney Sweep is thrilled. The Shepherdess, however, is terrified — it is too much for her. She begs the Chimney Sweep to take her back down. He swears he wants nothing more than to live in the real world. If she cannot join him, he will leave her behind.

In a desperate effort to win him over, the Shepherdess throws herself upon the Chimney Sweep and kisses him. Unable to resist her, he concedes, and takes her back down the chimney.

When they return to the table-top, they find everything as before. The Old Man's neck has been repaired. But now he can no longer nod. When Goat-legs again asks the Old Man for his consent to marry the Shepherdess, the Old Man stays perfectly still.

The Shepherdess is safe from the prospect of being Goat-leg's wife. The Chimney Sweep promises to love her until the day he breaks.

I read this story as a psychological tragedy: it is about the Shepherdess's inability to extricate herself from a dreadful and yet familiar world. She cannot face change, she is pulled back into what she knows. Change is too frightening. She has no idea how she might handle being free.

The Chimney Sweep is torn — he has to choose between freedom and his lover. Either choice dooms him to resentment and bitterness.

I chose to write the libretto in rhymed doggerel. It seemed like an appropriate amplification of the rather innocent surface of a truly terrifying fable. The verse is put into a language which was aimed at representing the porcelain stiffness of the two main characters, always strictly metered. Goat-legs speaks much more crudely than the Chimney Sweep, using salacious innuendo and some foul language.

Given the ensemble I wrote this piece for, I had to find a way of representing all four characters with the means I had available — only one sung role, with the other parts tailored to be appropriate for the rest of us.

As the only female musician involved in the project, I cast myself as the Shepherdess. Jeff Gavett, the baritone, was the Chimney Sweep. Will Lang, trombone, was the Old Man. And Goat-legs was represented by both Andy Kozar (trumpet), and by the bass clarinet player (at the time of the premiere, this was Carlos Cordeiro, subsequent performances by Adrian Sandi who took over the bass clarinet position after Carlos left Loadbang).

There were only two characters who could have actual lines, spoken or sung: the Chimney Sweep and Goat-legs.

Jeff, of course, had the only sung role, the most traditionally "operatic" part.

Seated as close together as possible, trumpet and bass clarinet spoke together in stereo, or played together, or one spoke while the other played.

Will sat most of the time upstage, standing only to deliver his nod represented by trombone slides, or to prepare for his fall from the table (executed with impressive commitment — you could actually hear the audience gasp when he hit the floor).

I conveyed the Shepherdess's actions through playing my harp and dancing alternatively (I have a professional dance background).

We worked with director Luke Leonard, whose imagination and exploratory and collaborative approach proved invaluable.

The music itself is largely unlike any music I had previously written. The use of an idiom which at times flirts with musical theatre (of a particularly archaic and austere variety) was new to me — a kind of Stravinskian/Kurt Weilian edginess you could say.

The piece begins with a prelude outlining the material which more or less develops and spins out the entire piece: four descending minor sixths related by semitone (these separate into two pairs gesturally). This chaining together of descending sixths implies a kind of head-butting of triads. For example: A, C-sharp, C, E outlines both A-minor and A-major; if you continue the chain with the next pair: E-flat, G, G-flat, B-flat, then there is the addition of the outline of E-flat minor and major.

This is a closed 8-note cycle, which comprises the octatonic set. I used this closed cycle to define tonal centers. The construction can modulate in a variety of different ways. One possibility (keeping the adjacent melodic intervals limited to an alternation of semitones with minor sixth) would be to use a semitone in ascent to after the deployment of one of both pairs of sixths, which then opens up a different octatonic set/tonal field.

But modulating between octatonic scales has very limited interest, unless you consider the various possible subsets and utilize them as active and profiled motives. In my case, I had a specific contrapuntal goal to which end the horizontal voice-leading had to be carefully handled and foregrounded quite prominently as material in motion. Also, the voicing of the total 8-note field draws the ear much more to the tritone relationship of two major-minor triads rather than the octatonic set as such.

The musical austerity at the outset of the piece helped suggest the idea of the characters being at the mercy of their own fragility and the limitations of their world. It has a kind of inexorability, a fatalistic cyclic grind.

I do not mean to imply that the piece is strictly systematic. It is by no means so. However, this reservoir of triads connected together in pairs was a highly appealing starting place and germinal idea to expand, develop, and generate much if not all (loosely speaking) of what follows.

It is important to mention that I later also make use of major sixths, thinking of them as being adjusted versions of the initial structural minor ones. You could explain their major property by suggesting that they represent a "skipping" of the higher note within the semitone dyad that connects the pairs of minor sixths. However, the use of differing qualities of the same interval within a motivic web that allows us to hear them as connected or analogous is a technique I have learned from Bartók among others, and I think of my case as similar to Bartók's, e.g. I would rather think of the major sixths as being variants developing organically from the minor ones as opposed to being systematically derived.

There are sections of the music which demand staying within and developing a quite explicitly triadic field, treated oftentimes quite functionally. For example, the Chimney Sweep's song "Very well, I'll take you down, we will return to the table..." lands as a simple sing-song melody in E-flat with naïve accompaniment, the baldest and boldest assertion of tonality in the piece — representative of both characters' emotional compromise and stultification.

The exact return of the prelude at the moment when the Shepherdess and the Chimney Sweep arrive back at the table signals the beginning of last segment in the piece — a thrice repeated ending sequence: obsessive, infirm, growing increasingly desperate and numb until the final iteration, which is by that point worn so fully into the ground it no longer seems conclusive… the Shepherdess's final stony stare into the abyss of a dark house.

Now that I have explicated at least some of the musical means I used in weaving of this piece, I will address some of the challenges we faced in mounting the work and finding pathways towards our characters.

One of the strangest aspects of transitioning from abstract concept to musical and theatrical space and reality was the integration of movement, which was part of the conception of the piece from its most nascent idea-phase onward.

Although movement is inherently part of theatre and opera, this was a specifically tricky situation in that none of us, except for Jeff, were accustomed to taking on acting and moving within our musical performative activities.

Normally in chamber opera or theatre, even if the musicians have active and dramatic roles in the piece, the heavy lifting, dramatically speaking, is done by the actors/singers. This is of course not without exception. A musical theatre version of Once, for example, requires that the cast also function as the orchestra (although in that case the cast comprises actors who are required to play instruments rather than the other way around). Also, some theatre works by Amy Beth Kirsten involve musicians fully engaged in the drama as characters. But, by and large, we instrumentalists are not often called upon to be actors, speakers, or dancers.

Andy and Carlos had to speak in semi-rhythmic pseudo-sprechstimme, often in unison. Finding the balance between a natural-sounding speech cadence and something truly un-lifelike was an interesting process — my notation was at first overly precise. We eventually arrived at a solution which adhered fairly strictly to my rhythmic notation but that allowed them a great deal of freedom in terms of manner of delivery. They became a truly terrifying beast together, shouting harshly at the top of their lungs.

A seemingly insurmountable difficulty applying only to me was the idea of switching back and forth between being a harpist and a dancer.

Although I am a trained dancer and a fairly seasoned performer of dance, I have never had to toggle back and forth between playing and dancing in one performance. I felt impossibly ungainly trying to duck behind the harp after executing a series of butterfly jumps or barrel turns.

Eventually Luke came up with the idea that to be behind the harp was to be trapped upon the table — a constant, unavoidable return. The first time the Shepherdess stands to dance is to be a disturbing moment, quickly and irretrievably breaking the audience expectation of what and who the Shepherdess is.

The challenge of Will's role as the Old Man was the need to hold the space despite having no physical action between his rather dramatic episodes. He did so admirably, feigning nodding off during rests in his part, and managing to continue to hold character even when participating in a purely musical interjection or interlude. Placed in the center of the stage, the Old Man is a poignantly tragic reminder — constant and immobile — of the pathos of the entire story.

Jeff was called upon to dance too. He does not have a background as a dancer but is an adept learner and possesses an innate grace that made it easy to choreograph his part, which we did as a kind of collaborative effort under Luke's guidance.

My own choreography changed and evolved quite a bit during the process of rehearsal. I learned how the Shepherdess moved — fragile and somewhat brittle until her moment of panic, when suddenly she becomes wild and flailing and — ironically — quite unfettered and free (this was also the most challenging and exhausting section to dance; I remember throwing myself into a chair at the end of that sequence feeling that I might not catch my breath in time to play).

It wasn't until the second performance or so that piece really hung together, in terms of musical and dramatic pacing as well as our conviction of what we were doing. I am not sure it would have been possible to digest the piece as performers before that first run, to understand from the inside how the piece truly unfolds. So much of the work is about estrangement, distancing, tension. You only discover these things through performance, at least in my experience.

In subsequent performances it fascinates me how different the piece feels each time. Our most recent performance in Sprague Hall at the Yale School of Music where I am on faculty was certainly our most refined and carefully rehearsed. I also think it was our most desperately committed. When the lights blacked out at the end, I was fighting back the tears the Shepherdess couldn't cry.

In conclusion, I will only add that the riskiness of this piece makes it one of my favorites in my output. I feel myself deeply compelled by the journey towards the absurd, the bitter and biting humor, the pathos cloaked within a simple story.

I found it was necessary to use means the of musical limitation and development described above to convey the general tone of the piece — the repetition, the inevitable harmonic and contrapuntal arc, the stylistic oddness. This, in conjunction with dramatic choices — made both by me as the creator of the piece, and by Loadbang and Luke Leonard — really allowed the aspects of the work to feel integrated and effective.

Lastly, I would be remiss if I ended this essay in any other way than to mention how fortunate I was to work with Luke and Loadbang on this strange piece. Luke's guidance and vision were both beautiful and necessary. And Loadbang — they are the most fearless, curious, flexible, creative and imaginative musicians one could ask for, and a joy to work with throughout.

CHAPTER 21

PRESERVING A SPACE

DAN LIPPEL

Despite the symbiotic bond that exists between them, there are several points of tension between the practices of performance and recording. The ephemeral, temporal nature of performance versus the meticulous permanence of recording is probably the most often cited point of divergence; performance is to recording what theatre is to film (not to mention how writing about music is like dancing about architecture). Despite a general understanding and acceptance of the larger role recording plays in the music field, the editing process is often shrouded in a cloud of skepticism. Through a balance in my career over the last fifteen to twenty years between performing, recording, and running a record label, I've come to see editing and the studio process as an organic counterpart to performance, and a forum to explore interpretation, creative implications, and occasional philosophical conundrums.

I was bitten by the recording bug in the summer of 2000, when I was living in Cleveland, Ohio, after finishing my master's degree. I embarked on my first classical studio recording project without a clue about what went into the making of a commercial CD. For the first time, I played a session which mixed takes of run-throughs, sections, and small phrases, as the engineer and producer (the excellent Alan Bise) guided me through what we would be able to stitch together later on in the editing process. When we had finished the sessions, Alan lent me his DAT machine and sent me tapes of the takes to map out the edit points. I was immediately captivated by this aspect of the process; the idea that I could compile a performance choosing from all of these takes was exhilarating. It mirrored the process of practicing an idealized interpretation, neutralized the factors that vacillated from one performance to another, and allowed me to hear possibilities emerging from subtle permutations between takes that suggested new ways of understanding the music. Of course, editing affords you the opportunity to map around mistakes and put together the cleanest version from the material you have. But I found this to be the most mundane application of the tool. What was truly intoxicating was the prospect of sculpting a performance so that the interpretation gleams with the shine of a deep relationship with the material. In real terms, this often translates into more takes on a given passage. A phrase might be clean and the score accurately rendered in one or two takes, but transcending those fundamental requirements and generating material that ignites the final edit with energy and expression often requires more material.

The part of me that spent countless hours in the practice room striving to shape a phrase so it responded perfectly to the music surrounding it felt a need to take an audio snapshot of that intention. One practices endlessly crafting a cadence so it convincingly expresses its role in the overall structure of a fugue, finessing a phrase so that it is shaped to highlight its unique characteristics, or drilling a virtuosic passage so it projects ease and rhythmic impetus, and here was an opportunity to choose which take reflected those goals most purely. I've never been deluded into believing that definitive interpretations exist, but the studio process can get you closer to definitive realizations of interpretive intentions. Fine editing provides the opportunity to sculpt those realizations, to choose the delicate final details of a performance that can never be notated in a score, and to capture them in a format that counteracts the fleeting nature of performance.

That first CD I had made featured a recital program of standard guitar repertoire by Bach, Takemitsu, Mertz, and Torroba, so everything I had discovered about the recording process to that point had spoken to the experience of crafting interpretations of music from the standard repertoire. After moving back to the New York area in the summer of 2001, I began my doctoral degree and continued in a direction I had been gradually moving in for a few years, focusing more and more on contemporary repertoire. Recording immediately took on a more grounded, concrete component for me, presenting an opportunity not only to capture the evolution with a piece, but to document its mere existence in a way that prioritized fidelity to the composer's intentions. My second recording project was a marriage of that impulse to share new repertoire and codify its existence with the desire to capture an interpretive connection. *Resonance*, co-produced with composer Peter Gilbert and later mixed and mastered by composer/engineer Ryan Streber, was the first release for what would later become New

Focus Recordings (the initial name was simply Focus Recordings before we discovered it was already was taken).

The engine of the contemporary concert music world runs on the fuel of premieres, and this need to document new work increasingly became the primary force behind my recording activity, and the direction of New Focus Recordings. The variables surrounding contemporary music concerts can be significant, and needless to say, they are not always conducive to realizing ideal performances for posterity through recordings. The studio provided a context where there was enough control over the environment to do justice to the demands of new and often very complex scores. This emphasis on a culture of premieres and brand new repertoire presented a challenge to my initial motivation for recording — how can one capture a deep relationship to an interpretation when the work is so new for everyone involved? As much as any other factor I've encountered, the focus on premieres threatens to disturb the delicate, organic balance between performance and studio recording. Many times I have been involved in scenarios, and indeed often responsible for them, where external pressures have resulted in a session on a piece that is not really ready to be recorded. For better or worse, the studio can accommodate this imbalance, facilitating the evolution of an interpretation after the session, when one could sculpt the performance out of moments that possess the spark of a more inhabited understanding. While it may be valuable to salvage material from a session on a piece that has not yet been internalized, editing can never manufacture deep musical understanding. Sessions like these fulfill the important work of documenting under represented music. But taken in the context of the larger case for recording as an aesthetic counterpart to performance, they represent a missed opportunity to wait until a richer stance on the music has been cultivated. And yet, all too often the practical prospects for multiple performances of new works are not encouraging, and an initial recording, even a hastily scheduled one, might be the piece's best chance at having a life beyond its premiere.

Discovering the capacities of editing has further implications for how one could approach a session itself from an interpretative point of view. I developed a conviction (since softened depending on context) that it was essential to get at least one or two run-throughs of a piece in a session, regardless of how clean they were, to make sure to have material that reflected the inhabited perspective of a full performance. (As an aside, I have always been amazed at how adept film actors and directors are at inhabiting the context of short scenes embedded in larger narratives. Obviously, there are no "run-throughs" in multi-location, multi-scene films, while remarkable examples of long takes confront the opposite problem of not having the option to splice). I continue to find that in choosing edits, large run-throughs are often the best option for transitional moments in a piece, because those takes reflect the sweep of the overall structure and not just a microscopic look at moments outside of context. On the other hand, certain hyper-local aspects of scores are facilitated in a studio setting that aren't as practical otherwise — a demanding passage that might be inconsistent live because of physical limitations, a pesky ensemble rhythm in chamber music that is much clearer when the group can start right as the passage begins, a quick instrument change that can be executed without rushing. Cultivating these pathways to a more faithful rendering of a score can be liberating, and over time I found myself developing an independent creative practice that related only to the recording process itself, no longer operating as a tool to "freeze" an idealized performance.

This brought up, and continues to provoke, intriguing questions. Where is the line past which the studio recording process becomes untethered to its essential parent, performance? What is the responsibility of the recording artist to the feasibility of live execution of a score? If something in the score is not practical or even possible to execute in a live performance, is it doing a disservice to the viability of the work and potential future performers to create a false expectation? The answers to these questions for me vary from project to project and are dependent on the ethos and spirit of the music. And I'm not entirely sure I want to arrive at a dogmatic stance on them. The tension that exists between the rarefied, controlled process that is studio recording and the unpredictability of performance, both inside and outside of the studio, is one of the ingredients that goes into making art through recordings. To rigidly define the boundaries between them discounts permutations that might have the potential to generate something magical. I couldn't assert that the meticulously detailed studio approach of late Glenn Gould or Steely Dan is any more or less artistic than live recordings of Sviatoslav Richter or Miles Davis' famous one take per tune Prestige sessions.

The tools available through various levels of editing software are no secret to anyone with some degree of exposure to the contemporary recording industry. So there is little reason to hide their use to create an idealized recorded performance. But editing together a series of takes to create a polished recorded performance is distinct from using the studio to assemble the illusion of a performance that is not in fact possible live. If a work presents itself as music to be performed by a soloist or ensemble, the appropriate presentation of a recorded document of that piece should be framed by what is actually achievable in a performance setting. The implications of this kind of studio trickery without transparency range from erecting a false expectation or goal post to reach in future performances of the piece, giving license to composers to write similarly impractical material based on their impression that it is possible or playable at a given tempo, or blurring a valuable line between physical capacity and technological manipulation that doesn't serve the future of a healthy, human performance culture. For instance, if the score lists a note that doesn't exist on the instrument in question without an alteration that would change the rest of the performance, this would seem to me to be a disingenuous use of studio capability unless there was some acknowledgment of the situation. Automated tempo adjustments sometimes enter into similar territory, though the specifics of context make for interesting points of discussion. I am less troubled by a tempo (or pitch for that matter) adjustment that smooths out an internal discrepancy between takes, especially when those aberrations are a function of the awkwardness of the studio process itself. Manufacturing a tempo that either isn't really possible or is clearly far beyond what the performer or ensemble is capable of strikes me as a more problematic use of the technology.

I can imagine exceptions where the ideal vision of a score is so compelling that there could be a justification for using the studio to actualize something that simply isn't possible — where the artistry lies in some Platonic ideal inherent in the construction of the score itself. In that scenario, I think it might appropriate to reveal the ruse so to speak, both to preserve the integrity of the process and also to call attention to the element of the score that is being accommodated. It is far easier to make these general assertions than to establish how to evaluate them on a specific basis, so it becomes largely a question of individual integrity to make that determination for one's own work. Additionally, some music is overtly the byproduct of either studio techniques or their mapping onto live performance models. In those instances, I think there is a strong case to use the studio to realize the work in the spirit of how it was conceived regardless of whether the changes are consistent with realistic performance (an example would be layered pieces like Reich's *Counterpoint* series, where the conception of the piece is born from the tools that the studio affords).

With the ups and downs of being in the music industry, I've found that holding onto some core values that I seek in my work has been really important, both as a guiding principle and occasionally a lifeboat. For me, one of those guiding principles is the idea that recording offers up a protected space to sculpt a truly personal sonic statement. My conviction that I want to preserve that space for my own work and make it available to others is at the heart of most of the decisions I make as a recording artist and label owner. I see this aspect of recording partly as a bulwark against the competing energies that can draw artists away from the work that they find most meaningful. It makes room for an impulse that I think is an important component of the performing artist's life, as a counterweight and a counterpart to the intensely ephemeral and extroverted features of performing. And once recordings are distributed and disseminated to listeners, they engage with them from a similarly personal, inward facing stance that cements the bond between artists and their audience and lays the foundation for an evolution of their connection to the music as well. It may be too much to hope that our recordings, stored progressively on LPs, tapes, CDs, digital files on hard drives and cloud services, and whatever new formats are headed our way, will lend us immortality in any lasting or meaningful way. But maybe more importantly, recording offers the opportunity to live *as if* we can save those creative intentions forever, even if it's an illusion. In that way, the process represents an ongoing opportunity to focus one's artistry with an eye towards perpetuity, while softening the existential burden of the inexorable temporal march.

CHAPTER 22

UNFOLDING BECOMING AIR

A Conversation Between Nate Wooley and Annea Lockwood, October 2020

ANNEA LOCKWOOD

Becoming Air was composed for Nate Wooley's project of commissioning new works for solo trumpet. Since its first performance at Issue Project Room, New York in 2018, *Becoming Air*, composed collaboratively by Annea and Nate, has continued to evolve, the recording session on September 27, 2020 with engineer Randall Dunn being the most recent version but probably not the last. A fortuitous side effect of working on the piece has been an ongoing discussion between the collaborators-become-friends; mostly in private, sometimes in public, and always with a great amount of warmth, surprise, and depth. This opportunity to continue the conversation in *Arcana* is very welcome and begins with talk of the recent recording session before dividing off into other topics, as it always joyously does.

Nate: The recording session is maybe the most unique situation we've had, because it's the only time that we've actually broken the piece down into its component parts; up to that point the piece was contained within the flow of twenty solid minutes of music. How did that feel for you? I was a little bit worried going into it about what that will mean. It's a piece that is inherently in parts, but it felt weird to take the parts apart.

Annea: For some reason, it felt entirely okay to me. But as the performer and one of the creators, in the studio performance of the piece it must have felt peculiarly semi-detached for you. And yet your realization of the piece didn't come across that way at all. The various parts flowed as you recorded them from one to another, in spite of the fact that we were chopping it up into those segments.

Nate: In the last couple of years, I've grown used to recording things, especially more composed work, that way. I've gotten used to doing a 9-bar section twice, then doing the next thirteen bars, and stitching it together. That works fine if you're doing a piece that's through composed, but there's so much improvisation in this piece.

Annea: When I'm listening to a performance I'm really absorbed in how it unfolds for you, through you and how your energy unfolds, and I'm interested in how the P.A. system is responding and the acoustics of the live space, so there are many aspects of the piece which I'm checking out. Whereas in the studio, I could listen to the actual flow of sounds and the relationships between, for example, all the noise content — all the noise timbres of the piece from the very delicate whistling and blowing across the valves through your work with the aluminum strip to such details as the breathier sound, that narrow-band beautifully balanced noise with which the feedback section ends. All of these were clearly interrelated. I could hear the relationships as we worked on the piece.

Nate: One of the positives of the recording situation is that you have the possibility of controlling the parameters a little bit. I was allowed to concentrate on how I wanted to shape a discrete chunk of material. And you and I have done the piece so much — and I always say "we" because to me we're always performing it together, even though you don't get to be onstage — that we know what it should feel like overall. In the studio, I don't have to worry about the P.A. or what the amplifier is going to do or concentrate on the visual component of picking up something in a performative way without dropping it. The downside of that is that the risk involved in all those things is part of the performance and the whole philosophical idea behind the piece, but not — as with Brian Ferneyhough or Kenneth Gaburo — about endurance or physical limitations. Did you feel like it took some of the chance component out of the equation; the seat of your pants quality that we've had in the performances?

Annea: No, it didn't, because to me a big part of the chance element lies in how the aluminum strip held against the bell responds to your movements for example, where the sound goes as a result and how much control you have or don't have over how the strip responds, rather than the tightrope element of the work in which you have a lot of physical, busy work to do going back and forth between the tam tam and the mic, the instrument and the various components of the instrument. It's always fascinating to see how really smoothly you handle that, but for me it's never been a big part of the piece, as it clearly is for you because you're implementing it all.

Nate: I think of your work as setting up opportunities to capture rare sounds. Like the river pieces are a container for the natural sounds that occurred in that moment. You may, as composer, modify the order or mix it in a certain way, but the content is the content and is something that you had no preconceptions about before you went to gather it. The aspect of *Becoming Air* that excites me compositionally is that same thing: you set up a form, you set up a container, and then it's different every single time.

Annea: And that container was based wholly on your way of working with sound and your own delight in discovery which I share.

Nate: But it's different for me because so much of the sound world that we're dealing with in this piece comes from an improvised music history. And, once you're outside of the jazz tradition of song forms, you're supposed to have jettisoned containers; that's what we supposedly love about improvised music. But, it's so interesting to use that language in a contained way; the challenge of making that work within some confines as opposed to in complete freedom. I think that was the thing that was exciting to me in the performances from last year and this spring — Café Oto, Oslo, Miller Theatre and Chicago — how open we were to changing the structure as we went. It's like we could freely change the dimensions of the room that those sounds fit into, just to see what happens to them in a new space.

I get the feeling that this is a natural part of how you compose, watching you work on the piece that you made with Yarn/Wire [*Into the Vanishing Point*] and preparing the solo piano piece [*Ear-Walking Woman*] with different performers. Is that true? How do you generally think about putting a piece together?

Annea: I frequently start with a broad structure, because it feels like firm ground in which to root a collaborative piece, or by listening, as with you. Listening to the sound world of a particular performer, the sound world which they themselves have really created, brings the sense of a structural flow to mind pretty easily, which is certainly what happened with us.

Yarn/Wire and *Into the Vanishing Point* was a different experience. That collaboration began much more abstractly with a concept about in some way addressing the vanishing insect populations of the world and what that implies for everything else, our shared concern about it and how we might move through a progression of expressing that concern together. For example, I think one of my very early ideas about framework was that it would be nice to start with a soft background bed of sounds through which each member of the group successively would emerge as a solo expression, and that whatever they came up with to create that expression would recur later in the piece.

Ear-Walking Woman, a prepared piano piece, evolved from throwing everything I've got in the basement into my piano down there which is in such terrible shape that it can tolerate anything, and finding sequences of sounds which I really loved, then forming them into phrases and short notated sections. I hand these over to the player to explore further with a particular implement, or a particular technique for eliciting sound asking "How can this sound change? How far can you take it? What can you discover?" All three pieces depend very much on the personalities and personal sonic explorations of the performers I'm working with; seeing that emerge is something that gives me such pleasure.

As a child I was somewhat self-isolating. Forming friendships and getting close to people was something it took me a long time to learn to do. But now, when I'm working with performers — and often I do form friendships with people I work with, as with you — it's always moving to me to see, to experience how open the people I work with allow themselves to be, and that encourages me to do the same.

Nate: I was self-isolating in the same way; still am to a certain extent, and there is something about the relationships that grow through working on a piece: *Becoming Air* is a prime example: the relationship is as much a part of the composition as any documentation of it.

Becoming Air really exists on three levels: first there is the piece itself, which is very interesting, but always only twenty minutes, a 20-minute chunk of a thing. Then there's the relationship that has come from working on it — a friendship that will outlive that twenty minutes — something beautiful in its own right. And, because that 20-minute chunk of a thing is rooted in the something-bigger of our friendship it's a real collaboration, not the author-speak version of that word that we often use, but the act of working together to create...

Annea: It's fundamentally collaborative.

Nate: Exactly, and because of that, when we perform it, the spirit of collaboration is disseminated to the audience, who are collaborating by being in the room. That sounds a little "new-agey", but it's true. Everybody in the room has made a choice to leave their houses and experience something born of communication and human bonds and the smallest, in some ways most insignificant part of it is that 20-minute chunk of a thing.

And, that collaboration has not just been between us, but, over time, we've worked hand in hand with the spaces in which it's been performed. I would be really interested to kind of get your take on it, because you have a different experience. One, you're a composer in the audience, so you have a different relationship to the performance happening in front of you and, two, it's almost always on a concert of your other pieces, so your attention is spread across the whole evening rather than *Becoming Air* as the concentrated moment that it is for me. Since we're moving backwards, let's start with Chicago [Frequency Festival in February 2020] and that experience for you and we'll kind of re-fold the unfolding of the piece in time.

Annea: Ah, Chicago. Let me start with visual snapshots that are coming into mind: how right it was to see — in a darkened space, a fairly good-size space but relatively informal — to watch you emerge from the back of that space just as if you simply materialized, so you then possessed the space. The acoustics were good, and I liked that you were relatively close to the audience. Although the seating was raked, it wasn't steeply raked so it felt as though you were on much the same plane as the audience. There was an implicit intimacy in that, as there was at Café Oto, which I like very much, which feels really right for the piece. And then it was a beautiful realization of our piece, so it was thrilling, I could just lie back and float in your sounds, which is a lovely way to listen.

Nate: It's striking to me how visual your work is without you specifically *making* it visual. I don't see your work as performative, but *Ear-Walking Woman*, for example, is very physical and interesting to watch without the movement taking anything away from the music. Our piece is visually arresting mostly because of that massive set up with tam tam and amplifier. The solo snare drum piece [*Amazonia Dreaming*] that Ryan Packard did in Chicago, and even the Yarn/Wire piece have very visual representations built into them. Yet, I never get the feeling that the visual component is the first thing on your mind.

Annea: I think it comes about just from my relationship with sound, which is, of course, for all of us at the bottom of the music we make. Thinking back, I have done a few pieces in which movement and the look of performance is important, but not for ages. One of them was *Shone*, a piece in which I had four performers from different countries wearing clothing which would make sound, such as mylar. Their actions and their songs were based on sound games which they had known as kids. And so, games being thoroughly physical and performative, that visual element was intrinsic to the piece. But usually it's similar to how I record rivers, which is as much as possible to get myself out of the way, and in the case of working with performers the movements are simply those necessary to elicit the sounds. Of course, it becomes a choreography, which is fun to watch, as it is with you — live performance, it's really a nice thing to watch, but the choreography arises from the practicalities rather than being an element laid over the performance. Again, as with the rivers where I want to bring listeners as close as possible to the sounds, to feel themselves inside the rivers, so with *Becoming Air* I want to allow listeners to be as close as possible to you, your being, how you are, what your relationship is to the sound, how does it manifest? And get myself out of the way.

Nate: I think we were talking during the recording about me missing the intimacy of noise concerts; people being attracted to the exhilaration of massive amounts of sound. This piece is very similar, but its delicacy and vulnerability are what attract the audience. That other music is all about strength but, with *Becoming Air*, you're attracted to the fragile humanity of it. I think there's a reason that both of us feel that the Chicago and Café Oto performances were really special: the people were right there, so close to the performance and you could feel them being drawn into the whistle sounds and the clicks and watching that physical dance of moving from different parts of the horn and dealing with the tam tam and those moments of stillness. Then there's this nice little payoff at the end with that big feedback squall, but it's really not that important in the grand scheme of the intimacy of the piece.

Annea: That's right.

Nate: It's very much like a dance. It's not a stylized dance, and it's not ritualized either. It actually feels like folk dance. It's very human: what I'm doing has a meaning and I'm enjoying doing it, but the point is that we're all in here together and we're sharing in a thing. I think that's a very hard experience to create.

Annea: And I like the down-to-earthness of it too; you need to move in a certain way to pick up something, pick up the next thing you're going to work with, so that's how it unfolds.

Nate: So that's an interesting point to me. I'm really interested in where you are now, making work that is deeply involved in collaboration and harnessing certain human experience, like the piece for the people in the sound-making clothes. It seems like, within your history as a composer, you've effortlessly moved from an education in modernist "paper-composing" to the broader work you're doing now. Maybe you've been able to move back and forth a little bit from time to time, like with the solo vocal work (*I Give You Back*) based on the Joy Harjo poem. Can you pinpoint where that shift came from?

Annea: Well, the *Glass Concert* was a radical break, after which I made many different sorts of pieces but didn't return to working on scored pieces until Thomas Buckner invited me to make a piece for him in 1987 and I wrote *Night and Fog* for Tom, J.D. Parran on baritone sax, and percussionist Michael Pugliese — three superb musicians. I loved the experience of working with them, and since then I've moved back and forth easily. I'm very interested in enabling the vulnerability of the performer, letting it come through. And, in a way, I don't see people as performers, they're always collaborators, so many of my pieces try to make room for that openness to happen in various ways.

The Joy Harjo poem, *I Give You Back*, as I read it, is very much a lament and a sort of exorcism. I made that song at a time when I myself was afraid, for reasons I've long forgotten because writing it actually dissolved those fears. Part way through I give the singer a cluster of pitches and invite her to improvise her own personal lament if she has experienced loss and grief which is still strong, or not — it's optional and not all singers take it — but it was important to me that the piece should be truly a lament, not a performance of lament.

But, speaking of vulnerability, that's important to both of us. I was just listening to the recording of *Seven Story Mountain VI* late at night, which was a perfect time. Everything in me was wide open and it seemed to me, experiencing it, that the musicians through whom that is being created are really vulnerable, willing to be that open, which is such generosity.

Nate: That's not something I initially intended to be part of the piece. In the first two versions, that vulnerability wasn't as important. It was just a way of structuring something. But, as the piece went on, it became more and more ecstatic, and that quality of the ecstatic feeling changed over time.

The first couple of versions were all about raw sound and just being overwhelmed by sound. We were young at that time, and more naive in a lot of ways. One of the violinists, Spencer Yeh, has done five of the six of them, and now a growing number of people have been involved in all the subsequent versions. In the performance, you could feel the people in the ensemble let go, and see the effect on them physically and emotionally, knowing that they really did that for themselves and they didn't do it for me. I just set up a situation in which they were feeling something, and they let it go.

As people have been added to the family that plays that piece it's become as much about the group of us coming together to have that emotional experience, as any of the compositional stuff. To me, there's always that core; how do I get those people to a place where we can have that experience? That's the most important bit. And then what can you add around it to make the audience feel something? But ultimately, if that core is not there, then it's not right.

Version VI is tied up with Peggy Seeger's lyrics and it's tied with political ideas and things like that, but ultimately, it's about the human beings on stage being super vulnerable and uncontrolled. And the minute we try and do something specific beyond that, then it isn't the piece anymore.

Annea: Then it becomes an artifact, right?

Nate: Exactly, then it becomes an object. It reminds me again of recording *Becoming Air*. I did the first pass through the feedback and was trying to control it. It was okay, but then you urged me to be less controlled; it reminded me that this is what this piece is about. It's not about the traditional virtuosity of reproducing the thing, but a virtuosity of failure; a virtuosity of being human. It's about this technical ability we have to be ourselves better than anyone else. And yet we can't do it that well. We have moments where we're opening ourselves up to the people around us, but they're rare. There's a virtuosity to being vulnerable, and that's very different from like coming out and playing all the notes.

Annea: There's a fluency about enabling yourself to open up.

Nate: To me, that comes from the way that we've structured the piece, but it also comes from our friendship and our understanding of each other's history. I don't know that I would be comfortable being that vulnerable with anybody else's work, and I find it's very revolutionary to work that way; much more so than a lot of crazy stuff on a page, because of how rare it is. There are people who work to recreate a kind of communal folk experience but it's still recreating a specific *folk* experience, whereas *Becoming Air* is experience that happens to be folk because it asks for a sort of communion between the audience and a human being. I can walk out on a stage and play solo and improvise, and the intimacy is there immediately because the spontaneity of it requires intimacy, but to perform a composed, reproducible piece of music in which that same relationship is available is really radical to me. And, hopefully expandable out beyond not only our experience with each other, but through a lot of other people making music in this way. This to me is a test case. It can be done.

Annea: Let's go back to *Seven Story Mountain VI*, which was a powerful experience the other night. This is the very sort of penumbra around music and sound which reminds me that music has been an agent of transformation, a channel of transformation for as long as humans have been around, probably; the openness that we're talking about is a willingness to remember that and to allow it to emerge. You do it, you and your collaborators, the amazing people in that recording, you and your collaborators do that flat out. By the time Megan Schubert and the other singers reached the Peggy Seeger text, the song — which is a treasure, it's an important song to have brought back again — by the time they get there and I've been through this enormous world of everybody being so intertwined and so free, that text and the solidity of the voices, the sturdiness of their sound, the way I can feel their legs are really rooted in the ground, "This is how we are", as a woman I felt such affirmation from that, which I would not have felt had the text dominated the piece from the beginning. The universe of increasing freedom, emotion, intensity that grew through the piece was essential to opening me up completely, so I was really open by the time the singers entered.

Nate: I'm glad, and that means a lot to me because it's something that I think we're both engaged in right now when we're working together, but separately too.

And, we bonded over a couple of things at the beginning of creating *Becoming Air*: maybe the most important was a shared love of seeing where a sound will go without trying to control it, but I feel like we are also both interested in the complexity of human relationship in the act of creating something together; how the relationship between different people affects the sounds they make. I've seen *Ear-Walking Woman* three times, with three different women performing it. I've seen you work with them and that relationship is always different. And the piece is always different. It's a different person and a different instrument yes, but it also has to do with the emotional connection between you and that person. I've seen two versions of the Joy Harjo piece. Again, totally different. It's exciting to me to see human relationship involved in composition in that way — an equal, caring relationship — and to have it affirmed that it can create some of the most complex music; a different complexity.

Annea: The opportunity to have enough time to make that sort of connection with a performer is very important to me and it makes a big difference to the actual discrete sounds which emerge and their shapes. For one thing, it makes a big difference to the timing, pacing. Talking of *Ear-Walking Woman*, I've had the experience of mailing the score out to a terrific pianist along with a care package of all the little tools needed — a pestle, super ball mallets, rocks, etc. — then a preliminary recording came back to me as just eight minutes long, and I thought *What! That's a catalog of sounds. There's no time to explore* — a misconception of the piece that could easily arise if you're working from the score alone. So, we went back and forth about it and the piece stretched and stretched as it needs to do, until you could hear the pianist listening so closely, giving the sounds all the time they needed, truly exploring, and it was beautiful. But from my early 20s I have realized that the score conveys just the surface of a piece. There's so much more to be unraveled and explored and a huge part of that process is the personality, the way the performer works, the way they like to work, so — connection. That connection is really vital, and nourishing.

CHAPTER 23

PERSPECTIVE OF AN AUTODIDACT

DAVE LOMBARDO

It starts with a sound, any sound. It can be the way a fork hits the floor. The reaction to the four prongs' fall creates a short pattern. I immediately memorize it, repeat it and create a rhythm. Or, I take a long drive and find myself rhythmically hypnotized by the car driving over a sequence of bumps on the road at 80 miles per hour… batoom, batoom, batoom batoom.

Perhaps it's a washing machine sloshing back in forth. Can you hear it?

Welcome to my brain; where this monotony thrives at its purest, most entertaining form.

It seems neverending. Through the years, I thought it might be the onset of a mental issue. Rhythm psychosis? Is there such a thing?

I've since moved on from that self-diagnosis and decided to embrace the realization that I am simply vulnerable to inspiration and therefore I will suffer the most. I believe I will always be consistently (sometimes oddly) inspired by simple, organic rhythms and sounds.

We all know that the heart beat, one's own pulse, was the first rhythm ever heard by early man. For me, I am certain that my biological roots of rhythm began in my mother's womb. Something must have triggered my obsession with drums and music. When does nature contribute to nurturing human interest? Scientists have proven that before a child is born it can hear muffled sounds. So, to that point, if a mother hears drums and it makes her feel uneasy — it is possible that the child would be born predisposed to feeling uneasy around drums. On the other hand, what if the mother enjoys them? I would expect the child would then come into the world embracing this sort of stimulation.

Although my parents were not musicians, they religiously listened to music. Dancing and live bands made them feel exuberant. I never saw them happier than when they were lost in a song. Immigrants from Cuba, everyday was a challenge trying to overcome a life lost to dictatorship. Thankfully, many of the other Cubans in our southeast Los Angeles neighborhood had decided to hold weekend social clubs. It was the place to be — a place where Latin and Rock bands would play — a place where immigrants felt at home.

While attending parties at the social club with my parents I would never watch the band from the front. I'd sit stage left, on the piano stool, observing and analyzing the moves of the percussionist and the drummer. One of most poignant moments in my life was when one of the drummers allowed me to play the drums during sound check. I was excited and electrified… I was hooked.

In my lineage drums are a highly respected instrument. I am of Caribbean origin where you are submersed into two religions, the Yoruba religion of West Africa and Roman Catholicism. Also known as Santeria, where drums, dance, rhythm and chants of the respected dieties are the equivalent of being on your knees in prayer.

I loved my culture whole-heartedly and dove deep into its rich musical history. The complex weave of ritualistic songs heavily influenced the core of my drumming. However, when you're an immigrant it is common to feel that you must hide much of whom you are to try and fit into your new unpigmented surroundings. To the outside world, I did my best to portray myself as an American. A young surfer/skateboarder, yearning for acceptance. I never thought I was doing this intentionally to abandon my roots, but it was noticed and would become evident from the words that were said to me by a childhood friend. "Tu lo que eres un Cubano repentido." Loosely translated, "You are not proud to be Cuban."

I lived in a household that spoke Cubano (Cuban Spanish) and spent much of my time trying to emulate words and phrases without an accent. Learning to copy and articulate your words perfectly without accent was difficult for my parents but easy for me. I found myself repeating words I would learn in elementary school with the personality in which I heard the word spoken. For example, if I heard a cowboy in a movie say a particular phrase I would repeat it in the same southern drawl and accent. As a child, I would mimic practically every English word I heard. I knew using the correct pronunciation was important because of how persistent my brothers were while teaching my parents to speak English. As I honed my new ability, it simultaneously crossed over and fostered my obsession…

the drums.

Before I had a drum set, I had drum catalogs from the local music store and I would flip through pages wishing I had one. But the one odd habit I developed was to visualize myself playing the drum set I was looking at in the book. As with learning English, I would vocally mimic drumbeats and rolls while imagining myself behind the drum kit I was viewing. This wouldn't happen with just the basic drum sets in the catalogs, but also with massive sets with eight tom toms and double bass drums — kits I knew we couldn't afford.

Around this time a high school friend, who was taking a psychology class, gave me a cassette that taught the ability to self-hypnotize — with the end result being a task or talent you aspired to achieve. I was very intrigued, but soon realized I had been doing the exact same thing *without* the cassette through visualization — mentally rehearsing and envisioning what I wanted, and what was to come.

As I collected birthday and Christmas gift money, I'd frequent the local record store and buy 45s of the music that I had discovered on the radio. The earliest ones I remember are Stevie Wonder/*Sir Duke*, Bachman Turner Overdrive/*Taking Care of Business*, Doobie Bros/*Long Train Runnin'*, The Emotions/*Best of My Love*, Ram Jam/*Black Betty* — all before the age of 12. I'm not afraid to admit that I also bought Disco Duck/Rick Dees and His Cast of Idiots.

Before I was able to make these purchases, I was basically seasoned and marinated in a world of eclectic music. My older brother Manuel introduced me to War, Tina Turner, Rufus with Chaka Kahn, My other older brother, Daniel, guided me down the path to Led Zeppelin, Rolling Stones, Big Brother and the Holding Company, Cream and Jimi Hendrix. My parents always had our home dialed in to the local Spanish radio station and would often have Celia Cruz, Benny Moré and Tito Puente spinning on their turntable.

In the midst of this perfect musical storm was my sister's husband Edward. He had the largest collection of albums I had ever seen. Salsa, Blues, Latin, Jazz, etc. He introduced me to the masters of music, the intellects and geniuses. It was overwhelming at times because Edward felt such an urgency to share this music with me. In retrospect I feel his urgency was simply because his time on earth was limited. I will always be grateful for his contribution to my musical landscape.

At some point during this informal, family-induced music lesson, an actual music school had opened nearby. My parents agreed to enroll me. I received a pair of drumsticks, a practice pad and sheet music with some rudiments. I had one lesson and felt I already knew more than what I was being taught. That was the end of that. By listening and imagining myself playing so many songs, I somehow managed to develop my rhythmic foundation... and clearly a short attention span for lessons. Thankfully, my dad appreciated my confidence and agreed to buy me a small 5-piece drum set. I felt that the sky was the limit. The kit was in my bedroom next to my stereo. Everyday after school I'd lock myself in my room and play along to my favorite records. Learning every part exactly how I heard it. I was able to distinguish the individual drums and cymbals because of the time spent looking through drum catalogs and reading the descriptions. I quickly picked up song structuring and was able to recognize/feel upcoming changes in music on the fly. I later discovered I had the ability to improvise with ease, completing rhythmic phrases and melodies with minimal musical hints.

As my confidence grew, so did my search for local musicians to jam with. By the time I was 15, I had played in a talent show and started a band called Escape that later changed their name to Sabotage. We played a couple shows at the high school, but I wasn't able to commit to too much more. Being raised by a father that had a strict work ethic, he insisted that I get a job. I can still hear him firmly telling me, "Yo no crio hijos vagos." ("I don't raise lazy sons".)

As soon as I had a driver's license in hand, I secured a job delivering pizza.

Somehow, with only limited shows under my belt, my drumming reputation was floating around. Friends would stop by my house and we would sit and listen to music while discussing local musicians that I should play with. They mentioned a guitar player that lived a few blocks away from me. On a whim, while making a delivery, I drove by the musicians' house where a guy with long hair was outside watering the lawn. I stopped and shouted, "Hey man, I heard you play guitar... I'm a drummer. Let's jam sometime. He responded, "Sure! Would you like to come by later and check out my guitars?" We exchanged numbers.

Within a couple weeks we started a band called Slayer.

I have spent very few moments wishing I had formal training. I have been in rooms where I was frowned upon for my lack of it. I have been ignored by reputable publications for my self-taught, Berklee-less resume. But I have always been unaffected by that. I would begin my musical journey all over again. Just like my family, I chose to go beyond the borders. I didn't know the rules. I didn't know I was supposed to color within the lines, so I didn't. I created freely, recklessly. No boundaries, no right or wrong. Those are the gifts of being an autodidact: unchecked passion, an all-consuming love of music, and a complete respect for the many gifted musicians before me. They were my teachers. My heartbeat was, and still is, my guide.

CHAPTER
24

ON MELISMA

CHARLIE LOOKER

Melisma, noun, (m'lizm)

Plural **melismata**

A group of notes sung to one syllable of text

Since the beginning of my work as a composer and vocalist, one aspect of my music, which has garnered particular attention, is my use of melisma. While this technique of text-setting is standard to many, if not most, vocal styles across world history, from gospel to Carnatic music, its use in a post-punk context is somewhat eccentric. The best-known precedent for this is Morrissey's florid, idiosyncratic style, which has indeed been an important touchstone for me. My main sources of melismatic influence, however, have been the sacred music of the Middle Ages and Renaissance and, to a lesser extent, contemporary R&B. In this essay, I will discuss the important roles melisma has played in several compositions from across my catalog, and its philosophical place in my thought in general. In my theorizing of melisma, two important reference points will be my favorite thinkers, Georges Bataille and Julia Kristeva. There is no single over-arching system of how I employ melisma. I do, however, have certain ideas about melisma's implications, which inform my use of the technique in all instances, even as these ideas spin off in various different directions. The central issue is the dialectic between language and pure sound. If, by the end of the piece, we seem to have wandered far afield, it will be because the aesthetic and theoretical connections I tend to find the most inspiring and fertile are those that many would describe as "a stretch". And what is melisma itself, if not a stretching?

Text-Setting, Abstraction, and Materiality

Techniques for the musical setting of text can be laid out as a spectrum of increasing complexity:

Recitative (also known as psalm note in the Christian liturgy, and rap-singing in R&B): one note per syllable, remaining on that single note for entire passages of text, chanted at a speed close to that of ordinary speech.

Syllabic: (the most common technique in popular music): one note per syllable, with melodic movement.

Neumatic: single syllables stretched into small groups of two to four notes.

Melismatic: one syllable stretched across many notes.

In European and African American musics, melisma is commonly used to express a moment of heightened emotion, whether it be joy, pain, erotic abandon, or religious ecstasy. In the early Christian liturgy, a site of particularly florid melisma is the final syllable of the *Alleluia*. This melisma, considered on its own, is known as the jubilus (also called the sequence). As its name and its place in the liturgy suggest, the jubilus is a moment of elevated joy, where the exaltation of God reaches an ecstatic peak. As melisma stretches out a single vowel sound, it effectively suspends the articulation of the word. The vowel opens like a portal within the word and we enter the realm of wordless melody. The jubilus exalts a power that is unnamable and it celebrates this limit of language's reach. Words ultimately fail to represent, describe, or even adequately praise God, and the jubilus takes us, for a moment, to a place too spiritual for language.

Medieval music has been a colossal influence on my work, and my use of melisma is often consistent with its role in that tradition. It could be said that its every instance in my work is, on some level, an ecstatic reaching beyond words, but one of the most deliberate and overt examples is the final section of *Ten Year Teardrop* (2012), from the Extra Life album, *Dream Seeds*.

This melisma on *ah* extends for three minutes, including several repetitions with different endings. In this case, the vowel isn't technically sung as a syllable within a word, but, coming as it does immediately after the lyric, "All praise be to God", it functions as a melismatic extension of the line's last word. *Ten Year Teardrop* dramatizes a riveting, deeply transformative dream of mine, which included the resurrection of a long-deceased loved one, as well as several archetypal mythological symbols. The dream fully solidified my ability to say that I believe in God. Melisma functions here exactly as it does in the jubilus, exalting the namelessness of God's glory. It seems fitting that this solemnly joyous outpouring would end the last song of what turned out to be the last Extra Life album.

Having established what melisma isn't (words), we can consider more closely what it is: pure sound. Writer and gospel music scholar Anthony Heilbut, in his discussion of melisma, describes how "the singer will worry a word to the point of abstraction".[1] Here, Heilbut attributes abstraction to the pure, non-linguistic musical sound of the melismatic vowel, relative to the words as words. Reviews of my own work have also described my melismatic vocal style as abstract, using the term in a way that is fairly consistent with its common use in visual art. As opposed to so-called representational art, abstract art doesn't represent anything other than itself. The essence of the work is immanent to the shapes, colors, and the physical materials of the medium itself. I would argue, however, that the use of these terms "abstract" and "representational" in art is inapt. The Merriam-Webster Dictionary defines the word "abstract" as: "expressing a quality *apart* from an object" (italics mine).[2] In art, representation *is* abstraction, not its opposite. Representational art uses objective materials to represent something apart from those materials. In the case of vocal music, pure sound is the medium's material; words are what is abstract, in that they use sound symbolically to signify things apart from the sound's own objective materiality. When a singer uses melisma to open up a word, allowing the irruption of non-signifying sound, the music has become *less* abstract, more material.

1. Interview with Mike Katzif for NPR, January 11, 2007.

2. Merriam-Webster Unabridged Dictionary, 2020.

This suspension, and temporary overtaking of the symbolic, verbal, and abstract by the material is essential to the sacred function of the jubilus. In my conception, it is not that God's glory is "above" the grasp of words, but in fact it is "below" it. The sacred does not lie in a rarefied, higher plane, more abstract than language. Rather, it lies immanent to the lowly, less abstract domain of the material, the purely sonic. My view of religion and the sacred is influenced by Georges Bataille's concept of *base materialism*, which he links to the spirituality of the Gnostics. Man's imperfect, mundane realm of structures, symbols, and ideas aren't redeemed by a transcendental, higher, universal idea from above, but are subverted, corrupted, and undone from below by a sacred, material baseness.[3] To refer to the wordless vocalizing of melisma as "pure" music is perhaps misleading. Its sacred purity lies in its pure materiality, untouched by the symbolic, the intellectual, the abstract. The Gnostic view is typically paradoxical: matter redeems by its purely unredeemed baseness.

3. Two other influences on my thoughts along these lines are Fred Moten's work on the aesthetics of the black radical tradition, and various alchemical and Hermetic writings, as analyzed by Carl Jung.

In *Ten Year Teardrop*, the role of melisma, and the ideas of words versus pure sound, abstraction versus materiality, retain some of the more Christian sense of redemption. An example of where my text-setting techniques serve Bataille's more Gnostic sensibility is *Black Sun* (2018) from my orchestral album *Simple Answers*. Lyrically, the song deals with depression, and I use the archetypal trope of being turned to stone to evoke Freud's death drive. Beyond any simplistic idea of suicidality, Freud describes the death drive as the organism's desire to return to an inorganic state.[4] Because the very first organic life arose out of inorganic matter, the death drive is a kind of primal nostalgia, a longing to be opened back up and fused with the plane of inanimate material from which we are originally descended.

4. Sigmund Freud, *Beyond the Pleasure Principle*, p. 308.

Black Sun's Freudian theme of returning, in death, to pure matter is expressed both by the text, and by the text-setting techniques I employ. The song begins with the speaker describing the feeling of being turned to stone, pulled by the death drive toward the inorganic. The text here is set syllabically, which renders the lyrics perfectly intelligible and foregrounded. In this non-melismatic setting, the abstract signifying of language is undisturbed, and the speaker is able to clearly articulate his depressed state. Despite the deadened affect of the speaker, and his desire to disappear, the verbal clarity of the syllabic text-setting makes him very present.

There is a fundamental link here between speaking and being, or being alive. The work of psychoanalyst/philosopher Julia Kristeva, which has remained an inspiration to me for years, relies heavily on the concept of the "speaking subject", which she inherits from Lacan and develops uniquely. The idea is that the child defines itself as a stable subject, with a demarcated boundary between inside and outside, by mastering speech, or the symbolic. To speak is to make oneself discrete from the world, from the maternal body, from all outside matter. In the first half of *Black Sun*, while the speaker longs to lose his boundary between self and world (to die, and return to matter), his ability to articulate this desire in song, to speak clearly with syllabic text-setting, is key to what marks him as still alive. Speaking maintains the boundary between the speaking subject and the inorganic materiality of the stone, and the syllabic (non-melismatic) text-setting with which he speaks maintains the boundary between his words and the pure sonic materiality of free melody.

Four minutes into the piece, there is a sudden upward shift in tempo, vocal register, and complexity of the vocal lines. The section opens with the repeated, "Send me a melody", followed by several longer lines where the last syllable of "melody" is extended into various melismata. Viewed one way, this plea for a melody could be directed at God, the wordless vocalizing expressing the unnamable mystery of his power, as in *Ten Year Teardrop*. However, I conceive of melisma's role here differently, less as an expression of God's power to deliver the subject from the death drive, and more as a figure for death itself.

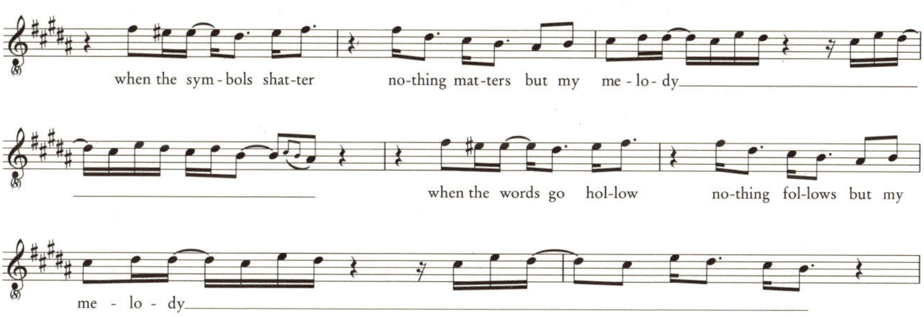

In the song's beginning, the depressed speaker articulates his suicidal desire to be turned into material; now, in the second section, his singing is being transformed from the verbal signifying of syllabically-set text into the non-signifying material of melisma.[5] The lyrics and their setting both describe and illustrate the shattering of the symbolic, and the assumption of absolute primacy by melody, pure sonic material. This dissolution, or at least disruption, of verbal signification by melisma brings the death of speech into speaking. If mastery of the symbolic is how the speaking subject demarcates and maintains his identity, then melisma's flirtation with the death of the symbolic, the irruption of non-symbolic melodic materiality, gives our depressed speaker a taste of what he wants. This brush with symbolic death is redemptive for the speaker. The flat, depressive affect of his earlier syllabic singing gives way to highly animated, rhythmically active melismata. The depressive subject, with his emotionally numb, yet functionally signifying speech, is revived by melisma's flirtation with the material, inorganic plane he longs to merge with in death. With respect to speech, and to speaking as constitutive of a subject's stable identity, melisma here brings a sacred taste of death into life.

5. "When the symbols shatter" is a reference to Death in June's 1992 album, *But What Ends When the Symbols Shatter?*. The band's notorious ongoing flirtation with Nazi aesthetics connects with *Simple Answers'* recurring themes of Jewish consciousness, including the song title *Black Sun*'s referencing of the Nazi *Schwarze Sonne* symbol. How all this relates to melisma in my work is elaborated later in the essay.

Continuity of Existence

Bataille writes, "We are discontinuous beings… but we yearn for our lost continuity… The quest for continuity of existence… signifies an essentially religious intention".[6] By "discontinuous", Bataille means that the default condition of human subjectivity is to be sealed off from the greater totality of all that exists. The impulse of religion (from the Latin *religare*, to bind together) is to fuse us with that primal continuity by erasing, or at least destabilizing, the boundaries of the self. From the Bataillean perspective, the Freudian death drive has a religious quality. Melisma is a fitting technique to render this sense of dark religiosity because, like the death drive, melisma also seeks the continuity of being. It does this both on the level of language and, more immediately, of the body itself.

6. Georges Bataille, *Erotism*, pp. 13, 16.

I've noted that melisma, by definition, must occur as a vowel sound. This might seem too obvious to require highlighting, as the purpose of melisma is melodic extension, melody is made of sustained pitches, and pitches can only be sung as vowels.[7] However, if the only

7. Technically, this is not phonetically accurate. When I say "consonants" here, it's really shorthand for the sub-groups *plosives* (such as p or b) and *voiceless fricatives* (such as s or F). One could sing melismatically with consonants such as *voiced fricatives* (such as V or z) or *nasals* (such as m or n). A melisma on m is simply humming.

function of melisma were to turn language into pure sound, this could be achieved just as well using a word's consonants, perhaps by shortening the vowels and over-enunciating non-pitched sounds like *p* or *t*. This would be a percussive effect, rather than a melodic one. The melismatic vowel, however, is the better vehicle for the singer's religious impulse toward the continuity of existence because it is literally a continuous movement of air through the body. Consonants are discrete, finite events, closing off air flow to the body, sealing the body more tightly, making it more "discontinuous" with existence's totality; the vowel, on the other hand, opens the body to the outside, to the continuum of matter. If the "spiritual" comes from the Latin *spiritus*, (breath), I don't view it so much as God's breath filling our bodies with its divine substance above the material world, but rather as our own breathing opening our bodies to fuse with the sacred continuity of matter.

Melisma's relationship to language and to (non-)signification also engages Bataille's sacred continuity of existence. To name something, to speak of it, to represent it with language, is to separate it from existence's greater continuity. Language and thought divide the continuum of existence into discrete things, and enter them into various relationships, while maintaining the seal of each thing's discontinuity. In some traditions, the intellect has been associated with the image of the sword, thought being a faculty of dividing. As melisma opens up the word and breaks the seal of its abstract symbolic function, it returns the word's sonic material to the greater undifferentiated realm of non-signifying sound. The continuous melismatic vowel could extent infinitely. In *Black Sun*, we discussed melisma as speech's death drive in music; this drive is toward existential continuity that destabilizes both the seal of the singer's body and the seal of the word as a signifier of something discrete.

Excess

> "There is in nature... a movement which always exceeds the bounds... Indeed it is by definition that which can never be grasped... But through the excess in him, that God whom we should like to shape into an intelligible concept never ceases, exceeding this concept, to exceed the limits of reason."
>
> —Bataille[8]

8. *Erotism*, p. 41.

Another poetic element associated with melisma in my work, which is very much in line with Bataille's concept of the sacred, is a sense of *excess*. With the band name Extra Life, I was consciously evoking overbrimming vitalism. While some have interpreted it as referring to an afterlife, a higher, second life to come, to me it was always more about the joyous and terrible (in both the antiquated and modern senses of the word) idea and experience of extravagant expenditure. The Extra Life piece *Voluptuous Life* (2010) is a hedonist anthem, calling for the Dionysian spilling of wine, tears, sperm, money, and vomit, in a total unleashing of all flows, whether they be libidinal, emotional, financial, or simply aesthetic.

The melisma on "flow" is very clear in its programmatic function. Not only is the melismatic vowel more fluid than syllabic singing on an aesthetic level, melisma also represents an overflowing excess with respect to language. Melisma disrupts the symbolic function of the word with a sonic materiality, which is *superfluous* to the system of signification. If language, as a system of relationships between discrete, abstract things, is a kind of economy, then melisma's materiality is a wasteful, non-recuperable expense, like an extravagant gift, spilling outside the system of exchange.

Bataille's concept of the erotic, which he closely links to the sacred and to the death drive, is based in excess. The lyric "Too much life, so much life that we die" evokes the Bataillean sense of an overflowing of vitality that can't be contained within the subject, and a kind of pulsion toward the hydraulic release of death, the organism's opening, returning to continuity with the inorganic. *Black Sun* depicted the depressive's lugubrious slouching toward this fusion with the outside; *Voluptuous Life* is its manic, excessive counterpart. Hedonism's excess vitalism pushes the subject toward the continuity of death, whether as the little death of orgasm, heart attack, or financial ruin; melisma's sonic excess bursts apart the word, flowing back into the continuum of sound.

Power

Melisma has also been a vehicle for me to express ideas and feelings surrounding human power dynamics. To consider power, especially in any hierarchical formation, is inherently political. However, this aspect of my work has never been a commitment to an ideological alignment or agenda. My thoughts on power are ambivalent and as a songwriter, I often inhabit several different perspectives within one piece. To engage this fraught psycho-political area, I have employed melisma in several ways in the past.

The Next Stab (2004), written for my very short-lived project Seductive Sprigs (two tenors and two electric guitars), uses the entire spectrum of text-setting techniques, from recitative to melisma, to fortify the text's narrative in very clear, specific ways. Written in the second person, but referencing my own experience, the song describes a scene of childhood cruelty, where your friend forces you into a cardboard box, seals it with duct tape, and stabs the box repeatedly with scissors. The opening lyrics wryly describe a naïve optimism about human nature which, under the banner of Reason, attempts to deny the unavoidable reality of sadistic violence.

The first few lines of text are mostly set syllabically, with a few neumatic moments (two or three notes on a syllable). In the spectrum of text-setting complexity I laid out earlier, these techniques fall in a middle ground, more mobile than recitative, without venturing into the open realm of melisma. With syllabic and neumatic setting, text is clearly intelligible, with a melody that is active, but still follows cadences similar to normal speech.

The clarity of this text-setting serves the "reasonable" perspective put forth by the opening lines. Your trust in your friend not to hurt you has yet to be betrayed. Your sense that people are mostly in control of their violent urges, and your faith that the primal will to dominate can at least be suspended in friendship is intact. In the syllabic singing of the text, signification prevails, with melody serving the function of language, not yet threatened by melisma's pure, non-signifying sound. Aesthetically, linguistically, and with respect to the social outlook of the speaker in the narrative, the piece begins in a stable, "functional" realm.

Your entering into the cardboard box is a turning point in both the narrative and the music. The characters' relationship of domination and subjugation is formed, and this power dynamic is rendered with a shift in the text-setting. The consistent syllabic setting of the piece's opening splits into a polarized oscillation between recitative (psalm note) and melisma. The lines describing your confinement in the box are set as rapid-fire psalm note chanting, while your friend's freedom is elaborated with extended melismata.

The programmatic function of juxtaposing the two starkly contrasting techniques is to evoke imprisonment versus mobility. In psalm note singing, the chanting is locked into the repetition of only a few notes, strict harmonic confinement, not stretching out into what one would even call melody. Melisma, on the other hand, roams with complete melodic freedom, never even repeating a note consecutively, just as our tale's aggressor freely moves around the room outside the box. The recitative here is also faster than the melisma, its hectic sixteenth notes pitted against the melisma's comparatively leisurely triplet eighths. You are panicked and sputtering in the dark while your friend paces arrogantly outside.

Beyond your physical imprisonment and its mirror in the psalm notes' strict harmonic and registral limitation, there is another level of confinement at work in the piece's text-setting. With respect to language and song, and relative to melisma, recitative is a confinement within pure signification. Here, pitch, rhythm, and pure sound in general are subservient to the signifying function of the words, even more so than in syllabic setting. Language, notoriously unable to represent reality as it truly is, and yet the "house of being" where we dwell, is a kind of prison.[9] Whether we are attempting to name the power of God in his unrepresentable highness, or to describe Bataille's continuity of being in its sacred, material baseness, language spells impotence either way. It is the abstract, the intellectual, unable to touch the terrible power of existence's totality. Speaking is the cage of the all-too-human, who, with his significations, representations, and abstractions, remains

9. Martin Heidegger, *Being in Time*, p. 217.

powerless in the face of Life's nameless outside.[10] Outside of the box, the tyrant roams; outside of the verbal and melodic confines of recitative's verbal signifying, melisma flows.

10. My reference points for these ideas include Immanuel Kant and Nick Land.

In my discussion of melisma so far, I have attributed to its sacredness a certain threatening aspect. Its status as sonic materiality threatens the function of the word as an abstract signifier. Its physical production as uninterrupted breath threatens the body's boundaries (more so than other vocal styles). Its sense of excess threatens the system of language as an economy. In those religious and erotic contexts, however, these "threats" are desirable and beautiful transgressions of boundaries. Even in *Black Sun*, where melisma represented a flirtation with death, it provided a redemptive, ritual fulfilment of the death drive, reanimating the depressed subject with a taste of the death he longed for.

In *The Next Stab*, however, melisma represents something actually threatening in the more standard negative sense of the word. The realm outside of the box isn't tempting you to dissolve into its sacred materiality, nor is it some erotic domain of ego-less ecstasy toward which our overflowing excess of desire pushes us. The unnamable outside, linked to melisma, is a source of real violence. In this song, you don't want to die or dissolve. You want to live and speak. You cower inside the box, inside language, hysterically stammering out your verbal barrage. The recitative is a desperate, vain scrambling to signify, in the face of what always trumps words, thoughts, and abstractions: the power of pure *action*. The sacred outside of language, which in other pieces of mine has meant God's glory, or the material world's undifferentiated continuum, in this piece means domination. Free from saying or thinking anything, the aggressor's melisma flows like his pure action, force, and will, his violent movement through/as the continuity of being. In comparison, words are the domain of the weak.

The Jew

This journey through my use and theorizing of melisma has taken us from the relatively traditional and familiar into far more idiosyncratic territory. Continuing from my use of text-setting to express themes of power in *The Next Stab*, we arrive at one of my personal obsessions: antisemitism, the figure of the Jew, and the complexities of Jewish consciousness. Jewishness, as perceived by both Jews and gentiles, both positively and negatively, correctly and falsely, occupies a conflicted place in my intellectual and emotional ecology. The entanglement of Jewishness with all of the ideas discussed thus far has been the subject of several of my songs over the years. Here, I will focus on a case where I specifically use melisma to engage those entanglements.

Ritual Fire (2018), from the *Simple Answers* record, addresses and expresses self-directed Jewish anti-Semitism. The song takes the idea of language as weakness encoded in the text-setting of *The Next Stab*, articulates it overtly, and ups the ante by racializing it.

Lyrically, this passage attributes true masculine power to wordlessness and thoughtlessness. In his essay *Ur-Fascism*, Umberto Eco diagnoses a fundamental psychological aspect of fascism as "... the cult of action for action's sake. Action being beautiful in itself, it must be taken before, or without, any previous reflection. Thinking is a form of emasculation."[11]

The actions of the truly powerful man are pure forces, uncorrupted by abstractions. He is "whole" in that thoughts do not divide his world into discrete, discontinuous things. As discussed earlier, ideas and language as representations are barriers to the continuity of being, to totality's wholeness. In the jubilus of the Christian liturgy, or in my own *Ten Year Teardrop*, the inability of language to represent God's unnamable glory is celebrated with ecstatic reverence. Conversely, in *The Next Stab*, and even more explicitly in *Ritual Fire*, language is mocked as weakness, from the point of view of a superior, supra-linguistic man, who wields the unnamable power of the continuity of existence.

11. Umberto Eco, *Ur-Fascism*, p. 6.

The phrase "danger and play" here comes from Nietzsche, as his definition of the true man's desire. The placement of the melisma on "play" is important and deliberate.[12] The unfettered actions of Nietzsche's *übermensch*, in all their violence and cruelty, are above all cheerful and playful.[13] Play exists outside the intellect and its confining gravitas. Its dangerous power is in its "pointlessness", its non-sense. A game may have rules but play itself is free, outside systems, or in the system's gaps. Language and the intellect *work*, both in the sense of functioning and of labor and productivity. Melisma *plays*, disrupting, fleeing, and dancing outside, and in excess of the seriousness of the rules of signification, like the übermensch's unthinking movement.

12. *Thus Spoke Zarathustra*, p. 48, Cambridge texts in the history of philosophy.

13. To use interchangeably Nietzsche's übermensch and simply the "true man" is sloppy, as the übermensch is a post-human figure, yet to even exist. But I'm comfortable eliding them here, as Nietzsche's "danger and play" can easily be attributed to both, and the "true man" seems like his idea of the least weak of a human we can hope for at the moment.

This kind of play, this sacred levity, is presented as something the Jew is incapable of. One need not be a fascist, or even an anti-Semite, to understand the stereotype (and reality) of Jews as a highly verbal, intellectual people, a people of the book. In Eco's analysis of fascism, the Jew becomes a lightning rod for distrust of the intellect and contempt for the impotence of abstraction and language in the face of pure action, real power, and play. The Jew inside all of us, with his weak and weakening words and ideas, must be destroyed, just as words themselves face their Final (dis-)Solution in the non-abstract, material power of melisma's playful movement.

The Symbolic and the Semiotic

The strange conceptual nexus of language, the intellect, fascism, Jewishness, and music, which motivates my use of melisma in *Ritual Fire* and elsewhere, is a configuration which has been with me for some time, but for years I only sensed it in the most vague, inchoate form. The ideas became crystallized for me, and my intuitions corroborated, by Julia Kristeva's work. Kristeva's analysis of the work and life of author Louis-Ferdinand Céline has been particularly resonant for me. Céline was a notorious anti-Semite and Nazi sympathizer, and Kristeva explains his racial animus as stemming from a "... *rage against the symbolic*, which... culminates in what Céline hallucinates and knows to be their foundation and forebearer — Jewish monotheism. When one follows his associations of ideas, his anti-Semitism [is a] sweeping away [of]... abstraction, reason, and adulterated power, con-

14. *Powers of Horror*, p. 178.

sidered emasculating."[14]

Kristeva's assessment of Céline is that he harbors great contempt for intellectualism, and that his antisemitism functions as a sublimation of this contempt. This is similar to the fascist psychology diagnosed by Umberto Eco, and expressed in *Ritual Fire*. Kristeva never endorses Céline's racial hatred whatsoever as an actual viewpoint; she is concerned with how it functions as an expression of his deeper ambivalence toward language and the symbolic, a conflict which she celebrates as central to Céline's brilliance. In various letters, when he isn't maniacally railing against international Jewry, Céline expresses his struggle with his own artistic medium:

> "... to resensitize language, to have it *throb* more than *reason* — SUCH WAS MY AIM... That doesn't happen without imparting to thought a certain melodious, melodic twist..."
>
> "At the precise point where emotion turns into sound, on that articulation between body and language, on the catastrophefold (sic) between the two, there looms up my great rival, music'."[15]

15. *Powers of Horror*, p. 190, or *Letter to Hindus*, May 29, 1947, *L'Hern.*

Like so many writers, not to mention philosophers, Céline expresses an almost jealous admiration for music, as an artform that exists in the liminal zone between language and body, sublimely negotiating the abstract and the material, reason and throbbing. Language's reasoning is its signifying, while its throbbing is something less abstract, more material, dangerous, erotic, and playful. Céline states that for language to throb, not only the words, but thought itself must become *melodic*. It must *play*. Like my depressive speaker in *Black Sun*, who pleads for a melody, both Céline and Kristeva understand "rhythm and music as being the only way out, the ultimate sublimation of the unsignifiable".[16]

16. *Powers of Horror*, p. 23.

Kristeva's analysis of Céline's work and thought is based, to a large extent, in her concepts of the symbolic versus the semiotic. As discussed earlier, the symbolic is the Lacanian idea of the space where the child enters the world of language, and forms himself as a speaking subject. Mastery of the symbolic is how one establishes one's own discrete identity, one's "discontinuity", to use Bataille's term. The semiotic, on the other hand, is a non-symbolic current of rhythms, tonality, gestures, and affects, which runs through language, but operates within the "gaps" of its symbolic functioning. It exists before language, rooted in far more primal, biological experiences of the pre-verbal infant, or the unborn, when the body itself has not yet been separated from the mother, from the continuity of existence. It is a more archaic flow within language, in dialectical tension with the symbolic.

> "... the semiotic functions within signifying practices as the result of a transgression of the symbolic... It requires the symbolic break to obtain the complex articulation we associate with it in musical and poetic practices..."[17]

17. *Revolution in Poetic Language*, p. 118.

For Kristeva, the semiotic lies in the musicality of everyday speech, and is a subversive quality with respect to signification. Speaking need not unravel into melisma, or even be sung at all, to be destabilized by pure sound, rhythm, and pitch. All speech is always musical. If symbolic mastery through language is how the subject solidly defines their discrete identity, then Kristeva's idea of the semiotic means that identity is never completely stable. It is disrupted at all times by the musical materiality of semiotic flows. This analysis of abstraction versus materiality in speech is quite a bit more radical than my own, as mine has focused on singing, which is by definition musical, with melisma being a very obvious extreme endpoint of the aesthetic spectrum. Kristeva identifies the less obvious, but ever-present semiotic, musical undercurrent of all language, explicating its radical implications for subjectivity itself. When I see colossal thinkers such as Kristeva or Céline attributing to music such dangerous, elusive, far-reaching power, I feel proud and fortunate to have been called to such a sublime medium.

Melisma in My Current and Future Work

In a sense, any vocal music is a mixed medium, at least relative to purely instrumental music. While I consider myself a composer way before a writer or a poet, and *way* before any kind of intellectual, the process behind most of my best work has begun with writing or harvesting text. The symbolic dimension of language in song is a dramatic sense of human presence, if not my own, then a speaker, character, or narrator. Lyrics tether the musical work to an aura of subjectivity, the individual; and, however simple or emotionally-based the lyrical content might be, text is always on some level intellectual compared to pure sound, simply to the extent that language, as

I've argued, is inherently abstract. In various examples from my work, I have shown how this realm of speaking subjectivity and the intellect can be a safe, stable home, a place of devout humility, a condition of weakness to be scorned, or a prison to be fled. In reflecting on all of these examples together, and in reflecting on my own foregoing analyses themselves, I notice something consistent: while melisma disrupts or suspends the symbolic, my discussion here has focused on the ways in which I use that disruption to ultimately serve the meaning of the text. Melisma may be a non-signifying, purely sonic, semiotic element, but when I use it to signify the *idea* of non-signification, it is still beholden to the text, to representation. The lyrics' complex systems of meaning often include the idea of meaninglessness, which melisma serves to represent. While melisma's materiality continually haunts and problematizes the abstract symbolizing of the lyrics, that haunting itself is often key to the abstract ideas the lyrics are articulating. My melismatic excursions programmatically feed back into what the songs are "about".

Of course, there is the other side of my use of melisma: text as simply a springboard toward the joy and power of writing pure music. Beginning my compositional process with lyrics belies the extent to which the text is just a pretext for my working with sound. When I am launched by the initial text into melisma, or further out into extended instrumental writing, my inspiration never remains held in the orbit of serving the original meaning of the text. Lyrics might come first in the process, but composition as pure sound, melody, and rhythm become the fundament, after the fact.

Over the years, my lyrical content has changed. So much of the Extra Life and Seaven Teares songbooks were rooted in autobiography and inner life, fortified by some philosophy. Across Psalm Zero's trajectory, and in *Simple Answers*, my lyrics became less personal, more political, outwardly directed, and overtly intellectual. However, I've grown tired of my personal narratives and dramatizing my own mishegas (despite how good I am at it), as well as "making people think". I have also lost interest in consciously and explicitly responding to the world outside. The political and social fabric has reached a level of complexity and fragmentation which I now find uninspiring to even attempt to address directly in song. In my current and upcoming work, I'm consciously moving toward far more vague, cryptic lyrical expressions, and even more importantly, simply writing less text. I am stripping my lyrics down to only what is necessary to open the floodgates of pure musical material. This is not to say that my new music will be so overtaken by rampant melisma as to have an entirely new quality. But the weight is shifting.

There may be an apparent irony to ending this dense philosophical and technical disquisition on my work with the announcement of a creative move toward the sidelining of text, personal reflection, and intellect. However, this is a part of why I'm writing more essays now; moving forward, these essays may branch out away from my own music, because, as my music increases power by shedding much of its text, there will probably be less and less to say about it.

CHAPTER
25

ON SOCIAL CONNECTION IN IMPROVISED MUSIC

THOMAS MORGAN

One of the greatest rewards of playing improvised music with others is the social connection it creates. This social aspect of music is a driving force in my life. As an introvert my natural inclination runs toward solitude, and musicians certainly have work to do alone, including practicing, studying, and composing. But music also brings one together with friends in a creative, intimate, and joyful shared activity. For me this complements solitary pursuits and gives them meaning. In this essay I offer a perspective on social connection in music and in particular how it stems from improvisation.

The boundary between improvised and composed music is less clear than it would seem. This is because no two performances can be the same; there are subtleties to be improvised even supposing the highest degree of organization. Still, I am primarily thinking about music in which improvisation plays a central part. One personal reason for this focus is that I felt a heightened sense of connection when I discovered jazz, a music defined by its use of improvisation. Also, practically all of my experience in the twenty-five years since then has been in this area. I believe there are specific reasons that jazz resonated with me, and they follow from the fundamental nature of improvisation: the fact that it happens in real time. There is often a composed framework for improvisation but much of the decision making still happens quickly, from moment to moment. This has some implications for an ensemble: it indicates that mutual support, trust, and respect are important. These are things that foster social connection.

Because improvisation happens in real time, there is little opportunity for analysis, judgment, or blame. By the time one analyzes the current state of the music, it has changed and the analysis has limited relevance. Similarly, judgment takes one's mind a step away from the matter at hand. These are distractions that inhibit the instantaneous reactions that have to happen when improvising. Even when the rate of change feels slow, many subtleties and nuances develop quickly; to miss them is to miss the music. Therefore, the nature of improvisation makes it beneficial to replace analysis and judgment with intuition and trust, following one's intuition to bring the current state of the music forward as well as one can and trusting that the other players are doing the same.

Trust is built by mutual support. Improvisation means adapting to continually changing circumstances, and often there arises a need or opportunity to try an untested idea. This carries some risk because anything new might not succeed. But if the new idea appears deficient strictly on its own merits, the other players can help by creating a complementary context or by taking up the idea themselves, adding what is missing or letting go what is inessential. This kind of support provides a basis for free and interactive exploration, keeping music lively, dynamic, and exciting. It makes it possible to take greater risks without fear of failure and it builds trust among the improvisers.

For musicians to support each other in improvisation there must be connection between them, and this is made possible by respect. The important thing is to be as aware as one can. No one can understand everything happening in any given moment, but with awareness one can develop a sense for what, if anything, could be added to augment the current picture. Also, some key details may emerge that suggest where the music could go next. Being receptive to the broad strokes and nuances of the other improvisers' playing results in more coherent music. Moreover, it communicates respect and creates an environment where all know that their contributions make a difference. Respect is as foundational for musical interaction as it is for human relationships and society. The acknowledgment of each individual's value allows the group to realize its potential.

In ensemble music where improvisation plays a large part, the need for connection is quickly made apparent. Much of the potency of improvised music comes from its interactive nature. It has the potential to go in dramatically different directions and the players have agency in deciding where to take it. So the improvisers' individual decisions, informed by their listening, are clearly evident. Lack of connection tends to result in discord as the players' decisions lead in diverging directions. This means that when learning to improvise, seeking common ground is an essential task. I believe this is a reason that jazz appealed to me from the start; even as a beginner I was compelled to form real musical connection with the other players.

Connection can exist in different degrees in each dimension of music, such as timbral, rhythmic, intonational, melodic, harmonic, gestural, emotional, and spiritual. Strong connection in one dimension tends to make up for weaker connection in another. Connection in a more fundamental, more physical dimension provides an especially solid foundation on which one can appreciate greater independence in other dimensions. For example, if timbres blend exceptionally well, intonation can diverge more widely; even unintentional discrepancies may be experienced as stimulating. Similarly, rhythmic coordination creates space for harmonic independence. In order to explain why some combinations succeed and others do not, one can come up with aesthetic theories. Still, the multitude of combinations means that any theory can only be provisional, and many untried paths through these dimensions will turn out to be surprisingly effective. An ensemble that nurtures flexibility and generosity can safely navigate these new paths.

Independence and contrast do not always mean a lack of awareness; connection can produce dissonance as well as consonance. Sometimes the perfect complement to an element is one that contrasts with it, building desirable tension and invigorating the music. For example, a dynamic element can call for a more static counterpoint. At other times one is inclined to take a linear approach and imitate another player's gesture, harmonize with it, and develop it. One can also try to achieve both things at the same time. Improvisers find personal ways of balancing these approaches, gaining experience in a process of trial and error.

When people play together interactively, a feedback loop is formed. What I pay attention to is how comfortable the other players seem, how freely they are offering their ideas, and how they are responding to mine. If there is a flowing interchange there is no need for thought. Playing feels more like being than doing. But if there is some stagnation I try to imagine what I could do differently that might release it. If one thing fails I try something else, and so on. One attraction of improvisation for me is the immediacy and simplicity of this feedback loop, which is made possible by direct connection between musicians.

A primary goal when starting to improvise in a group is finding common ground. This can be a specific rhythm, melody, or other musical element; it can also be an approach to developing these elements. If one comes upon a common reference point, one that is relatable to all present, this stimulates the flow of ideas and the reference point becomes a center from which to expand and explore. Whenever the music loses focus and needs grounding, the group can come back to the center. As the musicians continue to discover these points, they forge pathways between them and develop a network of shared vocabulary that makes up the group's identity. One feels the joy and camaraderie of cooperative exploration and discovery.

This has been an exploration of some of the reasons why collective musical improvisation is such a rewarding social activity. In short, improvisation progresses in real time without pause, and it soon becomes evident to someone learning to improvise that connection, trust, and respect provide freedom and safety in exploring the boundless possibilities that music offers. At times one feels that improvisation lacks coordination but if this is true with regard to some musical dimensions, robust connection in other dimensions can still make the music effective. The effect that musical connection has on improvisers and listeners is meaningful; it affirms and inspires trust and cooperation in human society. Experiencing this connection and cooperation is deeply enriching, and it is one of the things I love most about being a musician.

CHAPTER
26

FÅRÖ

Reflections Passed Walking on a Baltic Island in November

STEPHEN O'MALLEY

Connection to the environment; is it meaningful with the music? Does music have this solution? If it does, what is it? Or why is it? I am just beginning to ask these questions, which have already been asked millions of times.

Not sure at all, but music seems to be a solitary activity, an action performed by a so-called individual.

Not sure at all, but music also appears to be a spiritual activity, a group action bringing individuals to a triangulated, cubed, or a more complex geometric place of ideas.

Maybe it is a soul activity; but what is a soul?

* * *

An action of expression, a thrill of exchange, waves of the present concepts, of instincts or elemental states, related to the meditative, peak moments conditions, the high of an athlete, souls offer that ease of connection when one encounters awareness.

* * *

Am I just part of the environment, or do I have my own will and thoughts?

A radiant effect of music is distortion, the sonance, the saturation of the wave energy. It breaks and cracks the air and consciousness.

As Turrell reminds us, the optic nerve and light are an untrustworthy coupling but facilitate a rough bridge to engage with the phenomena of observation itself, of light energy and time.

Ben Rivers brings the sensation of the times movement as environment, his movement through his surroundings, the texture of visual grain, and a montage of clarifying visions of ghost states, temporal inertia and friction, the life's slow passage through those tunnels of perception.

With time we can play with elasticity, Not sure, but this seems to correspond to arrhythmic activity involving attention and patience. There are thresholds to be met with this attention, as in any work of focus and intention.

Andy Goldsworthy's rapport "The energy and space around a material are as important as the energy and space within. The weather — rain, sun, snow, hail, mist, calm — is that external space made visible. When I touch a rock, I am touching and working the space around it. It is not independent of its surroundings, and the way it sits tells how it came to be there."

Geology reminds that the circulation (of minerals) is essential (of matter), which occur at scales beyond measure or the comprehension of dimension, cyclic as far as non-event-based phenomena. Organisms were growing from particulates in the sea die and fall to the ocean floor, over aeons metamorphosis into strata of stone. The pressure of time enacts stone to flex and rise and folds into mountains, ascending to the sky, the minerals of rain and wind, water and gases corrode these mountains. Through the depth of tectonic forces, materials return to their raw form, returns into seas. Again organisms arise of these particulates. Repeat and erode.

However, what is music in this?

Playing around with metaphors has a colourful character but also stinks of pretentious distractions from the lack of actual skill or substance. (one of my specialities, so I have been accused). Low hanging fruit. Please take a few which look ripe, don't mind the orchard itself.

Distortion is an archetypal arcane form of sound.

It breaks the air.

It rends the matter.

It renders the mind.

It shreds the thoughts.

Thick wind on the peninsula, off the baltic. Breaking surf of the shattering wave.

Moaning winds in the roof the sun is shining brilliant mercury waves into my eyes. The sheep are kneeling.

Musical structure is a trained and disciplined mind, articulating pattern and transformations.

How does one train and discipline the mind to articulate musical structure well, anyway?

To perceive and let go, for the subject to reprieve, perceive.

It is also a brilliant way to exchange, shining.

But the experience of that rendering and rending of the air inescapable as a fundamental.

Warning, here comes another metaphor, another brain phantasm.

We can talk about the distortion, especially the significant fat loud slime crystal distortion, the kind that chews on the bone marrow and the vagus nerve, as being like geological matter and process.

Why do we need to do that?

It makes it feel like the environment.

Something "greater" than the space occupied. Or perhaps older, solid/not solid. Magmatic sheet rivers of minerals and stone. Plasma.

Hell, it is just an electric guitar; get a grip. No wonder metal get shit on as ridiculous, juvenile. Get a grip, man! It is just music. Fucking metalheads and their fantasy/delusion.

That rauk on Faro, they are a few hundred thousand-year-old rock pillars hewn of sea and wind melting those infinities of ancient carapaces pressed into stone strata on their road back into the sea.

The stones are magnificent. The island is a pile of rocks. Vegetation exerts great effort to stay up out of the stones. It is the inversion of lava bursting up through the jungle floor in Kauai.

Baltic waves fold back on themselves, the stones of the reef bringing reverse wave triangles. Waves from all directions.

The wind overcomes everything, blasting the body like the worlds most glorious infra sub ever conceived. You fall over, gravity diagonals.

Deepest pale violet ripples the air.

* * *

I want to remember the environment is in me; of course, it is somehow reassuring to state "I am not individual", truly it feels more like a fraudulent statement. It is not to be stated at all. The DNA won't allow that.

Why individually, a part of the more extraordinary environment.

We are the environment.

As Timothy Morton wrote about in his presentation of Hyperobjects and OOO in hyper objectivity (as my distortion mind-read); we are not the objective ones in nature, (and the vocabulary of others in words like nature) we ultimately misunderstand a place or space other than ourselves. The environment is all of this and all of that.

But in the hyperobjective that of environment, again its effect of time is enormous, 500 years, 5 million. When our threshold of music time is five or fifteen minutes, we are meeting only ephemerality and absence, emptiness, and it is barely a molecule of breath or a wave in the sea. A 3-hour performance is akin to a second of silent space.

We cannot separate from that; we can not conceptualize that.

You cannot begin to perceive an idea without a concept to show a lens on it.

* * *

So why not throw a concept net over the music this way.

On the one hand, it is 1-note with a folded wave, folding speaker distortion another hand feels that in the chest, another hand feels it in the eyes, another in the bones. The distortion addled marrow feels that. The vagus nerve inflames. Is the RNA feeling that? Is the wave itself, the distortion itching the genome? As the genome expresses, do these experiences recourse those streams of expression in some way. When the mind sits in those metaphors, are the memories of those archaic expressions?

Where am I going with this? Well, that is a beautiful wave over there.

How much moss is on the floor in this grove?

Q: Who's your favourite:
Dave Lombardo or Dale Crover?
A: Yes.
How about Verlaine?
Q: Paul?
A: No, Tom.

* * *

What are the purpose of music in that environment and the attention of the environment?

Perhaps it is enough to alter that environment for the few hundred minds, just a little bit. Togetherness is damned.

All of those people jammed in that warehouse space hyperextend experience. Rotate twenty degrees for ninety minutes. Deep vibration immersion, how does it feel? Is it in the chest, the eyes, the balls, the throat? Wherever it is, does this happen often? Here comes a threshold; the pain is gone, just let go of it. The moment glacier towers there in front of us, melting, a roar of calving tears across the periphery, then horizontal.

Then back on the street.

The idea of a connection of the sound energy in the air/gas through vibrating the body is not an idea. It is the matter.

The mind-body connection being something quite abstract, for we live above the neck. Those Jurassic vibrations are not plate-tectonics but maybe thinking about them out of time can provide a connection to something out of time altogether.

The abstraction of the environment and time is sure "out of time."

The phrase "out of time" is a bit Lovecraft. I'll try to avoid that as it reeks of metal lit 101 cliché.

(Like his writing though)

Or: The phenomenological Experience of the Distortion and the Noise

Alive, immaterial, plasma.

Looking for the new colours which never existed. The blood-red algae on the avalanche of stones. A crest of broken violet pastel shells, beginning their disintegration, reintegration, flares of beaming magenta crepuscule, plumes of purple vapour, liquid metal radiant.

Dumitrescu's phenomenological point of so-called-spectralism shows us that even the metaphor can invoke a possible purpose of a grander scale. He thinks it all sounds like the radiations of the Big Bang. 50 billion-year-old nebulas that blossom like a lover. He is a fantastic conductor, excellent shaman, sound poet, great dancer.

Even utterly absurd in practice. Like a dancer, in a choreography.

The elasticity of perspective, the dancer, always deeply touching all strings of existence around them.

They exist in the physicality. In that world.

The music is in mind.

But it is a mirror in the dance.

Mind-body awareness distortion tears that page and looks behind the edge.

It has not damaged; it is myopic atomism. A few moments of awareness it is atomizing the present, the pile of strings in the vibration field.

CHAPTER
27

BOW SMOKE BACK

Showing Up for the Recording Session and Delivering the Magic Take

LAURA ORTMAN

Making the violin bow smoke back signals how music became sculptural to me.

Growing up learning how to make drawings and paintings always enlivened me. Portraits made with a wood-burning tool and sketching body parts all over newsprint paper gave me intimacy.

It wasn't until I started making installation work and performance art sets out of my clothes and found wood; making new clothes and habitats sewing plastic tarp; adding sunset-colored seed beads that formed waves and skies along imaginary rivers — that I began making music for all this to accompany. Making performances with so much atmosphere through all these clear-colored tarps and sounds was overwhelming when through so many kinds of dynamic lighting…I began to see my violin as much as hearing it. The music appeared and the rest vanished.

Changed all formats of my storytelling to just music. Watched the over-rosining I loved to do look like plumes of smoke and spin my head with ideas of how violins come from beautiful trees and forests, such as the ones where I am from in Arizona. The hot sap off trees is formed into cakes of rosin. Finally gave me an understanding of the materials I use to create atmospheres. It made more sense than sewing plastic. The crazy rosin was so useful in making strong sounds that gave me weight to stay still and watch the atmospheres drift, like a cool song in the night. It could also help me stick to the softest and quietest textured bow stroke I know like the back of my hand.

At this point, I've heartily played the violin for forty years and have re-captured visualizations of the woods, rivers, and remote moments in my compositions for violin, and also Apache violin, amplified piano, electric guitar, various electric keyboards, field recordings, and singing through a megaphone.

Created a crumply loop of part of Mendelssohn's famous violin concerto here in New York eons ago on a tape and listened to it too many times. It became an obsession with where it goes in my world because I loved its rolling, lumbering bass line.

After several years of sampling it, it finally became a solid introduction for a new composition named *My Soul Remainer* featuring an exploratory violin, amplified Helpinstill piano, Casio keyboard, a roaring field recording of the underground NYC subways I live above, and ends with a heavily energized, serious but adamantly bright violin solo.

The ever-interpreting rosin on my bow makes this flame, flicker, and wave come to life. It builds what *My Soul Remainer* is and eventually brought to the wonderful studio of engineer Martin Bisi in Gowanus, Brooklyn, where it is recorded. It was one of the most difficult songs to record, but within a year we made it work. It became ready for the final part of its creation.

This recording circles back to the sculpting sound, visualizations, and creating living atmospheres.

I collaborate with two extraordinary Diné artists, former principal ballet dancer of the New York City Ballet Jock Soto and filmmaker Nanobah Becker, who used to live in New York too. We went out to the desert Southwest where we are all indigenously from and synched up the sounds of *My Soul Remainer* with the choreography and moving image direction we created a plan and a home for. We hiked an hour into the mountains near Eagle Nest, New Mexico where Jock lives joined by cinematographer Blackhorse Lowe (Diné) and gaffer Autumn Chacon (Diné) seeking tall trees, lakes, and waterfalls to shoot amongst.

In the evening we sparked a large bonfire for the final scene. We shot a final walk under the moon.

It was wonderful to be amongst this sparkly and glistening remindful smoke for the final part of how *My Soul Remainer* entirely came alive amongst my friends, collaborators, nature, and our stories of existence.

Vision, movement, and sound in this way carried us and lit our way home.

CHAPTER 28

COMPOSING, IMPROVISING AND CHILD-LIKE INTUITION

ALEX PAXTON

"Children know something that most people have forgotten."
—Keith Haring

Prologue

Queen Elizabeth II: I like chocolate in my tea,
can you say your name to me?

Me: Alex

Chorus: ALEX? Alex! that's a wonderful name!

Queen Elizabeth II: What sort of music do you write Alex?

Alex: Well, for me, my music is kind of like this;

#It's
like minimal but loads more notes like video-games but with more song like jazz but much more gay like gay old music but more current like yummy sweet but more stick like paint but more scratch like tapestry but filthily like prayer but more loud like loud groove and more rude like fingers and faces too but somehow more smelly like smelly things cooking with more chew and change like louder prayers that groove with like stinking-hot-pink in poo-brown but even more desperate-like than that like drums and dream musics, but (don't say butt) you have to listen to it tbh.

#It's
like

Birth of Crocodile, 2000
Water colour on paper 67 x 97 CM
Bhupen Khakhar

Queen Elizabeth II: Oh, how nice for you.

Alex: Sometimes when I read stuff, I like to check out stuff and listen to stuff. So here I am doing quotes and stuff. I also like to look at pictures. I hope that you like it.

"Sat here like an improviser with my hand rambling over the p..."[1]
TROMBONE TROMBONE TROMBONE TROM-
BONE TROMBONE

1. Virginia Woolf.

"Oh dear #it's Mr. Trombone and he's wearing a very silly hat indeed." —Mark Bassey

Mr. Trombone: I think it would be best enjoyed read out loud, in a whole host of silly voices and stuff like that.

The Numbing Vibrancy of Characters in Play
Exhibition of paintings on canvas
by Jadé Fadojutimi

Queen Elizabeth II: What a lovely idea.
Send in the clowns.

[Exit **Alex, Queen Elizabeth II** riding higgledypiggldy-back on **Mr. Trombone**]

ACT I

Like

"Kids make collage, housewives make collage, even if #it's just birthday cards. It is a democratic art." —Wangechi Mutu

[Enter **Joan Rivers**]

Joan Rivers: *(Alex in Drag): "Can we talk? let me tell you something!"*[2]

2. Joan Rivers.

Children at Round: Say the magic words, Shout the magic words. Shake the magic words. Daisies. Milkshake. Sellotape. Boom. Oo. Yatatata. How do you make your hair sip? How do you make your nose drip? How do you make your pet dress up and say "I'm ready!" 'cos #it's so so so so so so so so unfair! I'll be the next one that magic stuff happens to mmm yeah next time you'll see it will happen to be me.......also how do you make your dragon wings? How do you make your pudding sing? How do you make your mummy think you're so so funny? Terry Pratchett went to sea with a trumpet on his knee the only thing that he could see was figuring for letter D. But #it's so so so so so so so unfair. Next time, you'll see it will happen to be me.

A Pudding *(whispering)*: This is my pudding tummy, this is the tummy where I put my pudding when the main course tummy is full.

Chorus: #It's

kind of like words about music

...words for music like "*Ornithology for the birds.*"[3] I try to describe it, like it is in a form/language I only speak functionally, like "I'll be mother" — Mom what's for tea? ("Please put some tea into a pot, don't use a teabag please do not. Boil some water but you ought'(a) make sure #it's seething and scalding and boiling."[4]) sometimes I like 'em like in Neil Luck's work and wordmusic and musictheatre — pass the toast, that's breakfast to you and me, the beginning. "All hail" Bird, thane of no "*more Jay Jay automatons.*"[5] But (don't say butt) sometimes I like when words are best like in like "*YEAH YOU!*" —Elvin Brandhi

3. Gavin Bryars in *Arcana V.*

4. Django Bates.

5. Amiri Baraka (in 1968! *would you believe it*).

#It's

like, words about music are kind of like this:

...like sprawling lines of BraXton rhymes with PaXton (privileged-like rhyme) every note embedded with densely packed intelligence and story grim and wild and freely running triumph of self/Triumph of Time

Birtwistle. Still old. Still good. Harrison's clocks — tick tock Ellicott clock. Tick tock Shelton clock. Two clocks talking: "*And indeed, what they wanted to talk about all along, was the Ocean. Somehow they could not get to the Topik. Neither Clock really knows what it is, — beyond an undeniably rhythmic Being of some sort, — tho' they've spent most of their lives in Range of it, sometimes no more than a Barrel-Stave and a Hull-Plank away. Its Wave-beats have ever been with them, yet can neither quite sat, where upon it they may lie. What they feel is an attraction, more and less resistible, to beat in synchrony with it, regardless of their Pendulum-lengths, or even the divisions of the Day.*" —Thomas Pynchon, Mason and Dixon Henry Holt and Company, 1997, p. 122.

6. Luciano Berio.

#It's

...like **Alex:** *(sings to a tune so beautiful it makes wild "tulips grow in my garden"[6])* Once in the woods, I am safe there,

because nobody cares what I'm wearing there.
they will not dare start staring
at my salamander onesie
and the way I eat flies.

"Art it's supposed to be right in the community, where they can have it when they want it." —Amiri Baraka

Society: Sing this song right in the community 4,000 times a year every year, for seven years as part of your money making behaviour, in return we can give you some electricity and stuff like that.

Children at Round: (ecdeeccdeeeddcdeeeccdeecdeeeddccdedcedc)

Like, my mom's a real big fish
and she lives in the deep blue sea
she sings bubble bubble
she works all day
and then she comes home for tea
to see me ray doh,
like 3, 2, 1

"Ah music, a magic far greater than any we do here." —Albus

7. J.K. Rowling.

Dumbledore[7]

Children at Round: Like let me see your acting what let me see your acting who let me see your acting oh

let me see your acting no down down down in the loud sound-belly of the bird word — you heard

I I I I just wanna be me, C'mon and let me at me, do you get me, and don't pretend that I'm not acting doh ray me fah soh O Bird you shan't eat me.

Chorus: Let me see your acting no let me see your acting no let me see your acting no

let me see your acting no.

Children at Round: Like every time I dance on my hand I know that I'm not acting yeah and when I play in my band I know that I'm not acting how can I make you understand I know that I'm not acting laugh as you and I will laugh too then I know I'm feeling fine just to me I sing in everything I do, yeah

Facebook fake book fat cheque fact check YouTube Chu Chu fake news snooze

like me like me little pizza little pizza little bits of bitter twitter lets make friends

but (don't say butt) but but but but but but but is it really you?

"If you are squeamish, do not prod the beach rubble." —Sappho

Queen Elizabeth II: I love the way you pick your nose, with your tiny slimy toes.

Stay the way you are.

Joyce Grenfell dressed as a nursery school teacher *(**Alex in Drag**)*: *"George…Don't do that."*[8]

8. Joyce Grenfell.

(pause for laughter)

Queen Elizabeth II *(eating like a very hungry caterpillar)*: Let me share a

tip for those who know an urge to splash when one is eating ones "T": If you chew red sloppy food that splurges and splats — Just wear red clothes! and none of it will show. Don't bother wearing white 'cos #it's no good for you. If they see you in that light then say: "no, no, no"[9]. Don't let them get your art replaced by plain exquisite taste
fight the formless face of blank conformity.

9. Amy Winehouse.

[Exit **Queen Elizabeth II** riding higgledysquiggly-back to **Society**]

Children at Round: *(whispering)*: This is my ice-cream tummy, this is the tummy where I put my ice-cream when the pudding tummy is full.

"We're on the eve of the complete fall of western ideas and life values. We're in the process of developing more meaningful values and our music is a direct extension of this." —Anthony Braxton

ACT II

Like this

#It's

Like #Rainbow Story

like **Rhubarb & Custard** *(sing to a tune so beautiful it makes wild men grow tulips)*: Let's paint the town red, let's paint the town blue, let's paint the town orange too, 'cos I say so, let's sing a song now!. Ah, singing low, lullaby, lets make the town here! Smell the air and here is the rain! Feel all at once ah. Yes! do the rounds now. Get the loud sounds. Yes! Let me please do it to you, ah blue! Or orange. O you! Ah my favourite! Rainbow brown. I was promised rainbow brown. Mmm.This is all so long ago. This is all so long ago. This is all so very very very long ago. This is all so very very very very very long ago. Let me name you. Let me paint you. With my own home grown, rainbow brown. A rainbow! 'Cos I say so. All over your face and pallid bod. dob dob dob dob dob dob dob dob dob dob dob dob dob dob. Making, tasting, yeah. I Like it. Mmmm.

#Rainbow Story

like **Addictive Temptation:** No no no no no no no no no no no no no no give it to me now Muffin Muffin Muffin Muffin

"Postmodernism is both academic and popular, élitist and accessible."
—Linda Hutcheon

Muffin Muffin Muffin Muffin double yellow no no double yellow ah, ah, ah. Melty triple-chocolate-muffin dribbles in the fluff. Icky fluff. Sticky stuff. Yum yum yum.

Children at Round: *(whispering)*: This is my chocolate muffin tummy, this is the tummy where i put my chocolate muffin when the ice-cream tummy is full.

Queen Elizabeth II *(regurgitating her food and using her spit, bile and urine to make chrysalis)*: Enough fun?

like a niggling anxiety

Children at Round: *(sung to a tune so beautiful it makes men grow while shitting tulips)*:

You are so old. You are so old. You are so old. You are so old to me. If I live as many years as that.

I would still be much younger than you are. Look! Mozart had achieved so much more, when he was so much younger than you.Yeah. How come this raisin is so old and wrinkly but so much younger than you are? Would you like a raisin? I found one on the car floor.

Enough fun? no no no no no no no no yes no yes no no no no don't touch this yum yum yum yum yum yum yum umm yes you no yum yes you yum yum yum no don't touch this.

10. Samuel Beckett.

like

Winnie ***(Alex in Drag):*** *"Today is going to be another happy day."*[10]
—Winnie from *Happy Days*

#It's

Winnie the Pooh ***(Alex in Drag):*** *"Tut-tut it looks like rain."* —Winnie the

11. A.A. Milne.

Pooh[11]

like a **Lover:** ...umm...well...so what happened was...I left 'm and let the silhouette of cold-kettle and cigarette regret the bowl of alphabetti-spaghetti (microwaved merely for mother and formality) HESITATE before collecting my clear set plastic-bag-pound-shop-polythingummy-jacket, kept for the inevitable onset of precipitation, and ran with it! racing towards my expecting-spectating lover excitedly excreting perspiration. O HOW EXHILARATING not to fret or forget but CELEBRATE the sensual secreting of sweet freshly flesh sweating redolence, that at first lay low kept abated by slow biology yet only delayed by later bacterial changes when you bet once warm inside without warning it leapt and let out a mighty cry of "RAINY RAIN SMELLS!"

Queen Elizabeth II *(rolling up into a ball and waiting for her metamorphosis)*: Enough fun?

#It's like **Children at Round:** It's raining it's pouring the old man is snoring he went to bed and bumped his head and couldn't get up in the morning.

He tried to ignore it before he even saw it but gory bits of red raw brain were staining on the flooring.

He didn't heed the warning from the forming weather.
Ho hum, the rain is raining every bloody day.

I will do a drawing to others as a warning.
Hey ho for the rain is raining every bloody day.

Another Dead Straight Man (talking about sex to an all homophobic society):
"Soft sticky Gum Jelly Lips."[12] —Leopold Bloom

like

12. James Joyce.

Joan Rivers ***(Alex in Drag):*** *You know what it's like to stand up in front of your husband naked and say "what does this remind you of" and he says*

"Pancakes for breakfast."[13]

13. Joan Rivers.

(pause for laughter)

Children at Round *(whispering)*: This is my pancake tummy, this is the tummy where I put my pancakes when the chocolate muffin tummy is full.

#It's
like

My Dear Friend, 1983
Oil paint on canvas 112 x 112 CM
Bhupen Khakhar

Aa-Ah: My imaginary friend was called Alex and eventually we split up, he decided to live with his folks for another eleven years or so and work on his narcissism alone, whilst I went To The Lighthouse.

Lighthouseman: Lonely on the bladder-wrack, standing nobly soused in brine, a shinning foe of night's command, half lighthouse and half-man. Dancing to his droll sarabande, songs time has doused in sand and sad lamenting tears, the only lighthouse man. Mostly, the churning others misunderstand.

Turning his head, he longs for instead, another lighthouse-man. Shimmrin' in the bladder-wrack strands, glistnin' under sea and sand, stands, nearing tearful glee, the other lighthouseman.

"The most inquisitive and curious-minded of that family was called Smeagol. He was interested in roots and beginnings; he dived into deep pools; he burrowed under trees and growing plants; he tunnelled into green mounds; and he ceased to look up at the hill-tops, or the leaves on the trees, or the flowers opening in the air: his head and his eyes were downward."

—Gandalf the Grey[14]

14. John Ronald Reuel Tolkien.

Aa-Ah: Into the bare, dark below, without a stark prayer to show the scars of another who taught me how to sing and holler in the wind. Fleeing the gilded smile of the gloamin', feeling the gloomy cry of night, I said goodbye to my lover who taught me how to sing and holler in the wind. I said goodbye to my mother who listened to me sing and holler in the wind.

#It's

like a niggling anxiety.

Angryman: "*You suck. You're a no talent. If you really had talent go practice and then get yourself a gig instead of ruining the end of the day for everybody down here, you disgrace. You are everything that's gone wrong with this world. You're a self-consumed, no-talent, mediocre piece of shit. And I've earned my right to say it. Ok?*"[15]

15. Douglas Levison on YouTube.

The mushy splurge of organic juice that used to be **Queen Elizabeth II** *(whilst re-arranging her atoms)*: Enough fun?

like **Opera**!

Chorus: Eat me! Eat now.

Eat fruit. Eat flour. Eat flesh. Worship Bell!
Eat! Do obeisance and feed Bell!
[Enter **Daniella**]
Eat it!
Eat it immediately.
Eat twelve bushels of flour.
Eat four or (perhaps) forty sheep.
Eat six measures of oil or (perhaps) wine. Eat sheep. Eat Oil. Eat for the last time. Worship Bell!
Eat! Do obeisance and feed Bell!

Daniella: It never eat or drank anything!

Chorus: O king. You are so angry. See, your face! It is distorting.

King: Aaaaaaaaaarh!

Therefore, arrest the seventy priests of Bel and their wives
and their children
and put them to death!

"Money goes in, opera comes out." —Terry Pratchet

ACT III

I like it

#It's
like the **Children at Round:** Here it comes here it comes along the feeling of the line, Like a kitchen pulling a village behind it.

We are waiting, we'll be waiting our whole lives. We're waiting for Godot and God only knows we've forgotten the reason why. We'll be waiting for the next big thing. Ringadingding. Woo, wooo!

Poo, poo story line we don't need you half the time every time it's time to find the next be event.

Every time it's finally time to find out what happens next I find I'm much too busy. Here it comes here it comes along the feeling of the line, feeling I can fly.

#It's like
the **Children at Round** (*singing in a voice so mawkish it makes ice-cream melt in the freezer)*: When I can fly I'm giving you my scooter and when I have wings my computer's yours so I can concentrate on things that really matter like flying this close the to sun with my song.

#It's like **Hildegard von Willesden Green:** I don't know whether, like, this is a global phenomenon, but (don't say butt) in the UK all children have cleverly evolved scooters under their bio-bodies as a joyful usurper from the traditional leg walking chore that has been tyrannously dominant from darwinian dawn of man right up until 21st century. In Phillip Pullman's excellent Dark Material trilogy an elephant-based humanoid spices called the Mulefa evolve wheels in a symbiotic relationship with a plant producing seedpods. Perhaps it is pleasing to Pullman's obsessive, fetishistic and (ineluctable christian) pre-lapserian portrait of children, that it is *only* the children in our world who wheel freely on scooters like they are free from the tree-of-knowledge-based skill of trudging through life-like life like left right left right right right left.

#It's like **Chorus:** Pray. So we will pray. So we will pray. So we will pray.

We will play as well. We will play as well. We will play as well. We will play as well. And then we're gunna sing. And then we're gunna sing. And then we're gunna sing. And then we're gunna sing. Shout into the Silence! Shout into the Silence! Shout into the Silence! Shout into the Silence!

Sing I am. I am. I am. I pray.

Dragon: Like, when I was about 3 I remember asking some difficult questions like: "Why do baddies exist?" and she kept on saying "when you go to heaven you can ask God all these questions"

#It's

16. *Eraserhead* 1977 film by David Lynch.

like the **Lady in the Radiator:** "*Everything's fine in heaven.*"[16]

So the last two minutes of my *Music for Bosch People* goes like (over a massivefuckoffimproviseddrumsolo):

Alex possessed by the voice of **Johnny Rotten:** In! Hea! Ven! You! Can! Ask! Her! Ques! Tions!

In! Hea! Ven! You! Can! Ask! Her! Ques! Tions!
In! Hea! Ven! You! Can! Ask! Her! Ques! Tions!
In! Hea! Ven! You! Can! Ask! Her! Ques! Tions!
In! Hea! Ven! You! Can! Ask! Her! Ques! Tions!
In! Hea! Ven! You! Can! Ask! Her! Ques! Tions!
In! Hea! Ven! You! Can! Ask! Her! Ques! Tions!

TRANSMORPHICMULTIGENDEREDORGANICSPLODGE of BUTTERFLY-BOTTOM that used to be **Queen Elizabeth II** (whilst metamorphosing into a (**Festering Pile of Shit**)**:** Enough fun?

"*It's supposed to be as essential as a grocery store… that's the only way art can function naturally.*" —Amiri Baraka

He Took Enema Five Times a Day, 1999
Oil on Canvas 107 x 260 CM

Bhupen Khakhar

Another Gay Poet (talking about sex to an old homophobic society): O music!

O great redeemer!
Ineluctable modality of the audible:
At least that if no more, thought through my ears.
Come, thou glorious monarch of sound!

"I'm probably more famous for sitting on the toilet than for anything else that I do." —Frank Zappa

Amidst the clammer of strain and splat on porcelain,
A thousand twangling instruments
Will hum about my ears,
While I,
Relishing delightful religious rite and ribaldry,
Limp the gait of the gelded
And skid (still straining) into the streaky basin.
Splosh! Oh dear. Wipe. Drain. Cadenza. Cadence!
Rejoice! Amen!
Joy. Yes.

"I don't think what you see or feel in the world when you open your eyes for the first time ever leaves you." —Frank Bowling

Alex: Then they drank heartily and sang this verse:

like **Children at Round:** The cows smelt a lot like cows
Just like a lot of cows do
And when they'd stopped smelling like cows

They sang a lot like cows too. Moo moo moo moo moo moo Moo moo moo moo moo Moo moo moo moo moo moo Moo moo moo moo moo

The chickens smelt a lot...
"Chicken Lickin'" —Jozia's (age 5) idea
The T-Rex smelt a lot...

Rarrw rarrw rarrw rarrw rarrw rare
The mother smelt a lot like chocolate...
Love love love love love love

The Sweet Smell of his Hair Oil, 2002
Water colour on paper 72 x 45 CM
Bhupen Khakhar

Alex: Then the children went to the television to pray for stuff. The Television was singing a Christmas number one hit. The song was written by a popular composer.

Children at Round: #It's better to give than to receive. I want to give a pathway to enlightened living. It's is better to believe than to deceive and I believe in giving you the gift of giving so gimme good presents 'cos I've been good. Gimme good presents you know you should. Please! There — I said please! Two or more a gathered so you can hear my prayer. Gimme good presents to show you care! Please! Please, Mummy! Please! Please, Mummy! — I said "please!" Next year I will be good, I will be good, I pwomise. Next year I will be good, I will be good, I pwomise. Next year I will be good, I will be good, I pwomise. Next year I will be good, I will be good, I pwomise. It is better to partake than to perceive. I perceive there is not enough for everybody's greed and so it is obvious that everybody sees who it is that has the greatest need for even more stuff, so gimme good presents 'cos I've been good.

#It's

Joan Rivers (Alex in Drag): like I just did a composition workshop with Tyondai Braxton's *Uffe's Workshop* and the children sang: I love the way you chop the wood I love the way you cut x7 Even though it's really weird x3 we are not lazy!

Children at Round: I love the way you chop the wood I love the way you cut x7 Even though it's really weird x3 we are not lazy!

#It's
like a niggling anxiety.

like **Children at Round:** You are so old. You are so old. You are so old. If I live to see hover cars I will (probably) be still much younger than you are. Look! How come this ugly slug is so old and slimy but so much younger than you are? Would you like an ugly slug?I found one in my pencil-case? **Sara Kane** had achieved so much more, when she was so much younger than you. Yeah! old old very old old oldy oldy old! Oh so very old like dinosaur oldy old old! If I lived my entire life four times over I would still be much younger than you are. Look! How come this farty sock is so old and smelly but so much younger than you are. Would you like a farty sock I found one in your hand bag. Jimi Hendrix had achieved so much more, when he was so much younger than you. Yeah! You are so old! To me. When I am as old as you, I will have made the world a better place to live.

Look! How come this computer is so old and slow but so much younger than you are?Would you like a computer? I found one in my classroom Amy Winehouse had achieved so much more, when she was so much younger than you. Yeah!

These crisps are old but not as old as you are! Ha ha!
My brother is old but not as old as you are! Ha ha!
My phone is old but not as old as you are! Ha ha!

Smell!

Chorus: That smells of fish and dead fish and half-dead fish.

#IT'S LIKE
THE
OCEAN

*[Enter **Leonora Carrington** and her **Niece** hidden in an algorithmic labyrinth)*

Leonora Carrington (oozing malevolence): *You're trying to intellectualise something,*

Niece (cowardly): *I know*

LC (leering): *desperately!*

Niece (ignorantly): *Yeah*

LC (slow and sneering): *and you are wasting your time.*

Niece (naively): *OK I should know by now, shouldn't I.*

LC (losing evil): *too much effort, scrambling for human words): That is not a way of understanding! To make a kind of sort of errr-inter-little mini logic. You will never understand by that road.*[17]

17. Leonora Carrington and her long lost Niece.

Children at Round *(whispering)*: This is my candy tummy, this is the tummy where I put my candy when the pancake tummy is full.

Festering Pile of Shit: Enough fun?

The Q Symphony, 2002
Acrylic on board 92 x 76 CM
Leonora Carrington

ACT IV

Like me! Like me! Like me! Like me! Like me! Like me! Like me!

"One day everything will be as it should be" —Albert Ayler

#It's

#Rainbow story.

Children at Round: Like let's paint he town red, let's paint the town blue, let's paint the town orange too.

OMG wow wow, I don't believe it, oh my days what have you done?

"I often think about the way I see."[18]
Gimme red yellow! Oh.
David Hockney:[19]
#Rainbow story

18. David Hockney.

19. David Hockney.

[Exit **David Hockney**]

"There is no justice, just us." —Terry Pratchett, as quoted by Reni Eddo-Lodge in *Why I'm not talking to white people about race anymore.*

Children at Round: Got somefing in your eye, stop messing up my sky!
Got somefing on your knee, stop messing up my sea!
#Rainbow story.

"They are like complex musical scores from which certain melodies can be teased out and others ignored or suppressed, depending, at least in part, on who is doing the conducting. At this moment, all over the world – and most recently in America – the conductors standing in front of this human orchestra have only the meanest and most banal melodies in mind."
—Zadie Smith

Dogs can't see you when your blue,
they only see in black and white and like other funny smells.

Let's paint, yes let's, let me paint you please let's, let's be sad I'm not sad!
When I am sad I am reminded of how you seem right now.
Rainbow story.

Children at Round: Got somefing in your eye, stop messing up my sky!
Got somefing on your knee, stop messing up my sea!

Funny seas funny skies ha ha ha ha
funny lies funny knees
funny seas things that mean a lot to me.
Rainbow story.

#It's

Joan Rivers *(Alex in Drag)*: like when I just did this workshop on Pauline Oliveros' *Sonic Meditations* and the children said: Ahhhhhhhhhhhhhhhhhhh ahhhhhhhhhhhhhaahhhhhhhhhhhhhAhhhhhhhhhhhhhhhhhh ahhhhh-hhhhhhhhhaaaaahhhhhhhhhhhhh *(etc.)*

Children at Round: Ahhhhhhhhhhhhhhhhhhhahhhhhhhhhhhhh aahhhhhhhhhhhhhhAhhhhhhhhhhhhhhhhhh ahhhhhhhhhhhhhhaaaaah-hhhhhhhhhhhh *(etc.)*

Let's paint, yes let's, let me paint you, please let's, let's be snakes, I'm not a snake!

Snakes can't see you when you're blue
they only see in hot and cold and other cups of tea.
Rainbow story.

"I can't conceive the nucleus of all begins inside a tiny seed..."
—Stevie Wonder

Let's paint, yes let's, let me paint you, please lets, let's be trees, I'm not a tree!

"Trees, it turns out, have a completely different way of communicating: they use scent." —Peter Wohlleben. *The Secret Life of Trees.* Penguin Books Limited.

Trees can't see you when your blue
they only see in wind and rain and other types of song.
#Rainbow story.

"...But who am I to doubt or question the inevitable being,
For these are but a few discoveries
We find inside the Secret Life of Plants." —Stevie Wonder

Lady in the Radiator *(sung to a tune so beautiful it makes grown men shit* *crocodiles while eating tulips): "Brueghel thus outlined everything it was possible to outline; he showed that we must not read into the painting (Carnival Clashes with Lent) a meaning of history, which is precluded by the circularity and shifting interpenetration of the figures; that we must use it instead to listen to music, which creates a ritual order (including human sacrifice), then is represented as a simulacrum of order, finally passes over to the side of Lent and is sold like fish, compulsory nourishment."* —Jacques Attali

Festering Pile of Shit: Enough fun?

Eleven Secrets, 2015
Collage on vinyl. Dimensions: 30½ x 36 IN
Wangechi Mutu

like **Opera!**
Dragon Priestess: Eat me, Eat now,
Eat camel. Eat Cake. Eat pomegranate. Worship the living dragon. Look; he eats and drinks
Do obeisance and feed him.

Daniella: Eat cake.
Eat fat. Eat hair. Eat iron combs. Eat barley cakes. Eat pitch. Eat Flax. Eat nails.
Eat skins of camels filled with hot coals.
Eat it. Eat Cake. Eat it now!

Chorus: Behold! An almighty flatulence. See; the dragon bursts asunder!

*"**Roald Dahl:** Wha...no wizzpopping? None jullifying music?*
***Queen Elizabeth Ii:** Oh, do let him sing if he wants.*
***Sophie:** He doesn't want to sing."* —Roald Dahl, *The BFG*

Sophie: *"clowns shit (up the wall)"*[20]

20. Sophie Xeon.

[Exit all as if propelled by the force of the exploding dragon fart. Like balloons blown up and let go. **Festering Pile of Shit** rides higglldy-piggldy-pop-back on the crest of a wave]

[Enter **Jacob Collier, Little Nell, Rebecca Saunders** and **Sheol the Whale**]

Jacob Collier: *"She walked behind me sir, that I would not know how lame she was."* —Charles Dickens

Old fire side had smiled on that same sweet face." —Charles Dickens

"My face is the front of shop." —**Sophie** Xeon

Little Nell: *"Her little bird, a poor slight thing, the pressure of a finger would have crushed, was stirring nimbly in its cage."* —Charles Dickens Chickens Lickens.

"Yar, yar, yar, yar, yar." —Tricky Sam Nanton

That which used to be **Festering Pile of Shit** before finding redemption in the writing of Donna J. Haraway and becoming ***"Camille Compost Person"*****:** Enough.

#It's like the death of a whalewoman-man-mankind.

Sheol The Whale: There she blows, out of blue sea
On she goes, to flee those who pursue,
as Sheol knows when to slow
and forgo her full-fathomed freedom.

Softly she lows
to the blue sea, who swallows her song
and casts into the deep what is concealed and can not escape into sleep.

She'll steal away, she'll steal away, She'll steal away Sheol.

"Thar she blows" out of blue sea
faster he rows and thrusts into the deep
He only knows what is revealed.

There flows her full fathomed freedom

He'll steal away, He'll steal away, He'll steal away
He will slay Sheol.

#death #manmadeclimatechange #whalehunting #animalintelaggence #abuse #immortality #BookofJonah #religion #conquering #archiacleviathan #mobydick #callme #metoo #stewardoftheearth #heterosexuals #assonance #fuckthepatriarchy #songofthehumpbackwhaleII

"Little rabbit Foo-foo, running through the forest, scooping up the mushrooms and bobbing them on the head. bop bop bop bop bop bop bop."
—Micheal Rosen

"My face is the real shop front." —**Sophie** Xeon

Children at Round: So goodbye whale. You must go
out to sea,
into the blue where you belong.
Oh actually whale,
before you go
out to sea,
we must ask you…
We must ask you to show us the way of the whale song.

Chorus: Flashes of lightning are snorting out of her nose. From the might of her thrashing tale, boiling hot water flows. And low she breaches, throws up her mega monster belly and reaches, flipper first, to the sky…

Rebecca Saunders: *(spoken as fast as possible)* Like, *"for me, what's really important is enabling the listener to feel the magical physicality of sound, the timbre, the colour, the mass, the weight, of sound."*[21]

21. Rebecca Saunders.

Children at Round: …Then SMACK! Oooo! She flips a mega monster belly flop back on to the broken ocean skin(nn) below. SMELL!
That smells of fish and dead fish and half-dead fish.
That smells of weed fish and sea weed and fish wee.

That tastes of sandfish and fishy sand and just sand.

Camille Compost Person[22]: Enough poo.

22. Donna J. Haraway.

"My shop is the face I front." —**Sophie**

#It's like

Le Libre Développement De La Tete
pigments and acrylic on chain canvas 92 x 65 CM
Ody Saban

"**Carl** *kisses him.*
He makes love to **Rod**

Rod: I will always love you.
I will never lie to you
I will never betray you.
On my life.
(They both come.)

Tinker: You or him, Rod, what's it to be?

Rod: Me. Not Carl. Me.
Tinker *Cuts* ***Rod's*** *throat.*
Carl *struggles to get* ***Rod****. He is held.*

Rod: It can't be this.
(he dies)

TINKER: Burn him."
—Sarah Kane, *Cleansed, Complete Plays* p. 142. by Methuen Publishing, 2001

like **Windmill Woman:** Out in the air I go adorning where I know so well the old scorning spite Of cold morning light out in the air alone I rode into the forming night and called as she drew near smoke upon my breath and in my eye I saw the stormy pearls of fright beneath her angry tears and I awoke still bereft of her goodbye.

#It's like

"Now we must learn to judge a society by its sounds." —Jacques Attali

Like **Joan Rivers** ***(Alex in Drag)*:** Like when I just did this workshop on the opening of Stravinsky's *Rite of Spring* and how the children sang: "I want a Sainsbury's pizza now, give it to me-ee please." —Hetty's idea (age 8).

Children at Round: I want a Sainsbury's pizza now, give it to me-ee please

"I'm real when I shop my face." —**Sophie** Xeon

like **Opera**!
"Fuck opera. Fuck that shit." —***Alex***

Chorus: Eat, eat, eat, eat flesh. Eat the Adam. Eat red clay.

Daniella: Eat Daniel.
Eat me. Eat now.

Chorus: Eat Daniella. Eat flesh.

Children at Round: *(whispering)*: This is my vegetable tummy, it's very very small and not very much can fit in it at all.

Angel: Eat Daniella.
Eat, O Eat Daniella. Eat, Eat, Eat.
Eat the yummy stew the angel has sent you.
[**Daniel** shares the casserole with the **Chorus** (the lions), who no longer want to eat **Daniel**.]

Angel: Eat cake. Eat pomegranates. Eat mana. Eat fruit. Eat flour. Eat mixed wine.
Eat Casserole.
Eat for the last time.
Eat grass like an oxen. Eat nothing at all.

*[Chorus, **King** and **Daniella** creep up behind **Angel**]*

Tutti: Eat men. Eat women. Eat children See; they are devoured immediately!

Rebecca Saunders: *"I still eat Marmite and watch Sherlock."*[23]

23. Rebecca Saunders.

Children at Round: I love music. Munchy *munch* chew chew chew gulp *spittle* teeth graunch grind chop smack smile *blood love* and laugh; the language of mastication that binds the offal of man-kind into a faggot, regardless of epoch religion and race.

"Art allows you to imbue the truth with a sort of magic." —Wangechi Mutu

Children at Round: Love food, love music, love.

Joy. Yes. Yum. Mmmmmusic "is your own experience, your thoughts, your wisdom. If you don't live it, it won't come out of your horn." —Charlie Parker

Compost: Poo poo poo poo poo poo
RuPaul: *"Sashey away."*[24]

24. RuPaul Andre Charles.

"The Children of Compost insist that we need to write stories and live lives for flourishing and for abundance, especially in the teeth of rampaging destruction and impoverization." —Donna Haraway, *Staying with the Trouble*, Duke University Press, 2016

CHAPTER 29

VOICES IN THE SKIN

ALEXANDRIA SMITH

Sitting in darkness, I plug in and pull on my second skin, feeling it mold to the curves of my body and ignite its circuitry. I become a nexus of visual and sonic intensity; not an object of external gaze, but a powerful bioluminescent creature. The reptilian-like scales start to reflect the low levels of light that are still left, distributing them throughout the room. I place two galvanic skin response electrodes in series on my shoulder, secure the pulse sensor to my chest, and buckle the belt of the respiration sensor. Once I open my DAW and start getting signal; the transformation is complete. A familiar space becomes another universe. My interior readings become my epidermis. With each breath I take, low sub tones sound, vibrating in my chest. The rhythm of my pulse generates glitchy translations of trumpet sound. Paranormal utterances crawl out of the speakers and echo throughout space as they meet my skin and ears.

* * *

Over the past five years, I have built a bioartistic practice cultivated at the intersection of my foundation as a classically trained performer with my experience as a technologist, audio engineer, and researcher. In order to explore this interdisciplinary terrain, I have built an apparatus that integrates my diverse experience and interests; a second skin. With fabrics, elastics, clasps, LEDs, sensors, and my inner electricity, I constructed a wearable electronic that measures the discrete electric and resistive properties of three of my organs: my heart, my lungs, and skin. It translates their functioning into data streams that can be fed into audio and visual software that I have designed in open source environments. My interoceptive, proprioceptive, and exteroceptive processes have become part of a complex feedback loop.

This is a system for autonomous, empowered, embodied collaboration and the extension of one's instrument, not a means for achievement, domination, or control. I seek to explore ways in which biological data can aid in the feedback between my unconscious and conscious mind during performance, and perform with the voices inside my skin.

Layers

I remember my first experience ripping apart electronics; seeing the guts of a VCR when I was six years old. My mom spent the weekends fixing broken VCRs and televisions to sell at *Happy's* (the local flea market) in order to make extra money on the weekends while she completed hair school. When I wasn't running around in the woods surrounding the workspace with my brother, I watched her tinker around until the electronics *finally* worked. *Men in Black* (1997), her test video cassette, would start playing on the TV accompanied by a sigh of relief.

There were wires and belts, things that turned, lit up, and rattled, solder joints that became cold, and motors that got too hot. The intricacies of their many moving parts undoubtably played a role in getting them thrown to the curb, but they also made this machine incredibly interesting to me. I wondered if everyone knew how complicated something that seemed so simple on the outside was on the inside.

Tinkering has always been a part of me. It is how I have approached everything since I was a kid. When something didn't work, I tried every angle, version, corner, etc. until it did. Asking for help was not an option. This was also how I approached learning the trumpet until I started my conservatory training in New York City. It didn't matter how difficult a piece of music was, I heard the sound that I wanted to make in my head and tinkered around on the instrument until I *made* it happen. Tunnel vision gave me the virtuoso chops that I needed in order to move from southern Virginia and get a scholarship to go to Mannes the New School for Music.

Living in New York City was an incredible experience and education. There was art everywhere, all the time. I fell in love with many different types of music and wanted to play everything that I was hearing. However, I was training to become an orchestral trumpet player at the time which forced me to limit the ways in which I could tinker with sound. Much like fixing a VCR, my western classical training often required me to rip apart a technique that was considered "broken," and rebuild it into something that would fit within in "the box."

While I was rebuilding my orchestral trumpet technique, I started to make electronic music. In the beginning, I kept this practice separate from my trumpet playing; it was my escape after all! Hours and days were spent shaping the sounds of software instruments and layering them on top of each other to create complex, hybrid instruments and sonorities that didn't need to fit a specific paradigm. I would take what I was hearing in digital space and apply it to my experimentations with miking and amplifying acoustic instruments. My experimentations with electronic music and recording gave me the desire to approach the trumpet in this way. Instead of performing on the trumpet as a purely acoustic instrument, electronics would begin to form as a hybrid extension.

* * *

The layers between "acoustic" and "electronic" become blurred during the process of recording an acoustic instrument: a microphone takes the input of an "acoustic" sound (air pressure) and converts it into an electrical signal. Kinetic energy transforms into an electrical current that preserves or amplifies the fleeting phenomenon of sound. When the preserved signal is processed further in a Digital Audio Workstation (DAW)[1], the translated acoustic signal goes through another electrical conversion. What results is a hybrid, cyborg-like extension of the sound object. Digital and acoustic artifacts merge to create a sound that cannot exist without the other.

1. e.g. Ableton, Max MSP, Pure Data, etc.

The depth of a sound object, purely electric, acoustic, or a combination of both, cannot be separated from the context and history of its creation. This argument is further illustrated by Eve Kosofsky Sedgwick's unpacking of Renu Bora's theory of texxture. In music, texture is a cross-modal mapping of timbre, layers, harmonies, intensities, nuances, etc. that evoke the intricate tactile surfaces of the sound object that are present at the time of conception and reception. It doesn't necessarily *have* to be tied to its means of production. Texxture as delineated by Sedgwick is "the kind of texture that is dense with offered information about how, substantively, historically, materially, it came into being."[2] She further described this by evoking the image of a brick and a metalwork pot that "still bears the scars and uneven sheen of its making.[3]" Texxture is not a only a sonic attribute, but another critical

2. Sedgwick, Eve Kosofsky, and Adam Frank. 2003. *Touching feeling: affect, pedagogy, performativity.* Durham: Duke University Press. 14

3. ibid.

layer of meaning that will always remain attached to a sound object. It is a term that sets in motion music's affective qualities.

Close miking is one that texxture is put into dialog with music. One can envelop themselves into the timbral and intimate sonic complexities that are formed by the intricacies of sound production. Texxtures are artifacts that are crucial to the creation of the textural object, i.e., the music. However, these are often left unheard by the audience or the performer unless they make a conscious decision to have those sounds be a part of their sonic vocabulary. Texxture evokes the layers between the biological process of making and conceptualizing sound into analog and digital information. It becomes verbal as it brings the present, past, and future all to the same place at the same time.

In order to amplify this concept, I needed to build an environment where I could put my conscious mind in dialog with the muscle activity (motor memory) that was needed in order to play the trumpet, e.g., respiration, heart rate, flexion, etc., and make music with it. During the summer of 2015, I bought an Arduino starter kit and started to learn the basics of physical computing and C programming by watching hours of videos and reading through many forums. In the fall of that year, I started taking course work in the Design and Technology program at Parsons to further prototype this work. Over the next few years, I built my own audio and visual applications that responded to my pulse, arm and finger movement, and respiration. In these first experiments, these sensors were primarily being used as a controller, and that started to feel gimmicky to me. I was only scratching the surface potential of this data, and needed to further understand what these voltages were telling me. I have begun to explore ways in which biological data can be ethically observed and/or interfaced with in performance. How this data and musical expression can teach us about our conscious and unconscious mind.

Biofeedback

Biofeedback as defined by Dr. Barbara B. Brown is the "feedback of biological information to the person whose biology it is.[4]" It is a decentralized medical practice where the practitioner and the patient actively work together to bridge psychological and physiological sensations in real-time with the assistance of sensor data. This

4. Brown, Barbara B. 1974. *New mind, new body: bio-feedback: new directions for the mind*. New York: Harper & Row.

data isn't derived from a single reading like the one that you get when you get your blood pressure taken at the doctor's office, but rather a continuous reading of internal states. The healing starts to happen when the patient and practitioner formulate a training plan that gets repeated as a result of the acquired data and emotional reactions. In other words, biofeedback makes internal and the external bodily processes visible and audible to one's self.

Biofeedback is an interdisciplinary field, its discovery is rooted in a combination of psychic, biologic, social, humanistic, cybernetic, and physiological forces.[5] While it is primarily used as a tool for self-regulation and/or enhancement, it has also been used for strategic military operations, artistic applications, and to shed light on certain disabilities, e.g., epilepsy, PTSD, deafness, etc. Critical amounts of institutional funding aided in the growing awareness of biofeedback research after World War II. The United States Department of Defense (DOD) and Department of Veterans Affairs (VA) sought alternative treatments that would enhance a soldier's performance in battle and aid in the transition back to civilian life. Alvin Lucier's *Music for Solo Performer* (1965), one of the first pieces of music to incorporate EEG sensing, formed out of a collaboration with Edmond Dewan, a physicist at the Hanscom Air Force Base in Bedford, Massachusetts, who researched ways in which people can be taught to control their own alpha rhythms (brain waves) voluntarily.

5. ibid. 19

In the 1960s and early 1970s, many actors involved in establishing the field of biofeedback were shaped by the sociocultural movement that is sometimes referred to as the "new sensibility." It was deemed "the folk art of an electronic culture" by practitioner, Dorelle Markley Heisel; large bodies of research that addressed this practice started to emerge and converge through the late 1960s. The term, "biofeedback," was formed by an interdisciplinary group of EEG researchers: Joe Kamiya, Barry Sterman, Thomas Mulholland, and Barbara B. Brown. This group of researchers formed the Biofeedback Research Society (BRS) in 1969. In the early 1970s, it gained traction and society in the medical field and popular culture.

* * *

It is through the lens of Dr. Barbara B. Brown's research that I became excited about biofeedback. She presents considerable scientific evidence that supports the realizations I was having while performing with people that I feel a deep connection with and/or getting into a flow state. In her book, *New Mind, New Body* (1974), Brown unpacks the various aspects of biofeedback research, including involuntary and voluntary muscle control, the gap between our unconscious and conscious minds, reading sensor data to determine what it means, and so much more. Perhaps most importantly, I learned that an enormous depth of emotional intensity can be read and voiced from the surface of our skin. Even though the skin is our body's largest organ, it is the most mysterious and misunderstood.

Unlike respiration and heart rate, sensing skin conductance is less about measuring the timing or activity of a discrete organ, and more about detecting everything that is being communicated at the surface of our bodies by our autonomic nervous system.[6] Brown refers to the skin as our "emotional speaker,"[7] and illustrates the many coordinates of emotions and thoughts that are expressed by our skin that don't register with our conscious minds. She writes:

6. ibid. 108–109

7. ibid. 55

> "Emotional judgements expressed by the skin and those expressed by words are often at great odds. And more often than not the voicing of the skin cut through convoluted language and the pressures of consciousness with a remarkable accuracy about the nature of reality. Has man been so inordinately proud of his conscious mind that he has abnegated the beauties and extraordinary abilities of the subconscious? Is it possible that the genuine evolution of mind has taken place below the level of a consciousness busy with applying socially created brakes to the natural development of the psyche?[8]"

8. ibid. 88

The voices of the skin, according to Dr. Brown, can be considered the window into our unconscious.

These are a few of the questions that I am currently engaging with in my research: (1) Might our electrodermal activity (EDA) communicate things beyond our conscious understanding with other musicians (i.e., vibe and/or auras)? If so, make can I make sense of this and use it artistically? (2) If we understand skin conductance, can we communicate specific affective states? (3) How does the latency between our conscious and unconscious influence our musical choices? Is it important to understand and articulate the language of "skin talk," or should it perhaps remain somewhat mysterious? I built my second skin in order to put texxture, my biological signals (how they relate to my conscious and unconscious mind), and artistic expression onto the same plane, to explore how these processes are articulated and distributed.

My Second Skin

My design is a fluid interface, meaning that it continues to change over time as I continue to ask myself the following questions: (1) which methods of sensing would reveal interesting states while performing? (2) what considerations enable me to use them for liberation and self-observation, not a means for control? (3) how to make it affordable enough to build different variations for other artists that could potentially incorporate different methods of sensing? (4) what are some ways in which I can make a departure from the"usual" control/DAW relationship, i.e., let the sensors have their own way of connecting with sound instead of treating them like buttons, potentiometers, faders, etc.?

* * *

There are currently three different sensors located on my second skin which measure the following: respiration, pulse, and galvanic skin response. It is possible to add other methods of sensing; however, I am finding these three to be the most immediate interlocutors between my biological data and the sonic activities beneath the threshold of the unconscious. Embracing the DIY nature of this project, I work with what I have: my body, my curiosity, my lived experience, my sound, and some basic electronics.

After experimenting with pre-constructed clothing, I taught myself to design, sew, and tailor close fitting elastic material garments that can support circuits sewn in and completed with stainless steel conductive thread and insulated wire. Canvas and jersey are tough and relatively easy to sew on, so they were the first materials that I tried. Canvas, a fabric with a tight weave, was able to hold circuits well; however, it couldn't stretch with me. Jersey/t-shirt fabric would stretch with me too much, and couldn't hold the weight of the material. It didn't feel enough like skin. After many attempts at constructing the garment, I have found that polyester/spandex blend performance fabric and high performance athletic mesh functionally catalyzes my metamorphosis. It has a thick stretchy feel that maintains a smooth, reptilian-like texture.

Located on its epidermis is a mosaic of scales that are formed from shattered CDs[9]. Nested within these scales are eight RGB LED's that give a visual narrative of my embodied states; they pulse, flicker, and intensify based on the data that is being fed to them. They can also be turned off and not used at all. Three LEDs are connected to the respiration sensor, three are connected to the galvanic skin response sensor, and two are connected to the pulse sensor. The lacquer-coated aluminum on the underside of the compact discs disperse the light in multiple layers and dimensions of complexity. The color of the LEDs can be changed by moving the connected potentiometers. They change colors in ways that can adapt with my environment and musical ideas.

9. I originally wanted to make it out of glass but decided that was too dangerous.

The respiration sensor is located at the bottom of the wearable, under my ribcage. Built with the circuitry of a voltage divider, readings vary between gooey, viscous, erratic, intense, and expansive textures, decreasing in voltage as it stretches with my breath. The pulse sensor is placed under the wearable onto my chest. It measures inter-beat intervals (IBI)[10], which often result in jagged, rhythmic translations of these voltages. Galvanic Skin Response (GSR) readings are taken from two electrodes that are placed in series on my right shoulder. The readings are quite complex and can be as difficult to describe with written language as the unconscious itself.

10. The measurement time between successive moments of instantaneous heartbeat.

The sensors transform voltage readings that come from my body into discrete analog signals that get parsed into audio and visual applications. The data is read by an Arduino, an open-source microcontroller that I program using the C programing language, and can be sent to software such as Ableton Live/Max for Live, Max MSP, Pure Data (Pd), OpenFrameworks, projecting mapping software, etc. via a direct serial connection, serial to MIDI bridge, and open sound control (OSC). All of the data streams collected by the discrete sensing look, feel, and sound very different. For example, if you mapped each sensor to the same reverb, the output would vary in pace, smoothness, fluctuation, color, etc.

Working with these radically different readings has made it necessary to make a departure from the more common control methods that some DAWs favor, e.g., buttons, faders, potentiometers, etc. I have found that in order to make that departure, I must design my own instruments and effects. In other words, there aren't many pre-made software instruments or effects that translate well. For the best sounding results, it has been crucial to map these streams in ways that compliment their output(s). For example, mapping galvanic skin response (GSR) to reverb, delays, etc. is incompatible, often resulting in "clicks." However, these readings can be mapped to become an incredibly interesting sounding gate, a method to drive granular synthesis, and an operator of percussive MIDI instruments.

Bio-luminescence

I perform in complete darkness. A cave-like atmosphere. I slip on my second skin and feel it mold to my body. Even though we aren't alone, it feels very intimate. We start breathing together; my metamorphosis begins. A state of illusory anonymity is induced.

The symbiotic relationship between my exterior and interior readings are superimposed with the grain of my sound. The texxture of my biological data becomes my collaborator. We enter a sensual space where there are no barriers or filters left; our voices are coming through my skin. My inner circuitry becomes the fabric in which these are woven into, my emotional and physiological speaker. They enter a sonic space when my software instruments, processed trumpet timbre, and the intensities of my emotional world collide.

Every time I make music with my unconscious, I am performing with someone that seems familiar, but have never met before. It has taught me to not only listen with my ears, but also with my skin and everything that it conceals. Making music like this is vulnerable and can be unpredictable. Sonic complexity sits within the multi-dimensional registers that lie beneath the threshold of the conscious mind. Even though we both produce sound in a way that the other cannot and have our own musical language; we are not completely independent of each other. Instead of grasping for control, I dance with my unconscious and embrace the inevitable limits of autonomy. This practice is an acknowledgment of the multiplicity of my being, and the complexity of liberation.

Conclusion

My bioartistic practice is a texxtural means of expression that combines my interdisciplinary research in technology, recording, electronic music, biofeedback, and performing. It is an extension of my practice as a musician: improviser, trumpet player, multi-media artist, and researcher. Due to the fluid nature of this research, I will continue to evolve and expand up these ideas as I build wearable electronics for other people and perform in my second skin.

my bioartistic is:

non-hierarchal * layered * feminist * autonomous * personal * liberating * voluntary * conscious * felt *involuntary * practice-based research * embodied * healing * unconscious * aesthetic * anxious * dedicated * dangerous * conductive * improvised * powerful * rhythmic * biological * woven * vulnerable * crass * cinematic * collaborative * texxtured * athletic * silent * dissonant * cold * sensual * alien * ugly * honest * distant * out-of-control * depressed * wet * freakish * lavish * consonant * expansive * punk * embedded * surprising * fabric * beautiful * hot * mundane * altered * bold * soft * complex * hard * related * brave * old * splintery * unpredictable * textured * evanescent * abrasive * invisible * close * analog * digital * parched * full * scared * broken * shattered * fused * sheer * joyful * disembodied * mammal * reptilian * stretchy * meditative * virtuosic * hyper materialized * rambunctious * young * velvety * looped * energetic * tired * dry * saturated *mysterious * shimmery * natural * conditioned * continuous * unstable * interdisciplinary * sonic * visual * scientific * viscous * measured * distributed * open-source * disrupted * visible * human * resistant * ingrained * custom * in-conversation * thick * gentle * over-flowing * timbral * elastic * pivoting * growing

My bioartistic practice is not:

a means with which to surveil, dominate, or control data from the body to achieve someone else's goal or vision.

References

Brown, Barbara B. 1974. *New Mind, New Body: Bio-Feedback: New Directions for the Mind.* New York: Harper & Row.

Sedgwick, Eve Kosofsky, and Adam Frank. 2003. *Touching Feeling: Affect, Pedagogy, Performativity.* Durham: Duke University Press.

CHAPTER
30

YOU LOOK LIKE YOU WANT TO FLY

Harmonic Motion, Rhythm, and Form in the Music of Kerri Chandler's "Reel-to-Reel Session" and Brahms's "Violin Sonata No. 1 in G Major, Op. 78"

CONRAD TAO

I spent my first hours of 2020 dancing to a 10-hour DJ set of house and techno in Brooklyn. Since then, I've been listening to a lot of dance music and unpacking a deep connection I feel between this and the sensation of playing Brahms at the piano.

In particular, I've been listening to one set by house pioneer and virtuoso Kerri Chandler. Performed live on reel-to-reel tape machines and recorded for Resident Advisor's YouTube channel[1], the set runs a total of seventy-three minutes. Examining the way harmony works and changes across this set, across its large, symphonic timescale, has been very musically rewarding, and I think it offers something interesting to those of us who engage with older tonal classical music.

1. https://www.youtube.com/watch?v=YC7Mw8RjlXM

House music shares similar logics of tension and release found in classical functional harmony, but operates at a much slower pace. To fully appreciate the structure, you have to be *with* the music. Not just identifying what it is, but living with it in the body, being a part of the doing. This is music that privileges active participation. As you dance with it, the harmony might be heard and felt as corporeal, as a total musical body that you can engage with, that you can embody yourself if you let it in, changing with and in it over time.

At a party, the crowd is an active contributor to the energy of a set. As a pianist, I know this to also be true in the concert hall.

* * *

Chandler's set begins in harmonic stasis. A spoken prologue precedes two opening tracks in which phrasing manifests at the level of register — both pitch and frequency. The first music heard is a G minor chord, rhythmically looping in a recursive cycle one dotted quarter note long, while a hi-hat loop one half note in length clicks away up top.

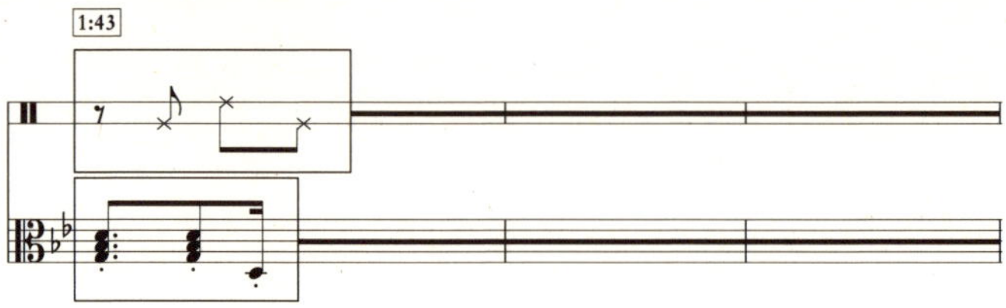

Photon Inc's *Generate Power (Jimpster Dub)* does not ever move away from this one chord. The central G minor is instead enhanced, added to, other layers contributing glimmers to the sound as the track develops. Most layers, including chords and vocal samples, register as single percussive impacts, locking into the groove. The bassline, when it arrives, bounces along at one note per beat, landing on — or is it propelled by? — a low D at the start of each bar, orienting the total harmony in second inversion.

This continues for a few minutes, until the bassline starts to expand with new pops of a low C, syncopated, adding a strut to the music's step. This is the start of Quell's *Real People*, which Chandler brings in subtly at first, briefly forming a compound melody as the basslines intersect.

At 5:04 comes a decisive break: a perfect fourth between G and C in the music's middle-high register that pulls the ear in a new direction. The G minor implication palpably lifts. A vocal sample, the first extending beyond initial percussive impact, warbles away, soaked in delay and reverb, beginning on a sustained G and eventually spilling out before it collapses into babbles. Now we are circling C minor, the implication further strengthened once an E♭ is introduced to the bassline at 6:58.

Real People is also harmonically static, but its positioning immediately after an extended G minor start gives it an expectant character. We might hear its C minor implication as the iv chord to the G root of *Generate Power*, or perhaps it's the other way around, the opening G minor retroactively cast as the v of C.

At 7:22, as the vocal sample sounds again, new pads enter, and for 8 bars, it seems as though we might be in for more of the same — these pads circle around a single A♭ minor seventh chord, looping at a 1-bar rate. But the motion is noticeably more active, carrying new cadential implication, and the chords produce a chromatic interaction with the G-C fourth still held over from *Real People*.

At this point, the music opens up. A synth sounds on a B♭ right in the middle of that aforementioned fourth, sliding up two octaves over the course of a single bar, bringing us up to the highest pitch heard yet and sustaining three more bars before looping back down, dropping two octaves again, continuing in 4-bar intervals. The chord progression expands, the initial obsessive motion towards A♭ minor now supplemented by a subsequent curling into A♭ Major, which is the first time we hear a chord cycle extend across two bars. When the 2-bar and 4-bar cycles are combined, the effect is polyphonic. The anticipatory tension, having already been built gradually by two single-chord tracks, increases exponentially, as though concentrating. Chandler mixes the bassline of *Real People* out of earshot; by the time the beat drops out for four bars, it is clear that we are listening for the imminent arrival of something.

That something is given, at 8:07, when the massive bassline of Demuir's *Philippine Sunrise* triumphantly arrives, bringing the beat back in with it. The rate of harmonic motion palpably kicks up a notch, key implications rotating rapidly, prismatically, twice a bar for a 2-bar loop. Below the pads' slide back and forth between A♭ minor and Major, rising broken chords strut in F Phrygian, over and over again, sometimes breaking their own rules and popping out of their self-imposed frame, cheekily and confidently reminding you they can.

This lets us hear the first three tracks together in a ii-V-i formation, G and C minor in relation to an F root, which the bassline cycles forward and up from, in contrapuntal interaction with the pads above it that first guided us into the track. We can think of its parallel harmony, this motion — perpetually rising, chromatically generating its own staying power, its own momentum — as a bodily, dancing phrasing.

* * *

I am reminded of the piano part of the last movement of Brahms's *Violin Sonata No. 1 in G Major, Op. 78*. Playing this movement feels like articulating a tunnel, the right hand mapping out a perpetually shifting intervallic space with which the music articulates itself, and within which subjectivities may speak. This dimensionality is opened by strategic rhythmic flattening; Brahms imposes a rigid sixteenth-note grid over the pianist's right hand. Within that grid he establishes a basic rule: the right hand plays shifting broken dyads, always from lower note to higher. The totality of the harmony is sounded between and across the notes.

The consequential phrasal layer of the right hand, then, is felt more than it is heard, or, more precisely, is only hearable, feelable across time.

* * *

Dancing along to harmonic stasis carries its own particular intensity. A track with only one chord usually articulates its composition across other dimensions: the entrance and exit of hi-hats up top, occasional moments of breath when the kick drum drops out, changing rhythmic patterns orchestrated within and across the unchanging harmony. You can feel the music shifting and changing, inviting you to move, while the chord keeps you rooted in the same place, producing a kind of corporeal polyphony.

After two opening tracks comprising single chords sustained in blocks, the sensation of a multi-bar *phrase* of chords given when Chandler drops *Philippine Sunrise* is powerfully freeing and opens up a heretofore unheard horizontal possibility.

With this arrival, Chandler suggests that harmonic motion is a parameter to observe over time, a phrasal layer within which to listen for change and expression. What is needed is attention to *feeling*: how it feels for a given chord to hit the body; how it feels to move through harmonic space *between* each individual chord or simultaneity; how it feels for that movement-between to then loop around and be made into its own recursive unit, which is then constituted as a foundational building block for the surrounding track and set; how it feels for that unit to evolve across the longer duration.

* * *

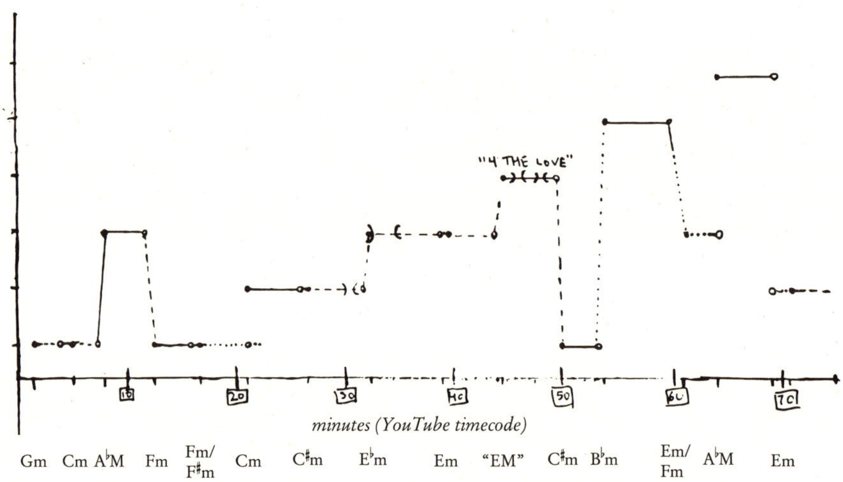

Figure 1. Rate of harmonic motion across Kerri Chandler's *Reel-to-Reel Session* for Resident Advisor (2020).

01:25 Photon Inc: *Generate Power (Jimpster Dub)*/
Kerri Chandler & Louie Vega: *Back to the Raw* (acapella)
05:03 Quell: *Real People*
08:07 Demuir: *Philippine Sunrise*
12:33 Tommy Bones: *South Africa Deep*
16:42 Dennis Ferrer: *Underground Is My Home*
21:04 Roland Clark: *Resist (Southern Divide Weekend Remix)*
26:31 Kerri Chandler: *So Let the Wind Come (Special Edit)*

32:30 Kerri Chandler: *Bar A Thym*/
Loleatta Holoway: *Love Sensation* (acapella)
39:00 Simbad feat. Steelo: *Soul Fever (Kerri Chandler Mix)*
44:00 Karizma/DJ Spen: *4 The Love*
49:39 Black Rascals: *Blaze Theme Track*
53:46 Urban Blues Project present Michael Procter:
Deliver Me (UBP Vocal Mix)
1:00:47 Louie Vega & The Martinez Brothers: *Let It Go (TMBLV Extended Dub)*
1:04:09 Mass Syndicate feat. Su Su Bobien: *You Don't Know (M.A.S. Collective Gospel Club)*
1:09:05 Kerri Chandler: *Track One*/Mustafa feat. Natalia:
Circles (acapella)

Figure 1 is a visual representation of how the rate of harmonic motion evolves across Chandler's set, with the *x*-axis representing chronological time and the *y*-axis representing six distinct rates of motion: static, 1-bar cycle, 2-bar cycle, 4-bar cycle, and finally, verse-chorus structures with two or three distinct cycles within them. Points with a closed circle mark the beginning of a new track; open circles mark the beginning of a transition. Continuous lines designate tracks with contrapuntal motion, dashed lines parallel motion, and dotted lines tracks with notably dissonant, possibly bitonal interactions (a rich capacity that I do not touch on in this essay, as it deserves its own full study.) Parentheses surround sustained moments where the beat drops out, a key indicator of large formal moments of breath. Underneath this graph, along the same *x*-axis, I've also laid out the key centers of each track.

Looking at this macro scale, we can observe that after his initial introduction of harmonic motion at 8:08 with *Philippine Sunrise*, Chandler embarks on a larger climb through harmonic-temporal space, during which chord cycles gradually lengthen for nearly forty minutes. This climb proceeds in pairs of tracks, first with a return to harmonic stasis, then with moving cycles lengthening methodically from *Resist* onwards. Within these pairs are inter-track semitone relationships between keys, marked by the following:

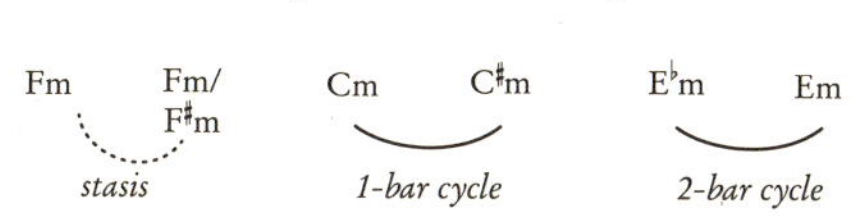

This gradual lengthening of chord cycles helps the music generate new expectations and gives it the capacity to upend its own precedents. Over the course of these forty minutes, the form is constantly opening up, the harmony discovering new temporal space to spill over into, to move in.

We can also speculate on the changing *type* of harmonic motion in the set. *Philippine Sunrise* and *Resist*, the first two tracks with active chord cycles, both move contrapuntally. But Chandler follows *Resist* with twenty minutes of parallel chords; although the contrast between contrapuntal and parallel motion is less extreme than that between stasis and motion, they still feel markedly different.

Tracks like Chandler's own *Bar A Thym*[2] illustrate the approach: choose the right melody, with just the right flattened scale degrees, and layer minor ninth chords — probably the most iconic chord in house music — over, around, or below every note of it, for maximum chromatic, prismatic effect.

2. 32:30.

Bar A Thym uses the majority of its cycle's 2-bar duration to travel to i; by comparison, the *Soul Fever* remix reaches its E minor tonic early, at an ostensibly stable halfway point in the cycle, landing on the downbeat of its second bar. But it stutters on that Em9, as though skidding from its excess momentum, four rapid flickers, the last one providing relief, opening up the window for the cycle to wriggle back to its starting Am9. Its parallel chords use the cadential logic of an imperative "return to i" to generate the cycle's momentum, which then needs freedom from the seeming stability of the tonic.

The chord cycles of *Bar A Thym* and Chandler's remix of *Soul Fever* both ultimately make use of all twelve pitches in the chromatic scale. When Chandler begins mixing the latter track in, blending the two cycles together at around 39:00, the cumulative harmonic effect is dizzying, E♭ minor and E minor key implications overlapping and colliding.

All the better then to make the eventual reintroduction of contrapuntal voice-leading really snap, so that when it arrives we will be made to revel in the sensation, the capacity for contrapuntal harmony to create a *need* for the return to i, voices wrapping around one another towards completion.

Except that isn't what happens, at least not immediately. Karizma and DJ Spen's *4 The Love*, arriving forty-four minutes in, about two-thirds of the way through the set, *does* reintroduce contrapuntal harmonic motion after twenty minutes of parallelisms. It also continues the methodical lengthening of chord cycles Chandler has previously established, with a cycle four bars long, the longest yet. Its harmonic rhythm draws attention to this length: three bars comprise a single, sustained Bm11 chord, followed by a final turnaround bar with rapid, chromatic, contrapuntal changes on each beat, the last of which is that very same Bm11, tied over, pulling us into the next 4-bar loop. Stasis and motion are put in direct contrast with one another, to lyrical effect.

Theoretically, this should feel like an enormous arrival, which it does, to an extent. From the outset, this track announces itself as consequential. As the parallel chords of the *Soul Fever* remix glide out of earshot, we are left with nothing but pulse for a sustained moment, the only instance of this in the entire set. Stereo information surrounding the recurring claps in the music's high register suggests vast, open space. As the beat pounds away, new chords come into view in the distance, gauzy with reverb. The kick then dramatically drops out and we get a manifesto:

> *"strictly for the love,*
> *strictly for the love,*
> *strictly for the love,*
> *strictly for the L-O-V-E..."*

We are at a point of formal significance; the track feels like a statement of intent for the set as a whole. But considering that it marks the return of contrapuntal harmony — so often valorized for its ability to teleologically thrust towards a tonic — *4 The Love* also feels surprisingly weightless and suspended, even once the kick comes crashing back in. The track might be heard as the only one in the set *without* a clear tonic. Every other track chosen, when reduced down to its core harmonic content through the frame of 12-tone equal temperament, carries within it a solid tonic, giving us the ability to identify their key centers, as in Figure 1. But *4 The Love* might be the single exception.

In Chandler's context, the Bm11 at the core of *4 The Love* does not suggest the finality of "i." The Bm11 instead acts as an implied v chord around a tonal center of E. This perception is shaped by what immediately surrounds *4 The Love* in the set: the *Soul Fever* remix is in E minor, while Black Rascals' following *Blaze Theme Track*[3] registers as C# minor, and is thus hearable as the relative minor to a possibility of E Major that never actually arrived.

3. 49:39.

The tension generated by the lack of an assured key center in *4 The Love* is only fully resolved two tracks later, with the arrival of Urban Blues Project & Michael Procter's *Deliver Me (UBP Vocal Mix)* at 53:46. I hear this track as the fulfillment of nearly everything that precedes it. It is not just that *Deliver Me* begins with an assured, satisfying B♭ minor tonic chord in root position; it is that it uses that tonic chord to fuel further motion. Functional harmony now carries new vigor and possibility as it leaps off i. This is the first track of the whole set to have something resembling a verse-chorus harmonic structure, with two distinct chord cycles. The harmony is thus able to explode open, pivoting at the chorus from a familiar i–iv–i–iv–V7 cycle to i–III7–VI–V7.

"I might be mistaken but you look like you want to fly
Give into the voice that is deep in your heart, it won't lie"
—Michael Procter, *Deliver Me*

After nearly an hour of tracks that obsess over looping cycles, rendering harmonic motion a hypnotic, long-term, ever-elongating carrier of phrasing, Chandler gives us an intra-track structure capable of switching between and composing with multiple harmonic phrases. The effect is thrilling; when danced with, the freedom found in the music is vast.

* * *

In Chandler's set, the arrival of motion *is* the resolution.

This is evident with the arrival of *Philippine Sunrise*, the track that first indicates that Chandler is communicating with evolving rates and phrases of harmony moving across time. It is evident with the arrival of Roland Clark's *Resist (Southern Divide Weekend Remix)*, which *re*introduces the possibility of harmonic motion after a sustained period of static unease. And it is most evident with *Deliver Me*, which unlocks arguably the most consequential capacity of the set: that the harmony can be composed into lyrical, changing forms.

Here, resolution is an invitation into an ever-complexifying multidimensionality. *Resolution*, the feeling of tension being released, is not marked by a single moment of completion, nor the cessation of motion. What is arrived at, worked towards, reveled in, is *freedom*, life, propulsion driven by a soulful joy, momentum produced by something beyond just anxious need, a utopic expression of what freedom could be.

An analogous point of resolution may be found, once again in Brahms's *G Major Violin Sonata*, this time in the first movement: bar 174, which marks the return of the second theme in the recapitulation.

Crucially, this arrival provides a release denied by the beginning of the recapitulation, which sneaks in at bar 156, contributing expectant tension by avoiding a clear reassurance of the tonic. Instead of arriving at a solid I, we accelerate *poco a poco* from stillness, almost imperceptibly — even incidentally — into the recap, landing on a G dominant seventh chord, V7 of IV. Brahms effectively slides us into the recap *in medias res* — bar 156, marking the start of Tempo I, references the *second* bar of the first theme. The secondary dominant V7/IV chord landed on further foregrounds this lack of stability while also providing momentum into the C Major chord of bar 157.

From bar 157 on, we are revisiting music from the exposition, nearly verbatim, but because Brahms has denied us both a solid tonic arrival *and* a solid first bar from which to launch our motion through harmonic space, reducing the G to the root of a different chord entirely, all of this familiar music carries a basic question: "Why are we back here?"

If we observe the changing rate of harmonic motion, we can find a distinct phrasal layer, essential to Brahms's lyrical traveling through harmonic space: one main chord per 6/4 bar from bars 156–163 (with one exception in bar 161), a repeated (with variation) chord cycle lasting nine quarter notes from bars 165–167, lengthening to a 2-bar cycle at 168, and then from bars 170–173 we linger on a single dominant seventh over D, the V7 of the movement's G Major key.

Brahms continues to imply a looping cycle, rhythms and gestures still obsessively ruminating as before, but starting at bar 170, expectation is generated by harmonic stasis. Despite the music's efforts to move away from the V7, we are always pulled back to it, as though by gravity; the harmonic motion in these bars amounts to neighbor-note relations that only serve to reinforce the centrality of the D root. By bar 172, the frozen A sustained by the violin, the result of its prior long-short gesture augmenting dramatically (a time-stretching sensation akin to the sustained rising B♭ that prepares us for the bassline of *Philippine Sunrise*) makes it clear that we are headed towards some inevitable resolution.

At bar 174, Brahms finally provides an unambiguous G Major tonic on a downbeat at the *start* of a phrase. This delayed arrival produces a satisfying release. The bulk of the work is finished, as was the case upon the arrival of *Deliver Me* in Chandler's set. This finishing doesn't mean that harmonic motion ceases; rather, resolution is achieved by shifting the impetus of that motion. In the recap's context, we are free to move in harmonic space, reveling in its sensations, hearing music familiar from the exposition but no longer with an insistent engine generating desire and need behind it, the momentum now simply driven by gravity and pleasure.

*   *   *

The intra-track harmonic variety of *Deliver Me* sets into motion a sustained climax, which does still have the feeling of a continual build, but it no longer feels as though Chandler is building in order to generate tension. Instead, we get some kind of joyous continuity, still gaining momentum but no longer necessarily for a specific purpose. Now, the music is simply reveling in what is possible, what has been made possible by the hour preceding.

This is exemplified by the penultimate track, *You Don't Know (M.A.S. Collective Gospel Club)*, by Mass Syndicate feat. Su Su Bobien, the most harmonically and structurally variegated of the entire set. Like *Deliver Me*, *You Don't Know* uses a verse-chorus song structure to switch between multiple chord cycles. It goes even further, in fact; the track has at least *three* distinct cycles, starting with a simple and beautiful organ progression, in which the tonic is suspended over throughout. The next two cycles are articulated primarily by the bassline: a "verse" cycle one bar long, in F minor, looping behind the vocal, building anticipation; and, most thrillingly, a "chorus" cycle *three* bars long, marking the first and only point in the set where Chandler breaks away from duple periodicities. This 3-bar phrase also insistently curls up towards an A♭ minor implication, giving the track as a whole three distinct but related key centers — A♭ Major, F minor, and A♭ minor — to play with.

This implies a global tonal coherence across the entire set, between *Philippine Sunrise*, which marks the introduction of intra-track harmonic motion, and *You Don't Know*, which most totally fulfills that motion's possibility. Between these two tracks lies the main narrative thrust of Chandler's set, the long climb through harmonic-temporal space that builds tension and sets up expectation. Both tracks are primarily in A♭ Major but make use of A♭ minor as well as relative F tonalities to produce a multidimensional harmonic space. The difference is that whereas *Philippine Sunrise* sounds these multiple dimensions simultaneously, with F Phrygian rising in the bass against A♭m-to-A♭M motion in the pads above it, *You Don't Know* sounds them in succession.

We can return to our map of the changing key centers across the set. In addition to this macro A♭ Major linkage, we can connect *Deliver Me* and *You Don't Know*, the two tracks with multiple chord cycles. With these connections traced out, a longer form emerges:

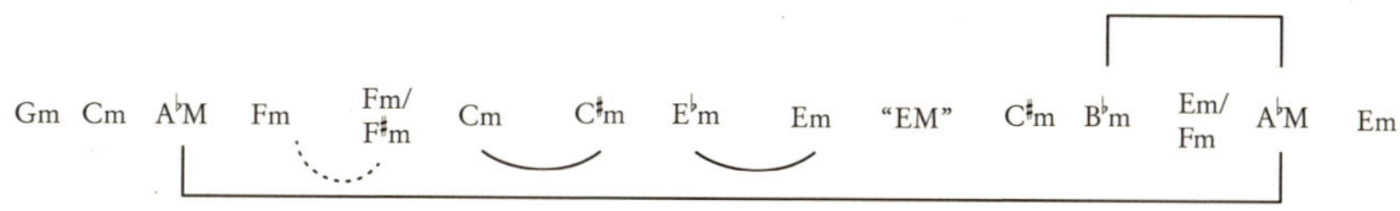

DJing is a mode in which improvisation and composition are tightly, and uniquely, interwoven. When a DJ auditions the next track of a set, listening to it over headphones, preparing it for a hopefully seamless, meaningful arrival, they are improvising ahead of time, designing live, and building an architecture at nearly the same time as others are in it. They are both with us in the present and thinking towards the future, dreaming of what might come next.

Spontaneity and form are tightly entangled. Each choice speaks to the past and influences the future in ways both known and not. The narrative is most felt when lived through, and lived in.

* * *

I feel a personal resonance with DJing as a mode of music-making. Years of making mixtapes and playlists for and with others have been formative; I know what it's like to spend hours finding the precisely right spot to place a track. That a piece can sound so different depending on its surroundings is, I think, one of the most fascinating and beautiful mysteries of music: I can easily imagine *4 The Love* sounding confidently like it's in B minor, given the right context. As a pianist, it reminds me of concert programming, which I approach as a kind of composition, mapping out a setlist as a constellation of works. My hope is that purposefully juxtaposing two pieces may illuminate something about both of them.

When I'm putting together a program, I tend to make my decisions intuitively, usually at a musical (as opposed to conceptual or thematic) level. I'm thinking about voice-leading between pieces, about different possible harmonic relationships that a given set of works might imply. I'm listening for unpredictably complex connections that might emerge. For the last couple of years, I've been placing Jason Eckardt's *Echoes' White Veil* before Beethoven's *Tempest Sonata (in D Minor, Op. 31 No. 2)* in my recital programs, with no space for applause in between. Emerging out of the resonant rubble that closes Eckardt's piece, the opening rolled A Major dominant chord of the *Tempest* sounds newly unfamiliar, and Beethoven's formal and sonic experimentation is foregrounded.

This articulates one of my core questions about what music *is*: when I put object B next to object A, when I put them in sequence, in time, what happens? How might meaning emerge between these two points? What is the substance of that meaning? This is a basic animating question in my practice.

Examining the way the rate of harmonic motion evolves across multiple scales of time in a composition (inter- and intra-track in Chandler's set, perhaps thinkable in other contexts as inter- and intra-phrase, or section) adds a valuable polyphonic dimension to how we might think about harmony and form in older tonal classical music. Voice-leading, harmony, melody, and rhythm are capable of speaking together in a powerful resonant relation, simultaneously vertical and horizontal, sonority as syntax and syntax as sonority, an unfolding succession of simultaneities.

* * *

Figure 2 is a harmonic reduction of the end of Brahms's *G Major Violin Sonata*, the coda of the third and final movement, starting from bar 140. Although the bulk of the movement is in G minor, at this point, just a bar ago, Brahms has lifted us out, changing the color dramatically, bringing us back to the sonata's global key of G Major.

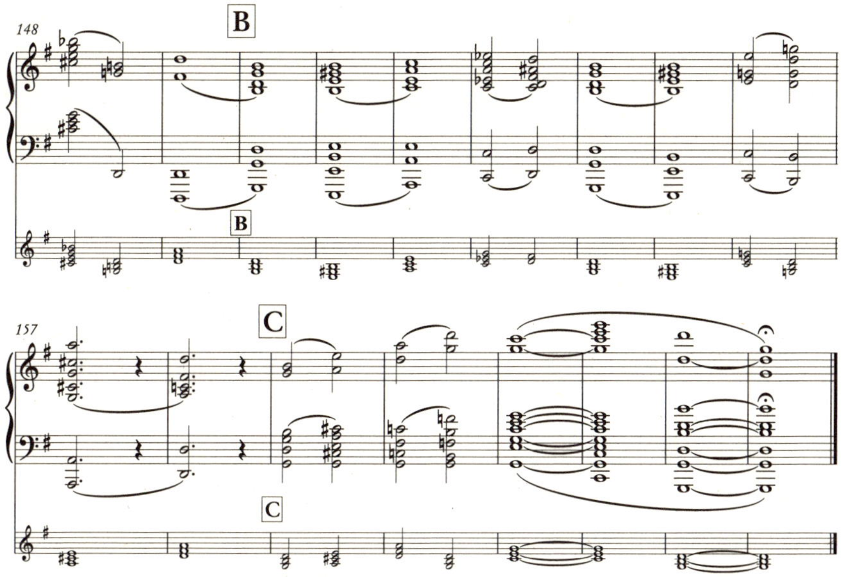

Figure 2. Harmonic reduction of Brahms, *Violin Sonata in G Major, Op. 78, III.* Allegro moderato, bars 140–end.

I've reduced this twice, once with registral information included across a grand staff, and once to chords in root position, triads as much as possible, so as to illustrate the fundamental harmony at the core of this coda. In bars 140–146, these fundamental triads are all parallel, all Major triads: the same cycle too, A-D-G-C, II-V-I-IV.

(Looking at bars 140–143, I am reminded of Kerri Chandler's track, "Rain," released in 1998. A happy coincidence: the Brahms G Major Violin Sonata is also known as the "Rain Sonata," or "Regensonate," because it shares material with Brahms's "Regenlied," Op. 59.

I see parallels in the way both of these tracks/movements use chromatic voice-leading to negotiate a series of cadences underneath, and in the way those gestures expand rhythmically. Perhaps there is a shared sense of how to musically open up the sensation of falling.)

Brahms expands and contracts the rate of harmonic motion in his coda. Bar 141 is a first attempt at augmentation, a secondary dominant (A7) leading to V7 (D7) on the third beat, which triggers a last-minute return to I that keeps the tonic from landing on a strong beat, creating the sensation of a "reset" and suggesting an enforced 2-bar periodicity. From here, the harmony moves in rhythmically consistent pairs, a series of 2-chord gestures, which I indicate in Figure 2 with slurs. The pair of quarter notes comprising the reflexive perfect V-I cadence in bar 141 is augmented twice, as though the cadence were frozen and then time-stretched across the next two bars, further elaborating the capacities of the 2-bar periodicity: we can land on a tonic on the downbeat, but only if it's on the second bar, not on the downbeat *of* the 2-bar period.

The chord cycle then restarts at bar 144, proceeding through the A-D-G-C sequence again, but the rate of motion has only diminished once, and is thus twice as slow as in bar 140. Because of this discrepancy, when the rhythm diminishes again on the third beat of 145, attempting to repeat the "reset" maneuver from bar 141, it does not coincide with a cadence. Instead, the last beat of bar 145 falls on a secondary dominant, which triggers a series of rapid cadences starting at bar 146. First we stay stuck, two loops of D-G, V-I in G Major. In the following bar, the harmony finally breaks out of the initially given A-D-G-C chord cycle, with two more cadences, V-i/ii (E-A) and V-I/IV (G-C), which careen us into bar 148's climactic C♯dim7, the top note of which functions both as B♭ and A♯ to enable voice-leading back into the tonic at bar 150, marked in my reduction as letter B.

Here, two of the coda's established patterns — 2-bar periodicity and harmony progressing in rhythmically consistent pairs — end up in generative conflict with one another. We finally get a G Major chord on the 1 of 1, the downbeat of the 2-bar period, but this is the second chord of its rhythmic pair. This builds subtle tension under the surface, because on the surface, everything is still and solid: the chords here stop traveling registrally, moving as little as possible. The obsessive initial chord cycle has been consummated by an assured tonic; everything seems to be in order. But underneath, the harmonic rhythm is trying to resolve itself in alignment with the 2-bar container, while remaining true to the core 2-chord-long harmonic-rhythmic gesture. At bar 153 a strategy emerges — double the harmonic rhythm here, and then the music will land on a tonic on bar 154, the start of a new period *and* a new pair. Solidity is found.

At bar 156, the 2-chord gesture rhythmically diminishes on a plagal cadence from IV to I, expanding the music's total range once again, the body coming back alive after six bars of near-stillness. From here, the music returns to the initial set of chords, A-D-G-C, but no longer needs to adhere to that precise sequence. The harmonic rhythm immediately stretches out again in bar 157, falling into a subdued, reflective V7 at bar 158, Brahms opening up a pronounced breath in the middle. I hear bars 156–158 as a single, extended 3-bar period. (I am reminded of the introduction of 3-bar phrases in *You Don't Know*.) It is as though, having united the subjectively changing rate of harmonic motion with the objective 2-bar periodicity in bar 154, the music can now fully unite with the form, play with it, speak through it.

There are two more cadences in bars 159 and 160, and the total harmonic range expands with each one, like a diaphragm expanding with deep belly breaths, and then one last instance of rhythmic augmentation brings us to our graceful, dignified close: a final plagal cadence, extended over four bars, tessitura expanding to its widest point, finally leading to contentment.

Through this network of harmonic gestures and unfolding processes, which manifest lyrically across both rhythmic and registral dimensions, Brahms brings us to a feeling of calm finality.

* * *

Chandler, too, provides a sense of calm finality with his coda at 1:09:05, a mashup of his own *Track One* with the acapella from *Circles,* sung by Natalia for a track originally produced by Mustafa. This is finality given via epilogue. After mixing the euphoric chords of *You Don't Know* rapidly out of view, Chandler lingers on a skeletal bassline for a while, opening up a new spaciousness. Natalia's vocal sails on top: "*I need something more/I need I need I need I need I need...*"

When the chords finally come in, they move in parallel motion once again, gliding and easygoing. There is little chromatic content to be found. In contrast to the joyous frenzy of the climactic stretch between *Deliver Me* and *You Don't Know*, here there is more space for a listener, a dancer, to linger in their own selves, to drift about their own interiority. After coming together in communal rapture, this comedown eases us back into being differentiated selves. The effect is like a gentle, reflective opening of a window out of the ecstasy built over the course of the preceding seventy-three minutes, a poetic invitation to leave that also feels like an invitation to continue.

Keep going, the music suggests — goodbye, but until next time, keep on going.

Appendix

Harmonic reduction of Kerri Chandler's *Reel-to-Reel Session* for Resident Advisor, 2020.

53:46 / B♭m
1:00:47 / Em/Fm
1:04:09 / A♭M
1:09:05 / Em

CHAPTER
31

WHY THE WORD JAZZ MATTERS

PAT THOMAS

In this time, cultural nuance is everything. Language is a revolutionary act. Its impact has far-reaching consequences. The word Jazz has had an interesting history. The current narrative suggest the etymology is of mysterious origin. This narrative is inaccurate, for it is Arabic in origin. The British Orientalist Henry George Farmer, in an article for the *Musical Standard* in 1924 about Arab musical influences on West African music, claimed the word Jazza, which means to cut as in cutting up the beat rhythmically, was the origin of Jazz. His reasoning was that a substantial part of West Africa was inhabited by Muslims who were the first slaves kidnapped and taken to the so-called New World, and as part of their cultural heritage they spoke and wrote in Arabic. This is also supported by the fact that the original spelling of the word Jass used in New Orleans is also of Arabic origin, and can be found in Hans Wehr's Arabic English dictionary (p. 125). Meanings include "spy", and "looking into things deeply to scrutinise". Islam has been established for over a millennium in West Africa, therefore it would seem a logical point of view to assume Africans used this word on arriving in North America. So why is there such resistance to this explanation?

The reason is the lack of genuine scholarly research in Jazz circles. Dr. Rudolph T. Ware in his seminal book *The Walking Quran*, a history of Islamic education in West Africa, suggests that "the study of Sub Saharan African Muslims has usually been framed either as 'Islam in Africa', a narrative in which Islam is an alien, external force, or as 'African Islam', which posits that Islamic practices in 'Black African' societies are by definition exotic and heterodox" (p. 19). I suggest that this view influenced Jazz Historians.

Gunther Schuller's *Early Jazz* has become the source book for Jazz historians, but unfortunately it is rife with errors about African Music and African History. Drawing on the false assumption of Islam as a foreign element in Africa he claims (p. 55) that "African speech, singing and playing are all marked by an open tone and natural quality. In this they are closer to European and Western tradition than to the Islamic, which is indeed characterised by a thin nasal wavering quality." Here Schuller is clearly ignorant of West Africa's Islamic legacy.

Here is a list of some of the languages spoken by West African Muslims:

Mandinka	spoken in Senegal and Gambia
Dagbanli	spoken in Northern Ghana
Fulbe	spoken in Senegal, Nigeria, Cameroon, Guinea
Fuuta	spoken in Guinea, Sierra Leone, Senegal
Hausa	spoken in Nigeria, Niger, Northern Ghana, Cameroon
Fulfulde	spoken in Mali, Nigeria, Guinea, Cameroon, Senegal
Yoruba	spoken in Nigeria

Along with these languages, Arabic is also used. All of these languages were written in the Arabic Ajami script. The Latin script was introduced with European Colonialism in the 19th century. These African Muslims were among the first and last slaves to enter North America. "When they reached the other side of the Atlantic ocean after a horrific journey, they introduced a second monotheistic religion into post Columbian America. Islam was also the first revealed religion freely followed as opposed to imposed Christianity by the Africans who were transported to the new world" (p. 1, *Servants of Allah* by Sylviane A. Diouf). Among the slaves in North America were Africans proficient in Arabic. We also know that literacy was discouraged by the slave masters, and punishment included the cutting out of the tongue, as well as violent beatings usually resulting in death. These Africans stood out among the slaves and clearly plantation owners felt threatened by their abilities to read and write. Diouf suggests that "if they were not the blank states or primitive savages they had been portrayed to be in order to justify their enslavement, then the very foundation of the system had to be questioned. North Americans felt compelled to deny the Africaness of the outstanding Muslims and portray them as Arabs." (Diouf p. 107–108)

There is no doubt that African-American music has been steeped in West African Muslim aesthetics regarding song and dance. The origins of the Ring Shout dance, found in the Sapelo islands in Georgia, clearly has aspects of the Dhikr and Hadrah still practiced in West Africa today by Sufi practitioners. Dhikr means "remembrance." The practitioners sit in a circle and recite from the Quran and mention some of the 99 names of God, chanted repetitively. Hadrah means presence and in this ritual the practitioners are standing in a circle, moving their heads from right to left, the legs moving slowly in a counter-clockwise manner. Also there is the fact that the Fulani Imam Bilali Muhammad ended up in North America and helped create a Muslim community. He was from Timba Futa in Senegal and spoke Fulbe and Arabic, two root languages that helped create the Gullah Dialect. Another clue is the counter-clockwise dance used in the Ring Shout, emulating the way pilgrims circumambulate the Kaaba for the Hajj in Mecca. Also in early black churches there was a preference for both genders to wear white at Sunday service — this is the practice of Muslims at Jummah, the congregation prayer held on Fridays throughout the Muslim world. Scholars such as Diouf have noticed the similarities between the melisma wailing in Gospel singing and the Adhan the Muslim call to prayer as practiced in West Africa. This style is found throughout Afro American Music, and clearly influenced the musical vocalisation approaches found in the music of Louis Armstrong, right up to Albert Ayler.

Islam is said to consist of three components:

1. Islam Shahada	proclamation of faith
2. Iman	the articles of faith
3. Ihsan Perfection	in the practice of the faith

Tasawuf, popularly known in the west as Sufism, is the science of tastes and spiritual unveiling. It is the means of perfection. The three dominant Sufi schools in West Africa are the Qadari Tijaniyya and Muraddiya Tariqahs. Tariqah means way. West Africa has a great legacy of Sufi masters right up to the present day. Among them is Abdul Qadir Kan (1727–1806), who had abolished slavery in Senegambia by 1786. Then there is the great Qadiri Fulani Shaykh Uthman Dan Fodio (1754–1854), who established the Sokoto Caliphate in today's Northern Nigeria. He also wrote major texts on Sufism, among them *The Sciences of Behaviour* and *The Book of Distinction*. He waged a Jihad against local rulers when he found out they had been selling Muslims to The Europeans. We also have the illustrious Shaykh Al Hajj Umar ibn sa'id Futi Tal (1797–1864). Who established the Tijaniyya Tariqah in Senegal. Among his numerous texts on Sufism is his magnum opus poem A reminder for the seekers and his text success for the students. Then there is the great Spiritual Master Shaykh Ahmadou Bamba Mbacke (1853–1927) who is the most successful pacifist of the 20th century. He waged a non-violent struggle against the vicious French regime and lived to see the Holy city Touba created and the French vanquished which led to the creation of modern day Senegal. Known as Servant of the Messenger he created a new Sufi Tariqah The Muridiyya, now the dominant Tariqah in Senegal. He is one of the most prolific writers of all time, best known for his poems honouring the prophet Muhammad — he wrote his masterpiece on *Sufism Pathways of Paradise* at the age of thirty years old. These great giants wrote in Classical Arabic.

Most scholars of the blues now acknowledge the influence of the West African Griot musical tradition. But they seem to be ignorant of the fact that the Jeli tradition is Islamic in origin. The Jelis are found only among the Mande people. Some of the countries they reside in are Niger, Nigeria, Ghana and Senegal, and the music of the Mande is inextricably linked with Islam. Every major Islamic festival is accompanied by drums and musical instruments. The Kora a 21-stringed harp like instrument made out of a calabash gourd cut in half, with eleven strings played by the left hand and ten played by the right hand, clearly influenced Blues Guitar picking styles in North America. The balafon is a polyphonic instrument of twenty-one keys played with mallets tuned either in the tetra tonic, heptatonic or pentatonic scale — the word consists of "balan" which means instrument and the verb "fon" which means to play. This instrument is found among Mande people of Guinea and Mali, and clearly played a major role in *Piano Blues* harmonic structure. The kontigo is the precursor of the banjo, a string instrument with five strings and a small neck.

The Jeli are the Master story tellers and have prodigious memories — no doubt this had an influence on blues music, and the importance of being able to tell your story through your improvisation in a jazz solo is essential.

We now know that the slaves from West Africa were not taken at random to the West Indies and North America — they had particular skills that their European slave masters needed. It's not a coincidence that the Fulani and Mandinka ended up in New Orleans and all of South Carolina as they had expertise in growing rice crops. It is a myth that these Africans were mostly unskilled labour. We need to acknowledge that the concept of

Race is a European invention. Three pillars of western thought Hume, Kant and Darwin, were all rancid racists — Darwin's *The Descent of Man* is nothing but a colonial handbook to justify colonialism and the genocide of non-European people. Thanks to the pioneering work of the late Sir Fred Hoyle and Michael Denton, we now know Neo-Darwinism is nothing but a White Myth masquerading as science.

The word Jazz matters especially in this time as it helps restore African agency. The false "either/or" dichotomy suggesting Africans couldn't objectively choose to be Muslims without losing their Africaness is incorrect. Indeed they helped in the creation of Afro American culture, and when we include the West African Muslim component many so-called mysteries disappear.

Bibliography

Carney, Judith A. *Black Rice the African Origins of Rice Cultivation in the Americas.* (Harvard University Press, 2001)

Charry, Eric. *Mande Music.* (The University of Chicago Press, 2000)

Cowan, J. M., editor. *The Hans Wehr Dictionary of Modern Written Arabic.* (1960)

Darwin, Charles. *The Descent of Man.* (Penguin Classics, 1871)

Denton, Michael. *Evolution Still a Theory in Crisis.* (Discovery Institute Press, 2016)

Diouf, Sylviane A. *Servants of Allah.* (New York University Press, 1998)

Farmer, Henry George. *The Arab Influence on Music in the Western Soudan.* (1924)

Hoyle, Fred. *Mathematics of Evolution.* (Acorn Enterprises LLC, 1987)

Schuller, Gunther. *Early Jazz.* (Oxford University Press, 1968)

Sosa, Foday Musa. *A Village Griot Boy and the World.* (Popliama Products, 2019)

Syed, Amis; Ware, Rudolph; Wright, Zachary; *Jihad of the Pen The Sufi Literature of West Africa.* (The American University in Cairo Press, 2018)

Valls, Andrew, editor. *Race and Racism in Modern Philosophy.* (Cornell University Press, 2005)

Ware, Rudolph T. *The Walking Quran.* (The University of North Carolina Press, 2014)

CHAPTER
32

TO IMPROVISE OR NOT TO IMPROVISE

HENRY THREADGILL

Some years back now, maybe as long as ten years I spoke with the director of a US orchestra — the point of that conversation had to do with me suggesting that I would lead some classes or workshops to teach the players an approach to improvisation. At that time I was considering writing something for that orchestra, however I had also decided that I didn't want to write 100% notated music anymore. What happened then was that my proposal was put before the players and their response was that they wanted to be paid for their time to learn something that they couldn't do. I found that was a position so far out of perspective that I had to withdraw from such an anti-intellectual-artistic attitude.

Now there are more components to my proposal than just me teaching or rather leading them into improvisation. The other aspects that I didn't get to meant bringing in more people to teach the players about improvisation not just in one genre but as many styles and approaches as possible. I really thought that a Bauhaus approach was necessary to bring a US orchestra into contact with everyday musical reality. Hence I had to drop such a "progressive idea or ideal" and leave things squarely set as they were and are.

At this time it appears that there has come into the public discourse the inequality of programing and conversation concerning improvisational history in regard to orchestras in the US. As a result there has been a sudden uptick of presenting black composers, women composers, and any other composers who have continually been left out of performing repertory. I still submit that the ground has not changed. Simply by programing the work of marginalized composers an organism that is not capable of handling contemporary music/art does not get fixed. For such an organism to be so big, all over this country, and not represent the work of the artist is totally preposterous and calls for a rethinking of this issue.

Without question, this is an attack on U.S. orchestras who play mainly (90 to 95% of its repertory) European music.

First this is not about European music. It is about federal and national support for an institution that does not represent the people in the country, yet it is supported by government and U.S. philanthropy. The support from the federal government and other institutions and philanthropies should be put towards a new paradigm. A model that could be set up with four regional orchestras around the country and hopefully to grow beyond that four.

There are some musical institutions that have been teaching students improvisation and feeding resources to this end. It is necessary to set up a broad oversight group that is charged with certifying that orchestras have the regional techniques and disposition to play music of U.S. composers with real seal and concern, not patronizing. There is no reason to try and change this large complex organism. Leave it to its own whatever. We as artists and listeners deserve better and why have a fight and struggle to change something that rejects change. A new model to fit the day is past due.

CHAPTER
33

THE BLUES ARE ALWAYS FREE

FAY VICTOR

I am not sure how I became a vocal improviser but somehow with deep faith and trust, I instinctively chose a path toward sound. This essay aims to shed light on that process especially for those that have no idea how to do this. I too had no idea.

The path was to delve into a musical world I had no prior knowledge of. Starting from jazz music which I didn't grow up with onto the world of wide-open musical spaces and possibilities that jazz was the portal to. Fortunately when the path was set, I was in a place with some space to make sense of it all. More on that later.

My musical starting line was a blurry and painful time in my life. I lost my mother suddenly just four years before when I was 19. I was lost and sad for a long time. I dropped out of college in upstate New York, went back and dropped out again. Getting back to New York City for good a couple years after that, I took a survival job at a bank near Grand Central Station. A shitty gig but I was glad for it as it paid the bills good enough.The job gave me something to do. I had no goals in my life then other than to try to stay alive and make sense of why my mother was gone.

Out of the blue, a co-worker that I befriended at the bank knew of a restaurant called Sheila's in Brooklyn that had live music a few nights a week with a singer featured some nights. For some reason, the co-worker suggested we go there to check out the scene, getting there on the night the singer was featured. That singer was the great, great Ulysses Slaughter of Brooklyn fame, may he Rest In Peace. Ulysses was a brilliant vocalist and showman plus a busy and popular singing teacher. We met that night and I sort of auditioned for him on the spot. After hearing me sing *the* one jazz tune I knew a cappella (King Pleasure's *Moody's Mood for Love*), Ulysses thought I had "something". That excited me as I loved to sing for fun and had done that forever, but I had no intention of doing anything with it.

Curious about what may be there and there was nothing else going on anyway, I worked to get him to take me on as a student. In the midst of that negotiation, Ulysses took me to a vocal jazz workshop at the Williamsburg Music Center in Williamsburg, Brooklyn. Every Saturday afternoon the workshop ran, hosted by Jimmy Sigler on piano and/or organ (the last accompanist of famed jazz and blues vocalist Dinah Washington) and Gerry Eastman on guitar or bass (brother of Julius Eastman). It was Gerry's place actually. I lived and breathed songs and jazz there rooted in the black community around this black music for about four years, rarely missing a Saturday. I cried when I had to. I literally fell in love with jazz music from going there. Ulysses would be there as well, lighting up the place with his sound and he did take me on as a student after all. I didn't realize how much I needed to feel part of a community, a new community of singers and musicians. I went head first into this music through performing it, interacting with the musicians around it, going out to hear bands and working my butt off as I started to build some repertoire and then sit in around town.

Amazing things started to happen. My heart lightened, I became a kinder person. I sensed that music was the catalyst to creating this feeling. Singing became the outlet for all I'd been through, especially since my mother died. I had a sense of direction again and hope, a new way of looking at life. The starkness of change before I started singing regularly and after was like winter and summer. I set on a path to become a mainstream jazz vocalist. Music was in charge, a guiding force and with no parents anymore, I needed the guidance. I welcomed the guidance. I vowed to go wherever music took me and stay true to that instinct. Music had already proven its healing force, so deserving of my faith and trust.

Amsterdam and the Blues

I moved to Amsterdam, The Netherlands in 1996, seven years after starting down this musical path, living in that country for eight years. Eight woodshedding years in hindsight, taking full advantage of living in a social democracy. Expenses were low, good quality food was reasonable and accessible. Work was fairly plentiful in and out of Holland as other countries in Euroland beckoned. Most importantly, I expanded my outlook on absolutely everything with time to take it all in. Long periods alone on trains and planes traversing the continent gave me time and distance to see where my life could go not to mention time to read lots of books. A favorite thing to me of living in the Netherlands was that people left you the fuck alone and I needed to be alone. I needed space in a safe place. I could finally confront the death of my mother there and ultimately I found that path to the music I was to make, starting with the Blues.

The Blues is a connecting spirit, a lingering feeling that never leaves me like a good security blanket I've grown to love. Singing the blues opens up my pores for the world to see inside. I say this now but back then, I was so afraid to sing the blues for real. A German guitarist heard me sing at a jazz festival and invited me to perform on an all Blues show with his group as a guest in Münster, Germany. As petrified as I was, I said yes. These were years when I never turned down work. I was just getting my name around and getting started, I couldn't afford to say no to any gigs. So scared as hell, I took the gig.

I prepped for the show best I could with my non-existent Blues repertoire, so little blues in my repertoire in a music that's supposed to be based on the Blues! I had a few blues "pastiche" tunes and I scrambled to get some more material together. It was pretty sad. In hindsight, I'm glad my first attempt at performing an entire Blues show was in Germany. The audience was so kind, they clapped for everything. Keeping it über-real, it wasn't a Black audience facing me down either. If so, I'm sure I would have been ignored after the third tune, especially with that band. That's just the truth. I'll never forget that night because I learned to respect The Blues like never before. It was about "what are YOU communicating to people?!" I can't lie singing The Blues. I've tried phoning it in, it doesn't work. It forced me more than any other music I perform to be completely honest and surrender to the feeling that NEEDS to be shared. To be 100% real in the expression. The Blues is Soul Space music. That show started an association with the guitarist who booked the show and before I knew it, other bands asked me to be featured with them as well. I sang so much Blues music in these years, learning how to communicate my own feelings and how to connect my voice with that expression. I realized that the Blues was the basis of all the music I'd been listening to my entire life from Calypso and Reggae to Soul, R&B and Funk. The more I leaned toward Blues expression as a vocalist, the more my musicality expanded, more connection and access to all the music I want to sing and improvise with. Deep immersion into the Blues opened that door to more expansive expressive ideas that I didn't associate with jazz, at least not at that time. I hadn't heard of Albert Ayler yet. Still, I thought about form in relation to expression. Like the Delta Blues musicians that played any number of bars to get their point across. 12 this time, 14 the next, 17 bars after that. The Blues are found everywhere. All this discovery and joy in this exploration and the ability to work it out on the bandstand. I got even more excited about the path. I also knew there was a missing component that I couldn't name but I could point to it. I simply had no language to improvise with outside of scat language (vocal improvisation connected to jazz that uses nonsense syllables) and the wails & hollers typically associated with Blues expression. I was looking for another way.

I like to scat and can do it well, yet I started to think about the sonic representation of scatting, which I believe strives to emulate the sound of instruments. I've seen vocalists over the years gesture to be a "trumpeter" or "trombonist" when scatting over jazz changes. Yet jazz music comes out of the black female voice. Out of the voices of the Black Blues singers of the 1910s and '20s specifically such as Bessie Smith, Ma Rainey, Ida Cox, Ethel Waters to name a few. The vocal sound is at the root of jazz music. Listen to the horns!! Early jazz musicians such as Louis Armstrong, Sidney Bechet, Coleman Hawkins, Lester Young honed their sound from listening to vocalists as a way to their own distinctive sounds. The incredible Ornette Coleman also got this memo, his sound was as vocal and as full of the Blues as they come. Looking at jazz music in this way, scatting feels like a disconnect from the point of view of authentic vocal expression. Scatting can feel expressly cerebral. I connect to my body and vocal sound much better when I use sounds that are truly representative of my vocal instrument. I know this now but as I toyed with what to use for language then, I stumbled upon an album of Luciano Berio's *Sequenzas*. *Sequenzas* are compositions from the Italian composer Luciano Berio for solo instruments. There is a *Sequenzas* for piano, cello, trombone, voice to name a few, fourteen *Sequenzas* in all. *Sequenza III* (1965) is the vocal *Sequenza*, written for and sung by Cathy Berberian, the great mid-20th century mezzo soprano whom Berio was also married to, though not at the time of this performance. I'd already heard Cathy Berberian on *Folk Songs*, a more well-known Berio album where Berberian sings on most of the pieces and I was struck by her impeccable technique and natural sound. A light went off when I heard the vocal *Sequenza* though. Although this was a through-composed piece, the language therein was what I was looking for: FIND AND APPLY SOUNDS THE VOICE MAKES NATURALLY.

I scoured the score of *Sequenza III* to understand how these sounds were made technically such as a gurgle, a burp, a laugh, a sigh or a cry. How can these vocal sounds be used in improvisation, while using good technique and vocal support. *Sequenza III* unlocked the nascent possibilities of what my vocal improvised language might sound like. The better trained my instrument was, the more risks I could take, the more sounds I could make. For example, I'd heard vocalizing with laughter and crying before yet it often came off on the kitsch end to my ears. I heard the great singer Tina Marsh (RIP) use laughter and crying in her improvisations where she developed the sound over a good period of time. In addition, these sounds came out of the context of the piece she performed. It was so good. In my desire to make improvisational choices that connect to an audience, the context is huge. I was gathering materials and trying to make sense of how I could use them as an improviser. Accessibility was about which materials communicate the idea the best. This is so crucial in my music-making, going back to the point: What am I trying to say to you? It may be a dream but I truly want audiences to feel part of the journey, to be pulled into the experience. But how?

One example that came about much later… There's a piece I wrote for the Fay Victor Ensemble entitled *Gunk*, a piece about coughing up the psychic "gunk" in your mind. Musically, it's based on a bass line in 9/8 that loosely cycles around. The bassist can play it, reference it or ignore it all together at times. The piece has static text that is improvised in performance with lots of space for improvisation over all. I considered what sounds I should make when I improvise to give the piece a wider context. The aim was for the improvisational materials to emphasize the text in a sound reinforcing way. In my improv, I used sounds such as *coughing* and *choking* to create a more visceral experience of "coughing up stuff". Listeners have commented on how powerful the words come across with the addition of these types of sounds in the improvisation. Audiences can really take a lot. I've pushed many audiences over the years and one thing I know for sure is that audiences can handle anything thrown at them as long as there is something for them to hold onto and the expression is strong. In the case of Gunk, the bassline is the safety net. That's it. And it works.

Jeanne Lee

Another deep influence of the vocal freedom puzzle.

One night I went to hear the great pianist Mal Waldron play with his trio at an amazing jazz venue, the Bimhuis in Amsterdam (Arjen Gorter–double bass; John Betsch–drums) for the first time. Mr. Waldron lived in Brussels, Belgium for many years, living there still in the years I lived in Amsterdam. He played at the Bimhuis regularly and when I was able I'd go to hear his shows there. Through the great and gregarious tenor saxophonist Sean Bergin, I got to meet Mr. Waldron and hang out backstage with him a few times after shows. He was so elegant and erudite. I gave him my latest record and he asked for my number, saying "If I hear something there, I'll call you." Mr. Waldron never did call. A couple years ago, a friend of Mr. Waldron's that cleared out his space after he died got in touch to say he found my note to Mr. Waldron with my number on it amongst his papers. Yeah, I cried.

That first time though, in 1998, Mr. Waldron invited a vocalist up to sit in that I'd never heard of. It was the late Jeanne Lee. Ms. Lee sat in for a few songs with his trio. I don't remember what she sang anymore yet it was this sense of hearing something far beyond my understanding of what jazz singing was then, but firmly a part of it. A different approach and sound from Betty Carter, the jazz singer I most admired and looked up to at this time or any other jazz singer I'd ever heard. Jeanne Lee sat in *and* entered the musical space with everyone. They all revolved together.

After this show, I looked for Ms. Lee's music, discovering the *Newest Sound Around*, her duo recording with pianist Ran Blake from 1962. The *Newest Sound Around* lived on repeat for months in those heady Amsterdam days. Inspired by her sound and how lithe her voice hung in the air in contrast to Ran Blake's playing. Like puffs of air above his chords. Ms. Lee made a duo record with Mal Waldron called *Caravan*, that was brilliant and more connected in a blues sense to each other. Listening to her was intoxicating and mysterious. I felt I knew but I knew I didn't. All the music and ideas swirled in my head. I began to experiment with my voice with the sounds I was now hearing. But my vocal instrument couldn't handle it. I suffered with intonation issues anytime I strayed too far off the beaten path. I hadn't studied with a teacher since I left New York City, now three years hence. It was time to give my instrument some attention.

So finding out that Jeanne Lee lived and taught in The Netherlands at The Royal Conservatory in Den Haag was a joy. Just as I reached out to the conservatory to connect with Ms. Lee, it wasn't but a week later when

I heard that Jeanne Lee had transitioned in Mexico. A devastating loss for our community. I still lament never getting to actually meet her, how timing affects everything in our lives. Still intent on solving my vocal issues, I studied with an opera teacher named Onno Van Dijk, who gave me the vocal technique that I have built on to this day. A great decision to study with him and I still see him when I go to Amsterdam. He understood that I wanted technique that facilitated my voice as an improviser and Onno helped me connect the technical dots to use my instrument in healthy ways while innovating my instrument. If you're a vocalist developing extended techniques, this is exactly what you're doing constantly. Creating a fluid way of improvising within and without structure. Curious to see how far I could take my own instrument, including composing that also focused on the inherent possibilities of the voice. The path broadened, the way cleared. I got more and more fascinated with sound than ever. I thought about all the languages in the world, some I could hear up close and swim in the sounds of them. How many sounds could there be? It's infinite really. If we consider all the sounds all the species on the planet make. If you've ever stood in the middle of a rainforest, the sound can be deafening, overwhelming. Just imagine it. In our own species, I think about languages such as Xhosa and Zulu, the Dutch language I was beginning to learn at the time and heard all around me. I paid attention to the sounds of other languages, the cadences and inflections. Mimicking them just for myself, for the sake of the sound. In Spain, India, Russia, Sweden, Austria. The attacks, the explosions, the sighs, the sounds made in languages for other living beings. All the amazing sounds possible with the human voice. All the ways the human voice represents the blues.

I felt like Ms. Berberian opened up language ideas for me and Ms. Lee's example helped me see how I could connect it all back to jazz and blues. Jeanne Lee made me believe that it's possible to sing absolutely anything you want.

I didn't give up on my jazz language work though. Studying piano and harmony with Curtis Clark. Sitting at the upright I had on at home on a daily basis between students figuring jazz music out harmonically. Singing every scale I was aware of. I learned to sing and play Charles Mingus' beautiful composition *Eclipse*, which hit me hard. It took a year to get that melody right while integrating the newfound techniques I got from working with my vocal teacher such as connecting my chest and head registers in a fluid way. Broadening my breath support, emphasis on using my resonators to connect my sound with more clarity. This worked great for tunes and improvisation, providing a bridge to build an approach such as *FreeSong*, which came up some years after I went down this vocal and improvisatory path. This is a "One Voice" idea, seamless connection between registers. A jazz or an improvising singer needs ease of access to one's entire range I believe. If I want to sing a 13th interval let's say, the aim is for the connection between the notes to sound seamless even if I'm using different registers in the connection of these notes. It builds agility and facility between registers to sound clear in the execution while having the ability to move all over the place from one idea to the next. It applies to ideas around vocal color and how approaches can change dramatically on the same breath. Technical approaches such as these help to relax my vocal instrument to create all the sounds that come through me without filter.

"You are on TOP of the music, you need to get IN the music" — Curtis Clark

I had a quintet in my final Amsterdam years which included my teacher and mentor on piano, the incredible pianist Curtis Clark and a guitarist named Anton Goudsmit. Anton was a highly sought-after player in The Netherlands and to me, one of the most soulful Dutch musicians I ever worked with to date. His passion always came through his playing, which had a fluid jazz-blues approach. He could negotiate all kinds of music from free to form and back. Having him in the band was important to the music and my own development as an improviser because he was already going the way I was trying to get to. Anton sang everything he played. If he was soloing you'd hear it more audibly and he'd mouth the sounds if someone else was in the spotlight. No matter the music, that's what he'd do. It dawned on me that there wasn't any filter between what came into his head and sung and what came through his fingers. We even talked about it. Gig after gig. That truly amazed me to witness someone so clearly in tune with head, heart and sinew. I wanted my music to flow out of me like THAT, to know that level of trust with myself.

The great European jazz master — pianist/composer Misha Mengelberg and I also connected around this time and he gradually became a mentor and friend. A dream at this time was to make a record of Monk and Nichols compositions with Misha on piano. Misha was into the idea and thus began a years-long friendship and connection. The recording I wanted to do never transpired but Misha encouraged me to write lyrics for Monk and especially Herbie Nichols tunes. I was moved and influenced by the Instant Composer's Orkest (ICP), co-led by Misha and drummer Han Bennink, which was a group that touted free wielding musical connections in a very outspoken way with absurdity and humor. No one seemed to take themselves too seriously even though the music was seriously good. In my search for expansion, I never thought about simply combining different jazz styles with another or what happens *in between* the tunes. I'd heard more avant garde music at this point but I hadn't heard Dixieland into Monk into Swing into Nichols into "let's sit at a table and have a small chat" — as if that were completely normal. Up until hearing ICP, most jazz musicians and groups I heard and loved felt firmly entrenched somewhere in some camp. Trumpeter Miles Davis gets a lot of credit for discarding that limiting point of view — rightfully so — yet I'd argue that his evolution was linear. He left things behind. This was different, ICP just seemed to do it all (sans the funk) and in one concert. I once heard Han Bennink say it was an "everything is everything"* approach, as a point of difference from the British improvising approach (pointillistic and precise) and the German improvisational approach (harsh and violent). Mind blowing for me to witness and consider.

* From *Afijn*, a documentary on Misha Mengelberg (2009).

What I admired about the ICP seemed quite far from what I was able to do on my own. But I was headed back home to NYC and coming home was about moving to a far bigger pond with more opportunities and the best teachers of the music up on the bandstand every night. I began going to sessions with musicians from the downtown scene in New York City whenever I got invited, just improvising with people like Roy Campbell (RIP), Sabir Mateen, Ras Moshe, Charles Gayle, Francois Grillot, Ken Filiano, Albey Balgocian and Daniel Carter and others affiliated with the Vision Festival and presenter Arts for Art. I enjoyed and learned so much improvising with instrumentalists. I learned how to insert myself in a musical way and which sounds made the most sense. Instrumentalists played with each other, interweaving their sounds and textures. Some players pull their sound to the back, others push out front, then others maybe play something completely disparate to the proceedings but that works too! This music sounded great to my ears, this improvised cacophony. I'd heard Albert Ayler by now.

It became more about *listening* and *responding* when I sing. Listening became a craft of a different level now. More than listening for the changes and the time feel. Listening for everything in and out of the music, the spaces. Listening for what the music needs and how can I contribute to that. Listening for the conversation. How can I make the music sound three-dimensional? Deepening my sense of ensemble connection, improvising with instrumentalists taught me how to take ownership over my own sense of time, space and phrasing in tandem with the ensemble. I got inside the music more from improvising with instrumentalists in all manner of settings. Getting inside to me means the expression became the focal point. The story. It's more than the ability to gain language and sounds. It was again the context for the sounds. The larger story at work. Something I share with vocal students is the inherent power of the voice. How familiar that sound is for every human. As a vocal improviser, you can bring in words whenever you want. They can be improvised words or words you bring with you to the bandstand with no predetermined time when you'll improvise with them. I've done this often and it's great to have language at certain moments and feel that on stage.

FreeSong

My husband, bass guitarist and composer Jochem van Dijk and I started a band to develop our compositions that channelled these vocal ideas in 2005 called the Fay Victor Ensemble (FVE). When Jochem and I started writing together in 1999, I wrote lyrics and he wrote the music. Over the years the roles became more collaborative although one thing never changed — the story comes first. The music we create is in service to that story. Performing with blues bands especially, I saw the power of the story, including the sonic delivery. The FVE rehearsed regularly because combining storytelling, form, dynamics, improvisation in one expression was very hard to do. Man. Many balancing issues to sort out as the music soared and I got drowned out in performance. OK in improvised passages but not OK for getting melodies or text to come across. We worked out as a group how to respond more organically. I had to educate my band members on this new approach because they weren't used to working with a vocalist this way and I barely had the language to give clear instructions. Or to even say what I was going for. It was frustrating to know things aren't working with no good way to express why. I used imagery a lot until I could better articulate our ideas.

Traditional notation was limiting and got in the way often in articulating ideas around improvisation: fuzziness, blurriness, improvising from one point to another and so on. My vision had no language yet and we struggled. Somehow, these wonderful strangers — Anders Nilsson (guitar), Ken Filiano (double bass) and Michael T. A. Thompson (drums) — had a certain faith and stayed with me. A few early shows gave glimmers of where the music was going. So we kept at it until that moment it came together and all that my husband and I were trying to put across through the writing and the band sound revealed itself. This was fluid and story-led inside/outside music. The FVE released three albums of original music in the end.

The second album of the FVE was named *The FreeSong Suite*. The album is made up of three "*rooms*" where the material in each *room* was recorded in the studio in real time together, like a set of music. The space between the "tunes" started to really matter for me and we were together for close to four years as a band at this point. I felt the trust was there to give that a try.

A couple years before releasing *The FreeSong Suite* (Greene Avenue Music, 2009), I started a quartet with Misha, Wolter Weirbos (trombone) and Ernst Glerum (double bass) called the FreeSong Quartet, working off of the idea of approaching the Herbie Nichols, Thelonious Monk and Duke Ellington pieces we performed as one continuous movement, moving from one tune into the other in an improvised flow. This was pretty difficult for me in the beginning because of hearing the first chords of the approaching tune. I worked out how to hear the starting pitch of the approaching song, which then freed everyone else to play what they felt. Sometimes it was like harmolodics, where the melody was a whole tone apart unintentionally yet very cool too. Or accidental counterpoint. It was and is still an amazing way to perform composed music. It took a few years to feel free in this expression from a harmonic, melodic and rhythmic place. Now I perform Herbie Nichols compositions often (Herbie Nichols SUNG is a project I have around Nichols' music) and any "tuneful" material can be approached in this way.

The FVE took the FreeSong concept to new heights as we'd have these engrossing streams of conscious flows in performance. FreeSong freed us from the definitive barriers of composition and improvisation. I truly enjoy when no one knows when the composition ends and the improvisation begins and vice versa. It's a rich dynamic to navigate with a group, requiring big ears and lots of trust. There's also no more of a thrilling exchange to leave the improvised space and land on something that everyone knows and hears, solid as a rock.

All these years later it's now clear that this was all happening at the same time. I was growing as an improviser with the musicians from the Downtown and Vision Festival scenes in NYC and composing very specific music to tell the stories I find important with the FVE fueled this growth. Both interactions fed off of each other to take me where I am today. The FVE facilitated the improvising and compositional language that grew over the ten years of the group's existence. Where the improvisation should be placed in this or that composition was a thing my husband and I discussed constantly about the FVE. Where would the improvisations take place in each piece and who would improvise in those places? Aiming to stay away from the solo-head-solo formula and consider different ways for improvised sections to interact with the rest of the composition.

One example of our thinking is the piece, *Exchange Rate* on the FVE's first album, *Cartwheels Through The Cosmos* (ArtistShare/Greene Avenue Music, 2007), *Exchange Rate* pivoted on a static dominant chord (A7) with quick harmonic shifts that came up and go away again. The groove hinged on a "fractured 6/8", inspired by Captain Beefheart's tune *The Clouds are Full of Wine (Not Whiskey or Rye)* from *Lick My Decals Off, Baby*. The bar lines were elastic, meaning they moved as we all moved. We dictated the time of each bar because there is no established tempo. We went through the piece together and when I stopped the groove kept going until I resumed singing the piece. There's only one improvisational space in *Exchange Rate* which is an ensemble improvisation. I used to say to the band, "if any one of us comes to the forefront that's cool for the music, let it go where it goes." No-one is making room for anyone else in the space other than what the music suggests. All designed to set up the story with a punchline that came at the end. *Exchange Rate* erupted out of the knowledge that cowrie shells were used as a primary currency in the African slave trade for hundreds of years. They were mined and taken from the Maldives and purchased on the congresses of the slaving countries of Europe such as Holland, England and Portugal. As a currency, cowrie shells were valued for their durability and more or less consistent size. Slavers would have the "currency" on hand when purchasing slaves from the large kingdoms on the African continent such as Dahomey. The words are meant to take the listener through an African inspired street fair of today, where one will see cowrie shells on many items, on people themselves. The final line questions the amount of cowrie shells I see and if it would have been enough to pay for **me** had I been sold into slavery myself all those centuries ago, making this a personal point as well as representative of the NOW.

On the FVE's final record *Absinthe & Vermouth (Greene Avenue Music, 2013)*, we went from being a quartet to a trio, sans drums. The way our writing was going and how the forms continued to billow out, going without a drummer felt right for the music. I believe it's good to not get attached to having any specific instrument in a band. It's about the project and what the music needs to communicate the ideas in play. Drums and bass are no exception. My current improvising quartet, SoundNoiseFUNK [with Joe Morris (guitar), Sam Newsome (soprano saxophone), Reggie Nicholson (drums)], has no bassist or anyone even trying to fill that role. We don't need one for *that* sound world.

In 2013, the same year *Absinthe & Vermouth* was released, The FVE was commissioned to compose a piece for Anthony Braxton Presenting Series through the TriCentric Foundation. We composed a piece called *Neighborhood Dynamics*, about gentrification from the inside out in Bedford-Stuyvesant, Brooklyn where my husband and I lived from 2003 until 2019. We saw the entire evolution of gentrification in our community and wanted to write about it, honored that Braxton selected our proposal. *Neighborhood Dynamics* featured the FVE + Nicole Mitchell (flutes) and Vincent Chancey (french horn). Inspiring to complete this work for a receptive audience, using many of the FreeSong vocal *and* genre approaches to date. For example, The first movement of *Neighborhood Dynamics* we start off the piece with a duo singing the blues that morphs into a sustained tone row based off of serialism. Seeing the two ideas as part of the same expression. And why not? *Neighborhood Dynamics* employed graphic scores illustrating demographic shifts, improvisation, a rock tune as points of expression through our experiential perspective. Braxton was enthusiastic with praise, really loved the piece and how we performed it as a group. I was stunned as we never wrote anything this large before (70-minute work) nor had we ever collaborated so well as a writing team, my husband and I. This moment was a career highlight to date, a way to look back at how far this idea of being an improvising vocalist and composer in as expansive a manner as possible had begun to work for me.

Later in 2014, I'd get the opportunity to perform Berio's *Sequenza III* at a Berio Festival at Columbia University put on by Ensemble Mise-En. The composed vocal piece that gave me notes of entry into an unknown improvising world. Forever grateful to all of the musicians and colleagues that allowed me to play with them, learn from them, share and grow with them. Now sound, noise and composition are all one thing and I'm performing it all. Everything is everything. Coming full circle indeed.

CHAPTER
34

LISTEN AND REACT

An Attempt to Organize Various Possible Manifestations of Improvisations Within Notated Composition

ANNA WEBBER

I am a composer, saxophonist, and flutist active in both improvised and composed music, mostly in music that is part of the jazz world, broadly speaking. In my music I try to find some common ground where complex notational systems overlap with improvisation in ways that feel natural despite whatever underlying compositional systems might exist, and to create music that connects with listeners on both an intellectual and visceral level.

When I began to get serious about composition, I questioned the need for improvisation in my music at all. I felt like I was spending all this time laboring over pacing and other various minute details just to open up sections of the music to the capriciousness of how someone else (or I) felt in the moment. In struggling with this dilemma, I kept coming back to the basic fact that I am an improvisor, and improvising is a deep-rooted and joyful part of my musical personality. I realized that rather than rescinding control, I have the ability as a composer to create the most perfect vessels for myself as an improvisor, as both the written notes and the improvisation are coming from the same mind. Simultaneously, I began to question the concept that had been instilled in me from the beginning of my jazz education as a woodwind player, whether consciously or subconsciously: that everything revolves around whoever is taking an improvised solo at a given moment. Also problematic was that my own opinion of how good I felt a given solo was — based on a myriad of musical factors, but also non-musical ones such as what I ate for lunch or how much sleep I had the previous night — could sooth or destroy my ego and how I felt about myself both as a musician and human, at least until the next opportunity to improvise.

I eventually came to the realization that improvisation doesn't have to be about the ego of a single soloist; there are many ways to include improvisation in a piece of music. It can be integrated within a score, and can be about building something together. This line of thinking is certainly not revolutionary — many composers in improvised traditions have thought this way for a long time, perhaps from the earliest occurrences of improvised music. But for me, this new awareness was crucial in overturning some norms passed on to me by a tradition of jazz education that attempts to place a radical art form into digestible boxes.

More and more, I am coming to the conclusion that this broadened definition of improvisation also mirrors my political worldview. While I don't think my music is inherently political, there seems to be something anti-capitalist in subverting the myth of the solitary genius composer, and instead allowing everyone's creative voice to be heard equally. And, by challenging the patriarchal image of the strongman improvisor, interweaving collectivism into improvisation holds something in common with socialist values.

* * *

Before going further, I want to define improvisation as it appears in my music. At its most inclusive, improvisation could be defined as "the composer asks the performer to make a decision". This is not the only definition — there are plenty of improvisational practices in which there is no single composer, for example — but for my music it works.

I write solo features too, but I try to remember that a solo feature is just one possible manifestation of improvisation, just one dot on a graph that details all extant forms of musical decision-making. Widening the definition of improvisation like this makes it less a question of "who's soloing?" and instead opens up several spectra of possibilities.

Clockwise

Clockwise is the title track from my 2019 album on Pi Recordings. The piece plays with various levels of density and determinacy, and deals with controlling specific variables of how decisions are being made. The form of the entire piece is basically symmetrical and, as far as determinacy goes, is as follows:

soloist with improvised accompaniment
soloist with written accompaniment
no improvisation

soloist with written accompaniment
written material with improvised accompaniment

In the section excerpted here, the bass flute is the primary improvisor, with the vibraphone, cello, and trombone being secondary accompanying improvisors. The upright bass part is fully notated, and operates as a sort of cantus firmus. The bass flute is given a set of pitches representing the harmony that is occurring, but no further instructions. Each of the secondary improvisors is each given two possible note choices per chord and told to interpret these notes through tremolos, bisbigliandi, flutter-tonguing, and the like. Their pitch content is controlled, their method of sound-production is controlled, and their level of density is controlled ("do not play all the time or on every chord"), but they all still have a certain amount of freedom.

Idiom VI, Movement I

The excerpted section of this piece, for large ensemble, has no primary improvisor. Rather, the ensemble works collectively to create a moving, scurrying carpet of improvised sound that is then interrupted by specific non-improvised objects. The parameters of this "carpet" are highly controlled: the pitches are specified, as are the dynamics, the approximate rhythms, the articulations, and the exact durations.

TRANSPOSED SCORE

Idiom VI, movement i

Anna Webber

Idiom II

Idiom II is from the album *Clockwise*. While the cello is the primary soloist in the first section here (letter C), the two tenor saxophones have background materials that are a combination of improvised and composed. The material is pre-determined, but the placement of it is up to the players. While box 1 is interpreted literally, boxes 2 and 3 are meant to merely be starting places, and not strictly interpreted. At letter D the saxophone background material from box 3 becomes the primary focus and a jumping off point into collective improvisation. The saxophones play their written line twice and then improvise rhythmically on a 16th note grid; at the same time the cello and trombone take over the former role of the saxophones by playing written background figures at a placement of their own choosing. Bass and drums are given text instructions ("popping noises") specifying the language-type with which they should begin improvising.

4
Idiom II - TRANSPOSED SCORE
C
OPEN
CELLO SOLO
PLAY VAMP SEVERAL Xs, THEN BREAK AWAY FROM IT
TENOR BACKGROUNDS:
All of these boxes are open and can be played in any order and/or played more than once
React to soloist, but also don't play all the time, leave space
1. play on cue, as written, but rubato
2 + 3. very loose, improvise with similar material; don't necessarily play this as written
3. continues through to letter E, which is on cue
CONTINUE IMPROVISING
(bass cues for reference — do not play)
Bass cues (do not play these) — ACCOMPANY CELLO SOLO
(play whole note 1st X only)
Groove as before/support soloist
Bass part for reference
OPEN
CELLO SOLO CONTINUES
OUT OF TIME
freely accompany
cello solo

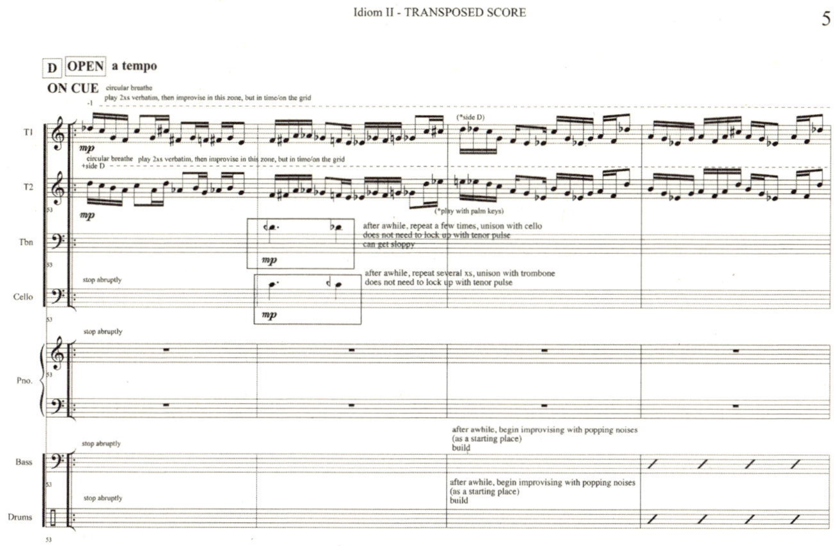

* * *

Manifestations of Improvisation

There are several sets of questions that I have found useful to ask myself as I compose in order to make sure I consider other options and remember that improvisation has many variables. I have tried to break each of the answers to these questions down into the smallest possible component parts, but it is important to recognize that none of these are likely to exist in total isolation, and the combinatorial possibilities should be explored. Additionally, it bears mentioning that the questions (and their subsequent answers) are not meant to be exhaustive, rather they represent a snapshot of some of the brainstorming I've done on the subject, and it is my hope that they can be added to, manipulated, adapted, and/or discarded as the reader sees fit.

1. Who is making the decisions? And, where does that person/do these people fall in the overall texture of the music?

Looking at the answers to these questions as two complementary spectra, one of which runs from "no one improvising" to "everyone improvising" and the other from "foreground" to "background", aids me in remembering the different roles specific people can play within the texture of a composition.

No improvisation
One person as primary improvisor

completely alone

solo feature (with either composed or improvised accompaniment, or some hybrid)

Two or more people as primary improvisors (small group to entire ensemble)

equal voices, improvising collectively

trading (4s, 8s, phrases, abstract)

with or without ensemble (again, either composed or improvised accompaniment, or a hybrid)

One, two, or multiple people as secondary or tertiary improvised texture

accompaniment behind a written melody or other composed structure

accompaniment behind a primary improvisation

comping in a traditional jazz sense

according to some new set of rules created by the composer

2. How much freedom is there in the decision-making?

The answers to this question can also be seen as a spectrum, this one running from "completely composed" to "completely improvised". What aspect of what an improvisor is doing is controlled? In a traditional jazz context the soloist is seemingly free to do whatever they want, but generally speaking they are (at least somewhat, and very much dependent on the aesthetic of the improvisor) cycling through a collection of pitch sets and harmonic milestones over a specified rhythmic grid, often using pre-determined "acceptable" language. I find that thinking about this question is especially useful in working out ways of incorporating secondary or tertiary improvisation in a piece.

Completely composed

Composed, but room to interpret

a single line (melody, bass line, etc.) that can be elaborated upon harmonically or rhythmically (or both)

a set of chord changes or voicings that can be expanded upon, or be interpreted loosely

a specific phrase or rhythm or gesture that can be placed, temporally, wherever the improviser deems it appropriate

Some specified variable, or set of variables

specified rhythm

a specific and defined rhythm or rhythmic grid

approximate, such as "play eighth notes" or "continue in

this approximate rhythmic vein"

- specified pitches or timbres
    - single pitch or timbre
    - pitch set, interval set, or timbre set, interpreted freely
    - pitch set, interval set, or timbre set, in a specific order
- specified way of making sound
    - "normal" playing, i.e., with pitches
    - specific types of sounds, i.e. multiphonics, air noises, inside the piano, etc.
    - speech
    - singing
- specified way of phrasing or playing, i.e. "play melodically" or "intense"
- specified language
    - unspoken, as in the above described traditional jazz solo
    - clearly outlined, like "bluesy" or "triadic" or "large intervals"
- specified tessitura
    - high register, low register, etc.
- specified grid — harmonic, rhythmic, etc., generally referred to as "form"
    - repeating/cyclic
    - through-composed

Specified starting place, ending place, and/or fragment within an improvisation

- abstract — mood, vibe, etc.
- energy level, dynamic
- specific melodic/rhythmic/timbral information

Completely open — entirely up to the improvisor

3. What information does the improvisor have to make these decisions?

This is similar to #2, but instead of referring to the aspect of a person's improvisation that is controlled, it refers to how the composer's ideas are translated on the page to the improvisor. I believe that notation can make a difference in interpretation and therefore is almost as important as the other elements in determining the outcome of an improvisation. Does the improvisor see chord changes? Do they see any sort of instructions at all? I refer to all of these information-types in isolation, but they can of course be used combinatorially.

No information

completely free, no references

or, the composer willfully withholds information about what is going on underneath the improvisor in order to achieve a specific effect

Text instructions

to create a specific mood or direction

to describe something about the improvisation that is not obvious from the notation

Given rhythmic structure

a defined tempo

a specific (possibly repeating) rhythmic grid

occasional important rhythmic accents (hits) outlined

Given harmonic and/or timbral structure

chord changes

spelled out harmonic information without the use of chord changes as shorthand

scales/pitch sets

specific voicings

abstract harmonic information, such as "clustery", "wide intervals", etc.

bass line/bass notes

ensemble cue parts

melody to be embellished upon or used as a reference

defined types of sounds that are being used in the ensemble (i.e., multiphonics, growls, air sounds, etc.)

4. Where does the decision-making happen within a composition? What purpose does it serve?

The placement of improvisation within a composition, both literal and abstract is, I think, incredibly important. The predictability of a head-solo-head form can become boring after a while, as can hearing multiple improvisors solo one after another on the same form. Similarly, using improvisation as linking material to go from one section to the next, a trick I am very guilty of overusing, gets tired quickly. Considering all these possibilities can make a huge difference in making a set of music varied and interesting for both performers and listeners.

Literal placement in a composition *(obvious, but worth considering!)*

beginning
middle
end
if there are multiple featured improvisors, are they all featured at the same place in the composition?

Metaphoric placement/compositional intent
energy creation/control
narrative development
linking material
to feature a specific musician or set of musicians
to keep musicians engaged and active
to create a specific texture
release of tension

* * *

Listen and React

In closing, I'd like to take a look at a final example from my work. Rebonds is from the album *Both Are True* by the Webber/Morris Big Band, a collaboration between myself and saxophonist/composer Angela Morris. An unfortunate truth in writing for big band or large ensemble is that not everyone is going to get a satisfying solo feature. In this context it is extra important to involve more people in various levels of the decision-making process, as it keeps the players engaged and interested. While Rebonds is a guitar feature from start to finish, two trumpets, two trombones, and two saxophones have staggered entrances behind the guitarist to create secondary improvised textures. They all have very specific instructions. The trumpets are told to "create a carpet of unpitched sound", the trombones to play "slow, quiet glissandi", and the saxophones to play "sparse whispery upper register trills and squeaks". The goal is to insert controlled chaos, and to help the guitar soloist build and maintain intensity. To take it a step further, later in the piece all six secondary improvisers have the instruction "listen and react." While they have freedom to go beyond their earlier parameters, they are still meant to be supportive of everything else that is going on.

"Listen and react" seems to me to be an excellent way of thinking about improvisation in general. Whether one is talking about collective free improvisation, traditional jazz improvisation, or anything in between, one should listen first, and react second. The goal of all of the above is to create frameworks in which the performers are free to listen and to react as themselves within a multitude of different situations. Organizing my thoughts about improvisation in this way has been helpful to me, challenging me to avoid compositional habits and to carefully self-examine my motivations for various decisions I am making. It has helped me to figure out ways of obscuring the distinction between written material and improvised material, which is often something I strive for. By trusting and including more minds as equal voices in the decision-making process it has also, I hope, made my music texturally and creatively richer, and more rewarding to perform.

CHAPTER 35

MUSIC AND VISUAL ART

CHRISTIAN WOLFF

They're different, as sound and visual experiences are different. This is how John Dewey puts it:

> The connections of cerebral tissues with the ear constitute a larger part of the brain than those of any other sense... It is a truism that the visible scene is evident; the idea of being clear, plain, is all one with being in view — in plain sight... The eye is the sense of distance — not just that light comes from afar, but that through vision we are connected with what is distant and thus forewarned of what is to come... The material to which the ear relates through sound is opposite at every point. Sounds come from outside the body, but sound itself is near, intimate. Sounds stimulate directly to immediate change because it reports a change. A foot-fall, the breaking of a twig, the rustling of underbrush may signify attack or even death... Sound is the conveyor of what impends, of what is happening as an indication of what is likely to happen. It is fraught much more than vision with the sense of issues; about impending there is always an aura of indeterminates and uncertainty... Vision arouses emotions in the form of interest — curiosity solicits further examination, but it attracts; or it institutes a balance between withdrawal and forward exploring action. It is sound that makes us jump.
>
> *Art as Experience*, 1934, Perigee paperback, 2005, pp. 247–8

* * *

At least since the early 20th century the work of visual artists and musicians can be variously connected. Debussy and impressionist art, for instance. John Cage was close to visual artists all his life. Cage also made a body of visual work, prints and watercolors (which are often quite beautiful, though I think less persuasive than his music: he uses for the artwork the same chance procedures as for his music, but the resultant art work is a fixed object, while in the music there is fluid presence and indeterminacy when it is performed, a process). Schoenberg made some quite impressive expressionist paintings. Earle Brown made some paintings, unexceptionally abstract. I've done some drawing. There are drawings by Gyorgy Kurtag. And there were Varèse, Carl Ruggles, Gershwin, and others, who produced art work. The music was better than the visual work. In the other direction, Duchamp made several quasi-musical pieces involving chance procedures, and Kurt Schwitters made the *Ursonata*. I can think of only one composer-visual artist whose work is equally strong in both activities, Chris Newman.

Newman, incidentally, supports himself with his art work. The economics of being a musician, even a quite successful one, and being a painter, are notably different. When did a piece of music last fetch millions, as some painters' works do routinely? Of course you can't hang a piece of music on your wall. There is a history of some visual artists helping financially to support musicians and musical activity.

Morton Feldman (who himself did no art work) is a composer one most associates with visual art. He was especially close to Rothko and Philip Guston. When he spoke or wrote, visual art often came into it. In the early years he would work on his graph pieces with the paper on the wall, like pictures in the making, so he could stand back and look them over. But at the same time sound as such and nothing more was essential to him. In a lecture in Toronto in 1982 he says "...my dream always when I write, is that I want to do it abstractly. Because I feel that if you finally do it abstractly nothing could equal it. No representational painting can equal maybe one or two paintings where Rothko made it...Same with Mondrian...So I have a total political conviction in that abstract sensation, without an iconic, iconography, no matter how startling, or no matter how fantastic it is..." [*Morton Feldman Says*, edited Chris Villars, p. 145]. The model of what he is saying is from the visual arts — abstraction vs. representation — but he's actually talking about his music. With the exception of *Rothko Chapel* no music of Feldman's refers to any art work, though there are pieces titled, in friendship and appreciation, *For Franz Kline*, *De Kooning*, *Piano Piece (to Philip Guston)*, *For Philip Guston*. *Rothko Chapel* is a peculiar piece in Feldman's work, ignoring, in its extended conclusion, abstraction, when it uses a sort of Hebraic tune he composed as a teenager, accompanied by a Philip Glass-like repeated modal figure in steady eighth-notes (not, I think, a convincing music). The visual element in Feldman that emerges extensively in his late work is connected, as he himself noted, to the patterning of Near Eastern rugs, and the process of their coloring that caused shifting intensities in a given color. The analogy of something visual, with specific physical features, but not any specific art work (though the individual rugs are works of art) with Feldman's later music is clear. And both operate in an entirely abstract way, involving just structure and procedure, repetition or looping with constant slight modifications in continuous but identifiably different patches. [Slight modification is a key feature in Feldman's musical textures: sometimes, just notionally, in the spelling of accidentals, where he means some kind of difference between, say, a G flat and an F sharp, or A double flat and a G, which of course on the piano are the same notes (and the piano is what Feldman always starts with). But mostly this is in the rhythmic patterning, which is continuously a little bit irregular (e.g. 3 beats in the time of 5, or 7 in the time of 4, etc.)]

So, what is it with abstraction and representation? You could say they may have overlaps. For instance, Velasquez paints a piece of lace: standing back you see a piece of lace, but when you get up close you see what look like random flecks of white paint (there is no photographic, literal representation). The latter by themselves are "abstract", but they also serve to make you see, a little further away, a representation, an image, of lace. Abstract painting may be just that, no recognizable image is there. Then again, abstract swirls of color and fluid shapes might suggest (most often) something of a natural landscape, say with de Kooning or Joan Mitchell or Helen Frankenthaler. Is there anything like this in music? There has been "representation" in music: storms or war-like conflict, countryside pastoral (via conventional associations of flutes and triplet rhythms), e.g. Beethoven's *6th Symphony* (the "pastoral"); Bach moving melody lines up (exaltation), or down (sorrow). And movie music. Most of this, though, is fairly trivial. Music is generally, when not combined with words in songs or drama (a whole other set of issues), regarded as abstract, non-representational. Abstract sensation, as Feldman said.

Then again, (abstract) music can evoke feeling, usually quite difficult to define, sometimes strongly, there. Occasionally I hear something in a piece of music that suddenly moves me quite unexpectedly to tears. And I can't explain this. It's a very direct un-mediated effect. John Dewey again: "in itself the ear is the emotional sense." Non-representational art may also suggest not only nameable images but also states of feeling, but these (at least in my experience) don't have the immediate effect that music has.

The equivalent of visual representation in music, apart from the literally imitated storms sounds and the like, would be recognizable quotations from music that listeners would be expected to recognize, collage effects. In art one could think of, say, Rauschenberg's use of newspaper images transferred to the canvas, where there would also be non-representational painting. Keith Rowe in his improvisation might suddenly, for a few minutes, play a recording of some baroque music. There is John Cage's *Variations 4*, using a heap of records, and before that *Credo in Us*. Both, and others, have used radios. The musical use of "found" or borrowed material may also be primarily a technical, compositional matter. Renaissance composers often use a tune or bit of traditional chant as compositional material, often in ways that are unnoticeable, e.g. the tune is presented at a fourfold slower speed so, even if you could hear it out of the contrapuntal texture, you could hardly recognize it. I sometimes do this too, but fairly briefly and often not quite noticeably, offering a fragment of a tune or rhythm, to get started on pitch and rhythm choices.

Music and visual arts, or any other arts may share basic presuppositions and attitudes. For instance, Jasper Johns makes several remarks about his work that make musical sense to me. Here is one, on being asked whether his paintings might suggest various particular meanings:

> I think it is quite possible that the paintings can suggest those things. I think as a painter one cannot proceed to suggest those things, that, when you begin to work with the idea of suggesting, say, a particular psychological state of affairs, you have eliminated so much from the process of painting that you make an artificial statement which is, I think, not desirable. I think one has to work and accept the kind of statement which results as unavoidable or as a helpless situation. I think that one wants from painting a sense of life. The final suggestion, the final statement, has to be not a deliberate statement but a helpless statement. It has to be what you can't avoid saying, not what you set out to say. I think one ought to use everything one can use, all of the energy should be wasted in painting it, so that one hasn't the reserve of energy which is able to use the thing. One shouldn't really know what to do with it, because it would match what one is already; it shouldn't just be something one likes.
>
> —From a 1965 interview with David Sylvester in *Writings, Sketchbook Notes, Interviews* [The Museum of Modern Art, New York, 1996]

* * *

In a recent letter, responding to my question about representation in music and visual art, Chris Newman, composer and visual artist, says more sharply what I've tried to outline above:

> ...recognizability of something which you can of course have in figurative painting but not in music — or can you? I think not. I mean of course you can have recognizability within the medium — like using Beethoven's *3rd* (which I am at the moment) but not as references to objects in "real life". I suppose figurative painting is always a portrayal which means its effect on you is always quasi-indirect, whereas music with its abstraction — it's like it's been unhinged — let off the hook & can get into any of those cracks & crevices. Of course the sounds of life are always being translated into musical terms, but that has more to do with a situation — a storm or something, than an object, & one could quote literally a real-life sound — but it always remains a quote & sounds a bit dinky.

* * *

Afterthought

When John Dewey says sound is what makes you jump he reminds that sound can also make you dance. Its effect is not only on the ear but on the body as a whole. What you see doesn't do that. But what you see can make you think, may trigger ideas, in a way that music doesn't quite give you time for.

CHAPTER 36

ON RHYTHM

MIGUEL ZENÓN

My grandmother used to have this beautiful glass figurine, sort of like a crystal ball with a red flower inside it. This same figurine served as my own personal drum set for a while as I banged away with pencils to the tune of one of my favorite commercials. This went on for a few days until the figurine crumbled under my rhythmic punishment, both angering and astonishing my grandmother.

"Why would you do that?" she asked, to which my 8-year-old self found no reply other than the obvious: "I just felt liked banging on it".

I think back to that memory frequently, remembering how it felt to mimic a drum pattern or to play along to a beat without really knowing what I was doing or what I was searching for. It turns out that what I was searching for was that natural high that comes from being "inside" a rhythmic structure: that rush you get when it just feels like you're part of it in every way.

* * *

But what does it mean to be "inside" a rhythm? What is it like to fit within that structure? For many, that connection is very physical, and it manifests itself through body movement and dance. Letting our bodies react to the sounds around us is one of the purest forms of human expression, and the act of dancing is something that can be found in every society and cultural group on earth, with virtually no exceptions. It comes in all shapes and forms, from solo to couples, from secular to religious. Some dances follow the beat of a drum; others give the dancer control over where those drums go. We can trace the evolution of dance from something that was most likely improvised at first and eventually formalized enough to be systematically turned into a "dance style." And even within one "style," you could find some serious variations, affecting how the dancer reacts to the groove or interacts with a dance partner, or even how much or how little our hips move as we find our place within the music.

Even though I started playing professionally at a very young age — mostly playing Salsa, Merengue and other forms of Caribbean Dance Music — I didn't really start dancing until I got to college. I felt very connected to this music way before that, and enjoyed watching (and making) people dance. But I didn't feel like I knew the steps well enough not to look ridiculous, at least to my eyes, on the dance floor. Of course, teenage inhibition as well as my distorted perception of my place within the social food chain played a big part here. I wasn't as worried about my inability to connect with the music at a rhythmic level as I was about what my friends might think if I took a wrong turn while on dance duty. Granted, many of my friends didn't mind looking foolish on the dance floor. In fact, they embraced the opportunity of letting their limbs take over while joking around. But that wasn't the case with me. I wanted to have a basic idea of what I was doing before jumping into the dance pool.

As is usually the case, many of my inhibitions dissipated as soon as I became a college student. Being far from home, with new friends (plus a roommate with some serious steps) got me dancing right away. I realize now that as soon as I started doing that, my relationship with rhythm became much deeper. It wasn't just about playing a rhythmic figure with your instrument — or even clapping or singing. Instead, I was taking in rhythm and interpreting it with my whole body. It also made me recognize my dance style, and specifically with Salsa, which is my dance music of choice: always on the beat, not a lot of spins, and the simpler the better.

I still dance now, although not as much as my wife would like me to. The feeling is still one of immersion within a rhythmic structure, bouncing off things as they come and go, just flowing through it.

* * *

If we define dancing as the act of letting our body naturally express movement as it reacts to rhythmic ideas, then the flip side of that would be a conceptual understanding of rhythm and of its virtually infinite possibilities — something closer to an intellectual analysis than to organic physical expression. I think of this as "rhythmic theory."

In Puerto Rico, as is the case in most of the Caribbean, music is really embedded in everyday life, and you can find it everywhere. Even though I grew up surrounded by all these sounds, I didn't encounter music theory — a formalized way to organize and define these sounds — until I attended music school. It was a very good school and my training was thorough and rigorous. It was at this school where I heard terms like "solfege", "harmony," and "counterpoint" for the first time. It was also where I learned to think about music in the same systematic way I could think about math or physics.

Years later, I started thinking about rhythm from this perspective, not only inspired by the ideas I was getting from listening to tons of Afro-Caribbean music from Puerto Rico and Cuba (mainly *Bomba*, *Plena*, *Rumba*, and *Batá* music), but also informed by my love for numbers. So, to my ears, a Jesus Alfonso quinto solo over a *Muñequitos de Matanzas* track or a Yubá from *Los Hermanos Ayala* went from being an amazing combination of sounds to a series of very specific rhythms and counter rhythms, all interacting with each other. It became clear to me how alternating subdivisions between triplets and eight notes (or 3s and 2s) was a very effective way of sparking rhythmic tension. Or how re-organizing those eight notes in odd groupings against the beat created an alternate rhythmic layer that somehow felt both floaty and precise.

This led to a very particular way of thinking about rhythm, inspired by theory and analysis. In the same way I could look at a John Coltrane solo and say something like, "If he plays this over a C7 chord, that means that if I transpose this up a perfect fourth I could also play it over F7" I could also say something like, "If I take three measures of 4/4, subdivided into eight notes, and accent those eight notes in groups of three, I end up with eight new 'accents' or cross rhythms (in this case dotted quarter notes), which could in turn become my new pulse (or quarter note) and lead me to modulate into a slower tempo."

So, a door was opened and through it came a whole new set of questions: What happens if my pulse is a dotted quarter, instead of a quarter? And if that happens over a 12/8 measure? Or 15/8? Or 21/8? What are my options then? How many layers can I work with? How about if my subdivision is not 2 or 3 to the beat, but 5 or 7?

To some, this way of thinking about music could be considered mathematical or dry, or even boring. But to me, it is nothing short of magical. It's kind of like looking at an amazing athlete, someone like Usain Bolt or Michael Jordan, admiring their skill and natural ability without really understanding how they do what they do, and then taking a peek inside, looking at their mechanisms to admire all the little details that make it work. That way of gazing into a rhythmic structure has become one of the most satisfying and informative musical experiences for me, and a priority when I listen to or create music myself. It's also another way of getting "inside" a rhythm: not just interpreting it, but understanding it fully.

* * *

A new friend (a neurologist and music lover) pointed out to me recently that the parts of our brain that are involved in generating movement interact heavily with the parts of our brain that generate feelings of joy or satisfaction. I found a lot of comfort in that. It made me think that we can experience rhythm with our intellect as well as with our body. It cemented my inclination to keep searching for ways inside rhythmic structures — ways that can challenge the mind, but also groove hard. The kind of music that will keep me banging pencils on my furniture, that will make my now 90-year-old grandmother dance in two rhythmic layers at once. Finding her way in.

ABOUT THE MUSICIANS

Born in Cleveland, Ohio, Susan Alcorn started playing guitar at the age of 12 and quickly immersed herself in folk music, blues, and the pop music of the 1960s. A chance encounter with blues musician Muddy Waters steered her towards playing slide guitar. By the time she was 21, she had immersed herself in the pedal steel guitar, playing in country and western swing bands in Texas. Soon, she began to combine the techniques of country-western pedal steel with her own extended techniques to form a personal style influenced by free jazz, avant garde classical music, Indian ragas, Indigenous traditions, and various folk musics of the world. By the early 1990s her music began to show an influence of the holistic and feminist "deep listening" philosophies of Pauline Oliveros. Though mostly a solo performer, Alcorn has collaborated with numerous artists including Pauline Oliveros, Eugene Chadbourne, Chris Cutler, Joe Giardullo, Caroline Kraabel, Ingrid Laubrock, Le Quan Ninh, Josephine Foster, Joe McPhee, Ken Vandermark, LaDonna Smith, Mike Cooper, Walter Daniels, Ellen Fullman, Jandek, George Burt, Janel Leppin, Michael Formanek, Ellery Eskelin, Fred Frith, Maggie Nicols, Evan Parker, Zane Campbell, Mary Halvorson and Nate Wooley. She has written on the subject of music for the UK magazine *Resonance and CounterPunch*. Her article *The Road the Radio, and the Full Moon* was included in *The Best Music Writing of 2006* published by Da Capo Press. In 2016, she was voted "Best Other Instrument" by the International Critics Poll. In 2017 she received the Baker Artist Award, and in 2018, along with saxophonist Joe McPhee, she was the recipient of the Instant Award in Improvised Music. She lives in Baltimore, Maryland with her husband, photographer David Lobato.

Oren Ambarchi is a composer, multi-instrumentalist and musical polymath who has been releasing records with the frequency of someone who prefers studio time to sleep. His longform compositions have featured many friends and collaborators constituting some of his most adventurous work to date and demonstrating his slippery capacity for stylistic shapeshifting whilst retaining his singular musical language. In his spare time Ambarchi runs the Black Truffle label. For more information, please see www.orenambarchi.com www.blacktrufflerecords.com

Susan Alcorn

Oren Ambarchi

In a career that spans six decades, pianist Ran Blake has created a

Ran Blake

unique niche as a composer, performing artist, and educator. With a characteristic mix of spontaneous solos, modern classical tonalities, the great American blues and gospel traditions, and themes from classic film noir, Ran's singular sound has earned a dedicated following all over the world. His legacy includes nearly six decades as a groundbreaking educator at New England Conservatory. Ran Blake's teaching emphasizes what he calls "the primacy of the ear," an innovative approach that elevates the listening process to the same status as the written score. Musicians of note who have studied with Ran include Ricky Ford, Dominique Eade, Matthew Shipp, Frank Carlberg, John Medeski, Isaac Wilson, Alonzo Harris. While Ran Blake's teaching has been a major part of his musical legacy, his work as a composer and performer is the source of his recognition as a wholly individual artist — and the basis of his MacArthur "Genius" Award in 1988. He has performed in forty-eight states of the US, throughout Europe and Scandinavia. His nearly fifty recordings have built a huge following around the world.

PETER BLEGVAD is an illustrator, writer, musician, broadcaster and teacher, born in New York City, now based in London. His cartoon strip, *Leviathan*, ran in the *Independent* on Sunday from 1991–'98 and *The Book of Leviathan* was published in 2000 by Sort Of Books in the UK and by Overlook Press in the US. Two Chinese and a French translation have been published since. He has been writing and recording music since the mid-'70s with Slapp Happy, Faust, Henry Cow, John Greaves, The Golden Palominos, John Zorn, Andy Partridge and others. As a broadcaster, he created many dozens of "eartoons" (audio cartoons) for BBC Radio 3, winning a Sony award in 2003. He won another in 2012 for *Use It or Lose It* a radio play about dementia made with composer Iain Chambers. In 2014 Uniformbooks published Blegvad's book *Kew. Rhone.* about the eponymous 1977 album. A book about his lifelong epistemological project, *Imagine, Observe, Remember* was published in 2020 by Uniformbooks/Amateur Enterprises. Related works have been exhibited in Kunstverein Hannover and Kunsthalle Düsseldorf (2004), in the Kunsthalle Luzern (2007), in Extra City, Antwerp (2010) and elsewhere. His latest album is *Go Figure* (2017) on the ReR MegaCorp label. The Peter Blegvad bandbox (six CDs with an 80-page booklet) was released on the same label in 2018. He was Awarded the *Ordre de la Grande Gidouille* by the Collège de 'Pataphysique, Paris, in 2000. In 2010 he was elected president of the London Institute of 'Pataphysics.

Peter Blegvad

Tyondai Braxton

TYONDAI BRAXTON is an American composer of electronic and notated music. He studied music composition at The Hartt School of the University of Hartford in West Hartford, Connecticut with Robert Carl, Ingram Marshall. His work ranges from solo pieces to music for large orchestra and electronics. Braxton is also the co-founder of the experimental rock band Battles. Braxton has been commissioned for compositions by ensembles and organizations such as The BBC Concert Orchestra, The Finnish Radio Symphony Orchestra, The Bang on a Can All Stars, Kronos Quartet, Alarm Will Sound, Yarn/Wire, Carnegie Hall, Black Mountain College and many more. His critically acclaimed work, *Central Market* (Warp Records), has been performed by world renowned orchestras such as The LA Philharmonic, The Wordless Music Orchestra, and BBC Symphony Orchestra. Notable collaborations include performing as a duo with Philip Glass for the festival All Tomorrow's Parties, collaborating visual artist Thomas Demand presenting work at Los Angeles County Museum of Art and Prada Foundation at Venice Biennale in 2017, His multimedia project *HIVE* for 3 percussionists and 2 modular synth performers was commissioned by and premiered at the Guggenheim NYC in 2014 followed by the recording released in 2015 HIVE1 (Nonesuch Records). In 2018 Braxton premiered *Telekinesis* for large orchestra, choir and electronics at The Southbank Centre's Queen Elizabeth Hall in London with the BBC Concert Orchestra and BBC Singers. The Finnish Radio Symphony Orchestra performed the piece in February 2019 in Helsinki, Finland as apart of the Music Nova Festival. As a solo performer of electronic music he has performed all over the world, most notably at Mutek Festival Montreal, Manchester International Festival, The Elbphilharmonie Hamburg, Sydney Opera House in Sydney, Australia, Big Ears Festival in Knoxville, Tennessee, The Broad in Los Angeles California, and Sonar Festival in Barcelona, Spain.

Mexican born vibraphonist, marimbist, improviser and composer Patricia Brennan is a member of Grammy nominated John Hollenbeck Large Ensemble and Michael Formanek Ensemble Kolossus. She is also a member of Phalanx Ambassadors, a project led by pianist Matt Mitchell, the Webber/Morris Big Band, and Tomas Fujiwara's 7 Poets Trio along with cellist and composer Tomeka Reid. She has also collaborated with pianist Vijay Iyer as a member of Blind Spot. Other projects led by Iyer that Brennan has performed include his large ensemble project Open City and several small ensemble performances along with renowned musicians like bassist Reggie Workman and trumpeter Wadada Leo Smith. Patricia's own projects include the newly recorded solo project *Maquishti*, and *Moch*, a collaborative duo with percussionist, drummer and turntablist Noel Brennan (DJ Arktureye) plus special guests. Patricia Brennan is a BlueHaus Mallets artist and currently teaches at the New School for Jazz and Contemporary Music and at the Jazz Studies program at NYU Steinhardt.

Patricia Brennan

John Butcher

John Butcher is a saxophonist whose work ranges through improvisation, his own compositions, multitracked pieces and explorations with feedback, unusual acoustics and non-concert locations. He is well known as a solo performer who attempts to engage with a sense of place. *Resonant Spaces* is a collection of performances recorded during a tour of unusual locations in Scotland and the Orkney Islands. His first solo album, *Thirteen Friendly Numbers*, includes compositions for multitracked saxophones, whilst later solo CDs focus on live performance, composition, amplification and saxophone-controlled feedback. After publishing a PhD (1982) in quantum chromodynamics, Butcher left academia and took off with music. He has since collaborated with hundreds of artists, some for many decades. To name a few: Derek Bailey, John Stevens' SME, Steve Beresford, Matthew Shipp, Akio Suzuki, Rhodri Davies, Gerry Hemingway, Polwechsel,

Magda Mayas, Tony Buck, Gino Robair, Otomo Yoshihide, Eddie Prévost, Okkyung Lee, John Edwards, Paul Lovens, John Russell, Mark Sanders, Ståle Liavik Solberg, Christian Marclay, Phil Minton, and Andy Moor. Compositions have been varied. Three for his own large ensembles at HCMF (including *somethingtobesaid*), saxophone quartets (*Rova & Quasar*), a piece for Futurist Intonarumori, *Tarab Cuts* (based on pre-WWII Arabic recordings, and shortlisted for a British Composer's Award), *Good liquor caused my heart for to sing* for the London Sinfonietta and *Fixations and the Open Road* for CEPRO (in a XVI convent in Mexico City). Butcher also values playing in occasional encounters — ranging from large groups such as Butch Morris' London Skyscraper, the WDR Sinfonieorchester and the EX Orkestra, to duo concerts with David Toop, Sophie Agnel, Joe McPhee, Keiji Haino, Akira Sakata, John Tilbury, Fred Frith, and Yuji Takahashi.

Ben Coniguliaro

Ben Coniguliaro (con-ju-lare-o) is a self-taught multi-instrumentalist, songwriter and composer based in New York. Over the last five years, Ben has produced over twenty releases under a variety of different monikers and for numerous collaborative projects. Wyxz (pronounced: wix-iz) and Sun Colored Chair are two of Ben's most musically adventurous projects, taking influence from a wide variety of artists in the progressive music culture. All of his catalog has been self-released until the release of the Wyxz album *Odyx* in 2020 on Tzadik's Spotlight series. Ben plans on releasing many more albums in the future and continuing to refine his creative approach and musical appetite, while also expanding his palette and repertoire by collaborating with other like minded creators. While Ben excels as a guitarist, he has also been a drummer for close to his entire life, giving him a substantial foundation of both rhythmic and harmonic knowledge.

Amir ElSaffar

Amir ElSaffar is a composer, trumpeter, santur player, and vocalist working at the intersections between jazz, Western classical, and Maqam music of Iraq and the Middle East. An expert jazz trumpeter with a classical background, ElSaffar has created techniques to play microtones and ornaments idiomatic to Arabic music that are not typically heard on the trumpet. He is also one of the few musicians in his generation to master the centuries-old Iraqi maqam tradition, which he performs actively as a vocalist and santur (Iraqi hammered dulcimer) player. As a composer, ElSaffar has created a unique microtonal harmonic language that merges the Arabic maqam modal system with contemporary Western harmony. He tours internationally with several ensembles, including his 6-piece Two Rivers Ensemble and 17-piece Rivers of Sound Orchestra, which combine elements of jazz, contemporary music, and Maqam. ElSaffar has received commissions in the US and Europe, composing works for symphony orchestras, string quartets and small chamber ensembles, large and small jazz ensembles, Middle Eastern music ensembles, as well as hybrid projects with Raga, Flamenco, and Subsaharan African trance music. ElSaffar is a recipient of the Doris Duke Performing Artist Award and United States Artists Fellowship, and is currently a Hodder Fellow at Princeton University, where he is working on his first opera, *Ruins of the Encampment.*

Born into a musical family, KENNY GROHOWSKI grew up in Miami, Florida, where his early days were spent listening to the likes of Richie Ray & Bobby Cruz, Tony Williams *Lifetime* and *Emergency*, Rush, Stravinsky, and any and all music that came his way. By age 12, he began to study theory and percussion with Peter Webster, Steven Kirkland, and the Acuña family, leading to his enrollment into the New World School of The Arts program and eventual tenure at The New School University Jazz & Contemporary Music program in New York City. While attending The New School, Grohowski began to work with the likes of Lonnie Plaxico, Daniel Bernard Roumain (DBR), and Andy Milne in their respective ensembles while ingratiating himself into the broader musical world of New York. From there, Grohowski would go on to work with George Colligan in his late fusion trio, Mad Science, Concord recording artist Benny Reid, Bill T Jones, Rez Abbasi's Junction, The Ze Luis Quartet, composer Jorge Sylvester, and many others, all while branching out musically from his musical beginnings. Joining forces in 2007 with DBR alumni Earl Maneein to form a violin-driven metal band called Resolution 15, Grohowski's foray into the world of Heavy Metal as a performer began. His years spent in the NYC Metal scene with Resolution 15 and subsequently the band Hung, would lay the foundation for his later work in ensembles such as Imperial Triumphant, Secret Chiefs 3, as well as John Zorn's Simulacrum trio and Abraxas, where he would have the opportunity to more fully explore the connections Jazz and Metal and various aboriginal musics and rhythm. In 2017, he briefly joined the legendary Fusion/Jazz Rock ensemble Brand X, leading to his later collaborations with acclaimed bassist Percy Jones. Grohowski currently resides in Brooklyn, New York.

Kenny Grohowski

Tom Guralnick

TOM GURALNICK is the founder and Executive Director of the Outpost Performance Space based in Albuquerque, New Mexico. He has been an arts presenter and performing musician for more than forty years. From 1970, until his retirement from performing in 2003, Guralnick toured nationally and internationally as a solo saxophonist as well as with his own innovative trio, the TG3. In the thirty-two years since Outpost's founding, it has become a nationally respected presenting arts organization which offers a uniquely eclectic mix of jazz, experimental, folk & roots, and international music in its own intimate and elegant performance space as well as in larger venues in the community. Outpost has presented close to 3,000 concerts by artists ranging from Roscoe Mitchell; to Taj Mahal Pops and Mavis Staples, Mighty Clouds of Joy, Odetta, and Sonny Rollins. Outpost also hosts extensive educational programs and youth performance opportunities as well as visual arts exhibits in its Inpost Artspace Gallery. Guralnick is also the Artistic Director of the New Mexico Jazz Festival (Albuquerque & Santa Fe) since 2006. He was an early member of the Western Jazz Presenters Network, an organization which has been block-booking jazz in the western United States since 1995. In 1976, upon moving to New Mexico from Boston, Guralnick ran the New Mexico Jazz Workshop establishing it as an Albuquerque-based, jazz presenting organization, producing concerts by Cecil Taylor, Dexter Gordon, Art Pepper, Sun

Ra, and more. In April of 2016, the Jazz Journalists Association (JJA) named Guralnick a "Jazz Hero." And in 2018 he received a Lifetime Achievement Platinum Music Award from the New Mexico Music Commission.

Mark Helias is a renowned bassist and composer who has performed throughout the world for more than four decades. After his studies at Rutgers University (BA 1974) and The Yale School of Music (M.M. 1976), he began his international career in the Anthony Braxton Quartet. Up to the present time he has performed with a panoply of world class artists including: Edward Blackwell, Anthony Davis, Dewey Redman, Marcel Khalife, Abbey Lincoln, Oliver Lake, Andrew Cyrille, Marilyn Crispell, Julius Hemphill, Don Byron, Uri Caine, Roswell Rudd, Bobby Bradford, Barry Altschul, Ray Anderson, Jane Ira Bloom, Jason Moran, John Zorn, Nasheet Waits, Don Cherry, David Krakauer, Cecil Taylor, and Gerry Hemingway. Helias has written music for two feature films as well as chamber pieces and works for large ensemble and big band. His orchestra piece *Stochasm* was premiered by the American Composers Orchestra in June of 2011. He has produced many recordings for other artists including Ray Anderson, Tony Malaby, Bobby Previte, Jerome Harris, David Ades and Mark Dresser. Fifteen albums of his music have been released since 1984. In 2020 Mr. Helias released his first solo bass album Available Light, as well as a live trio album with Open Loose *The Third Proposition*, and a sextet recording entitled *Roof Rights*. His most recent release is a duo with saxophonist Tim Berne entitled *Blood From a Stone*. His trio, Open Loose with Tony Malaby and Tom Rainey, has become an archetypal improvising ensemble on the New York scene. He continues performing and recording with BassDrumBone, a 43-year collaboration with Gerry Hemingway and Ray Anderson. Mr. Helias performs solo bass concerts and can also be heard in the innovative bass duo, The Marks Brothers, with fellow bassist Mark Dresser. He teaches privately and at SIM (School for Improvisational Music).

Mark Helias

David Hertzberg

David Hertzberg is a composer from Los Angeles. His opera *The Wake World*, based on the story by Aleister Crowley, was co-presented by the Barnes Foundation and Opera Philadelphia in the fall of 2017, and went on to win the Music Critics Association of North America's Best New Opera Award. The work's debut recording was released in the spring of 2020 on Tzadik. The spring of 2018 saw yet another opera premiere, *The Rose Elf*, after the fairytale by Hans Christian Andersen, presented inside the catacombs of Green-Wood Cemetery in Brooklyn. He is currently at work on his third opera, *Grand Hotel*, a collaboration with director Yuval Sharon and the Los Angeles-based company The Industry. Recent seasons have seen premieres at Carnegie Hall, Lincoln Center, and the Kennedy Center, with ensembles including the American Composers Orchestra, New York City Opera, and the Pittsburgh and Kansas City symphonies. Recent distinctions include a Guggenheim Fellowship, the Andrew Imbrie Award from the American Academy of Arts and Letters, and residencies at MacDowell and Yaddo. He also served as Composer-in-Residence for Opera Philadelphia, and studied at The Juilliard School and the Curtis Institute of Music.

Violinist STEFAN JACKIW has appeared as soloist with the Boston, Chicago, Cleveland, New York, Philadelphia, and San Francisco symphony orchestras, among others. Abroad, he has appeared with the London Philharmonic, the Philharmonia Orchestra, the Seoul and Tokyo Philharmonic, and the Deutsches Symphonie-Orchester Berlin. He is also an active chamber musician. Together with pianist Conrad Tao and cellist Jay Campbell, Stefan is a member of the Junction Trio. He is also a regular collaborator with pianist Jeremy Denk, with whom he has a forthcoming recording of the complete violin sonatas of Charles Ives. Stefan also recently recorded the Beethoven *Triple Concerto* with Inon Barnatan, Alisa Weilerstein, Alan Gilbert and the Academy of St. Martin in the Fields. Recently, Stefan gave the world premiere of American composer David Fulmer's *Violin Concerto No. 2 "Jubilant Arcs"*, written for him and commissioned by the Heidelberg Festival with the Deutsche Kammerphilharmonie under Matthias Pintscher. Next season, he will premiere a new violin concerto, written for him by Conrad Tao. Born to physicist parents of Korean and Ukrainian descent, Stefan Jackiw began playing the violin at the age of four. His teachers have included Zinaida Gilels, Michèle Auclair, and Donald Weilerstein. He holds a Bachelor of Arts from Harvard University, as well as an Artist Diploma from the New England Conservatory, and is the recipient of a prestigious Avery Fisher Career Grant.

Born in 1970 in Chicago, DAN KAUFMAN grew up in Madison, Wisconsin. In high school, he studied classical guitar with Dániel Biró; at the University of Wisconsin, Madison, he studied classical guitar with Javier Calderon. In 1991, he moved to New York City. He formed Barbez in 1997. For the past fifteen years, he has been honored to play with his cherished bandmates Pamelia Stickney, John Bollinger, Danny Tunick, Catherine McRae, Peter Hess, and Peter Lettre. In 1999, he began recording with Martin Bisi, who has recorded and mixed virtually all of his work since. His current projects are Barbez, John & Dan (with John Bollinger), and Shibboleth (with Gustavo Costa and Henrique Fernandes.) In 2003, he began an ongoing collaboration with director John Jesurun, performing music for his long-running serial play, *Chang in a Void Moon*. Performances for choreographer (and beloved wife) Juliette Mapp's *One* and composed the music for her show, *The Making of Americans*. Over the years, he has been privileged to perform with Dawn McCarthy, Fiona Templeton, Rebecca Moore, David Cale, Eszter Balint, Sim Cain, Catherine Jauniaux, Corey Fogel, Josh Matthews, Sarah Bernstein, Matteo De Cosmo, Martin Bisi, Dan Coates, Carl Maguire, Ka Baird, Michele Amar, Nils Frykdahl, Dafna Naphtali, Tony Nozero, Shahzad Ismaily, Velina Brown, Shelley Hirsch, and Steve Mackay. He is the author of *The Fall of Wisconsin*, which was published by W.W. Norton in 2018.

Stefan Jackiw

Dan Kaufman

Derek Keller

Born from his uncommon versatility as an award winning composer and performer (guitar/voice), DEREK KELLER's music explores the myriad of possibilities in the coexistence, inter-mingling, and hybridity between contemporary concert music, jazz and rock. Lately, he has been crafting multimedia works in his Modular Music Project. These pieces combine live performance, formal modularity, and the audience's mobile devices to create music along the deterministic-improvisational-aleatoric continuum. Through communicative flexibility between himself, the performers and the audience, the series seeks to address socio-political challenges of our contemporary moment. Keller has received commissions from Loadbang, SACRA/PROFANA, City Water, the Empyrean Ensemble, Fondation Royaumont, Redfish-BlueFish, NOISE, JitaZax, Cantoria, Cappella Gloriana, the Athens Master Chorale, Colin McAllister (guitar), Mark Menzies (violin), and Morris Palter (percussion). His music has been performed in the Americas, Europe, China, and Australia, and at notable festivals such as The World Saxophone Congress, June in Buffalo, SoundOn (La Jolla, CA), and the Festival of New American Music (CSUS). In addition to being a composer, Keller is an accomplished guitarist. He studied with John Sutherland, master-classed with Christopher Parkening, and won or placed in competitions across the country. With his own ensemble, he has performed at festivals, including the Festival of New American Music (2019, '13, '12, '07), In The Flow (2011, '08, '06), and the 2007 Spring Festival of New Music at the University of California, San Diego. Keller holds a Ph.D. in music composition from the University of California, San Diego (2004) and is an Assistant Professor of Music at Southern Oregon University.

Richard Kessler

Richard Kessler's career in the arts spans nearly four decades including work as an educator, musician, teaching artist, advocate, and organizational leader. Richard Kessler holds a dual appointment as the Executive Dean for the College of Performing Arts at The New School and Dean of Mannes School of Music, where he also oversees the School of Jazz and Contemporary Music and the School of Drama. As Dean of Mannes, Richard Kessler developed and implemented a comprehensive plan aiming to make Mannes the most progressive music conservatory in the world. The plan, expanded to include all three performing arts schools at The New School, leaves little untouched and has resulted in a significantly expanded curriculum that rethinks the nature of performing arts education in the 21st century. Prior his appointment as Dean of Mannes, Kessler served as Executive Director of The Center for Arts Education, Executive Director of The American Music Center and before that, Vice President of Artsvision, an international arts education consulting company, where he was a chief architect of The Annenberg Foundation's Challenge to the Nation School Reform Initiative that sought to restore K–12 arts education to the largest school district in the United States. Kessler was a professional trombonist who was awarded the 1990 Walter W. Naumburg Chamber Music Award and taught brass chamber music at the Manhattan School of Music. Kessler commissioned, premiered, and recorded works by composers in Arvo Part, including Anthony Davis, Pauline Oliveros, John Harbison, and Richard Danielpour. Kessler is the board chair of Chamber Music America. Richard Kessler has been recognized with awards from the United Federation of Teachers, ASCAP, Music at the Anthology, and was the keynote speaker for the College Music Society's 2018 Summit on 21st Century Music School Design. Kessler is a graduate of the Juilliard School, where he received his undergraduate and graduate degrees.

Pauline Kim Harris aka PK or Pauline Kim is a Grammy nominated violinist and composer who lives in New York City with violinist and life partner, Conrad Harris of Flux Quartet. The youngest student to have ever been accepted into the studio of legendary violinist, Jascha Heifetz, she has appeared throughout the US, Canada, Europe, Asia and Australia as soloist, collaborator and music director. Known for her work with classical avant-punk violin duo, String Noise, she has toured extensively with Orpheus Chamber Orchestra and continues to collaborate with leading new music ensembles in New York City. Pauline Kim was the first Music Director for the Bill T. Jones/Arnie Zane Dance Company and has been the featured artist for choreographers David Parker and Pam Tanowitz. As a composer, Pauline deconstructs and re-embodies tactile connection between memory and sound. Her music creates a multi-dimensional sonic matrix, transporting the listener to an alternate co-existence. Through composition, she introduces an environment that alters the listener's emotional identity to what they are experiencing. Pauline Kim was an associate artist at the Atlantic Center for the Arts and had her debut residency at The Stone — New School in 2019. In addition to being a fellow at the Norman Bird Sanctuary — Mabel Residency, she was also awarded the EtM Con Edison Residency in 2019. Pauline's debut album, *Heroine* — a reimagining of the Bach *Chaconne* and Ockeghem's *Deo Gratias* was released on Sono Luminus with worldwide distribution on September 27, 2019.

Pauline Kim

Ulrich Krieger

Ulrich Krieger is an internationally renowned German-American composer and saxophonist living in Southern California. He is known for his originality and innovation in composed and free improvised contemporary music. Krieger's compositions are widely performed by ensembles in Europe, USA and Asia. He works in variety of contexts; chamber music, experimental music, free improvisation, electronic music, reductionism, noise, ambient, rock and metal. He has been active in pushing the boundaries of saxophone playing in general and the function of the saxophone in rock and noise in particular. In his distinct style of amplified saxophone playing, Krieger processes refined acoustic and quasi-electronic sounds by amplifying his instrument in various ways. He gets down to the grains of the sounds, changing their identities and structures from within. In addition to Krieger's solo practice, he is leading his own death-doom-noise-metal band Blood Oath and has performed extensively with his groups Metal Machine Trio (with Lou Reed) and Text of Light (with Lee Ranaldo). He has further collaborated and performed with Faust, John Zorn, Merzbow, Thomas Köner, Robert Henke (Monolake), Laurie Anderson, Carl Stone, Christian Marclay, Phill Niblock, Radu Malfatti, Michael Pisaro, Berlin Philharmonics, Ensemble Modern, PARTCH Ensemble, and many more. He is professor for composition, Experimental Sound Practices, and rock music at CalArts, where his special field of interest is the cross-pollination of new art music and avant garde rock. Krieger's recent focus lies on the fringes of contemporary rock culture, in the areas of limbo where noise, metal, silence, and experimental chamber music meet. Not accepting stylistic categories. His compositional approaches include micro-sounds, microtones, reductionism, "instrumental electronics" (instrumental music evoking the soundworld of electronics), drone, and noise; forms that often demand elaborate and nuanced amplification. For more information, please see www.ulrich-krieger.com

Hannah Lash's music has been performed at such major venues as Carnegie Hall, Los Angeles Walt Disney Concert Hall, Lincoln Center, the Times Center in Manhattan, the Chicago Art Institute, Tanglewood Music Center, The Aspen Music Festival & School, among others. In 2016, Lash was honored with a Composer Portrait Concert at Columbia University's Miller Theatre, which included commissioned works for pianist Lisa Moore (*Six Etudes and a Dream*) and loadbang (*Music for Eight Lungs*). In the 2017–2018 season, Lash's *Piano Concerto No. 1 In Pursuit of Flying* was given its premiere performances by Jeremy Denk and the Saint Paul Chamber Orchestra; the Atlantic Classical Orchestra debuted *Facets of Motion for orchestra*, and *Music for Nine*, *Ringing* was performed at the Music Academy of the West School and Festival. Last season, Paul Appleby and Natalia Katyukova gave the world premiere of *Songs of Imagined Love*, a song cycle commissioned by Carnegie Hall. Hannah Lash's chamber opera, *Desire*, recently premiered at Miller Theatre to great acclaim. Hannah Lash's *Concerto* for piano and harp was premiered in November by the Naples Philharmonic. Most recently, Hub New Music premiered Lash's *The Nature of Breaking*, written for Hub New Music and Hannah Lash to perform together as a mixed ensemble with harp. Hannah Lash's music is published exclusively by Schott Music Corporation (New York).

Hannah Lash

Daniel Lippel

Guitarist Daniel Lippel has a multi-faceted career as a performer, recording artist, and label owner. He has premiered more than fifty solo and chamber works, many written for him, recording several on his label, New Focus Recordings. Recent performance highlights include recitals at Le Poisson Rouge (NY), Sinus Ton Festival (Germany), National University of Colombia (Bogota), and the New York and Cleveland Classical Guitar Societies, and chamber performances on the Mostly Mozart Festival, Ojai Festival, Ottawa Chamber Festival, Aspekte Festival (Salzburg), and Kunst Universitaet Graz (Austria). Lippel has been a member of the International Contemporary Ensemble (ICE) since 2006, counter)induction since 2019, FretX duo with Mak Grgic since 2015, as well as a guest with many other ensembles. He has worked closely with many eminent composers including Mario Davidovsky, Nils Vigeland, and John Zorn, and collaborated with several prominent mid-career composers, including Dai Fujikura, Tyshawn Sorey, Reiko Fueting, Du Yun, Cory Smythe, Mikel Kuehn, Ken Ueno, and Wang Lu. In addition to New Focus, he appears on recordings on several other labels including Kairos, Bridge, Innova, Sono Luminus, Albany, Tzadik, Wergo, and New World, and as a producer on several New Focus releases. He was the classical guitarist on several international tours and recordings with Mice Parade, an eclectic indie group that integrates elements from world music. As an educator, Lippel has given guitar masterclasses and presentations at institutions including the Hanns

Eisler Hochschule (Berlin), Curtis Institute, Sydney Conservatorium of Music (Australia), San Francisco Conservatory, Cleveland Institute of Music, Peabody Institute, University of Texas at Austin, and New York University. He received the DMA from the Manhattan School of Music studying with David Starobin, writing his dissertation on the guitar works of Mario Davidovsky.

Annea Lockwood's compositions range from sound art and environmental sound installations to concert music. In addition to *Becoming Air*, the collaboration with Nate Wooley, recent works include *bayou-borne, for Pauline*, a sextet based on a map of Houston's bayou system, *Wild Energy* with Bob Bielecki, a sound installation focused on geophysical, atmospheric and mammalian infra and ultra sound sources at the Caramoor Center for Music and the Arts, Katonah, and *Into the Vanishing Point*, co-composed with the ensemble Yarn/Wire, a meditation on the large-scale disappearance of insect populations. Water has been a recurring focus of her work and her three installation sound maps of rivers, the Hudson River, the Danube and the Housatonic River, have been widely presented. She is a recipient of the SEAMUS Lifetime Award 2020.

Dave Lombardo (born February 16, 1965 in Havana, Cuba) is a 3-time nominated, 2-time Grammy Award winning Cuban American drummer, deemed one of the most significant drummers of our time. Lombardo is most widely known as an aggressive and exceptionally skilled heavy metal drummer, but over time he has proven that his unique gift far surpasses the confines of being labeled. His use of the drums have been called "astonishingly innovative" and earned him the title "The Godfather of Double Bass". Over his career, he has had a significant influence on the metal scene and has inspired many modern metal drummers, particularly within both death metal and thrash metal. As an original and founding member of Slayer, Lombardo has performed with Slayer on seven albums, including their groundbreaking 1986 release *Reign In Blood* and their 2006 release *Christ Illusion*, for which he received critical praise. Lombardo's music career has spanned more than thirty-five years, during which he has been involved in the production of over forty-five commercial recordings crossing a number of major genres with bands such as Fantômas, Grip Inc., Mr. Bungle, Testament, Apocalyptica, Dead Cross, Suicidal Tendencies, John Zorn, in addition to Slayer. Lombardo's most recent endeavors have found him in a variety of compelling adventures; recording drum tracks for various television shows and films, creating an art collection called *Rhythm Mysterium* that has been shown in Los Angeles, New York City, Sydney and Melbourne Australia, in addition to unveiling an extraordinary visual and audio experience with his First Edition Book, *LOMBARDO*. Lombardo is clearly showing no signs of slowing down. With the underground rumblings of more surprises on the way, 2021 promises to be one of his most provocative and inspiring years to date.

Charlie Looker has been active in underground and experimental music circles for the past two decades as a composer, vocalist, gui-

Annea Lockwood

Dave Lombardo

Charlie Looker

tarist, and producer. His music brings together diverse influences and styles including metal, pop, industrial, early music, improvisation, and classical composition. Born and based in New York City, he has received commissions from various ensembles, however most of his output has been with his own bands. Looker was a founding member of the experimental collective Zs, establishing his roots in the 2000s' Brooklyn DIY scene. In 2007 he formed his own band Extra Life, which recorded three albums and several EPs, and toured the US and Europe extensively, before dissolving in 2012. Since then, Looker's main performing vehicle has been metal/electronic project Psalm Zero. Other ongoing projects include medieval folk quartet Seaven Teares; Period, an improvising trio with Mike Pride and Chuck Bettis; and Nothing Human, Looker's all-electronic moniker. In 2018, Looker released the first record under his own name, *Simple Answers*, a song cycle for three singers, 17-piece chamber orchestra, and electronics, on his own imprint Last Things Records. This concept album, dealing with fascist psychology, stand-up comedy, and addiction, was performed in its entirety at National Sawdust (Brooklyn), and was praised by the *The New York Times*, Pitchfork, and NPR. Looker's credits as an arranger, sideman, collaborator, and producer include M Lamar, Dirty Projectors, Tyondai Braxton, Lingua Ignota, Mick Barr, Jherek Bischoff, S.E.M. Ensemble, William Parker, Kate Miller-Heidke, Amanda Palmer, and Mivos Quartet. As a composer in a concert music context, Looker has received fellowships and commissions from the Brooklyn Philharmonic, Yarn/Wire, the Ostrava New Music Days festival, and Experiments in Opera. In 2011 he was voted one of the top 100 American composers under 40 by WNYC. In 2015, Looker was an Artist-in-Residence at The Stone (New York City).

Thomas Morgan is a double bass player with a unique approach to the instrument and an exceptional musical understanding. He has played on more than a hundred recordings and toured all over the world as a member of bands led by Bill Frisell, Jakob Bro, Craig Taborn, Masabumi Kikuchi, Jim Black, Dan Weiss, Paul Motian, John Abercrombie, Dave Binney, Steve Coleman, and Tomasz Stanko, among many others. It is Thomas Morgan's extraordinary way of being in the moment in music and putting his own signature on it that has made him one of the most in demand jazz bassists on the international scene.

Thomas Morgan

Stephen O'Malley

Stephen O'Malley is a guitarist, producer, composer, and visual artist who has conceptualized and participated in numerous drone and experimental music groups for over two decades — SUNN O))), KTL, and Khanate being among his best-known projects. Wildly prolific, O'Malley's oeuvre defines remarkable breadth, complexity and multidisciplinary interests. It includes collaborations with a wide range of experimental musicians and composers, including Scott Walker, choreographer Gisèle Vienne, the authors Dennis Cooper and Alan Moore, Alvin Lucier, Fujiko Nakaya, Jim Jarmusch, experimental music research centres IRCAM, INA-GRM (Paris), EMS (Stockholm) and many others. O'Malley is also a vigorous live performer and has toured around the world.

LAURA ORTMAN (White Mountain Apache, lives and works in Brooklyn, New York) is a soloist and vibrant collaborator who works across recorded albums, live performances, filmic and artistic soundtracks, and is versed in amplified violin, Apache violin, piano, electric guitar, keyboards, percussion, often sings through a megaphone, and is a producer of capacious field recordings. She has performed at The Whitney Museum of American Art and The Museum of Modern Art in New York, The Toronto Biennial in Ontario, the Musée d'Art Contemporain de Montréal, and the Centre Pompidou, Paris, among countless established and DIY venues in the US, Canada, and Europe. In 2008 Ortman founded the Coast Orchestra, an all-Native American orchestral ensemble that performed a live soundtrack to Edward Curtis' film *In the Land of the Head Hunters* (1914), the first silent feature film to star an all-Native American cast. Ortman's video collaboration *My Soul Remainer* is in the collection of the Baltimore Museum of Art in Maryland. Awards: 2020 Jerome@Camargo Residency, 2019 Whitney Biennial, 2017–18 Jerome Foundation Fellowship, 2016 Art Matters Grant Awardee, 2016 Native Arts And Culture Foundation Fellowship, 2014 Rauschenberg Residency, 2015 Social Engagement Residency At Iaia's Museum of Contemporary Native Arts Santa Fe, Artist-in-Residence, Issue Project Room NYC, 2008 First Nations Composers Initiative Grant.

Laura Ortman

Alex Paxton

ALEX PAXTON (1990) is a composer and improvising trombonist based in the UK. Alex's work draws upon a range of classical, experimental, electronic & folk music traditions to create a unique and explosive voice. He was elected to the 9th International Composition Seminar with Ensemble Modern (*Ilollipop*), has won a Royal Philharmonic Society Composition Prize (*Od Ody Pink'd*), Dankworth Jazz Prize, Leverhume Art Scholar Prize (*Now We Are Duh-Dur*) and Harriet Cohen Music Award (*Purple-Tree Tapestry*) and appointed as London Symphony Orchestra Panufnik Composer, *Spake* represented the Orchestral section of the International Society of Contemporary Music. His albums to date: *Music for Bosch People* released on Birmingham Record Company/NMC label, and *Happy Music for Orchestra*. He is featured on the Listen Pony Label (*Tellsong*) and Spotify playlists (eg: Nonclassical). He has performed his music as a soloist with leading orchestras including: Ensemble Modern (*Ilollipop*), London Sinfonietta, The Philharmonia Orchestra (UK), Royal National Scottish Orchestra & Ensemble x.y. Further works include pieces for the London Symphony Orchestra, London Philharmonic Orchestra, Kammer Klang, Bournemouth Symphony Orchestra, Psappa, National Youth Jazz Orchestra (UK). Music theatre works include the operas *For the Love of Thornstien Shiver*, *Bel and the Dragon*, *Woolf Music*, *Equivocal Harriet*, *Noggin the Whale* and *Raven's Child* and were hosted by English National Opera, Helios Colective, Tête à Tête Festival, Second Movement Opera. His Dreammusics Ensemble uniquely combines electronic sounds with leading virtuosic improvising-musician/notated-musician soloists. Alex has extensively written music for community settings and for young performers: *Muffin* and *Fly, Like A Kitchen*. Alex has worked across the UK as an educator in creative-music settings and is composition tutor on the National Youth Orchestra (UK). Alex studied as a scholar at the Royal Academy of Music and the Royal College of Music in London. "Manic, brilliant beauty." Listenpony Records.

ALEXANDRIA SMITH is a trumpeter, technologist, audio engineer, and multimedia artist that enjoys working at the intersection of all of these disciplines. Her current research and performance interests engage with building, designing, and performing with wearable electronics that ethically translate embodied, biological data into interactive sonic and visual environments. Recent projects include performing on Billy Martin's record *Guilty* (2020), performing at the VI Semana Internacional de Improvisación in Ensenada, Baja California, curating a residency at The Stone at the New School, performing in the premiere of Alvin Lucier's *Orpheus Variations* for solo cello, seven wind instruments, and seven dancers, teaching at the Festival de Música Nueva; Ensenada, Baja California, and commissions by Kathryn Schulmeister and Ilana Waniuk.

CONRAD TAO has appeared worldwide as a pianist and composer. In addition to his recital and concerto performances as a solo musician, Tao maintains active collaborations with the Junction Trio, his ensemble with violinist Stefan Jackiw and cellist Jay Campbell, with dancer and choreographer Caleb Teicher, and with improviser and vocalist Charmaine Lee. At the 2019 New York Dance and Performance Award ("Bessies"), Tao and Teicher received the award for Outstanding Sound Design/Music Composition, for *More Forever*, their evening-length work for Teicher's company. Tao's 2020 began with the world premiere of his piece *Spoonfuls* by the Iris Orchestra, performances of his concerto *The Oneiroi in New York* with the Seattle Symphony, and his debut solo recital at Disney Hall, performing works by Rzewski and Copland as part of the LA Phil's Power to the People! Festival just before the COVID-19 pandemic caused an industry-wide shutdown. With traditional performances on hold, Tao maintained a busy schedule of streamed performances: two shows for the Library of Congress with Teicher and the JACK Quartet, a virtual recital for Tanglewood, several shows with the Junction Trio, and duo performances with Jackiw, among others. Tao was also announced as a 2020–2021 Kaufman Music Center Artist-in-Residence, working with students there and presenting a series of seven free digital "Performance as Process" events, and hosted additional masterclasses, workshops, and talks with composition and piano students at the Juilliard School, Peabody Conservatory, Music Academy of the West, Amherst College, Emory University, and Columbus State University. Tao is a recipient of the Avery Fisher Career Grant, and was named a Gilmore Young Artist in 2012. Born in Urbana, Illinois, in 1994, he has studied piano with Emilio del Rosario in Chicago and Yoheved Kaplinsky in New York, and composition with Christopher Theofanidis.

Alexandria Smith

Conrad Tao

Cory Smythe

Pianist CORY SMYTHE has worked closely with pioneering artists in new, improvisatory, and classical music, including saxophonist-composer Ingrid Laubrock, violinist Hilary Hahn, and multidisciplinary composers from Anthony Braxton to Zosha Di Castri. Smythe has been featured at the Newport Jazz, Wien Modern, Nordic Music Days, Approximation, Concorso Busoni, and Darmstadt festivals, as well as at Lincoln Center's Mostly Mozart festival, where he was recently invited to premiere new work created in collaboration with Peter Evans and Craig Taborn. He has received commissions from the Trondheim Jazz Orchestra, Milwaukee's Present Music, the Banff Centre for the Arts, the International Contemporary Ensemble, of which he is a longtime member, and the Shifting Foundation, which supported his 2018 release, *Circulate Susanna*. Smythe received a Grammy Award for his work with Ms. Hahn and plays regularly in the critically acclaimed Tyshawn Sorey Trio.

Pat Thomas (b. 1960, Oxford) began playing piano at the age of 8. He studied classical music and reggae was an early interest. Thomas was inspired to take up jazz after seeing legendary pianist Oscar Peterson on television at 16, by 1979 Thomas was performing seriously as an improviser has played with Mike Cooper, Geoff Hawkins, Lol Coxhill, Tony Oxley, Steve Beresford, Alex Ward, Derek Bailey, Eugene Chadbourne, Jimmy Carl Black, Evan Parker, John Zorn, Joe Gallivan, John Butcher, Okkyung Lee, Bill Dixon, Roy Campbell, Marshall Allen, Moor Mother, Axel Dörner, Luke Stewart, Matana Roberts. Current activities include solo piano; Black Top with Orphy Robinson; Scatter with Phil Minton, Roger Turner, Dave Tucker; Valid Tractor with Lawrence Casserley, Dom Lash; Shifa with Rachel Musson, Mark Sanders; Bleyschool with Tony Orrell, Dom Lash; Educated Guess with Thurston Moore, Dave Tucker, Mark Sanders; Ahmed with Seymour Wright, Joel Grip, Antonin Gerbal; a duo with Steve Noble; a trio with William Parker, Hamid Drake; and Bagman with Raymond Strid, Sture Ericson. He received the Paul Hamlyn Foundation Award for Composers in 2014.

Pat Thomas

Henry Threadgill

For over forty years Henry Threadgill has been celebrated as one of the most original, forward-thinking composers and multi-instrumentalists in American music. His 4-movement work, *In for a Penny, In for a Pound*, received the Pulitzer Prize for Music in 2016, one of only three jazz compositions to ever be so honored. A Chicago native, Mr. Threadgill studied at the city's American Conservatory of Music, majoring in composition, piano, and flute. A Vietnam veteran, he performed with the U.S. Army Concert Band. Mr. Threadgill is a founding member of the Association for the Advancement of Creative Musicians (AACM), dedicated to the performance of its members' original music. Mr. Threadgill has also received a Guggenheim Fellowship, the Aaron Copland Award, and the Doris Duke Impact Award. *Down Beat* magazine's *International Jazz Critics Poll* has five times distinguished him with its Best Composer Award. The Jazz Journalists Association honored him with its 2002 Composer of the Year Award and its Lifetime Achievement Award. Mr. Threadgill has released over thirty critically acclaimed albums. Mr. Threadgill's orchestral pieces, 1987's *Run Silent, Run Deep, Run Loud, Run* and 1993's *Mix for Orchestra* premiered at the Brooklyn Academy of Music. His many commissions include

Mordine & Co. Dance Theater, Carnegie Hall, the New York Shakespeare Festival, Talujon Percussion Ensemble, Junge Philharmonic Salzburg Orchestra, the Biennale di Venezia, and the American Composers Orchestra. He has been Composer-in-Residence at University of California-Berkeley and the Atlantic Center of the Arts. Through the years, Mr. Threadgill has led, performed, and recorded with numerous groups, most recently Zooid and the Double Up Ensemble. In 2015, a 2-day festival at New York's Harlem Stage celebrated works spanning Mr. Threadgill's career performed and reinterpreted by an all-star collection of musicians.

Brooklyn, NY-based sound artist/composer Fay Victor hones a unique vision for the vocalist's role in jazz and improvised music regarding repertoire, improvisation and composition. Victor has an "everything is everything" aesthetic, using freedom of expression to inform the appropriate musical response and viewing the vocal instrument as full of possibilities for sound exploration. Victor embraces these ideas in real time, aiming to push the vocal envelope to expand even further. On Victor's eleven critically acclaimed albums as a leader, one can hear the through line of her vocal approaches unfurl over time. Victor's work has been featured in media outlets such as *The Wall Street Journal*, *The New York Times*, *The San Francisco Chronicle*, *Rolling Stone* Magazine and *The Huffington Post*; Victor's performed with luminaries such as William Parker, Roswell Rudd, Dr. Randy Weston, Nicole Mitchell, Misha Mengelberg, Moor Mother, Myra Melford, Archie Shepp, Marc Ribot and Tyshawn Sorey to name but a few; Performance highlights include The Museum of Modern Art and The Whitney Museum of American Art (NYC), The Hammer Museum (LA), The Kolner Philharmonie (Germany), De Young Museum (SF), Symphony Space (NY), The Earshot Jazz Festival (Seattle), The Winter Jazz Festival(NYC) and the Bimhuis (Netherlands). Victor has been awarded prizes such as the 2017 Herb Albert/Yaddo Fellow in Music Composition, a 2018 Artist-in-Residence in Composition (Headlands Center for the Arts) and a 2020 Jazz Coalition Commission Fund Grantee. Victor is currently on the Faculty of the New School of Jazz and Contemporary Music and has given many workshops/clinics/masterclasses around the world. For more information, please see www.fayvictor.com www.patreon.com/freesongsinger @freesongsinger on Instagram, Facebook and Twitter.

Fay Victor

Anna Webber

Anna Webber (b. 1984) is flutist, saxophonist, and composer whose interests and work live in the aesthetic overlap between avant garde jazz and new classical music. Her most recent album, *Clockwise,* featuring a septet comprised of several of the most creative musicians working in New York's avant garde, was released on Pi Recordings (February 2019). Webber's other projects include her Simple Trio, with John Hollenbeck and pianist Matt Mitchell, and the Webber/Morris Big Band, co-led with saxophonist/composer Angela Morris. This ensemble released its debut album, *Both Are True*, on Dave Douglas' Greenleaf Music in April 2020. She has performed and/or recorded with projects led by artists such as Dan Weiss, Jen Shyu, Dave Douglas, Matt Mitchell, Ches Smith, and John Hollenbeck, among others. Webber is a 2021 Berlin Prize Fellow and a 2018

Guggenheim Fellow. She was top of the Rising Star — Flute category in *DownBeat* Magazine Critic's Poll in 2020. She has additionally been awarded grants from the Shifting Foundation (2015) and the New York Foundation for the Arts (2017), and residencies from Exploring the Metropolis (2019), MacDowell Colony (2017, 2020), the Millay Colony for the Arts (2015), and the Brush Creek Foundation for the Arts (2014). Webber is originally from British Columbia.

Christian Wolff, (b. 1934, Nice, France), lived mostly in the U.S. since 1941. Studied piano with Grete Sultan and, briefly, composition with John Cage, from whom, along with Morton Feldman, David Tudor, and Earle Brown, he got support and encouragement. Then long-term association with Frederic Rzewski and Cornelius Cardew. Taught classics (Latin & Greek) at Harvard, then classics and music at Dartmouth. Currently 250 pieces in work list, published by C.F. Peters; music on over eighty CDs. Collection of writings and interviews in *Occasional Pieces* (Oxford University Press, 2017).

Miguel Zenón is a Puerto Rican saxophonist, composer, band leader, music producer, and educator. He is a multiple Grammy Award nominee, and the recipient of a Guggenheim Fellowship and a MacArthur Fellowship. Zenon has released twelve recordings as a leader, including the Grammy nominated *Sonero: The Music of Ismael Rivera* (2019), *Yo Soy La Tradición* (2018) and *Típico* (2017). As a sideman he has worked with jazz luminaries such as The SFJAZZ Collective, Charlie Haden, Fred Hersch, Kenny Werner, David Sánchez, Danilo Perez, The Village Vanguard Orchestra, Kurt Elling, Guillermo Klein & Los Guachos, The Mingus Big Band, Bobby Hutcherson and Steve Coleman. Zenón has been featured in publications such as *The New York Times*, *The Wall Street Journal*, *The Los Angeles Times*, *The Boston Globe* and *The Chicago Tribune*. In addition, he topped both the Jazz Artist of the Year and Alto Saxophonist categories on the 2014 *Jazz Times Critics Poll* and was selected as the Alto Saxophonist of the Year by the Jazz Journalist Association in 2015, 2018, 2019 and 2020 (when he was also recognized as Arranger of the Year). As a composer he has been commissioned by SFJAZZ, NYO Jazz, The New York State Council for the Arts, Chamber Music America, Logan Center for the Arts, The Hyde Park Jazz Festival, The John Simon Guggenheim Foundation, MIT, Jazz Reach, Peak Performances, PRISM Quartet and many of his peers. Zenón has given hundreds of lectures and master classes at institutions all over the world and is a permanent faculty member at The New England Conservatory, The Manhattan School of Music and serves as the current Artist-in-Residence for the Zucherman Institute at Columbia University. In 2011 he founded Caravana Cultural, a program which presents free-of-charge Jazz concerts in rural areas of Puerto Rico.

Christian Wolff

Miguel Zenón

John Zorn

Born and raised in New York City, John Zorn is a composer, performer, artist, and aesthetic philosopher who has forged an independent path through stylistic domains that range from the classical avant garde to many popular idioms. His work is remarkably diverse and draws inspiration from Art, Literature, Film, Theatre, Philosophy, Alchemy and Mysticism as well as Music. He founded the Tzadik label in 1995, runs the East Village performance space The Stone and has edited and published ten volumes of musician's writings under the title *Arcana*. Honors include a MacArthur Fellowship, the Cultural Achievement Award from the National Foundation for Jewish Culture and the William Schuman Prize for composition from Columbia University. He was inducted into the Long Island Hall of Fame by Lou Reed in 2010 and has received honorary doctorates from the University of Ghent, SUNY Purchase and New England Conservatory.

RECOMMENDED LISTENING

Susan Alcorn

Uma Loveletter
Curandera Uma Sounds
Concentration Recorded
And I Await the Resurrection of the Pedal Steel Guitar Olde English Spelling Bee
Soledad Relative Pitch
A&B Iorram
Evening Tales Mystra
Invitation to a Dream Astral Spirits
Prism Mirror Lens VG+
Pedernal Relative Pitch

Oren Ambarchi

Simian Angel Editions Mego
Hubris Editions Mego
Quixotism Editions Mego
Sagittarian Domain Editions Mego
Audience of One Touch
In The Pendulum's Embrace Touch
Grapes From The Estate Touch
Triste Southern Lord
Suspension Touch
Insulation Touch

Ran Blake

Indian Winter Soul Note
Driftwood Tompkins Square
Cocktails at Dusk — A Noir Tribute to Chris Connor Impulse!
Ghost Tones: Portraits of George Russell A-Side
Live at the Kitano Sunnyside
Down Here Below, Vol. 2: A Tribute to Abbey Lincoln with Christine Correa RedPiano Records
Chabrol Noir: A Tribute to Claude Chabrol with Ricky Ford Impulse!
Town and Country Sunnyside
The Newest Sound You Never Heard: European Recordings 1966–67 A-Side
Gray Moon RedPiano Records

Peter Blegvad

Sort Of Polydor
Kew. Rhone. Virgin
The Naked Shakespeare Virgin
Downtime 1988
King Strut And Other Stories Silvertone Records
Unearthed Sub Rosa
Just Woke Up ReR Megacorp
Hangman's Hill ReR Megacorp
Orpheus (The Lowdown) Ape House
Gonwards Ape House

Tyondai Braxton

History That Has No Effect JMZ
Battles — EP C / B EP Warp
Battles — Mirrored Warp
Central Market Warp
HIVE1 Nonesuch

Oranged Out EP Beatink Records

Patricia Brennan
Sonnet Valley of Search
Maquishti Valley of Search

John Butcher
Resonant Spaces Weight of Wax
The Geometry of Sentiment Emanem
Cavern with Nightlife Weight of Wax
Invisible Ear Weight of Wax
Thirteen Friendly Numbers Unsounds
At the Hill of James Magee Trost
somethingtobesaid Weight of Wax
Routing Lynn Ftarri
Crucial Anatomy Trost
Scrutables Weight of Wax

Ben Coniguliaro
Seated self-released
Odyx Tzadik
The Birth of the Sun self-released
YiY self-released
Weakworks self-released
Wickman self-released

Amir ElSaffar
Safaafir: Maqams of Baghdad independent release
Two Rivers Pi
Radif Suite w/Hafez Modirzadeh Pi
Inana Pi
Alchemy Pi
Crisis Pi
Rivers of Sound: Not Two New Amsterdam

Kenny Grohowski
Seasons of Being Sunnyside
Eleven Clean Feed
Alphaville Century Media
Baphomet Tzadik
Spirit Driven Four (Friends of Unseen Rain)
Axiom Music Box Publishing
So Alive Village Records - Sony Japan
Shapeshifters Moonjune
Behind The Vibration Cuneiform
Cuban Reflection Padrón Music

Tom Guralnick
Albuquerque: Solo Saxophone Cleo Records
Sonistruction UBIK Sound
Broken Dances for Muted Pieces Nonsequitur
TG3: Pitchin' Voxlox
Then Voxlox
Tom Guralnick, David Moss & Steve Feld. Duos & Trios

Mark Helias
The Signal Maker Intakt
Loopin' The Cool Enja
Fictionary GM
The Third Proposition Radio Legs
The Current Set Enja
The Marks Brothers W.E.R.F.
Anthony Braxton Quintet — Basel hatOLOGY
The Struggle Continues ECM
Strange Unison Radio Legs
Atomic Clock Radio Legs

David Hertzberg
The Wake World Tzadik
The Rose Elf Swan Studios NYC

Dan Kaufman
Barbez Important Records
Insignificance Important Records
Mexico City Impressions

Important Records
Force of Light Tzadik
Bella Ciao Tzadik
For Those Who Came After Important Records

Stefan Jackiw
Ludwig Van Beethoven: Triple Concerto Decca Gold
Johannes Brahms: Complete Violin Sonatas Sony

Derek Keller
Horse Thieves: 'Bout Damn Time Derek Keller Music
Sound Check Four UCSD, Dept. of Music
Impositions and Consequences Tzadik
Remedy Centaur
Solos and Duos for Guitar Old King Cole

Richard Kessler
Urban Dances for Brass Quintet Koch International

Pauline Kim
Giga Concerto New Focus Recordings
A Lunch Between Order and Chaos Chaikin Records
Alien Stories Infrequent Seams
AnnCela Express New World Records
String Noise Black Truffle Records
Fabric of String Noise Cold Blue Music
Heroine Sono Luminus
You Scream a Rapid Language Infrequent Seams
The Book of Strange Positions Northern Spy
Lemma Tzadik

Ulrich Krieger
Yggdrasil-Soli Winds Measure Recordings
Wall of Sound I-Iii Sub Rosa
Faust — Fresh Air Bureau B
Winters In The Abyss Pogus
[Urban Dreamings] Mode
/Raw:Respace/ Xi
Fathom Sub Rosa
A Cage of Saxophones, Vol. 3 & 4 Mode
Metal Machine Music Asphodel

Hannah Lash
Monodramas analog arts
The American Harp Azika
Poetry of Places Reference Recordings
Filigree New Focus Recordings
Garlands for Steven Stucky Bridge Records

Daniel Lippel
Mirrored Spaces New Focus Recordings
...through which the past shines New Focus Recordings
Aufs Lautenwerk: J.S. Bach on Well Tempered Guitar MicroFest Records
Dai Fujikura: ICE Kairos
Electric Counterpoint New Focus Recordings
Abandoned Time New Focus Recordings
FM New Focus Recordings
Sustenance New Focus Recordings
Resonance New Focus Recordings
Bach: BWV 998, 1003, 1010 New Focus Recordings

Annea Lockwood
The Secret Life of the Inaudible

Gruenrekorder
Tiger Balm/Amazonia Dreaming/Immersion Black Truffle
Ground of Being/Buoyant/Dusk/ Ear-Walking Woman Recital
A Sound Map of the Housatonic River 3 leaves
In Our Name/Jitterbug/Thirst New World
A Sound Map of the Danube Lovely Music
Thousand Year Dreaming/ floating world Pogus
A Sound Map of the Hudson River Lovely Music
Women in Electronic Music: World Rhythms (reissue) New World
*Becoming Air/Into the Vanishing Poin*t Black Truffle

Dave Lombardo

Reign in Blood Def Jam/Geffen
World Painted American Recordings
The Director's Cut Ipecac Recordings
Suspended Animation Ipecac Recordings
Xu Feng Tzadik
Power of Inner Strength Metal Blade Records
The Gathering Spitfire
World Gone Mad Suicidal Records
Dead Cross Ipecac Recordings
The Raging Wrath of the Easter Bunny Demo Ipecac Recordings

Charlie Looker

A Horizon Made of Canvas Astral Spirits Records
Sparta Last Things Records
Simple Answers Last Things Records
Surveillance Punishment and the Black Psyche Negrogothic Records
Power Ballads Northern Spy Records
II Public Eyesore Records
Score — The Complete Sextet Works: 2002–2007 Northern Spy Records
Dream Seeds Northern Spy Records
Made Flesh LOAF Records
Secular Works Planaria Records

Thomas Morgan

Epistrophy ECM
Small Town ECM

Stephen O'Malley

Rift.Canyon.Dreams Merciless
Things Viral Southern Lord
Monoliths & Dimensions Southern Lord
V Editions Mego
Soused 4AD
Gruidés DDS
Eternelle Idole Shelter Press
ĀKASA-DĀTU Ideologic Organ
Cylene Editions Mego
Life Metal Southern Lord

Laura Ortman

Dust Dives Alive Bandcamp
My Soul Remainer Bandcamp
Someday We'll Be Together Bandcamp
Laura Ortman, Live at St. Marks Church, NYC 12/18/15 Bandcamp
Tens of Thousands Bandcamp
Wmat Bandcamp

Alex Paxton

Music for Bosch People Birmingham Record Company/NMC
Happy Music for Orchestra Dreammusics
Tellsong Listen Poney
Corncrack Dreams

Non-Classical Label

Conrad Tao
The Juilliard Sessions Warner Classics
Voyages Warner Classics
Pictures Warner Classics
American Rage Warner Classics
David Lang: the loser Cantaloupe
Junction Trio: Live self-released

Pat Thomas
Nur Solo Piano Emanem
Strong Language Lunge Emanem
The Tony Oxley Quartet Incus
Company 91 Volume 1 Incus
Black Top Free #3 Babel
The Elephant Clock of Al Jazari Otoruku
Super Majnoon Ahmed Otoruku
Shifa Live in Oslo 577 Records
4 Compositions for Orchestra FMR
Powerfield Field Recordings FMR

Henry Threadgill
X-75 Volume 1 Arista/Novus
When Was That? About Time
Just the Facts and Pass the Bucket About Time
Spirit of Nuff...Nuff Black Saint
Live at Koncepts Taylor Madet
Where's Your Cup? Columbia
Tomorrow Sunny/The Revelry, Spp Pi Recordings
In for a Penny, In for a Pound Pi Recordings
Double Up, Plays Double Up Plus Pi Recordings
Woven Serenade Pi Recordings

Fay Victor
We've Had Enough! ESP-Disk
Barn Songs Northern Spy Records
Wet Robots ESP-Disk
Absinthe & Vermouth Greene Avenue Music
Kaiso Stories Silkheart Records
BARE Greene Avenue Music
The FreeSong Suite Greene Avenue Music
Cartwheels Through The Cosmos Greene Avenue Music
Lazy Old Sun: LIVE/Life in the Lowlands Greene Avenue Music
Darker Than Blue Timeless Records

Anna Webber
Rectangles Out of Your Head Records
Both Are True Greenleaf Music
Clockwise Pi Recordings
Binary Skirl Records
Simple Skirl Records
EAVE Astral Spirits
Refraction Pirouet Records
Percussive Mechanics Pirouet Records
Third Floor People NOWT Records

Christian Wolff
Bread and Roses Mode
Look She Said Mode
Early Piano Music Matchless Recordings
Percussionist Songs Matchless Recordings
(Re)MakingMusic, Works 1962–1999 Mode
Ten Exercises New World Records
8 Duos New World Records
Pianist Pieces Sub Rosa
Burdocks Tzadik
American Dream New World Records

Miguel Zenón

Sonero: The Music of Ismael Rivera Miel Music
Yo Soy La Tradición Miel Music
Típico Miel Music
Identities are Changeable Miel Music
Oye!!! Live in Puerto Miel Music
Rayuela Sunnyside
Alma Adentro: The Puerto Rican Marsalis Music
Esta Plena Marsalis Music
Awake Marsalis Music
Jíbaro Marsalis Music

John Zorn

The Bagatelles Tzadik
Azoth Tzadik
The Turner Études Tzadik
Gnosis Tzadik
Heaven and Earth Magic Tzadik
Teresa de Ávila Tzadik
Chaos Magic Tzadik
The Song of Songs Tzadik
Nostradamus Tzadik
Meditations on the Tarot Tzadik